TREASURY OF GREAT

HORSE STORIES

TREASURY OF GREAT
HORSE STORIES

EDITED WITH AN INTRODUCTION BY ROGER CARAS

A COLLECTION OF TALES THAT CELEBRATES
THE MAJESTIC BEAUTY OF THE HORSE

BRISTOL PARK BOOKS / NEW YORK

First Bristol Park Books edition published by BBS Publishing Corporation
in 1999.

This edition distributed by:
Bristol Park Books
252 W. 38th Street
NYC, NY 10018

Bristol Park Books is a registered trademark of
Bristol Park Books, Inc.

Library of Congress Catalog Number: 98-73942

ISBN 10: 0-88486-417-0
ISBN 13: 978-0-88486-417-2

Printed in the United States of America

CONTENTS

Contents

CONTENTS

Contents

ACKNOWLEDGMENTS

"Of Horses and Their History" by Cleveland Amory. From *Ranch of Dreams* by Cleveland Amory, copyright © 1997. Reprinted by permission of the Viking Penguin, a division of Penguin Putnam, Inc.

"Tea and 'Biscuit" by Jon L. Breen. Copyright © 1991 by Jon L. Breen. From *Cat Crimes.* Reprinted by permission of the author.

"Rescue" by Walter Farley. Copyright © 1941, renewed 1969 by Walter Farley. From *The Black Stallion* by Walter Farley, Reprinted by permission of Random House, Inc.

"The Njuggle" by Laura Frankos. Copyright © 1995 by Laura Frankos. First published in *Orphans of the Night.* Reprinted by permission of the author.

"The Blue Roan" by Molly Gloss. Copyright © 1989 by Molly Gloss. First published in *New Frontiers.* Reprinted by permission of the author and the author's agent, Virginia Kidd.

"For a Horse" by Will James. Copyright © 1938 by Will James. Reprinted by permission of the Will James Art Company, Billings, Montana.

"Once a Cowboy" by Will James. Copyright © 1940 by Will James. Reprinted by permission of the Will James Art Company, Billings, Montana.

Acknowledgments

"A Wayside Adventure" by C. S. Lewis. Copyright © 1954 by the Estate of C. S. Lewis. First published in *A Horse and His Boy*. Reprinted by permission of HarperCollins Publishers.

"One Ten Three" by Barry N. Malzberg. Copyright © 1990 by Barry N. Malzberg. First published in *Horse Fantastic*. Reprinted by permission of the author.

"A Miracle of Evolution" by James Michener. Copyright © 1993 by James Michener. From *Creatures of the Kingdom* by James Michener. Reprinted by permission of Random House, Inc.

"We'll Have Fun" by John O'Hara. From *And Other Stories* by John O'Hara. Copyright © 1963 by John O'Hara. Reprinted by permission of Random House, Inc.

"My Friend Flicka" by Mary O'Hara. Copyright © 1941 by Mary O'Hara. Reprinted by permission of the author and her agent, John Hawkins & Associates, Inc.

"Malish" by Mike Resnick. Copyright © 1991 by Mike Resnick. Reprinted by permission of the author.

"The Summer of the Beautiful White Horse" by William Saroyan. Copyright © 1938, renewed 1966 by William Saroyan. From *My Name is Aram* by William Saroyan. Reprinted by permission of Harcourt Brace and Company.

"The Cat Who Wasn't Black" by Josepha Sherman. Copyright © 1998 by Josepha Sherman. First published in *Black Cats and Broken Mirrors*. Reprinted by permission of the author.

"The Most Magical Thing About Rachel" by Nancy Springer. Copyright © 1991 by Nancy Springer. First published in *Horse Fantastic*. Reprinted by permission of Random House, Inc.

"Murder at the Race Course" by Julian Symons. Copyright © 1966 by Julian Symons. Reprinted by permission of the agent for the author's Estate, Curtis Brown Group, Ltd.

"Classical Horses" by Judith Tarr. Copyright © 1991 by Judith Tarr. First published in *Horse Fantastic*. Reprinted by permission of the author.

INTRODUCTION

The horse is synonymous with power in the mysteries and mystique cherished by man. Is that justified by our history in the company of the beast? Who else opened the world for our exploration and the exploitation of all the wonders we encountered? Horses bore us on their backs, as they did the terrible burdens that we insisted travel with us. They have been our war machines as well as our fleetest messengers. They carried us into battle, we fought from their backs, and they fell along side us.

In our art, our literature, in every form of description and awe we have created, we have heralded the horse as we have few other animals or other artifacts of our endlessly emerging culture.

The tales we tell speak of sparks flying from their hooves as they race across the heavens and of the fire flashing from their eyes. The chariots they pull after them are made from gold and silver, and gods of incredible manliness and beauty hold the reins and the whips. The thunder of their hooves can flatten mountains and cities and deafen nations. Yes, power and the horse, the horse and power, they are one and the same.

In a less violent context, the horse is the epitome of beauty, grace, and style. No domestic animal has been sculpted so often nor so well. The equestrian statue, a famous or powerful leader on a magnificently stylized

horse, is often the hallmark of power and prestige. The names of horses—
Alexander the Great's Bucephalus, Robert E. Lee's Traveler, Cortes's El
Morzillo, Napoleon's Marengo, the Duke of Wellington's Copenhagen—
they are a few that have lasted longer than the names of any other domesticated animals. Name if you can the greatest sheep, goat, or cow that
ever lived. Only if you are a life-long scholar of a species is that task
likely to be possible. You will remember some dogs, certainly largely
fictional heroes, but the names of the horses people rode remain in our
minds and hearts apparently forever.

There are fictional horses, too, and some of them appear in this remarkable collection. Flicka is here, Black Beauty, and Strider. But real or
imagined, a fantasy we share or a part of the real history of mankind,
these horses are unforgettable. As proof of that, generations have already
passed down some stories of legendary horses for centuries, while others
have been retold for millennia. In a very real sense they are classic horses.
This collection is an acknowledgment of that concept, the idea that
horses both real and imagined can come down to us as classics not to be
forgotten.

Horses are arguably the most beautiful animals we have taken into our
folds. They have been of truly incredible value in our economic endeavors
and in our exploits imagined or very real. They have been indispensable
companions and the great enablers of history. There have been other
beasts of burden and battle and other long-legged coworkers of exploration, but there has been no other animal with the fire, the flare, and the
magic of the great beasts who star in the stories within these pages.

John O'Hara

WE'LL HAVE FUN

It was often said of Tony Costello that there was nothing he did not know about horses. No matter whom he happened to be working for—as coachman, as hostler, as blacksmith—he would stop whatever he was doing and have a look at an ailing horse and give advice to the owner who had brought the horse to Tony. His various employers did not object; they had probably sometime in the past gotten Tony's advice when he was working for someone else, and they would do so again sometime in the future. A year was a long time for Tony to stay at a job; he would quit or he would get the sack, find something else to do, and stay at that job until it was time to move on. He had worked for some employers three or four times. They would rehire him in spite of their experience with his habits, and if they did not happen to have a job open for him, they would at least let him bed down in their haylofts. He did not always ask their permission for this privilege, but since he knew his way around just about every stable in town—private and livery—he never had any trouble finding a place to sleep. He smoked a pipe, but everybody knew he was careful about matches and emptying the pipe and the kerosene heaters that were in most stables. And even when he was not actually in the service of the owner of a stable, he more than earned his sleeping privilege. An owner would go out to the stable in the morning and find that the chores had been done. "Oh, hello, Tony," the owner would say. "Since when have you been back?"

"I come in last night."

"I don't have a job for you," the owner would say.

"That's all right. Just a roof over me head temporarily. You're giving that animal too much oats again. Don't give him no oats at night, I told you."

"Oh, all right. Go in the kitchen and the missus will give you some breakfast. That is, if you want any breakfast. You smell like a saloon."

"Yes, this was a bad one, a real bad one. All I want's a cup of coffee, if that's all right?"

"One of these nights you'll walk in front of a yard engine."

"If I do I hope I'll have the common sense to get out of the way. And if I don't it'll be over pretty quick."

"Uh-huh. Well, do whatever needs to be done and I'll pay you two dollars when I get back this evening."

The owner could be sure that by the end of the day Tony would have done a good cleaning job throughout the stable, and would be waiting in patient agony for the money that would buy the whiskey that cured the rams. "I got the rams so bad I come near taking a swig of the kerosene," he would say. He would take the two dollars and half-walk, half-run to the nearest saloon, but he would be back in time to feed and bed down the owner's horse.

It would take a couple of days for him to get back to good enough shape to go looking for a steady job. If he had the right kind of luck, the best of luck, he would hear about a job as coachman. The work was not hard, and the pay was all his, not to be spent on room and board. The hardest work, though good pay, was in a blacksmith's shop. He was not young any more, and it took longer for his muscles to get reaccustomed to the work. Worst of all, as the newest blacksmith he was always given the job of shoeing mules, which were as treacherous as a rattlesnake and as frightening. He hated to shoe a mule or a Shetland pony. There were two shops in town where a mule could be tied up in the stocks, the apparatus that held the animal so securely that it could not kick; but a newly shod mule, released from the stocks, was likely to go crazy and kill a man. If he was going to die that way, Tony wanted his executioner to be a horse, not a God damn mule. And if he was going to lose a finger or a chunk of his backside, let it be a horse that bit him and not a nasty little bastard ten hands high. Blacksmithing paid the best and was the job he cared the least for, and on his fiftieth birthday Tony renounced it forever. "Not for fifty dollars a week will I take another job in a blacksmith's," he swore.

"You're getting pretty choosy, if you ask me," said his friend Murphy. "Soon there won't be no jobs for you of any kind, shape or form. The ottomobile is putting an end to the horse. Did you ever hear tell of the Squadron A in New York City?"

"For the love of Jesus, did I ever hear tell of it? Is that what you're asking me? Well, if I was in New York City I could lead you to it blindfolded, Ninety-something-or-other and Madison Avenue, it is, on the right-hand side going up. And before I come to this miserable town the man I worked for's son belonged to it. Did I ever hear tell of the Squadron A!"

"All right. What is it now?" said Murphy.

"It's the same as it always was—a massive brick building on the right-hand side—"

"The organ-i-zation, I'm speaking of," said Murphy.

"Well, the last I seen in the papers, yesterday or the day before, this country was ingaged in mortal combat with Kaiser Wilhelm the Second. I therefore hazard the guess that the organ-i-zation is fighting on our side against the man with the withered arm."

"Fighting how?"

"Bravely, I'm sure."

"With what for weapons?"

"For weapons? Well, being a cavalry regiment I hazard the guess that they're equipped with sabre and pistol."

"There, you see? You're not keeping up to date with current happenings. Your Squadron A that you know so much about don't have a horse to their name. They're a machine-gun outfit."

"Well, that of course is a God damn lie, Murphy."

"A lie, is it? Well how much would you care to bet me—in cash?"

"Let me take a look and see how much I have on me?" said Tony. He placed his money on the bar. "Eighteen dollars and ninety-four cents. Is this even money, or do I have to give you odds?"

Murphy placed nineteen dollars on the bar. "Even money'll be good enough for me, bein's it's like taking the money off a blind man."

"And how are we to settle who's right?" said Tony.

"We'll call up the newspaper on the telephone."

"What newspaper? There's no newspaper here open after six P.M."

"We'll call the New York *World*," said Murphy.

"By long distance, you mean? Who's to pay for the call?"

"The winner of the bet," said Murphy.

"The winner of the bet? Oh, all right. I'll be magnanimous. How do you go about it? You can't put that many nickels in the slot."

"We'll go over to the hotel and get the operator at the switchboard, Mary McFadden. She's used to these long-distance calls."

"Will she be on duty at this hour?"

"Are you trying to back out? It's only a little after eight," said Murphy.

"Me back out? I wished I could get the loan of a hundred dollars and I'd show you who's backing out," said Tony.

In silence they marched to the hotel, and explained their purpose to Mary McFadden. Within fifteen minutes they were connected with the office of *The World*, then to the newspaper library. "Good evening, sir," said Murphy. "This is a long-distance call from Gibbsville, Pennsylvania. I wish to request the information as to whether the Squadron A is in the cavalry or a machine-gun organ-i-zation." He repeated the question and waited. "He says to hold the line a minute."

"Costing us a fortune," said Tony.

"Hello? Yes, I'm still here. Yes? Uh-huh. Would you kindly repeat that information?" Murphy quickly handed the receiver to Tony Costello, who listened, nodded, said "Thank you," and hung up.

"How much do we owe you for the call, Mary?" said Murphy.

"Just a minute," said the operator. "That'll be nine dollars and fifty-five cents."

"Jesus," said Tony. "Well, one consolation. It's out of your profit, Murphy."

"But the profit is out of your pocket," said Murphy. "Come on, we'll go back and I'll treat you. Generous in victory, that's me. Like Ulysses S. Grant. He give all them Confederates their horses back, did you ever know that, Costello?"

"I did not, and what's more I don't believe it."

"Well, maybe you'd care to bet on that, too? Not this evening, however, bein's you're out of cash. But now will you believe that the ottomobile is putting an end to the horse?"

"Where does the ottomobile come into it? The machine gun is no ottomobile."

"No, and I didn't say it was, but if they have no use for the cavalry in a war, they'll soon have no use for them anywhere."

"If you weren't such a pinch of snuff I'd give you a puck in the mouth. But don't try my patience too far, Mr. Murphy. I'll take just so much of your impudence and no more. With me one hand tied behind me I could put you in hospital."

"You're kind of a hard loser, Tony. You oughtn't to be that way. There's more ottomobiles in town now than horses. The fire companies are all motorizing. The breweries. And the rich, you don't see them buying a new pair of cobs no more. It's the Pierce-Arrow now. Flannagan the undertaker is getting rid of his blacks, he told me so himself. Ordered a Cunningham 8."

"We'll see where Flannagan and his Cunningham 8 ends up next winter, the first time he has to bring a dead one down from the top of

Fairview Street. Or go up it, for that matter. There's hills in this town no Cunningham 8 will negotiate, but Flannagan's team of blacks never had the least trouble. Flannagan'll be out of business the first winter, and it'll serve him right."

"And here I thought he was a friend of yours. Many's the time you used his stable for a boudoir, not to mention the funerals you drove for him. Two or three dollars for a half a day's work."

"There never was no friendship between him and I. You never saw me stand up to a bar and have a drink with him. You never saw me set foot inside his house, nor even his kitchen for a cup of coffee. The rare occasions that I slept in his barn, he was never the loser, let me tell you. Those blacks that he's getting rid of, I mind the time I saved the off one's life from the colic. Too tight-fisted to send for Doc McNary, the vet, and he'd have lost the animal for sure if I wasn't there. Do you know what he give me for saving the horse? Guess what he give me."

"Search me," said Murphy.

"A pair of gloves. A pair of gauntlets so old that the lining was all wore away. Supposed to be fleece-lined, but the fleece was long since gone. 'Here, you take these, Tony,' said Mr. Generous Flannagan. I wanted to say 'Take them and do what with them?' But I was so dead tired from being up all night with the black, all I wanted to do was go up in his hayloft and lie down exhausted. Which I did for a couple of hours, and when I come down again there was the black, standing on his four feet and give me a whinny. A horse don't have much brains, but they could teach Flannagan gratitude."

After the war the abandonment of horses became so general that even Tony Costello was compelled to give in to it. The small merchants of the town, who had kept a single horse and delivery wagon (and a carriage for Sunday), were won over to Ford and Dodge trucks. The three-horse hitches of the breweries disappeared and in their place were big Macks and Garfords. The fire companies bought American LaFrances and Whites. The physicians bought Franklins and Fords, Buicks and Dodges. (The Franklin was air-cooled; the Buick was supposed to be a great hill-climber.) And private citizens who had never felt they could afford a horse and buggy, now went into debt to purchase flivvers. Of the three leading harness shops in the town, two became luggage shops and one went out of business entirely. Only two of the seven blacksmith shops remained. Gone were the Fleischmann's Yeast and Grand Union Tea Company wagons, the sorrels and greys of the big express companies. The smooth-surface paving caused a high mortality rate among horses, who slipped and broke legs and had to be shot and carried away to the fertilizer plant. The horse was retained only by the rich and the poor; saddle horses for the rich, and swaybacked old nags for the junk men and fruit peddlers. For Tony Costello it was not so easy as it once had been to find a place to sleep. The last livery stable closed in 1922, was converted into a public garage, and neither the rats nor Tony Costello had a home to go to, he said. "No decent, self-respecting rat will live in a garridge," he said. "It's an inhuman smell, them gazzoline fumes. And the rats don't have any more to eat there than I do meself."

The odd jobs that he lived on made no demands on his skill with horses, but all his life he had known how to take proper care of the varnish and the brightwork of a Brewster brougham, the leather and the bits and buckles of all kinds of tack. He therefore made himself useful at washing cars and polishing shoes. Nobody wanted to give him a steady job, but it was more sensible to pay Tony a few dollars than to waste a good mechanic on a car wash. He had a flexible arrangement with the cooks at two Greek restaurants who, on their own and without consulting the owners, would give him a meal in exchange for his washing dishes. "There ain't a man in the town has hands any cleaner than mine. Me hands are in soapy water morning, noon, and night," he said.

"It's too bad the rest of you don't get in with your hands," said Murphy. "How long since you had a real bath, Tony?"

"Oh, I don't know."

"As the fellow says, you take a bath once a year whether you need it or not," said Murphy. "And yet I never seen you need a shave, barring the times you were on a three-day toot."

"Even then I don't often let her grow more'n a couple days. As long as I can hold me hand steady enough so's I don't cut me throat. That's a temptation, too, I'll tell you. There's days I just as soon take the razor in me hand and let nature take its course."

"What stops you?" said Murphy.

"That I wonder. Mind you, I don't wonder too much or the logical conclusion would be you-know-what. My mother wasn't sure who my father was. She didn't keep count. She put me out on the streets when I was eight or nine years of age. 'You can read and write,' she said, which was more than she could do. With my fine education I was able to tell one paper from another, so I sold them."

"You mean she put you out with no place to sleep?"

"Oh, no. She let me sleep there, providing she didn't have a customer. If I come home and she had a customer I had to wait outside."

"I remember you telling me one time your father worked for a man that had a son belonged to the Squadron A. That time we had the bet."

"That was a prevarication. A harmless prevarication that I thought up on the spur of the moment. I ought to know better by this time. Every time I prevaricate I get punished for it. That time I lost the bet. I should have said I knew about the Squadron A and let it go at that, but I had to embellish it. I always knew about the Squadron A. From selling newspapers in the Tenderloin I got a job walking hots at the race track, and I was a jock till I got too big. I couldn't make the weight any more, my bones were too heavy regardless of how much I starved myself and dried out. That done something to me, those times I tried to make a hundred and fifteen pounds and my bones weighed more than that. As soon as I quit trying to be a jock my weight jumped up to a hundred and fifty, and that's about what I am now."

"What do you mean it done something to you?" said Murphy.

"Be hard for you to understand, Murphy. It's a medical fact."

"Oh, go ahead, Doctor Costello."

"Well, if you don't get enough to eat, the blood thins out and the brain don't get fed properly. That changes your whole outlook on life, and if the brain goes too long without nourishment, you get so's you don't care any more."

"Where did you get that piece of information?"

"I trained for a doctor that owned a couple trotters over near Lancaster. Him and I had many's the conversation on the subject."

"I never know whether to believe you or call you a liar. Did you get so's you didn't care any more?"

"That's what I'm trying to get through your thick skull, Murphy. That's why I never amounted to anything. That's why poor people stay poor. The brain don't get enough nourishment from the blood. Fortunately I know that, you see. I don't waste my strength trying to be something I ain't."

"Do you know what I think, Tony? I think you were just looking for an excuse to be a bum."

"Naturally! I wasn't looking for an excuse, but I was looking for some reason why a fellow as smart as I am never amounted to anything. If I cared more what happened to me, I'd have cut my throat years ago. Jesus! The most I ever had in my life was eight hundred dollars one time a long shot came in, but I don't care. You know, I'm fifty-five or -six years of age, one or the other. I had my first woman when I was fifteen, and I guess a couple hundred since then. But I never saw one yet that I'd lose any sleep over. Not a single one, out of maybe a couple hundred. One is just like the other, to me. Get what you want out of them, and so long. So long till you want another. And I used to be a pretty handsome fellow when I was young. Not all whores, either. Once when I was wintering down in Latonia—well, what the hell. It don't bother me as much as it used to do. I couldn't go a week without it, but these days I just as soon spend the money on the grog. I'll be just as content when I can do without them altogether."

. . . One day Tony was washing a brand-new Chrysler, which was itself a recent make of car. He was standing off, hose in hand, contemplating the design and colors of the car, when a young woman got out of a plain black Ford coupe. She was wearing black and white saddle shoes, bruised and spotted, and not liable to be seriously damaged by the puddles of dirty water on the garage floor, but Tony cautioned her. "Mind where you're walking, young lady," he said.

"Oh, it won't hurt these shoes," she said. "I'm looking for Tony Costello. I was told he worked here."

"Feast your eyes, Miss. You're looking right at him," he said.

"You're Tony Costello? I somehow pictured an older man," she said.

"Well, maybe I'm older than I look. What is there I can do for you?"

She was a sturdily built young woman, past the middle twenties, handsome if she had been a man, but it was no man inside the grey pullover. "I was told that you were the best man in town to take care of a sick horse," she said.

"You were told right," said Tony Costello. "And I take it you have a sick horse? What's the matter with him, if it's a him, or her if it's a her?"

"It's a mare named Daisy. By the way, my name is Esther Wayman."

"Wayman? You're new here in town," said Tony.

"Just this year. My father is the manager of the bus company."

"I see. And your mare Daisy, how old?"

"Five, I think, or maybe six," said Esther Wayman.

"And sick in what way? What are the symptoms?"

"She's all swollen up around the mouth. I thought I had the curb chain on too tight, but that wasn't it. I kept her in the stable for several days, with a halter on, and instead of going away the swelling got worse."

"Mm. The swelling, is it accompanied by, uh, a great deal of saliva?"

"Yes, it is."

"You say the animal is six years old. How long did you own her, Miss Wayman?"

"Only about a month. I bought her from a place in Philadelphia."

"Mm-hmm. Out Market Street, one of them horse bazaars?"

"Yes."

"Is this your first horse? In other words, you're not familiar with horses?"

"No, we've always lived in the city—Philadelphia, Cleveland Ohio, Denver Colorado. I learned to ride in college, but I never owned a horse before we came here."

"You wouldn't know a case of glanders if you saw it, would you?"

"No. Is that a disease?" she said.

"Unless I'm very much mistaken, it's the disease that ails your mare Daisy. I'll be done washing this car in two shakes, and then you can take me out to see your mare. Where do you stable her?"

"We have our own stable. My father bought the Henderson house."

"Oh, to be sure, and I know it well. Slept in that stable many's the night."

"I don't want to take you away from your work," she said.

"Young woman, you're taking me *to* work. You're not taking me away from anything."

He finished with the Chrysler, got out of his gum boots, and put on his shoes. He called to the garage foreman, "Back sometime in the morning," and did not wait for an answer. None came.

On the way out to the Wayman-Henderson house he let the young woman do all the talking. She had the flat accent of the Middle West and she spoke from deep inside her mouth. She told him how she had got interested in riding at cawlidge, and was so pleased to find that the house her father bought included a garage that was not really a garage but a real stable. Her father permitted her to have a horse on condition that she took complete care of it herself. She had seen the ad in a Philadelphia paper, gone to one of the weekly sales, and paid $300 for Daisy. She had not even looked at any other horse. The bidding for Daisy had started at $100; Esther raised it to $150; someone else went to $200; Esther jumped it to $300 and the mare was hers.

"Uh-huh," said Tony. "Well, maybe you got a bargain, and maybe not."

"You seem doubtful," she said.

"We learn by experience, and you got the animal you wanted. You'll be buying other horses as you get older. This is only your first one."

They left the car at the stable door. "I guess she's lying down," said Esther.

Tony opened the door of the box stall. "She is that, and I'm sorry to tell you, she's never getting up."

"She's dead? How could she be? I only saw her a few hours ago."

"Let me go in and have a look at her. You stay where you are," he said. He had taken command and she obeyed him. In a few minutes, three or four, he came out of the stall and closed the door behind him.

"Glanders, it was. Glanders and old age. Daisy was more like eleven than five or six."

"But how could it happen so quickly?"

"It didn't, exactly. I'm not saying the animal had glanders when you bought her. I do say they falsified her age, which they all do. Maybe they'll give you your money back, maybe they won't. In any case, Miss Wayman, you're not to go in there. Glanders is contagious to man and animal. If you want me to, I'll see to the removal of the animal. A telephone call to the fertilizer plant, and they know me there. Then I'll burn the bedding for you and fumigate the stable. You might as well leave the halter on. It wouldn't be fair to put it on a well horse."

The young woman took out a pack of cigarettes and offered him one. He took it, lit hers and his. "I'm glad to see you take it so calmly. I seen women go into hysterics under these circumstances," he said.

"I don't get hysterics," she said. "But that's not to say I'm not in a turmoil. If I'd had her a little while longer I *might* have gotten hysterical."

"Then be thankful that you didn't have her that much longer. To tell you the truth, you didn't get a bargain. There was other things wrong with her that we needn't go into. I wouldn't be surprised if she was blind, but that's not what I was thinking of. No, you didn't get a bargain this time, but keep trying. Only, next time take somebody with you that had some experience with horses and horse-dealers."

"I'll take you, if you'll come," she said. "Meanwhile, will you do those other things you said you would?"

"I will indeed."

"And how much do I owe you?" she said.

He smiled. "I don't have a regular fee for telling people that a dead horse is dead," he said. "A couple dollars for my time."

"How about ten dollars?"

"Whatever you feel is right, I'll take," he said. "The state of my finances is on the wrong side of affluence."

"Is the garage where I can always reach you?" she said.

"I don't work there steady."

"At home, then? Can you give me your telephone number?" she said.

"I move around from place to place."

"Oh. Well, would you like to have a steady job? I could introduce you to my father."

"I couldn't drive a bus, if that's what you had in mind. I don't have a license, for one thing, and even if I did they have to maintain a schedule. That I've never done, not that strict kind of a schedule. But thanks for the offer."

"He might have a job for you washing buses. I don't know how well it would pay, but I think they wash and clean those buses every night, so it would be steady work. Unless you're not interested in steady work. Is that it?"

"Steady pay without the steady work, that's about the size of it," he said.

She shook her head. "Then I don't think you and my father would get along. He lives by the clock."

"Well, I guess he'd have to, running a bus line," said Tony. He looked about him. "The Hendersons used to hang their cutters up there. They had two cutters and a bob. They were great ones for sleighing parties. Two-three times a winter they'd load up the bob and the two cutters and take their friends down to their farm for a chicken-and-waffle supper. They had four horses then. A pair of sorrels, Prince and Duke. Trixie, a bay mare, broke to saddle. And a black gelding named Satan, Mr. Henderson drove himself to work in. They were pretty near the last to give up horses, Mr. and Mrs. Henderson."

"Did you work for them?"

"Twice I worked for them. Sacked both times. But he knew I used to come here and sleep. They had four big buffalo robes, two for the bob and one each for the cutters. That was the lap of luxury for me. Sleep on two and cover up with one. Then he died and she moved away, and the son Jasper only had cars. There wasn't a horse stabled in here since Mrs. moved away, and Jasper wouldn't let me sleep here. He put in that gazzoline pump and he said it wasn't safe to let me stop here for the night. It wasn't me he was worried about. It was them ottomobiles. Well, this isn't getting to the telephone."

During the night he fumigated the stable. The truck from the fertilizer plant arrived at nine o'clock and he helped the two men load the dead mare, after which he lit the fumigating tablets in the stalls and closed the doors and windows. Esther Wayman came up from the house at ten o'clock or so, just as he was closing the doors of the carriage house. "They took her away?" she said.

"About an hour ago. Then I lit candles for her," he said.

"You what?"

"That's my little joke, not in the best of taste perhaps. I know that this fumigating does any good, but on the other hand it can't do much harm. It's a precaution you take, glanders being contagious and all that. You have to think of the next animal that'll be occupying that stall, so you take every precaution—as much for your own peace of mind as anything else, I guess."

"Where did you get the fumigating stuff?"

"I went down to the drug store, Schlicter's Pharmacy, Sixteenth and Market. I told them to charge it to your father. They know me there."

"They know you everywhere in this town, don't they?"

"Yes, I guess they do, now that I stop to think of it."

"Can I take you home in my car?"

"Oh, I guess I can walk it."

"Why should you when I have my car? Where do you live?"

"I got a room on Canal Street. That's not much of a neighborhood for you to be driving around in after dark."

"I'm sure I've been in worse, or just as bad," she said.

"That would surprise me," he said.

"I'm not a sheltered hothouse plant," she said. "I can take care of myself. Let's go. I'd like to see that part of town."

When they got to Canal Street she said, "It isn't eleven o'clock yet. Is there a place where we can go for a drink?"

"Oh, there's places aplenty. But I doubt if your Dad would approve of them for you."

"Nobody will know me," she said. "I hardly know anybody in this town. I don't get to know people very easily. Where shall we go?"

"Well, there's a pretty decent place that goes by the name of the Bucket of Blood. Don't let the name frighten you. It's just a common ordinary saloon. I'm not saying you'll encounter the Ladies Aid Society there, but if it didn't have that name attached to it—well, you'll see the kind of place it is."

It was a quiet night in the saloon. They sat at a table in the back room. A man and woman were at another table, drinking whiskey by the shot and washing it down with beer chasers. They were a solemn couple, both about fifty, with no need to converse and seemingly no concern beyond the immediate appreciation of the alcohol. Presently the man stood up and headed for the street door, followed by the woman. As she went out she slapped Tony Costello lightly on the shoulder. "Goodnight, Tony," she said.

"Goodnight, Marie," said Tony Costello.

When they were gone Esther Wayman said, "She knew you, but all she said was goodnight. She never said hello."

"Him and I don't speak to one another," said Tony. "We had some kind of a dispute there a long while back."

"Are they husband and wife?"

"No, but they been going together ever since I can remember."

"She's a prostitute, isn't she?"

"That's correct," said Tony.

"And what does he do? Live off her?"

"Oh, no. No, he's a trackwalker for the Pennsy. One of the few around that ain't an I-talian. But she's an I-talian."

"Are you an Italian? You're not, are you?"

"Good Lord, no. I'm as Irish as they come."

"You have an Italian name, though."

"It may sound I-talian to you, but my mother was straight from County Cork. My father could be anybody, but most likely he was an Irishman, the neighborhood I come from. I'm pretty certain he wasn't John Jacob Astor or J. Pierpont Morgan. My old lady was engaged in the same occupation as Marie that just went out."

"Doesn't your church—I mean, in France and Italy I suppose the prostitutes must be Catholic, but I never thought of Irish prostitutes."

"There's prostitutes wherever a woman needs a dollar and doesn't have to care too much how she gets it. It don't even have to be a dollar. If they're young enough they'll do it for a stick of candy, and the dollar comes later. This is an elevating conversation for a young woman like yourself."

"You don't know anything about myself, Mr. Costello," she said.

"I do, and I don't," he said. "But what I don't know I'm learning. I'll make a guess that you were disappointed in love."

She laughed. "Very."

"What happened? The young man give you the go-by?"

"There was no young man," she said. "I have never been interested in young men or they in me."

"I see," he said.

"Do you?"

"Well, to be honest with you, no. I don't. I'd of thought you'd have yourself a husband by this time. You're not at all bad-looking, you know, and you always knew where your next meal was coming from."

"This conversation *is* beginning to embarrass me a little," she said. "Sometime I may tell you all about myself. In fact, I have a feeling I will. But not now, not tonight."

"Anytime you say," said Tony. "And one of these days we'll go looking for a horse for you."

"We'll have fun," she said.

Judith Tarr

CLASSICAL HORSES

I

The yard was full of Lipizzans.

I'd been driving by, missing my old mare and thinking maybe it was time to find another horse, and I'd slowed because I always do, going along any row of fence with horses behind it, and there they were. Not the usual bays and chestnuts and occasional gray, but a herd of little thick white horses that weren't—but couldn't be—but were.

They weren't the Vienna School. They came from somewhere in Florida, Janna told me afterward, and they'd been doing something at the armory, and they needed a place to board for the night. I didn't know Janna then. I wouldn't have stopped, either, just gone down to a crawl and stared, except for the two horses in the paddock. It wasn't that they were wild with all the running and clattering. It was that they were quiet. A chestnut and a gray, not big, just about Morgan-sized, and maybe Morgan-built, too, but finer in the leg and shorter in the back than most I'd seen—and of course you don't see a gray Morgan. But as upheaded as any Morgan you'd want to look at, with a good arch to their necks, and ears pricked sharply forward, watching the show.

I pulled over without even thinking about it. I remember wondering that it was odd, me staring at two perfectly nice but perfectly normal horses, with all those white stallions taking turns around the yard and being walked into the barn. The gray would be white when he was older, there was that. He had a bright eye, but calm. When one of the Lipps circled past his fence, his head came up higher and he stamped. Then he lifted himself up, smooth and sweet as you please, and held for a long breathless while. He was, I couldn't help but notice, a stallion.

The chestnut watched him with what I could have sworn was amusement. His ears flicked back and then forward. His muscles bunched. He soared up, even smoother than the gray, and lashed back hard enough to take the head off anyone who might have dared to stand behind him.

Levade, capriole. Then they were quiet again, head to tail, rubbing one another's withers like any old plow horses.

I got out of the car. No one looked at me or even seemed to have noticed the demonstration in the paddock. I wandered toward the fence. The chestnut spared me a glance. The gray was too busy having his neck rubbed. I didn't try to lure them over. I leaned against the post and watched the stallions, but with a corner of an eye for the ones in the paddock.

There was an old surrey on the other side, with a tarp half draped over it, half folded back. Someone sat in the seat. She was old, how old I couldn't tell; just that she was over sixty, and probably over seventy, and maybe eighty, too. It didn't keep her from sitting perfectly straight, or from looking at me with eyes as young as her face was old, large in their big round sockets, and a quite beautiful shade of gray. She didn't smile. If she had, I might have ducked and left.

As it was, I took my time, but after a while I went over. "Hello," I said.

She nodded.

I supposed I knew who she was. I'd heard about a woman who had a farm out this way. She was ninety, people said, if she was a day, and she still drove her own horses. Had even been riding them up till a little while ago, when she broke her hip—not riding, either, but falling down in her house like any other very old lady. She had a cane beside her, with a brass horse's head.

"Nice horses," I said, cocking my head at the two in the paddock.

She nodded again. I wondered if she could talk. She didn't look as if she'd had a stroke, and no one had said anything about her being mute.

"Not often you see two stallions in a paddock together," I went on.

"They've always been together."

Her voice was quiet and a little thin, but it wasn't the old-lady voice I might have expected. She had an interesting accent. European, more or less.

"Brothers?" I asked.

"Twins."

I stared at them. They did look a lot alike, except for the color: bright copper chestnut, almost gold, and dapple gray, with the mane and tail already silver.

"That's rare," I said.

"Very."

I stuck out a hand, a little late, and introduced myself. Her hand was thin and knobby, but she had a respectable grip. "You're Mrs. Tiffney, of course."

She laughed, which was surprising. She sounded impossibly young. "Of course! I'm the only antique human on the farm." She kept on smiling at me. "My yard is full of Lipizzans, and you notice my two ponies?"

"Big ponies," I said. "If they're that. Morgans?"

"No," she said. She didn't tell me what they were. I didn't, at that point, ask. Someone was standing behind me. Janna, I knew later. She wanted to know what to do about someone named Ragweed, who was in heat, and Florence had categorically refused to move her Warmblood for any silly circus horse, and the show manager wanted to know if he could use the shavings in the new barn, but she wasn't sure what to charge him for them, if she let him have them at all, since no one had told her if there was going to be a delivery this week.

It went on like that. I found myself dumping feed in nervous boarders' bins and helping Janna pitch hay to the horses that had been put out to pasture for the night. There were people around—this was a big barn, and the guests had plenty of grooms of their own—but one way and another I seemed to have been adopted. Or to have adopted the place.

"Do you always take in strangers?" I asked Janna. It was late by then. We were up in the office, drinking coffee from the urn and feeling fairly comfortable. Feeding horses together can do that to people. She'd sent the kids home, and the grooms were gone to their hotel or bedded down in the barn. Even Mrs. Tiffney had gone to the house that stood on the hill behind the barns.

Janna yawned till her jaw cracked. She didn't apologize. She was comfortable people, about my age and about my size, with the no-nonsense air that stable managers either learn early or give up and become bitchy instead. "We take in strays," she said. "Plenty of cats. Too damn many dogs. Horses, as often as not. People, not that often. People are a bad lot."

"Maybe I am, too," I said.

"Mrs. Tiffney likes you," said Janna.

"Just like that?"

Janna shrugged. "She's good at judging animals."

"People-type animals, too?"

Janna didn't answer. She poured more coffee instead, first for me, then for herself. "Do you ride?" she asked.

"Not since the winter. I had a mare up at Meadow Farm; Arab. Did dressage with her. She got twisted intestine. Had to put her down." It still hurt to say that.

Janna was horse people. She understood. "Looking for another?"

"Starting to."

"None for sale here right now," she said. "But some of the boarders take leases. There's always someone wanting a horse ridden. If you want to try one of them, take a lesson. . . ."

I tried one, and then another. I took a lesson. I took two. Pretty soon I was a regular, though I didn't settle on any particular horse. The ones that came up weren't quite what I was looking for, and the ones I might have been interested in weren't for sale or lease, but I had plenty of chances to ride them.

What I was mostly interested in was just being there. Someone had put up a sampler in the tackroom: "Peaceable Kingdom." Tacky and sentimental, but it fit. There were always dogs around and cats underfoot. Janna gave most of the lessons, but she had a couple of older kids to help with the beginners. I didn't do any teaching. I did enough of that every day, down in the trenches.

There were thirty horses in the two barns, minus the one-night stand of Lipizzans. The farm owned a few ponies and a couple of school horses, and Mrs. Tiffney's pair of stallions, who had a corner of the old barn to themselves. They weren't kept for stud, weren't anything registered that anyone knew of. They were just Mrs. Tiffney's horses, the red and the gray—Zan and Bali. She drove them as a team, pulling a surrey in the summer and a sleigh in the winter. Janna rode them every day if she could. Bali was a pretty decent jumper. Zan was happier as a dressage horse, though he'd jump if Janna asked; and I'd seen what he could do in the way of caprioles. Bali was the quiet one, though that wasn't saying he was gentle—he had plenty of spirit. Zan was the one you had to watch. He'd snake his head out if you walked by his stall, and get titchy if he thought you owed him a carrot or a bit of apple. Bali was more likely to charm it out of you. Zan expected it, or else.

I got friendly with most of the horses, even Florence's precious Warmblood, but those two had brought me in first, and I always had a soft spot for them. They seemed to know who I was, too, and Bali started to nicker when I came, though I thought that was more for his daily apple than for me. If Mrs. Tiffney was there, I'd help her and Janna harness them up for her to take her drive around the pastures and down the road, or sit with her while she watched Janna ride one or the other of them. The day she asked me if I'd like to ride Bali—Janna was saddling Zan then—I should have been prepared, and in a way I was, but I was surprised. I had my saddle, I was wearing my boots; I'd been riding Sam for his owner, who was jetsetting in Atlantic City. But people didn't just ride Mrs. Tiffney's horses.

I said so. She laughed at me. "No, they don't. Unless I tell them to. Go and saddle Bali. He'll be much happier to be with his brother."

He was that. I felt as if I was all over his back—first-ride nerves, I always get them in front of the owner. But he had lovely gaits, and he seemed determined to show me all of them. Fourteen. I'd counted once at Meadow Farm, when I watched the riding master. Walk: collected, working, medium, extended. Trot: ditto. Canter: ditto. And then, because Mrs. Tiffney told me to do it, and because Janna was there to set my legs where they belonged and to guide my hands, the two gaits almost no one ever gets to ride: passage, the graceful, elevated, slow-motion trot; and piaffe, "Spanish trot" that in Vienna they do between the pillars, not an inch forward, but all that power and impulsion concentrated in one place, in perfect control, to the touch of the leg and the support of the hand and the will of the rider that by then is perfectly melded with that of the horse.

I dropped down and hugged Bali till he snorted. I was grinning like an idiot. Janna was grinning, too. I could have sworn even Zan was, flirting his tail at his brother as he went by.

Mrs. Tiffney smiled. She looked quite as satisfied as Bali did when I pulled back to look at him, though I thought he might be laughing, too. And told myself to stop anthropomorphizing, but how often does anyone get to ride a high-school horse?

II

Not long after that, Mrs. Tiffney taught me to drive. I'd never learned that, had always been out riding when chances came up. It was easier than riding in some ways. Harder in others, with two horses to think of, and turning axes, and all those bits and pieces of harness.

We didn't talk much through all of this. The horses were enough. Sometimes I mentioned something that had happened at school, or said I'd have to leave early to have dinner with a friend, or mentioned that I was thinking of going back to grad school.

"In what?" she asked me.

"Classics, probably," I said. "I've got the Masters in it, but all I teach is Latin. I'd like to get my Greek back before I lose it. And teach in college. High school's a war zone, most of the time. You can't really teach. Mostly you just play policeman and hope most of your classes can read."

"Surely," she said, "if they can take Latin, they can read English?"

She sounded properly shocked. I laughed sourly. "You'd think so, wouldn't you? But we're egalitarian at Jonathan Small. Anyone who wants anything can take it. Can't be elitist, now, can we? Though I finally got them to give me a remedial Latin class—remedial reading, for kids who can't read English. It does work. And it keeps them from going nuts in a regular class."

"Democracy," said Mrs. Tiffney, "was never intended for everyone."

I couldn't help it. I laughed. I couldn't stop. When I finally did manage to suck in a breath, she was watching me patiently. She didn't look offended. She didn't say anything further, either, except to ask me to turn around and put the team into a trot.

When we'd cooled the horses and cleaned the harness—she insisted on doing it herself, no matter what anyone said—she invited me to the house. I almost refused. I'm shy about things like that, and I had classes in the morning. But maybe I had amends to make. I shouldn't have laughed at her.

From the outside it was nothing in particular. A big white frame house with pillars in front: New England Neoclassical. Janna had the upstairs rear, which I'd seen already, steep twisty staircases and rooms with interesting ceilings, dipping and swooping at the roof's whim, and a fireplace that worked.

Downstairs was much the same, but the ceilings were halfway to the sky, rimmed with ornate moldings, and there seemed to be a fireplace in every room, even the kitchen. There were books everywhere, on shelves to the ceiling, on revolving shelves beside the big comfortable chairs, between bookends on tables and mantelpieces. And in through the books there were wonderful things: a bust of a Roman senator, a medieval triptych of angels and saints around a Madonna and child, an African mask, a Greek krater, a bronze horse that must have been Greek, too, and hanging from the ceiling, so surprising that I laughed, a papiermaché pterodactyl with carefully painted-in silvery-gray fur.

Mrs. Tiffney wasn't going to let me help her with the cups and cookies, but she didn't try too hard to stop me. She did insist that I get comfortable in the living room while she waited for the water to boil. I wandered where she pointed, past the den and the library I'd already seen, to the front room with its wide windows and its Oriental carpet. It was full of books as all the other rooms were, and its fireplace was marble, cream-pale in the light from the tall windows. There was a painting over it, an odd one, perfectly round, with what must have been hundreds of figures in concentric circles.

When I came closer I saw that it wasn't a painting, precisely. More of a bas-relief, with a rim that must have been gold leaf, and inside it a rim of beautiful blue shading to green and gray and white, sea-colors, and in the center a field of stars—I picked out the gold dots of constellations, Orion and the Dipper, and the moon in silver phases—and between them more people than I could begin to count; doing more things than a glance could take in. They had a classical look, neoclassical more probably, not quite elaborate enough to be baroque, not quite off-center enough to be medieval.

I found my finger creeping up to touch, to see if it was really real. I shoved my hand in the pocket of my jacket.

A kettle shrieked in the kitchen. I almost bolted toward it. Hating to leave that wonderful thing, but glad to escape the temptation to touch it.

"Did you know," I said to Mrs. Tiffney as she filled the teapot, "that you have the shield of Achilles in your living room?"

She didn't look at me oddly. Just smiled. "Yes," she said. "I thought you'd recognize it."

I picked up the tray before she could do it, and carried it back through the rooms. The shield—yes, it was a shield, or meant to be one, clearly and, now that I noticed, rather markedly convex—glowed at me while Mrs. Tiffney poured tea and I ate cookies. I don't remember what the cookies tasted like. They were good, I suppose. I was counting circles. There was the city at peace, yes. And the city at war. The wedding and the battle. The trial, the ambush. The field and the vineyard. The cattle and the lions. The sheep and the shepherds. The dancing floor and the dancers.

"Someone," I said, "made himself a masterpiece."

Mrs. Tiffney nodded. She was still smiling, sipping tea, looking sometimes at me and sometimes at the marvel over her mantel.

"People argue," I said. "Over how it really was supposed to be. Your artist went for the simplest way out—the circles."

"Sometimes simplest is best," Mrs. Tiffney said.

I nodded. The cattle were gold, I noticed, with a patina that made them look like real animals, and their horns looked like tin, or something else grayish-silvery. Base metal; probably, gilded or foiled over. Whoever this artist was, whenever he worked—I was almost ready to say seventeenth century, or very good twentieth with a very large budget—he knew his Homer. Loved him, to do every detail, wrinkles of snarls on the lions' muzzles, curls of hair on the bulls' foreheads, bright red flashes of blood where the lions had struck.

"This should be in a museum," I said.

Mrs. Tiffney didn't frown, but her smile was gone. "I suppose it should. But I'm selfish. I think it's happier here, where people live, and can touch it if they want to, and it can know the air and the light."

Pure heresy, of course. A wonder like this should have the best protection money could buy, controlled climate, controlled access, everything and anything to preserve it for the ages.

But it was beautiful up there in this living room, with late daylight on it and a bit of breeze blowing through. I got up without thinking and went over to it, and touched it. The figures were cool, raised so that I could have seen them without eyes, and they wove and flowed around one another, a long undulating line that came back to where it began.

I wasn't breathing. I drew a breath in slowly. "I've never," I said, "seen a thing like this. Or anything that came close to it."

"There's only one like it in the world," Mrs. Tiffney said. She bent forward to fill my cup again. I sat back down, took another cookie.

"And you say you don't believe in democracy," I said. "If keeping this out of a museum isn't democratic, then what is?"

"This is simple sense, and giving a masterpiece the setting it loves best." She sipped delicately from the little china cup. "It's been in my family for a very long time. When it first came to us, we promised its maker that we would care for it as he asked us to do, never to hide it away and never to sell it, or to give it except as a gift to one who could love it as he loved it. It was the eldest daughter's dowry, when such things were done. Now I'm the last," she said, "and it goes to no daughter after me."

I was still wrapped up in the wonder of the thing, or I would never have said what came into my head. "Janna says you have daughters. Two of them. And granddaughters."

"Stepdaughters," she said. She didn't seem offended. I was my husband's second wife. We had a son, but he died early, and he had no children. My husband's children were never quite sure what to make of me. Now that I'm old, you see, I'm permitted to be eccentric. But when I was younger, with children who resented their father's marrying again so soon after their mother died, I was simply too odd for words. All my antiquities, and my books, and that dreadful garish thing that I *would* hang in the parlor—"

"It's not garish!"

She laughed. "It's hardly in the most contemporary of taste; especially when contemporary was Art Deco. And pockets full of coins of the Caesars, and gowns out of the *Très Riches Heures,* and once, as a favor to a friend, a mummy in the basement: oh, I was odd. Alarmingly so. The mummy went back home with as many of her treasures as we could find. I, unfortunately, lacked the grace to do the same."

"So you are Greek," I said.

She nodded.

"The artist—he was, too?"

"Yes," she said, "very. He wouldn't sign his work. He said that it would speak for itself."

"It does," I said, looking at it again, as if I could begin to help myself. "Oh, it does."

III

That was in the early spring. In late spring, just after lilac time, I came to ride Bali—those days, I was riding him almost every day, or driving them both with Mrs. Tiffney—and found the place deserted except for one of the stablehands. She was new and a bit shy, just waved and kept on with the stall she was cleaning.

The stallions were both in their stalls. Usually they were out at this time of day. I wondered if they'd come up lame, or got sick. Zan didn't whip his head out the way he usually did and snap his teeth in my face. Bali didn't nicker, though he came to the door when I opened it. His eyes were clear. So was his nose. He didn't limp as I brought him out. But he wasn't himself. He didn't throw his head around on the crossties, he didn't flag his tail, he didn't grab for the back of my shirt the way he'd taken to, to see me jump. He just stood there, letting me groom him.

I looked in Zan's stall. Zan looked back at me. Nothing wrong with him, either, that I could see or feel. Except that the spirit had gone out of him. He actually looked old. So did Bali, who was still young enough to be more a dapple than a gray.

"You look as if you lost a friend," I said.

Zan's ears went flat. Bali grabbed the right crosstie in his teeth and shook it, hard.

I had a little sense left. I remembered to get him back in his stall before I bolted.

Mrs. Tiffney was in the hospital. She'd had another fall, and maybe a heart attack. They weren't sure yet. I wouldn't have got that much out of anybody if Janna hadn't driven in as I came haring out of the barn. She looked as worn as the horses did, as if she hadn't slept in a week.

"Last night," she said when I'd dragged her up to the office and got coffee into her. "I was downstairs borrowing some milk, or she'd have gone on lying there till God knows when. The ambulance took forever to come. Then she wanted the paramedics to carry her up to her own bed. I thought she'd have another heart attack, fighting them when they took her out."

I gulped coffee. It was just barely warm. My throat hurt. "Is she going to be all right?"

Janna shrugged. "They don't know, yet. The harpies came in this morning—her daughters, I mean. Aileen isn't so bad, but Celia . . ." She rubbed her eyes. They must have felt as if they were full of sand. "Celia has been trying for years to make her mother live somewhere, as she puts it, 'appropriate.' A nursing home, she means. She's old enough for one herself, if you ask me."

"Maybe she thinks she's doing what's best," I said.

"I'm sure she is," said Janna. "What's best for Celia. She'd love to have this place. She'd sell it for a golf course, probably. Or condos. Horses are a big waste of money, she says. So's that great big house up there on the hill, with just two women living in it."

"And kids," I said, "in the summer, when you have camp."

"Not enough profit in that." Janna put down her half-empty cup. "She married a stockbroker, but Mrs. Tiffney always said Celia did the thinking for the pair of them, in and out of the office. If she'd been born forty years later, *she'd* have been the broker, and she probably wouldn't have married at all."

It still wouldn't have done Mrs. Tiffney any good, I thought, after I'd bullied Janna into bed and done what needed doing in the barn and driven slowly home. Mrs. Tiffney's horses didn't look any brighter when I looked in on them, just before I left, though, Bali let his nose rest in my palm for a minute. Thanking me, I imagined, for understanding. Just being a horse, actually, with a human he'd adopted into his personal herd.

Mrs. Tiffney wasn't allowed visitors, except for immediate family. In Janna's opinion, and I admit in mine, the hospital would have done better to bar the family and let in the friends. Aileen did answer Janna's calls, which was more than Celia would do; so we knew that Mrs. Tiffney hadn't broken her hip again but she had had a heart attack, and she was supposed to stay very, very quiet. She'd been asking after her horses. Janna was able to pass on some of the news, though Aileen wasn't horse people; she didn't understand half of what Janna told her, and she probably mixed up the rest.

I actually saw her with her sister, a few days after Mrs. Tiffney went to the hospital. They'd come to the house, they said, to get a few things their mother needed. I think Celia was checking out the property. They were a bit of a surprise. The slim blade of a woman in the Chanel suit turned out to be Aileen. Celia was the plump matronly lady in sensible brogues. She knew about horses and asked sharp questions about the barn's expenses. Aileen looked a little green at the dirt and the smell. She didn't touch anything, and she walked very carefully, watching where she put her feet.

I was walking Bali down after a ride. He was still a bit off, but he'd been willing enough to work. If he'd been human, I'd have said he was drowning his sorrows. I brought him out of the ring for some of the good grass along the fence, and there was Aileen, stubbing out a cigarette and looking a little alarmed at the huge animal coming toward her. Little Bali, not quite fifteen hands, kept on coming, though I did my best to encourage him with a patch of clover. He had his sights set on another one a precise foot from Aileen's right shoe. She backed away.

"I'm sorry," I said. "He's got a mind of his own."

"He always did," said Aileen. She eyed him. He flopped his ears at a fly and took another mouthful of clover. "You must be Laura—Ms. Michaels, that is. My mother has told me about you."

For some reason I wanted to cry. "Has she? She's talking, then?"

"She's very frail, but she's quite lucid. All she can talk about, most days, is her horses, and that dreadful platter of hers. You've seen it, she says. Isn't it gaudy?"

"I think it's quite beautiful," I said a bit stiffly—jerkily, too. Bali had thrown up his head on the other end of the leadrope, near knocking me off my feet, and attacked a fly on his flank. For an instant I thought he was going after Aileen. So did she: she beat a rapid retreat.

But she didn't run away completely. She seemed to come to a decision. "Mother has asked to see you. Celia said no, but I think you should go."

I stood flatfooted. Bali was cropping grass again, not a care in the world. "Why?" was all I could think to ask.

"You ride her horses," said Aileen.

IV

Mrs. Tiffney looked even frailer than Aileen had warned me she would, white face and white hair against the white sheet, and tubes and wires and machines all doing their inscrutable business while she simply tried to stay alive. I'd been not thinking up till then. I'd been expecting that this would go away, she'd come back, everything would be the way it was before.

Looking at her, I knew she wasn't coming back. She might go to a nursing home first, for a little while, but not for long. The life was ebbing out of her even while I stood there.

She'd been asleep, I thought, till her eyes opened. They were still the same, bigger than ever in her shrunken face. Her smile made me almost forget all the rest of it. She reached out her arms to me. I hugged her, being very careful with her tubes and wires, and her brittle bones in the midst of them.

Aileen had come in with me. When I glanced back to where she'd been, she was gone.

"Aileen was always tactful," Mrs. Tiffney said. "Brave, even, if she saw a way to get by Celia."

Her voice was an old-lady voice as it never had been before, thin and reedy. But no quaver in it.

"And how are my horses?" she asked me.

I had fifteen minutes, the nurse at the desk had told me. I spent them telling her what she most wanted to know. I babbled, maybe, to get it all in. She didn't seem to mind.

"And my ponies?" she asked. "My Xanthos and Balios?"

I'd been saving them for last. I started a little at their names. No one had told me that was what they were. Then I smiled. Of course the woman who had Achilles' shield—as genius had imagined it, long after Achilles was dead—would name her horses after Achilles' horses. She'd had a pair like them, Janna had told me, for as long as anyone had known her. Maybe it was part of the family tradition, like the shield on the wall.

"They're well," I answered her, once I remembered to stop maundering and talk. "They miss you. I had Bali out this morning; Janna and I did a pas-de-deux. We walked them past the surrey after, and they both stopped. I swear, they were asking where you were."

"You haven't told them?"

She sounded so severe, and so stern, that I stared at her.

She closed her eyes. The lids looked as thin as parchment. "No. Of course you wouldn't know. And they'd have heard people talking."

"We've been pretty quiet," I said. And when she opened her eyes and fixed them on me: "We did talk about it while we put the horses out. We'll tell them properly if you like."

"It would be a courtesy," she said, still severely. Then, with a glint: "However silly you may feel."

I didn't know about feeling silly. I talked to my cats at home. I talked to the horses when I rode them or brushed them. "I'll tell them," I said.

She shut her eyes again. I stood up. I was past my fifteen minutes. The nurse would be coming in to chase me out, unless I got myself out first. But when I started to draw back, she reached and caught my hand. I hadn't known there was so much strength in her.

"Look after my horses," she said. "Whatever happens, look after them. Promise me."

I'm not proud to admit that the first thing I thought of was how much it would cost to keep two horses. And the second was that Celia might have something to say about that. The third was something like a proper thought. "I'll do my best," I said.

"You'll do it," she said. "Promise!"

Her machines were starting to jerk and flicker. "I promise," I said, to calm her down mostly. But meaning it.

"And the shield," she said. "That, too. They go together, the horses and the shield. When I die—"

"You're not going to die."

She ignored me. "When I die, they choose to whom they go. It will be you, I think. The horses have chosen you already."

"But—"

"Look to Xanthos. Balios is the sweet one, the one who loves more easily, who gives himself first and without reservation. Xanthos is as wise as he is wicked. He was silenced long ago, and never spoke again, but his wits are as sharp as they ever were."

I opened my mouth. Closed it. She'd gone out of her head. She was dreaming old dreams, taking the name for the thing, and making her very real if by no means ordinary horses into horses out of a story. I'd done it myself when I was younger: little rafter-hipped cranky-tempered Katisha was the Prophet's won chosen mare, because she was a bay with one white foot and a star. But that hadn't made her the first of the Khamsa, any more than Mrs. Tiffney's wishing made her horses Achilles' horses. Or her shield—her neoclassical masterpiece—Achilles' shield.

They were treasures enough by themselves. I almost said so. But she was holding so tight, and looking so urgent, that I just nodded.

She nodded back. "The first moonlit night after I die, make sure you're at the barn. Watch the horses. Do whatever they ask you to do."

What could I do, except nod?

She let me go so suddenly that I gasped. But she was still breathing. "Remember," she said, no more than a whisper.

Then the nurse came charging in, took a look at the monitors, and ordered me out. The last I saw of Mrs. Tiffney was the nurse's white back and Mrs. Tiffney's white face, and her eyes on me, willing me to remember.

V

She died two days later, early in the morning of a gray and rainy day. She went in her sleep, Janna told me, and she went without pain. When I saw her laid out in the casket—and how Celia could think the shield was gaudy and reckon peach satin and mahogany with brass fittings tasteful, I would never understand—she was smiling. The funeral parlor was so full of flowers I could barely breathe, and so full of people I couldn't move, though it tended to flow toward the casket and then away into clumps on the edges. I recognized people from the barn, wide-eyed, white-faced kids with their parents, older ones alone or with friends, looking intensely uncomfortable but very determined, and the boarders in a cluster near the door. They all looked odd and half-complete in suits and dresses, without horses beside them or peering over their shoulders.

I said a proper few words to Celia, who didn't seem to recognize me, and to Aileen, who did. Celia didn't look as triumphant as I suspected she felt. Her mother had been such a trial to her for so long, and now the trial was over. She'd get the property and the estate—she'd have to share with Aileen, of course, and there'd be bequests, but she'd hardly care for that. She'd administer it all, if she had anything to say about it.

"She lived a full life," a woman said behind me in the syrupy voice some people reserve for funerals. "She died happy. Doesn't she look wonderful, Celia?"

There was a knot in my throat, so thick and so solid that I couldn't swallow. I said something to somebody—it might have been Janna, who didn't look wonderful, either—and got out of there.

The horses were real. They didn't make empty noises, or drown me in flowers. Bali stood still while I cried in his mane, and when I wrapped my arms around his neck, he wrapped his neck around me.

Finally I pulled back. He had an infection, or something in the new hay had got to him: his eyes were streaming. So, when I turned around, were Zan's. I sniffled hard and got a cloth for them and a tissue for me, and wiped us all dry. "All right," I said. "So you're crying, too. Horses don't cry. You've got an allergy. What is it, mold in the hay?"

Bali bit me. Not hard enough to do damage, but hard enough to hurt. I was so shocked that I didn't even whack his nose; just stood there. And he shouldered past me. He didn't have a halter on. I'd come in to the stall to get him, forgotten the halter on its hook, and started bawling. I grabbed for him. He kept on going.

Zan arched his neck, oh so delicately, and bared his long yellow teeth, and slid the bar on his door. I lunged. He was out, not moving fast at all, just fast enough to stay out of my reach.

I snatched halters on the way by. Zan pirouetted in the aisle and plucked them both out of my hands, and gave me a look that said as clear as if he'd spoken, "Not those, stupid." Then he spun again and waited.

I heard Mrs. Tiffney's voice. I was imagining it, of course. *Watch the horses. Do whatever they ask you to do.*

They certainly weren't acting like normal stallions on the loose. Bali was waiting, up past Zan, with his most melting expression. Zan— there was no other word for it—glared. His opinion of my intelligence, never very high to begin with, was dropping fast.

And it was dark, but there was a moon, a white half-moon in a field of stars like the ones in the center of the shield. Which was resting against the barn wall, just outside the door to the yard. And where the surrey used to stand was something else. I told myself it was the moon that made the old-fashioned black carriage look like something ages older and much smaller, and not black at all. Not in the least. That was gold, glimmering in the light from the aisle. And gold on the harness that lay on the ground beside it.

"But," I said, "I don't know *how* to yoke up a chariot."

Zan snorted at me. Bali was kinder. He went up to the pole that rested on the ground and positioned himself just so, and cocked an ear. After a minute Zan did the same, but his ears were flat in disgust. If he was choosing me, whatever that meant, he wasn't going to make it easy.

The harness wasn't that hard to figure out, once I'd had a good look at it. Or as good as moonlight and aislelight would give me. The yoke, of course, instead of collars. The bridles were familiar enough, and the reins.

I ran those the way they seemed to want to run. The horses were patient, even Zan.

When they were harnessed, I stood back. I don't know what I was thinking. Nothing, by then. Except maybe that this wasn't happening. Something in the combination of moonlight and barn light made the horses shine. Bali, of course, with his silver mane and tail and his pewter coat. But Zan, too, a light that seemed to grow the longer I stood there, not silver but gold, lambent in the dark.

"Immortal horses," I said. "Bright gifts the gods gave to Peleus, and he to his son, and his son—" I broke off. "But the gods are dead!"

Zan shook his head in the bridle, baring his teeth at me. Bali watched me quietly. His ear slanted back. *Get in the chariot,* he meant. And how I knew that, I didn't want to know. No more than how I knew to pick up the shield—heavy as all heaven, but lighter than I'd expected, even so—and hang it where it best seemed to fit, by the left side of the chariot. I picked up the reins. They weren't any different from driving the surrey, though I was standing up in a vehicle that seemed no heavier than an eggshell, and no better sprung than one either, for all its pretty gilding. I didn't pretend that I was telling the horses where to go. They started at a walk, maneuvering carefully out of the yard where I'd seen Lipizzans, so long ago it seemed now, though it wasn't even nine months. Hardly long enough to carry a baby to term.

They took the way I'd driven so often, down the road a bit and into the woods. The moon didn't quite reach through the new leaves, but the horses were shining, silver and red-gold, bright enough to light the woods around them. The track was clear and smooth. They stretched into a trot.

The wind was soft in my face. It was a warm night, the first after a week of damp and rain, and everything smelled green, with sweetness that was apple blossoms, growing stronger as we went on. By the time we came out into the orchard, my lungs were full of it.

The trees were all in bloom, and the moon made them shine as bright almost as Bali's coat. He was cantering now, he and his brother, and the chariot rocked and rattled. I wrapped the reins around the post that seemed made for just that, and concentrated on hanging on. If I'd had any sense at all I would have hauled the horses down to a walk, turned them around and made them go back home. But all the strangeness had caught up with me. My head was full of moon and night and apple blossoms, and old, old stories, and the shield-rim under my left hand and the chariot's side under my right, and the horses running ahead of me, the chestnut, the gray, Xanthos, Balios, who couldn't be, who couldn't begin to be, but who surely were.

And I'd inherited them. I'd had the letter this morning, in her firm clear hand, with a date on it that made me start: the day after I'd first seen the shield. The shield was mine, if the horses chose me; and they were mine, too, and the wherewithal to keep and house them. That was how she put it. Tonight, in the way the moon's light fell, I knew that Janna had an inheritance, too; that Celia would be very surprised when the will was read. Oh, she'd have a handsome sum, and she'd grow richer than she'd been to begin with, once she'd invested it. And Aileen had a sum as large, which she wouldn't manage a tenth as well, unless she handed it over to Celia. But the land was Janna's, and the barn, and the horses, and the house, and everything that went with them, except Xanthos and Balios and the shield that a god had made to protect a legend in battle.

The moon had made a seer of me. I'd wake up in the morning with a headache and a sour stomach, and maybe a little regret for the dream I'd lost in waking.

It didn't feel like a dream, for all its strangeness. The night air was real, and the branch that whipped my face as the horses turned, mounting the hill. From the top of it, over the orchard that surrounded it, you could see for miles, down to the river on one side and over the ridges on the other, rolling outward in circles, with towns in the hollows, and fields full of cows, and the Riccis' vineyard with its rows of vines on poles; and maybe, through a gap in the last ridge, a glimmer that was the ocean. Here was higher than the hill Mrs. Tiffney's house stood on: it lay just below, with the barns beyond it. In the daytime you could see the rings and the hunt course, and the riders going through their paces like a dance.

Tonight the orchard was like a field of snow, and the hills were dark with once in a while a glimmer of light, and where Mrs. Tiffney's house stood, a shadow with a light at the top of it. Janna, home where she belonged, alone in the quiet rooms.

I found I couldn't care that she might be checking the barn, and she'd find the lights on and Mrs. Tiffney's horses missing. Or maybe she wouldn't. Maybe it was all dark and quiet, the doors shut, the horses asleep, everything asleep but me, and the horses who had brought me here. I got down from the chariot and went to their heads, smoothing Bali's forelock, venturing—carefully—to stroke Zan's neck. He allowed it. I slid my hand to the poll, round the ear, down past the plate of the cheek. He didn't nip or pull away. I touched the velvet of his nose. He blew into my palm. His eyes were bright. Immortal eyes. "How do you stand it?" I asked him. "Bound to mortal flesh that withers and dies, and you never age a day? How many have you loved, and however long they lived, in the end, all too soon, they died?"

He didn't speak. He'd been able to, once. I saw it in his eyes. Dust and clamor and a terrible roil of war, the charioteer cut down, the loved one—loved more than the master, for the master owned them, but the charioteer belonged to them, Patroklos who was never strong enough to fight his prince's battle—and the bitterness after, the prince taking vengeance, and the stallion speaking, foretelling the master's death. He'd grieved for the prince, too, and the prince's son in his time, and his son's son, and how it had come to daughters instead of sons—that he wasn't telling me. It was enough that it had been.

Bali rested his nose on my shoulder. Zan nipped lightly, very lightly, at my palm. Claiming me. The wind blew over us. West wind.

I laughed, up there on the hilltop, with the wind in my hair. Little no-name no-pedigree horses: by west wind out of storm wind, or maybe she had been a Harpy, like Celia and her sister. I belonged to them now. And a gaudy great platter that owned me as much as they did.

I'd cry again in a little while. I'd lost a friend; I owed her grief. But she'd be glad that I could laugh, who'd known exactly what she was doing when she filled her yard with Lipizzans and lured me in, and snared me for her stallions.

I leaned on Xanthos' shoulder, and Balios leaned lightly on mine. They were shining still, and brighter than the moon, but they were warm to the touch, real and solid horses. We stood there, the three of us, mortal I and immortal they, and watched the moon go down.

Barry N. Malzberg

ONE TEN THREE

I am in the paddock inspecting the horses and thinking as one tends to do increasingly at this stage of life of time's winged chariot drawing near even though these are the flat races at Ozone Park, Queens, when the filly being escorted through and around the small tunnels of grass and dirt looks at me and says distinctly, I am a lock in this race. I would not turn me down. At eight to one I am a distinct overlay.

This communication is stunning; it is a shock. It is a voice within my head and yet outside my head if you follow what I am saying. Turning my head to the right, then to the left, inclining it toward the seat of purpose so to speak I note that none of the denizens of paddock observers seem to have shared this insight. Camped in their customary oblivion they are looking at figures, making notes on the entries, engaging in deep discussion with one another or with themselves, etc. The usual paddock business in short.

I am speaking to you, the filly says. She lifts her head and looks at me with powerful, soulful eyes. This is a direct communication within the confines of a relationship. I tell you, I cannot lose this. You had better get down on me. It is five minutes to post.

The name of this filly, one of eight in a maiden special weights in Man's Fate. I should make this part of the exposition clear, also that this is the name of a famous book by Andre Malraux who is a Frenchman not connected to the Dreyfus case, a work of philosophy of some significance published around the time of World War II. Also that the field is still within the paddock, circling and taking the air five minutes until post because this is deep, foul winter at South Ozone Park in Queens, gray and eight degrees at first post and it is agreed that exposure of jockeys to elements for the customary duration of the ten minute parade to the post would be most cruel. Also, the jockeys are participants in a union not available at this time to horses. That is all the exposition that is necessary in this context except to add that my name is Fred and that it has not been my history to have had conversations with horses, much less self-announced and prospective winners.

That's what you say, Fred, Man's Fate says to me. The fact is that you have had conversations with horses for most of your adult life. The difference is that this is the first time that a horse has responded to *you*. Man's Fate gave a little whinny at this final confidence or perhaps the word is whicker and said, Take it or leave it, Fred. All your life you have been looking for a tip and now when you have one you search for qualification.

Man's Fate became a popular post-existentialist text in upper level college philosophy courses during the 1960s. I know this, too, it is remarkable the detritus of information which can accumulate to one through decades of assiduous following of the horses. Noting that the bearer of that name is a chestnut filly with a noseband and red blinkers, that she in addition has a shadow roll and rear *and* front bandages, a normally bad sign, I shrug, tip my head in what I take to be a courteous gesture, turn from the paddock and its spare, cold-stricken onlookers and make my way through the sinister aspect of this unpleasant racetrack to the enclosure of the lower grandstand. Careful study of the *Racing Form,* a copyrighted publication of the well-loved Annenberg family informs me that Man's Fate worked out in one ten three over five and a half furlongs Wednesday past and has not previously experimented with blinkers. A three-year-old by Sinatra out of Keep the Faith whose sire was Never Bend, the filly has had only one previous race, much earlier this year at Thistledown where she finished eighth in a ten horse field, beaten by multiples of lengths at a distance of four furlongs, maiden special weights. There are no other figures accompanying the one ten three and the name of the trainer, W.L. Mariposa, is unknown to me as is that of the owner which is the same. The jockey is Stevens, an undistinguished journeyman, riding two pounds overweight at 116. One ten three is an outstanding workout for six furlongs but something less than distinguished for five and a half and Man's Fate finished her four furlong gambol in March, my calculations assure me, in something in excess of 54 seconds.

This is not encouraging, I say aloud on the line. These are not quantifying signs.

The man in front of me says, Could you not stick your paper in my ear? You are reshaping my earlobe unpleasantly.

I am sorry, I say, readjusting the Racing Form. It is still not encouraging.

That is for sure, the man with the rearranged ear says, rubbing it thoughtfully. It is not encouragement which brings us out here. One might say it is the reverse. He stares earnestly at the program in his right hand. But in that case, he says, why bet the race?

This is a powerful and intelligent question which accompanies me all the way in the brief line to the window, having no answer of distinction, I bet twenty dollars on the filly to win, twenty dollars to place and forty to show, all of this with the dim feeling that it is not my senses which have departed so much as my capital. Nonetheless, the ticket which is pushed over the counter to me, has the reassuring heft and feel of a prayerbook, some kind of Talmudic investiture slammed out of cold steel to my purchase. In the old days a bet such as this would have required several tickets of pink, gray, and green hue, but we are living in the sullen and apocalyptic nineties now, the era of Off Track Betting and computerized simulcasting equipment and have sacrificed colors and varying denominations as well as most of our convictions. We older followers of the horse, that is to say. I have no idea whether this is true of those who have entered the arena after new totalizer equipment and off track betting. There is very little communication amongst the generations—even less than there is between the man and the horse—and I am perfectly happy to leave it that way.

I ascend the escalator to the brittle and crumbling spaces of the upper grandstand. Aqueduct will be closed soon, the rumors say, Belmont will become an all-year track and Aqueduct will become an extension of what I grew up calling Idlewild Airport. Where Kelso's hoofs grazed, stewards will wink and anti-terrorist patrols will run their careful radium. In the meantime, in these exhausted days of the millennium and my own career, I continue to bet and now, it would appear, converse lately with horses. I return to my seat which has been occupied by folded shards of newspaper during this customary expedition to the paddock and also by the right hand of my companion and sometime wife Henrietta who has had her own problems with the late millennium.

You took your time, she said. It's one minute to post.

Well, I know that, I say. A horse was talking to me in the paddock. It wouldn't have been polite to leave.

Henrietta takes this with the same stolidity and lack of fundamental expression which has characterized our relationship from the first and shrugs. Did you bet? she says.

Yes, I did. I got down in time.

You bet the horse that spoke to you, I suppose.

Well, yes, I say. That didn't seem unreasonable. She said that she was ready to win.

And you trusted her.

Well, I say, apologetically at that, a horse never spoke to me before. It was kind of a new thing. So I thought I'd take a chance. You want to know which one?

No, Henrietta says, why don't you keep it a secret for luck? She looks at her own *Form* spread out on her lap. I am glad I decided to pass this race. Even by maiden special late winter standards, these are a bunch of cats and dogs. One ten three for *five* furlongs. That's milk horse time.

I think you mean five and a half, I say.

Henrietta looks at the form, runs her pencil to a figure. Okay, she says. Five and a half, right. Not that this makes any difference.

Meanwhile, as this affectionate and gently marital conversation has ensued, the horses have approached and been loaded into the starting gate far across what will some day be tarmac. The fog and gloom of this part of the country at this time of the year obscure any natural view of these proceedings, but the closed circuit televisions, several hundred of them, provide the view in color. Man's Fate is somewhere in the middle, the four horse, being loaded willingly enough. I put my hand into the pocket with the ticket, squeeze it for luck. A last flash of the odds board brings the filly down to six to one. Perhaps I am not the only person with whom she has had conversations.

We will have to do something to invigorate our marriage, Henrietta says. I was reading this article in REDBOOK about bringing the sparkle back. We are doing too many of the same things at the same time.

I think they'll break any second, I say.

You have to constantly find new activities and shared interests, Henrietta says. I don't think we've had a new interest in seventeen years.

The doors of the starting gate are open, the bell stopping all wagers sounds, and the fillies lurch into motion. Man's Fate is somewhere in the middle of the pack.

I was never that interested in horses, Henrietta says. Dog shows, maybe, and movie stars. I wanted to get a degree in art history when I started college. It's a funny way from there to here.

Watch the screen, I say.

You watch it, Henrietta says. I am considering basic facets of my life.

The race goes on. Having already demonstrated impatience with expository material and its necessity, I will simply point out that Man's Fate, hanging on the outside all the way, finally gets to the center of the track at the stretch turn and then begins to canter unpleasantly, losing her action. Soon enough she is bearing out and sometime shortly after that the horses have crossed the finish line, carrying away my eighty dollars and the first metaphysical experience I have had since I looked deep into Henrietta's eyes some years ago and realized that I had forgotten her maiden name and the circumstances under which we met.

There is a dull growling in the upper grandstand, neither sonorous nor menacing but post-autumnal in its sourness and elisionary aspect. There simply are not many in attendance in South Ozone Park on bleak Wednesdays in January and those who have come have exhausted most of their energy simply by making that appearance. I guess I will go downstairs, I say.

Did you lose? Henrietta says. You don't seem very enthusiastic. I guess that you did not make this one.

That would be a fair assumption, I say. Civility must rule. Passion comes and mostly goes but civility is the last ghost at the reception.

I would not have expected otherwise, I say. Still, it was an interesting experience.

You see, even if they speak to you they give you wrong information. You have a credulous face, Fred. Everyone can lie to you.

I suppose so, I say. I heave upright, give Henrietta an absent caress on the shoulder that if extended to its logical conclusion might not have been so tender and amble away, take the down escalator, emerge at the ground level, ease my way through the few stragglers waiting for the race to become official so that they can get on the payout line. I walk on the concrete lawn some day to be a point of debarkation and walk to the rail where the unsaddled Man's Fate, snorting through her shadow roll, is being escorted by a groom up the track. She gives me a contemptuous look. The look is purely contemptuous. One does not need to anthropomorphize to understand that glare. Bad conditions, she says. I got shuffled back.

You weren't shuffled back, I say. You weren't impeded. They have the monitors all over now, nothing gets by me like in the old days. You broke late, fell back, bore out. I am shouting somewhat uncontrollably, I fear. Three old men look at me with some interest and then scurry away. You have no excuses, I say.

Man's Fate shakes off her escort, rears merrily, drops to her knees and snorts, then commences a lazy gallop. I have to scuttle to keep up with her. All right, she says, bearing in somewhat to the rail. All right, I lied to you a little. I had no idea at all whether I was going to win or not. But I thought it would be an interesting experiment.

Interesting experiment? To lose me eighty dollars?

What do dollars mean to a horse? Man's Fate says. The groom curses, runs after her, she shakes her reins and canters away. I don't care about your idiot quantifications. I wanted to talk to one of you, that was all. I always thought it would be interesting and so I did, that's all. It's like interspecies communication.

Communication? I lost eighty dollars! You made a fool of me!

Man's Fate shakes her head gaily, dances by the groom, reverses field, moves up the track again. Sauntering counterclockwise, she begins to move to very good speed, favoring her left foreleg only slightly now.

You made a fool of yourself, she says. I was only the medium for your stupidity. What do you want of a horse, anyway? You think this is an easy job?

The filly is now in a full gallop, showing no effects of her loss, no indication of heat in her left foreleg. This is serious business, I realize. She is really running.

She runs all around the track, a mile and an eighth. I clock her in one forty six and two which is outstanding time. For the six furlongs bringing her to the top of the stretch, she is by my own figures exactly one ten three, race horse time indeed.

She done it for spite. The whole thing for what? Animal liberation?

Henrietta is silent all the way home. The horse-laugh fills the spaces in my head. No sign of the eighty in the wallet, though. The exchange of eighty for a horselaugh is a definite clue that I am moving down in class.

Nancy Springer

THE MOST MAGICAL THING ABOUT RACHEL

The sorrel horse of sunset
And the silver horse of dawn,
Neither of them is mine.
The black horse of the north wind,
The blood bay of the south,
Neither of them is mine.

The stallion of the high sky
And the great brown mare of earth,
Neither of them is mine;
But the spotted horse with wild white eyes,
Him I ride to paradise,
To paradise.

—Rachel's song

"The most magical thing about horses," Wilsy would gush to the parents, "is the way they give people back to themselves." I always snorted and shook flies off my head at this point, but nobody paid attention to me. They had to listen to Mrs. Wilson while she burbled on: "As Winston Churchill said, there is something about the outside of a horse that is good for the inside of a man." She always gave a little speech on the first night of each summer's eight weeks of Horseback Riding for the Handicapped. And I always stood there, a placid wall-eyed pinto gelding, saddled, sedate and patiently waiting, thinking, *Give me a break. Horses are not about people and their pathetic insides. Horses are about wind and sky and mares in heat and the great herd always galloping somewhere. Magical—what does she know of magic? What does any human know of the sun mare with her wings of flame, of the moon stallion's cold changing eye, of the black mane blowing behind the stars? Give humans back to themselves, indeed. Who is going to give horses back to themselves?*

Nevertheless, every year when they put a child on me, I plodded around the ring tamely. And every year the children started off wobbly in body or mind or both, and always over the course of the summer weeks their heads came up as if they were foals growing—for all of which I cared nothing, yet I did it all. The sun mother plodded through her daily rounds, and so could I. There was a sense in me of a fate working itself out, of a time coming, a debt being built which some season would be repaid.

Yet when that summer came, the moon stallion did not neigh and break free from his tether. The sun mother did not leap from her course and dash off to search for her missing colt, the one who eternally wanders beyond the edge of the world. It all started very quietly.

"The most magical thing about horses," Wilsy invoked as usual. She liked that word, magic, and used it in her farm name: Magic Acres. Every horse on the place had "Magic" plastered onto its so-called name. "This is Magic Make a Cake," she introduced me, and she helped this year's assigned rider up the mounting ramp and onto my back.

It was a young woman, the only adult in the handicapped riding class, and at once I scented her thoughts: about justice and poetry and sex. It startled me that she, one of the wobblies, was thinking about these primal things, but why shouldn't she? A wobbly wants to live, too. I smelled her thinking about sex, I felt her looking at some of the male humans and sizing them up and imagining the ecstatic act with them, and I could tell by something wistful in the tilt of her body that she had never done it. Because her head lolled sideward and her shoulders hunched, because her hands wavered in air and her spindly legs pitched her in all directions as she walked, no one had ever wanted her. Or not the way she wished to be wanted. Dreaming fool.

Wilsy was holding forth. "As Winston Churchill said, there's something about the outside of a horse—"

"It wasn't Churchill," muttered the young woman on my back. "It wasn't Abe Lincoln either."

"—that's good for the inside of a man."

"It was some other sexist God-given gung-homocentric."

"Rachel?" Mrs. Wilson turned toward me and my rider. "You said something?"

"I said I'm not a man."

Wilsy blinked but recovered rapidly. "Well, of course Churchill meant everyone. He knew how good horseback riding would be for all of us." She clapped her hands. "C'mon, everybody! Into the ring!"

The women walking with Rachel were curious about her and asked her questions they would never have asked a child: What is your handicap? Cerebral Palsy. Oh, that's too bad. Do you have to use a wheelchair? No. Crutches? No. Leg braces? No. Well it could be worse, then. Can you live by yourself? No. Why not? I fall a lot. Do you have a job? No. Why not?

"Try to find a job when you look like you're drunk all the time," Rachel said.

She would have made a good front-of-the-herd mare. There was bite to her, and kick. They didn't like it—I had noticed Wilsy and her friends expected the wobblies to be sweet and grateful. They started talking to each other past this Rachel person as if she wasn't there, and she started talking to me.

"It's the damn truth," she told the back of my head. "You're cute when you're a kid, you're a poster child, but once you grow up, forget it. No life for you. No job, no lover, no kinks, no lambada, no fun. Handicapped people are supposed to be thinking about other things, like nuns." I swiveled my ears, listening to her, and she smoothed my mane with one of her wobbly hands. "No free pony rides, either. So how long you been doing this, horse?"

Too plodding long.

"What did she say your name was? Cake Mix? That's no fair. Just because you've got spots." She was quite serious. I liked that. "Just because you remind her of a marble cake, no dignity for you. When color is the most superficial thing about a person. A horse, I mean. Tell you what. Just between you and me, let's find you another name."

Fine by me.

"You let me know when I say the right one, okay?"

Sure. Whatever.

"Okay. Possibilities: Colorado, like the river. Desperado. Chippewa Condor. Chippewa Wings."

I flung up my head and started to tremble, for in the poetry of her searching voice I felt a mystic sort of mastery, I felt her power. It was as if—I had never thought about it before, because horses change names whenever they change owners, we are like slaves that way—but now I sensed that there indeed was an innate name for me, a true name from the wide fields beyond the stars, the great grasslands I had run before my birth; perhaps I had even chosen it myself! And forgotten it since—but if this Rachel woman found it, I would remember, and everything would change.

I stood like some general's bronze horse scenting battle, with my legs stiff, my neck crested, my ears pricked so high their tips nearly touched, quivering—we could stand still now, for we had been lined up with the others in the center of the ring, we were supposed to be doing exercises, but no one wanted to tell Rachel what to do, and she continued to stroke my mane and say names to me.

"Medicine Hat," she said. "Cochise. Sun Dancer, Rain Dancer, Ghost Dancer. Shaman."

Shaman.

SHAMAN.

The name shot through me like the touch of a cattle prod. I reared up. Those hands of hers were useless for grasping with, yet somehow she did not fall off—the fire of the name had fused us into oneness. She was the lightning, I was the storm. She was the passenger, I the psychopomp who would take her to the spirit realm.

I knew what I had to do. I went mad. Wilsy was rushing toward me to grab my reins, afraid I would throw my rider, and I leapt from a standing start into a gallop, with bared teeth and flattened ears I charged her, roaring a horse's roar deep in my chest. She squealed and side-stepped—I knocked her down with my shoulder, racing past her, and I did not bother to jump the ring's fence—I went through it, splintering the rails like so many straws. People screamed. Through the commotion I heard Wilsy piping thinly, like a bird, "Stop! Cake, what do you think you're doing?" Her voice had no power over me at all. I bucked my way across the pasture, tail flying. Somewhere far behind me Wilsy wailed, "Oh, my God, what's the matter with him? He's always been such a good horse." On my back Rachel was gasping and giggling. I neighed the way my god might neigh some day when she wants to end the world, I nickered a horse laugh and reared again so that both of us looked upward, toward where the stallion of the high sky reared over us all with his white mane floating on the smooth blue arch of his neck.

"Cake, no!" Wilsy and her gang caught up to us, as I meant they should. I charged her again. My mouth was foaming and my white weird eyes were ablaze with pale fire, I could feel it, but she stood her ground, shouting, trying to turn me—Wilsy is brave, I'll give her that. I flattened her, but managed not to step on her, and she got up still shouting. "My God, I think he's rabid. Hang on, Rachel! Sam!" That was her husband. "Samuel, get the gun! Quick!"

"Shaman," Rachel whispered to me, "get out of here, they're going to shoot you!"

I knew it, and instead of running in crazed hightail circles any longer I stopped where I was and sank gently to the ground. Rachel snatched her legs up in time to keep them from being caught and crushed under me, then sat where she was, still on my back, as I shivered and groaned and laid my head down. I felt weak and in pain—it was not all my idea, what was happening; it was the fate in me taking charge of my body. "Shaman," Rachel breathed to me, "it will be all right, I promise you," and she stayed with me. I heard frightened children crying some-where, and I sensed how a mob of humans ringed me like a stake fence, but no one else wanted to come near me. Only Rachel touched me, straddling me and stroking my neck till the moment when Sam ran up and shot me between the eyes.

* * *

"Oh!" Rachel exclaimed from my back. "Oh! Oh, I *see!* They are all more than one color, like you."

I could see now, too. My spirit had carried her spirit up through the seven levels of cloud and loud bells and blinding light, and now they all awaited us, the great ones, particolored, as she had said. The stallion of night and the north wind was shining pure black, but starred all over with flecks of snowflake white. Dawn was a roan filly, pearl gray mottled with pink. Sunset was a yellow dun streaked with red. Earth was a gentle shaggy mare, brown with pinto markings, oceans, not unlike mine. There were many others: sky, south wind, the colts of all the skittish breezes, dappled moon, sun mother—I could not look at the sun mother, she blazed too bright. Her mane and tail stood up like feathers and streamed like fire. And while two colors or more were in the others, all colors seemed to be in her.

I understood much, but not the purpose of the journey. What did these great ones require from Rachel? On my back her body was taut as that of a wild filly being tamed. Through the quivering of her knees against my shoulders I could feel her excitement, her fear.

"Rachel," a voice of fire spoke, "you have done well to bring Shaman back to me."

It must be hard for you humans with your weak senses to understand how a horse can hear such things. You know only the surface of all that is, but a horse, even a broomtail bronc, can see the ghosts of ancestors in the air, can know by a prickling in the nostrils how a thundercloud has the soul of a predator, can hear a rider's thoughts through the reins, can smell in the night the thin pale manes of the stars. The sun mother's voice was palomino flame hanging in stardark, but I heard it burning in my bones.

She said, "You have done nobly, Rachel. Now do this: Bring my colt back to me." Yearning blazed hot in the words. She said, "Shaman will take you to the place where the world stops and the far fields start. Dream of my son as you travel, and name him, and call him by name so that he will come to you. Find him, my daughter."

Rachel said, "Am I your daughter?" Then I knew even more than before that there was magic in Rachel; she, too, could hear words of fire! But I did not yet know the most magical thing about Rachel.

She spoke on; her voice shook, but she raised it boldly. She said, "If I am your daughter, why am I a wobbly weakling of a human sitting on a spotted horse? Do not tell me to go questing for your son on Shaman's back. I want four strong legs of my own to run on. I want to gallop over oceans and clouds and mountains and never be tired and never fall down again. I want to be strong, and I want for once to be beautiful."

There was a long silence, and the sun mother's fire darkened, as if this was a thing that could cause trouble. Yet her voice when she finally spoke burned as gentle as a lover's warm gaze. "Very well," she said. "You will be like me, and beautiful. Get off Shaman."

Rachel looked down. Seven levels of sky yawned below her. And she sensed, rightly, that she did not know how to tread those cloud-meadows as I did. It took hooves to run with the blue stallion.

"You must get down if I am to change you," sun mother said. "You will not fall, I promise you."

But Wilsy was not there to help her, or anyone with hands to steady her wobbly body as she got down off my back. She had to do it alone, and I could feel her shaking with effort and fear as she tried to make her wayward arms and legs obey her. I stood foursquare and rock-steady on my footing of ether while with her awkward fingers Rachel clutched my mane, slipping herself down my shoulder. But then a spasm of her arm jerked her hand away from me, she lost her grip, she screamed. Panicked, I lunged to help her—

Sun mother was quicker, and true to her word. Before Rachel's feet touched the ether through which they would have plunged, they were no longer bony weakling human feet but strong hard hooves. She stood in horse form beside me, and she was indeed very beautiful, with a body rounded and shapely and the shining chestnut color of a deer in summer, all except her face, which blazed entirely white. Her tail was full, dark and long, her mane tawny, fine and so long it hung down off her neck over one shoulder to her fetlocks. Out of her white blaze, half hidden by the long spirals of her fawn-colored forelock, her eyes gazed, huge and dreaming, the gray-blue color of violets in twilight.

She moved a few short paces, trying her hooves, dancing them. She flung up her comely head and neighed. "When I have found him," that neigh cried, "my reward will be this: I shall be his bride."

The fiery voice of the sun mother replied, "That is why I have called you daughter. Go now."

"Willingly."

She ran across the wide tallgrass honey-colored fields of paradise. She ran across the black plains between the stars, and leapt from prong to prong of the horseshoe moon, and whipped the sky's white mountaintops with her mane and tail, ecstatic from the running, the leaping. Her legs wandered in all directions as she ran, for she was still Rachel and would always be; nothing, not even the power of the sun mother, could change that. She still wobbled—but now her wavering leaps were a sweet thing to see, like the curveting of a foal yet unborn in the meadows of heaven. She never fell. This is the difference between four legs and two, there is not so dire a need of balance. She could be Rachel, and yet be winsome and strong and full of joy.

I did not stay behind to converse with my gods, but ran by her side, for I was in love with her.

When we reached the earthly mountaintops at the edge of the world her hooves rang on the stone as she leapt from peak to peak. "Chosen One," sang the ringing of her hooves, calling. "Sun Runner, Star Son, Milord, my Prince, come to me."

I was in love with her, but she was in love already with her dream of him.

We reached the ocean at the edge of the world and ran on top of the waves. The wind from beyond the world lifted her long fine fawn-colored mane until it rippled and swelled like the ocean. "Prince of Passion," the billowing of her mane sang. "Crown Colt, Glory Horse, True Quest, Light in the West, come to me."

Very well, I thought, very well. Her dream of him would not match the truth should we ever find him. It could not possibly. No such horse could be.

We reached the huge heavy fall of water over the edge of the world into the chasm, the abyss, of beyond. The depth of the abyss frightened me as seven levels of high sky had not. I hung back, but Rachel leapt onward, and I had to follow. She flung herself into a black void, and the void supported her as she galloped down past a world's worth of thundering water. The salt spray of that water stung her nostrils so that they flared and shone red with her blood, and her blood sang, "Fire in the West, Skyfire, Sunfire, Far Star, Wandering One, come to me."

Constantly I ran by her side, but I did not speak to her of my love. How could I? She would give me only pity. I was a gelding.

Her very breath sang to the stallion of her dreams, "Wandering Spark, Flame in the Dark, Comet, Dark Comet—"

He came to her, streaking across the black void he came, and he was all her dreams wished him to be, and more.

His mane of soft white fire made a crown of glory for his princely head. His white-fire tail streamed vast behind him. Except for mane and tail he was utter black, yet shone so that he seemed bright, white. His eyes were deep as night, glimmering as if with starglow. The blessing of his father the moon lay like a cloak of light on his great shoulders. His jewel-black hooves were winged with light.

She stood motionless at the sight of him, and I knew how her breath stopped, I could scent her terror and hope and delight. I knew all thoughts of her errand had flown out of her. Nothing was left but exaltation.

He came before her dancing on those winged hooves. He arched his white-fire crest and breathed on her the holy heat of his nostrils. I heard no words in that message. There was no need. The comet-curve of her neck answered his, the white blaze of her forehead answered him, her mane mingled with his, the meeting of their heads and necks formed a shape like a heart. Into the vastness beyond the world they went away together, and I stood on nothingness and watched them go.

Then I went back to the mountains at the edge of the world and waited for her. I knew there were other things I could have done: I could have gone back to the wide fields of sky and spent the rest of my spirit life talking with my gods, learning the secrets of all their mysteries. Or, if I wished to cling to my sadness, I could have gone back to haunt the earthly fields of Magic Acres, where in a muddy pasture my body lay buried. But I did neither. Though I felt frozen with defeat, my heart would not let me go away. On the stony top of the tallest mountain I took my place, I lay watchful on the keel of my chest, put my nose to my foreknees and waited.

I waited for a long time. The sun mother ran her course again and again. Seasons passed.

It was her colt, Dark Comet, that starfire wanderer, who brought Rachel back to me. Across the sorrel dapplings of the sunset I saw her coming with him out of infinitude. I lifted my head, and found I had become part of the stone of the mountaintop—I crackled like thunder as I got to my feet, and boulders fell down. Like a monument on four pillars of stone I stood there, and they came before me as if before an altar or a throne.

"It is your choice," the stallion of her dream said to Rachel. Like his mother's, his voice was made of fire, but his was passionfire. It could burn, but he controlled it for her sake. He loved her the way a stallion loves a young mare running in the wind.

Rachel spoke to him, or perhaps to me, naming her choices, and her voice was made of the breath in her warm wide nostrils. "If you come back with me, the world will end," she said.

"It will burn up like dry grass." The words were simple and white-fire true—I knew to my stone bones that they were true. The flying of a comet in the sky of the world is an omen of doom. We shamans know that the world will end when a comet flies into the embrace of the sun.

"Yet I will do it if you command me to," he said. "But if you do not, then someone must tell my mother of the danger, what I have become, so that she understands I may not see her again."

Rachel went on, "If I stay with you, then our foal will become like you, another eternal wanderer in the cold."

"Yes. And you will grieve as my mother grieves."

"I will grieve anyway because I must leave you." Now her voice was a young mare's cry of despair. "I cannot leave you. How can I leave you?"

"Ask Shaman," he said.

"What am I to do, all my life without you?"

"Ask Shaman."

"Shaman," she begged, and the moment my name left the poet-fire of her mind, I was myself again, a spotted horse standing on a mountaintop waiting for her. I neighed with gladness—I should not have done it when she was so wretched, but I could not help it, I was so filled with joy to be with her, and I could not keep from stretching out my neck to nuzzle her.

"Shaman will be with you, all your life without me. If you wish it so. You must choose, beloved." Dark Comet's voice had gone very low, barely a glimmer, very gentle.

Rachel hid the white blaze of her face against the slope of my shoulder. She could not say it, but this was her choice. The foal. The world. And me, though it could scarcely be said that she loved me.

"You are very brave," Dark Comet breathed to her. "Good-bye, my love." And he was gone, a white teardrop of fire flying across the void to the far darkness where he would endlessly wander. Rachel trembled against me, not lifting her head to see him go. Her trembling increased, her arms hugged my neck, her hands tangled in my mane—she was a frail human woman again, crying on my shoulder.

"Shaman," she wept.

I am here. I would always be there, always be hers.

"Shaman, it was beautiful, so beautiful. Can you understand?"

Yes. I could, for in a way I loved him, too.

She wept a while longer, then lifted her head, and I knelt before her. I got down on the stone so that she could climb onto me for the long journey back.

Sun mother was a spotted horse made partly of fiery anger, partly of black despair.

"I want my colt!" Her wrath roared out in flames ten miles long. "Let the world end, what do I care?"

She did not, in fact, burn up the earth, though the people who lived on it remembered for years afterward the scorching drought of that summer. But the fire of her fury sent her pantheon running in terror, drove Rachel and me away from her so that we reeled in pain across the seventh level of clouds. Long whips of flame pursued us. I smelled my own singed hair and squealed in fear. Rachel cried out, "Don't! You're burning me. Don't kill me! The baby—I'm carrying his baby!"

"You! And you are but a useless human!"

Now I was angry, enraged for Rachel's sake, and I lashed my tail so that its angry whistling shouted back at the sun mother, "Rachel is the bravest and most magical of humans."

"Be her cuckold, then, Shaman, as you are so fond of her!" Sun mother lunged at us, and her leaps carry far; before I could do more than whinny in terror her great wing of fire had closed over me. For a moment I thought I was dead a second time. Pain took me apart. But it did not kill me. I felt a great change—everything about me rotated on a new axis, my limbs took on a different angle to my body, my head no longer nodded in front but sat squatly atop me, my back grew short and useless for carrying—Rachel slid off me, screaming, falling. Her fumbling hands caught at my mane, or rather my hair, and hung on for just a moment— it was enough. I turned, I caught her in my arms. We fell together.

We fell slowly back to earth. I was, after all, yet Shaman, just as she was always Rachel. I am the psychopomp; I have power to die, and travel to the spirit world, and come back alive. And I had power to bring Rachel back with me.

I have said she did not love me. But during that journey she held tightly to me, and we talked, and I think she began to love me a little.

"Where am I to go?" she asked me. "What am I to do?"

"Home," I told her. "The people, your mother, the others, they will be glad to see you back. Your body has been lying all this time in a hospital bed. They will make glad shoutings when it opens its eyes and speaks to them."

"But I cannot bear it. After I have run across the ocean and between the stars, to go back to a place where there is nothing for me, no life's work, no lover, not even a home of my own—"

"I will be there with you," I told her, "if you let me."

Erect, clutching one another, we drifted down through the lowest level of sky, spiraling like maple wings. I held Rachel by the waist. She kept her hands on my shoulders, but pulled back her head to look at me. Her smile was wry.

I said, "Am I a very strange looking man?"

"You are a particolored man." Her gaze wandered over me. "Your hair is like your mane used to be, part dark and part light. Your face is part brown, part white. So are your shoulders. And your eyes are pale." Her smile softened. "You are different. But so am I."

"Still pinto," I remarked, and then I knew what she had maybe not yet thought of. Clothing covered me, the ballooning trousers of a clown, but I did not have to look. I knew.

She saw my face change. "What is it?" she asked.

"Nothing."

"Shaman, tell me what is wrong."

I had to turn my eyes away. "Still a pinto and still a gelding," I told her. "I am no threat to your memories of Dark Comet, my lady."

She was silent, but she put up one hand and stroked my piebald hair. We had come through a long night together. Her face was very pale yet shining in the dawn light. Her hair was the bright chestnut color of a deer in summer.

She said, "I mind it mainly for your sake."

"But you deserve better, Rachel."

Straw-colored pastureland floated up to meet us. On a hilltop of Magic Acres we landed as gently as dandelion seed, and I forced my hands to release her.

I said, "You will find a young stud who can give you what you crave." I said, "I ought to go away from you and let it happen."

She put out her hand to me and said, "No, stay, Shaman. Do you love me?"

"You know I do."
"Then stay."

All of which made me her lover, in a sense of the word. I slept in her bed with her. We did things together which gave us both pleasure. I loved her.

Her mother, her friends, Wilsy, all the others, thought I was the one who had impregnated her. She let them think it. They wondered who I was, where she had met me. She let them wonder.

We had a home of our own. Only a room, really. And no jobs, only food stamps, welfare. No one wanted either of us. But we were happy. Out of the three things—a home, a lover, a life's work—we had two. Not bad. And we had memories. We spoke often of the fields of paradise, and of the mountains at the edge of the world, and of treading the clouds of sunset; and of Dark Comet.

And we had the child coming.

The burning heat of that summer gave way to a winter that was worse. Sun mother's wrath had taken another form, that was all. She turned her back, she gave us only her chilly shoulder for comfort, she let us freeze. That was a winter neck-deep in cold and snow.

On the night when Rachel felt the child coming, the streets lay three feet deep in snow. I ran down to the bar on the corner to use the phone, but the place was locked up. I pounded on people's doors—someone answered me, but after all that the phone was out, the lines were iced down somewhere. I left messages and ran back, cursing my own slowness, remembering how once on four long strong legs I had been able to race doves in flight. It is a pathetic thing being a human and not a horse. The mares foal without great pain, but Rachel lay on our bed panting and moaning between the times when she had to scream.

There was no heat, no electricity, only a puny fire in a kerosene burner. No one came to help us. Rachel's agony went on all night and through the next day, and I tried to get help again and again, but there were many who needed it, and no one came for us. Rachel was brave. She never cursed her too-narrow body or my clumsy attempts to comfort her. She never cursed the sun mother or the snow or her child or its father.

Night came again, white with snow. The child, when it slid out of her into my hands at last, shone white as the snowlight through the window, but also black with her blood. It was beautiful and misshapen, with a head too long to be quite human, a neck too long and silkily maned, legs too long and folded. It lay in my arms, and gazed at me with eyes made of white fire. They spoke to me, those eyes, as no infant's eyes ought to speak.

So many enslaved, the white fire said. *My father cannot save them. He cannot even show them his face—he burns too bright. So many enslaved. And I—I am mute.*

"Sweetheart," Rachel whispered from her bloodied bed—she heard it, too. "You are not mute to us."

But to all others I am. I cannot name them. Save them, mother, as you have saved Shaman. Give them names.

Rachel did not answer, for she fainted. I was a fool, I should have been tending her, within the next hour she very nearly died, of bleeding—I could not stop her bleeding. She lay senseless and I was weeping with despair when people finally came to help us, white-coated people with shots and oxygen who took her away to a hospital. The child they shuddered over and left with me.

It thrived, and all goodness be thanked Rachel lived, and came home to us, and we were a family.

Years passed in which we were happy together. We never forgot we were oddlings, freaks—we did not expect much. Therefore it did not matter that Rachel had only me for a lover; she had my love. It did not matter that there were no jobs for us—we had our child to tend. And it did not matter that our child was very strange, stranger than Rachel, stranger than me. To us she was beautiful, with her long pale face and her willowy neck with the chestnut hair growing wispily far down its nape.

I looked into the child's white-fire eyes sometimes and asked, "Little one, do you love me?" And always, though she held my hand as she tried to walk on her awkward legs, always the answer was *No.* For her name was Spirit, and she could not love, not any more than she could speak. Her eyes always looked far away, toward where her father wandered the dark. *But,* she would add, *my mother loves you.*

"Truly?" I could not hear this quite often enough to fully believe it. *Truly. She loves you, Shaman. I lay under her heart for eleven months. I know.*

Of the three of us, Spirit was the only one who seemed not happy. Rachel and I came to understand in a wordless way that in a sense she was not ours, that someday she would fly away and we would let her go.

Often the child could not sleep, and Rachel would hold her and rock her in the shadowy night and sing to her:

> *My Spirit leaps on the mountains,*
> *My Spirit runs amid the mountains,*
> *Under a horseshoe moon.*
> *Beautiful are the farthest mountains*
> *Under a hoofprint moon.*

> *Where the sunrise is,*
> *There is my Spirit running on silver.*
> *Where the sunset is,*
> *There is my Spirit running on gold.*
> *Where the moonlight is,*
> *There is my Spirit shining.*

> *My Spirit leaps on the mountains.*
> *My Spirit runs in the far dark sky*
> *Beyond, where slowly the stars spin by*
> *Beyond, where the comets fly.*

The child was a mute starlight voice from her father's realm, and we accepted this.

Rachel did as Spirit said, becoming a namer of horses. At first she did it for nothing and no reason except that Spirit had told her to. Also, it gave her pleasure. "I name you Manito," she would call to a big old Roman-nosed rat-tailed Appaloosa grazing by the road, and he would fling up his head and prance with joy at being real. "I name you Red

Swan," she would whisper to a gangly lop-eared fuzz-faced foal at its mother's side, and as it grew its wild beauty would appear.

Later, Rachel began to understand that this was a huge, serious task, her life's work at last. And people began to pay her to come name their foals and the new horses they bought, to send her their pictures in the mail, because word got around: The horses she named became magnificent.

As for me, I took joy in the days, and ate greens more than most normal people do, and waited. No one wanted to hire a piebald freak. But the world might yet need a shaman.

When Spirit was five years old, she started going to a special school for wobblies, and that summer things came round full circle: with the others from her school she went to ride horseback at Magic Acres.

Wilsy welcomed Rachel with moist eyes. Dear, horrible old Wilsy. She who hoped she would go to heaven, who believed it would be a sweet-smelling orderly place with just rewards, she who thought of a horse as a thing meant to be good for humankind. I am sure she never dreamed who or what she was talking to when she greeted me.

She brought out a blue roan pony for Spirit—one thing I will say for Wilsy, she always kept glorious colors of horses. A blue roan pony with a black mane but a blazing white tail. "Her name is Magic Muffin," she chirped at Spirit, who stared straight ahead at the horizon, where a vast stallion's breath blew white across the sky. "She's a big cuddly blueberry muffin," Wilsy tried again. I had to turn away to keep from groaning. Spirit gazed. Wilsy got the child into her helmet and safety belt and onto the pony, and Spirit stared out over its small pricked ears. Its eyes were strange, I noticed, gray as slate. Walleyes, like mine.

"The most magical thing about horses," Wilsy began her speech, "is the way they give people—"

"The most magical thing about Rachel," I interrupted, "is the way she gives horses back to themselves."

And Rachel smiled a frail wisp of a smile and said to the blue roan, "Your true name is Dark Omen."

And Dark Omen bugled out a neigh fit to shake mountains, and reared up. Wilsy shrieked and grabbed at her head—and missed—but

Rachel and I stood hand in hand, watching. And sitting on the pony Spirit was lovely, her thin mane flying at the back of her head, Spirit rode her mount unflinching, rapt, her gaze on the stars where they hid behind seven levels of sky. "Good-bye, little one," Rachel said, but Spirit did not look at us as Dark Omen carried her rocketing skyward, white tail streaming like fire, out of our sight within a moment.

"Gone to wander with her father a while," Rachel murmured.

But we were the only ones who seemed to see. Others were screaming and crying over the thrown body on the ground, the blue roan pony running wild. Wilsy was babbling to us over and over, "I'm sorry, I'm sorry."

"She'll be back someday," I told the Wilson woman, though not to comfort her. I was only saying what was true.

Rachel knew it, too. "Yes," she said dreamily, "She will be back. And we will live to see it, beloved. We will live long. And then when it happens, we will die."

We walked away, hand in hand. And there were tears on my pinto-spotted face, but I smiled because my beloved was brave and clear-eyed and full of poetry. She knew what I knew: that a comet, like a shaman, is one who journeys to return—even if the world should burn.

Deep in her throat Rachel began to murmur a song.

> *The sorrel horse of sunset*
> *And the silver horse of dawn,*
> *Neither of them is mine. . . .*

James A. Michener

A MIRACLE OF EVOLUTION

Fifty-three million years ago, while the new Rockies were still developing and long after diplodocus had vanished, in the plains area where the twin pillars formed, an animal began to develop that in later times would give man his greatest assistance, as well as pleasure and mobility. The progenitor of this invaluable beast was a curious little creature, a four-legged mammal, and he stood only seven or eight inches high at the shoulder. He weighed little, had a body covering of part-fur, part-hair and seemed destined to develop into nothing more than an inconsequential beast.

He had, however, three characteristics that would determine his future potential. The bones in his four short legs were complete and separate and capable of elongation. On each foot he had five small toes, that mysteriously perfect number that was the same for most of the ancient animals, including the great dinosaurs. And he had forty-four teeth, arranged in an unprecedented manner: in front, some peglike teeth as weak as those of diplodocus; then a conspicuous open space; then at the back of the jaw, numerous grinding molars.

This little animal made no impression on his age, for he was surrounded by other, much larger mammals destined to become rhinoceroses, camels and sloths. He lived in seclusion in the shady parts of such woods as had developed and fed himself by browsing on leaves and soft marsh plants, for his teeth were not strong and would have quickly worn down had they been required to chew rough food like the grass that was then beginning to develop.

If one had observed all the mammals of this period and tried to evaluate the chances of each to amount to something, one would not have placed this quiet little creature high on the list of significant progenitors; indeed, it would have seemed then that the beast might develop in a number of different ways, none of them memorable, and that the little fellow might survive a few million years and then quietly vanish.

The curious thing about this forerunner of greatness is that although we are sure that he existed and are intellectually convinced that he had to have certain characteristics, no man has ever seen a shred of physical evidence that he really did exist. No fossil bone of this creature has so far been found; we have a large collection of bones of diplodocus and her fellow reptiles, all of whom vanished, but of this small prototype of one of the great animal families, we have no relics whatever. Indeed, he has not yet even been named, although we are quite familiar with his attributes; perhaps when his bones are ultimately found—and they will be—a proper name would be paleohippus, the hippus of the Paleocene epoch. When word of his discovery is flashed around the world, scholars and laymen in all countries will be delighted, for they will have come into contact with the father of a most distinguished race, one that all men have loved and from which most have profited.

Perhaps thirteen million years after paleohippus flourished, and when the land that would contain the twin pillars had begun to form, the second in line and first-known in this animal family appeared and became so numerous in the area that hundreds of skeletons would ultimately be laid down in rock. Because of this, scientists would know this small creature as intimately as they know their own puppies.

He was eohippus, an attractive small animal about twelve inches high at the shoulder. He looked more like a friendly dog than anything else, with small alert ears, a swishing tail to keep insects away, a furry kind of coat and a face that was somewhat long in order to accommodate the forty-four teeth inherited from his ancestor. The teeth were still weak, so that the little creature had to content himself with leaves and other soft foods.

But the thing that marked eohippus and made one suspect that this family of animals might be headed in some important direction was the feet. On the short front feet, not yet adapted for swift movement, the five original toes had been reduced to four; one had only recently disappeared, the bones that had once sustained it vanishing into the leg. And on the rear foot there were now three toes, the two others having withered away during the course of evolution. But the surviving toes had tiny hooves instead of claws.

One could still not predict what this inconspicuous animal was going to become, and the fact that he would stand second in the sixty-million-year process of creating a noble animal seemed unlikely. Eohippus seemed more suited to be merely a family pet.

And then, about thirty million years ago, when the land that was to form the twin pillars was being laid down, mesohippus developed, twenty-four inches high at the shoulders and with all the basic characteristics of his ancestors, except that he had only three toes on each of his feet. He was a sleek animal, about the size of our collie or red fox. The forty-four teeth kept his face long and lean and his legs were beginning to lengthen, but his feet still contained pads and small hooves.

Then, about eighteen million years ago, a dramatic development took place. Merychippus appeared, a handsome three-toed animal forty inches high, with a bristly mane, long face and protective bars behind the eye sockets.

He had one additional development that would enable the horse family to survive in a changing world: his teeth acquired the remarkable capacity to grow out from their socket as they wore down at the crown. This permitted the proto-horse to quit browsing on such leaves as he found and to move instead to grazing on the new grasses that were developing on the prairies. Grass is a dangerous and difficult food; it contains silica and other rough substances that wear down teeth, which must do much grinding in order to prepare the grass for digestion. Had not merychippus developed these self-renewing grinders, the horse as we know it could neither have developed nor survived. But with this almost magical equipment, he was prepared.

These profound evolutions occurred in what is now known as Colorado on the plains that surrounded the site of the twin pillars. There on flatlands that knew varied climates, from tropical to subarctic, depending on where the equator was located at the time, this singular breed of animal went through the manifold changes that were necessary before it stood forth as the horse as we know it.

One of the biggest changes in the antecedents of the horse appeared about six million years ago, when pliohippus, the latest in the breed, evolved with only one toe on each foot and with the pads on which his ancestors had run eliminated. It now had a single hoof. This animal was a medium-sized beautiful horse in almost every sense of the word, and would have been recognized as such, even from a considerable distance. There would be minor refinements, mostly in the teeth and in the shape of the skull, but the horse of historic times was now foreshadowed.

He arrived as equus about two million years ago, as splendid an animal as the ages were to produce. Starting from the mysterious and unseen paleohippus, this breed had unconsciously and with great persistence adapted itself to all the changes that the Earth presented, adhering always to those mutations that showed the best chance of future development. Paleohippus, of the many capacities; eohippus, of the subtle form; merychippus, with the horselike appearance; pliohippus, with the single hoof—these attributes persisted. There were dozens of other variations equally interesting that died out because they did not contribute to the final form. There were would-be horses of every description, some with the most ingenious innovations, but they did not survive, for they failed to adjust to the Earth as it was developing; they vanished because they were not needed. But the horse, with its notable collection of virtues and adjustments, did survive.

About one million years ago, when the twin pillars were well formed, a male horse with chestnut coloring and flowing tail lived in the area as part of a herd of about ninety. He was three years old and gifted with especially strong legs that enabled him to run more swiftly than most of his fellows. He was a gamin by nature and had left his mother sooner than any of the other males of his generation. He was the first to explore new arrivals on the prairie and had developed the bad habit of leading any horses that would follow on excursions into canyons or along extended draws.

One bright summer morning this chestnut was leading a group of six adventurous companions on a short foray. He took them across the plains that reached out from the twin pillars and northward into a series of foothills that contained passageways down which they galloped in single file, their tails flowing behind them as they ran. It was an exhilarating chase, and at the end of the main defile they turned eastward toward a plain that opened out invitingly, but as they galloped they saw blocking their way two mammoths of extraordinary size. Fourteen feet tall at the shoulders, with monstrous white tusks that curved downward from the head, the great creatures towered over the horses. The tips of their tusks reached sixteen feet, and if they caught an adversary, they could toss him far into the air. The two mammoths were imposing, and had they been ill-disposed toward the horses, could have created havoc, but they were placid by nature and intended no harm.

The chestnut halted his troop, led them at a sober pace around the mammoths, coming very close to the great tusks, then broke into a gallop that would take him onto the eastern plains, where a small herd of camels grazed, bending awkwardly forward. The horses ignored them, for ahead stood a group of antelope as if waiting for a challenge. The seven horses passed at full speed, whereupon the fleet antelope, each with a crown of four large antlers, sprang into action, darting after them.

For a few moments the two groups of animals were locked in an exciting race, the horses a little in the lead, but with a burst of speed the antelope leaped ahead and before long the horses saw only dust. It had been a joyous race, to no purpose other than the challenge of testing speed.

Beside the grazing area on which the antelope had been feeding there was a family of armadillos, large ratlike creatures encased in collapsible armor. The horses were vaguely aware of them but remained unconcerned, for the armadillo was a slow, peaceful creature that caused no harm. To their surprise the round little animals stopped searching for slugs and suddenly rolled themselves into a defensive position. Some enemy, unseen by the horses, was approaching from the south, and in a moment it appeared, a pack of nine dire wolves, the scourge of the plains, with long fangs and swift legs. They loped easily over the hill that marked the horizon, peering this way and that, sniffing the air. The wolf serving as the scout detected the armadillos and signaled his mates. The predators hurried up, inspected the armor-plated round balls, nudged them with their noses and turned away. No food there.

With some apprehension, the horses watched the nine enemies cross the grassland, hoping that they would pass well to the east, but this was not to be. The lead wolf, a splendid beast with a sleek gray coat, spotted the horses and broke into a powerful run, followed instantly by his eight hunting companions. The chestnut snorted and in the flash of a moment realized that he must not lead his six horses back into the canyons from which they had just emerged, for the two mammoths might block the way, allowing the dire wolves to overtake any straggler and cut him down.

So with an adroit leap sideways he broke onto the plains in the direction the antelope had taken and led his troop well away from their home terrain. They galloped with purpose, for although the dire wolves were not yet close at hand, they had anticipated the direction the horses might take and had vectored to the east to cut them off. The chestnut, seeing this maneuver, led his fellows to the north, which opened a considerable space between them and the wolves.

As they ran to safety, they passed a herd of camels that were slower-moving. The big awkward beasts saw the apprehension of the horses and took flight, although what the cause of the danger was they did not yet know. There was a clatter on the prairie and much dust, and when it had settled, the horses were well on their way to safety, but the camels were left in the direct path of the wolves. The lumbering camels ran as fast as they could, scattering to divert attacks, but this merely served to identify the slowest-moving and upon this unfortunate animal the wolves concentrated.

Cutting at him from all sides with fearful teeth, the wolves began to wear him down. He slowed. His head drooped. He had no defense against the dire wolves and within a few moments one had leaped at his exposed throat. Another fastened onto his right flank and a third slashed at his belly. Uttering a cry of anguish, the camel collapsed, his ungainly feet buckling under the weight of the wolves. In a flash, all nine were upon him, so that before the horses left the area, the camel had been slain.

At a slow walk they headed south for the hills that separated them from the land of the twin pillars. On the way they passed a giant sloth, who stood sniffing at the summer air, dimly aware that wolves were on the prowl. The huge beast, twice the size of the largest horse, knew from the appearance of the horses that they had encountered wolves, and retreated awkwardly to a protected area. An individual sloth, with his powerful foreclaws and hulking weight, was a match for one wolf, but if caught by a pack, he could be torn down, so battle was avoided.

Now the chestnut led the other horses into the low hills, down a gully and out onto the home plains. The sight of the twin pillars—white at the bottom where they stood on the prairie, reddish toward the top, and white again where the protecting caps rested—was reassuring, a signal of home, and when all seven of the troop were through the pass, they cantered easily back up to the main herd. Their absence had been noted and the older horses came up to nuzzle them. The herd had a nice sense of community, as if all were members of the same family, and each was gratified when others who had been absent returned to safety.

Among the six followers accompanying the chestnut on his foray was a young dun-colored mare, and in recent weeks she had been keeping close to him and he to her. They obviously felt an association, a responsibility each to the other, and normally they would by now have bred, but they were inhibited by a peculiar awareness that soon they would be on the move. None of the older animals had signified in any way that the herd was about to depart this congenial land by the twin pillars, but in some strange way the horses knew that they were destined to move—and to the north.

What was about to happen would constitute one of the major mysteries of the animal world. The horse, that splendid creature which had developed here at the twin pillars, would desert his ancestral home and emigrate to Asia, where he would prosper, and the plains at the pillars would be occupied by other animals. By the year 6000 B.C. he would become extinct in the Western Hemisphere.

The horses were about to move north and they knew they could not accommodate a lot of colts, so the chestnut and the mare held back. But one cold morning, when they had been chasing idly over the plains as if daring the dire wolves to attack them, they found themselves alone at the mouth of a canyon where the sun shone brightly; he mounted her and in due course she produced a handsome colt.

It was then that the herd started its slow movement to the northwest. Three times the chestnut tried unsuccessfully to halt them so that the colt could rest and have a fighting chance of keeping up. But some deep instinctive drive within the herd kept luring them away from their homeland, and soon it lay far behind them. The dun-colored mare did her best to keep the colt beside her, and he ran with ungainly legs to stay close. She was pleased to see that he grew stronger each day and that his legs functioned better as they moved onto higher ground.

But in the fifth week, as they approached a cold part of their journey, food became scarce and doubt was cast on the wisdom of this trek. The herd had to scatter to find forage, and one evening as the chestnut and the mare and their colt nosed among the scrub for signs of grass, a group of dire wolves struck at them. The mare instinctively presented herself to the gray wolves in an effort to protect her colt, but the fierce beasts were not distracted by this trick, and cut behind her to make savage lunges at her offspring. This enraged the chestnut, who sprang at the wolves with flashing hooves, but to no avail. Mercilessly, the wolves attacked the colt, whose piteous cries were cut off almost instantly.

The mare was distraught and tried to attack the wolves, but six of them detached themselves and formed a pack to destroy her. She defended herself valiantly for some moments while her mate battled with the other wolves near the body of the colt. Then one bold wolf caught her by a hamstring and brought her down. In a moment the others were upon her, tearing her to pieces.

The whole group of wolves now turned their attention to the chestnut, but he broke loose from them and started at a mad gallop back toward where the main herd of horses had been. The wolves followed him for a few miles, then gave up the chase and returned to their feast.

Unlike reptiles, mammals have some capacity for memory, and as the trek to the northwest continued, the chestnut felt sorrow at the loss of his mate and the colt. But he did not grieve long because he was soon preoccupied with the problems of the journey.

It was a strange hegira on which these horses were engaged. It would take them across thousands of miles and onto land that had been under water only a few centuries earlier. For this was the age of ice. Vast glaciers crept from the North Pole to areas that are now Pennsylvania and Wisconsin and Wyoming, erasing whatever vegetation had developed there and carving the landscape into new designs.

At no point on Earth were the changes more dramatic than at the Bering Sea, that body of ice-cold water which separates Asia from America. The great glaciers used up so much ocean water that the level of this sea dropped three hundred feet. This eliminated the Bering Sea altogether, and in its place appeared a massive land bridge more than a thousand miles wide. It was an isthmus, really, joining two continents, and now any animal that wished, or man, too, when he came along, could walk with security from Asia to America—or the other way.

The bridge, it must be understood, was not constructed along that slim chain of islands which now reaches from America to Asia. Not at all. The drop of ocean was so spectacular that it was the main body of Asia that was joined substantially to America; the bridge was wider than the entire compass of Alaska.

It was toward the direction of this great bridge, barely existent when the true horse emerged, that the chestnut now headed. In time, as older horses died off, he became the acknowledged leader of the herd, the one who trotted at the head on leisurely marches to new meadows, the one who marshaled the herd together when danger threatened. He grew canny in the arts of leadership, homing in on the good pastures, seeking out the protected resting places.

As the horses marched to the new bridge in the northwest, to their right in unending procession lay the snouts of the glaciers, now a mile away but, later on, a hundred miles distant, but always pressing southward and commandeering meadowlands where horses had previously grazed. Perhaps it was this inexorable pressure of ice from the north, eating up all the good land, that had started the horses on their migration; certainly it was a reminder that food was getting scarce throughout their known world.

One year, as the herd moved ever closer to the beginning of the bridge, the horses were competing for food with a large herd of camels that were also deserting the land where they had originated. The chestnut, now a mature horse, led his charges well to the north, right into the face of the glacier. It was the warm period of the year and the nose of the glacier was dripping, so that the horses had much good water and there was, as he had expected, good green grass.

But as they grazed, idling the summer away before they returned to the shoreline, where they would be once more in competition with the camels, he happened to peer into a small canyon that had formed in the ice, and with four companions he penetrated it, finding to his pleasure that it contained much sweet grass. They were grazing with no apprehension when suddenly he looked up to see before him a gigantic mammoth. It was as tall as three horses, and its mighty tusks were like none he had seen at the pillars. These tusks did not stretch forward, but turned parallel to the face in immense sweeping circles that met before the eyes.

The chestnut stood for a moment surveying the huge beast. He was not afraid, for mammoths did not attack horses, and even if for some unfathomable reason this one did, the chestnut could easily escape. And then slowly, as if the idea were incomprehensible, the stallion began to realize that under no circumstances could this particular mammoth charge, for it was dead. Its frozen rear quarters were caught in the icy grip of the glacier; its front half, from which the glacier had melted, seemed alive. It was a beast in suspension. It was there, with all its features locked in ice, but at the same time it was not there.

Perplexed, the chestnut whinnied and his companions ambled up. They looked at the imprisoned beast, expecting it to charge, and only belatedly did each discover for himself that for some reason he could not explain, this mammoth was immobilized. One of the younger horses probed with his muzzle, but the silent mammal gave no response. The young horse became angry and nudged the huge beast, again with no results. The horse started to whinny; then they realized that the great beast was dead. Like all horses, they were appalled by death and silently withdrew.

But the chestnut wanted to investigate this mystery, and in succeeding days he returned timorously to the small canyon, intrigued by a situation that he could not understand. The puzzle completely eluded him, so he returned to the grassy area and led his herd backward toward the main road to Asia.

It must not be imagined that the horses migrated to Asia in any steady progression. The distance from the twin pillars to Siberia was only thirty-five hundred miles, and since a horse could cover twenty-five miles a day, the trip might conceivably have been completed in less than a year, but it did not work that way. The horses never chose their direction; they merely sought easier pasturage, and sometimes a herd would linger in one favorable spot for eight or nine years. They were pulled slowly westward by mysterious forces, and no horse that started from the twin pillars ever got close to Asia.

But drift was implacable, and the chestnut spent his years from three to sixteen on this overpowering journey, always tending toward the northwest, for the time of the horse in America was ended.

They spent four years on the approaches to Alaska, and now the chestnut had to extend himself to keep pace with the younger horses. Often he fell behind, but he knew no fear, confident that an extra burst of effort would enable him to join the herd. He watched as younger horses took the lead, giving the signals for marching and halting. The grass seemed thinner this year, and more difficult to find.

One day, late in the afternoon, he was foraging in sparse lands when he became aware that the main herd—indeed the whole herd—had moved on well beyond him. He raised his head with some difficulty, for his breathing had grown tighter, to see that a pack of dire wolves had interposed itself between him and the herd. He looked about quickly for an alternate route, but those available would lead him farther from the other horses; he knew he could outrun the wolves, but he did not wish to increase the distance between himself and the herd.

He therefore made a daring, zigzag dash right through the wolves and toward the other horses. He kicked his heels and with surprising speed negotiated a good two-thirds of the distance through the snarling wolves. Twice he heard jaws snapping at his fetlocks, but he managed to kick free.

Then, with terrible suddenness, his breath came short and a great pain clutched at his chest. He fought against it, kept pumping his legs. He felt his body stopping almost in midflight, stopping while the wolves closed in to grab his legs. He felt a sharp pain radiating from his hind-quarters where two wolves had fastened onto him, but this external wolf-pain was of lesser consequence than the interior horse-pain that clutched at him. If only his breathing could be maintained, he could throw off the wolves. He had done so before. But now the greater pain assailed him and he sank slowly to earth as the pack fell upon him.

The last thing he saw was the uncomprehending herd, following younger leaders, as it maintained its glacial course toward Asia.

Why did this stallion that had prospered in Colorado desert his comfortable homeland for Siberia? We do not know. Why did the finest animal America developed become discontented with the land of his origin? There is no answer.

We know that when the horse negotiated the land bridge, which he did with apparent ease and in considerable numbers, he found on the other end an opportunity for varied development that is one of the bright aspects of animal history. He wandered into France and became the mighty Percheron, and into Arabia, where he developed into a lovely poem of a horse, and into Africa, where he became the brilliant zebra, and into Scotland, where he bred selectively to form the massive Clydesdale. He would also journey into Spain, where his very name would become the designation for gentleman, a caballero, a man of the horse. There he would flourish mightily and serve the armies that would conquer much of the know world, and in 1519 he would leave Spain in small, adventurous ships of conquest and land in Mexico, where he would thrive and develop special characteristics fitting him for life on upland plains. In 1543 he would accompany Coronado on his quest for the golden city of Quivira, and from later groups of horses brought by other Spaniards some would be stolen by Indians and a few would escape to become feral, once domesticated but now reverted to wildness. And from these varied sources would breed the animals that would return late in history, in the year 1768, to Colorado, the land from which they had sprung, making it for a few brief years the kingdom of the horse, the memorable epitome of all that was best in the relationship of horse and man.

D. H. Lawrence

THE ROCKING-HORSE WINNER

There was a woman who was beautiful, who started with all the advantages, yet she had no luck. She married for love, and the love turned to dust. She had bonny children, yet she felt they had been thrust upon her, and she could not love them. They looked at her coldly, as if they were finding fault with her. And hurriedly she felt she must cover up some fault in herself. Yet what it was that she must cover up she never knew. Nevertheless, when her children were present, she always felt the centre of her heart go hard. This troubled her, and in her manner she was all the more gentle and anxious for her children, as if she loved them very much. Only she herself knew that at the centre of her heart was a hard little place that could not feel love, no, not for anybody.

Everybody else said of her: 'She is such a good mother. She adores her children.' Only she herself, and her children themselves, knew it was not so. They read it in each other's eyes.

There were a boy and two little girls. They lived in a pleasant house, with a garden, and they had discreet servants, and felt themselves superior to anyone in the neighborhood.

Although they lived in style, they felt always an anxiety in the house. There was never enough money. The mother had a small income, and the father had a small income, but not nearly enough for the social position which they had to keep up. The father went into town to some office. But though he had good prospects, these prospects never materialized. There was always the grinding sense of the shortage of money, though the style was always kept up.

At last the mother said: 'I will see if *I* can't make something.' But she did not know where to begin. She racked her brains, and tried this thing and the other, but could not find anything successful. The failure made deep lines come into her face. Her children were growing up, they would have to go to school. There must be more money, there must be more money. The father, who was always very handsome and expensive in his tastes, seemed as if he never *would* be able to do anything worth doing. And the mother, who had a great belief in herself, did not succeed any better, and her tastes were just as expensive.

And so the house came to be haunted by the unspoken phrase: *There must be more money! There must be more money!* The children could hear it all the time, though nobody said it aloud. They heard it at Christmas, when the expensive and splendid toys filled the nursery. Behind the shining modern rocking-horse, behind the smart doll's house, a voice would start whispering: 'There *must* be more money! There *must* be more money!' And the children would stop playing, to listen for a moment. They would look into each other's eyes, to see if they had all heard. And each one saw in the eyes of the other two that they too had heard. 'There *must* be more money! There *must* be more money!'

It came whispering from the springs of the still-swaying rocking-horse, and even the horse, bending his wooden, champing head, heard it. The big doll, sitting so pink and smirking in her new pram, could hear it quite plainly, and seemed to be smirking all the more self-consciously because of it. The foolish puppy, too, that took the place of the teddy-bear, he was looking so extraordinarily foolish for no other reason but that he heard the secret whisper all over the house: 'There *must* be more money!'

Yet nobody ever said it aloud. The whisper was everywhere, and therefore no one spoke it. Just as no one ever says: 'We are breathing!' in spite of the fact that breath is coming and going all the time.

'Mother,' said the boy Paul one day, 'why don't we keep a car of our own? Why do we always use uncle's, or else a taxi?'

'Because we're the poor members of the family,' said the mother.

'But why *are* we, mother?'

'Well—I suppose,' she said slowly and bitterly, 'it's because your father had no luck.'

The boy was silent for some time.

'Is luck money, mother?' he asked, rather timidly.

'No, Paul. Not quite. It's what causes you to have money.'

'Oh!' said Paul vaguely. 'I thought when Uncle Oscar said *filthy lucker,* it meant money.'

'*Filthy lucre* does mean money,' said the mother. 'But it's lucre, not luck.'

'Oh!' said the boy. 'Then what *is* luck, mother?'

'It's what causes you to have money. If you're lucky you have money. That's why it's better to be born lucky than rich. If you're rich, you may lose your money. But if you're lucky, you will always get more money.'

'Oh! Will you? And is father not lucky?'

'Very unlucky, I should say,' she said bitterly.

The boy watched her with unsure eyes.

'Why?' he asked.

'I don't know. Nobody ever knows why one person is lucky and another unlucky.'

'Don't they? Nobody at all? Does *nobody* know?'

'Perhaps God. But He never tells.'

'He ought to, then. And aren't you lucky either, mother?'

'I can't be, if I married an unlucky husband.'

'But by yourself, aren't you?'

'I used to think I was, before I married. Now I think I am very unlucky indeed.'

'Why?'

'Well—never mind! Perhaps I'm not really,' she said.

The child looked at her to see if she meant it. But he saw, by the lines of her mouth, that she was only trying to hide something from him.

'Well, anyhow,' he said stoutly, 'I'm a lucky person.'

'Why?' said his mother, with a sudden laugh.

He stared at her. He didn't even know why he had said it.

'God told me,' he asserted, brazening it out.

'I hope He did, dear!' she said, again with a laugh, but rather bitter.

'He did, mother!'

'Excellent!' said the mother, using one of her husband's exclamations.

The boy saw she did not believe him; or rather, that she paid no attention to his assertion. This angered him somewhere, and made him want to compel her attention.

He went off by himself, vaguely, in a childish way, seeking for the clue to 'luck'. Absorbed, taking no heed of other people, he went about with a sort of stealth, seeking inwardly for luck. He wanted luck, he wanted it, he wanted it. When the two girls were playing dolls in the nursery, he would sit on his big rocking-horse, charging madly into space, with a frenzy that made the little girls peer at him uneasily. Wildly the horse careered, the waving dark hair of the boy tossed, his eyes had a strange glare in them. The little girls dared not speak to him.

When he had ridden to the end of his mad little journey, he climbed down and stood in front of his rocking-horse, staring fixedly into its lowered face. Its red mouth was slightly open, its big eye was wide and glassy-bright.

'Now!' he would silently command the snorting steed. 'Now, take me to where there is luck! Now take me!'

And he would slash the horse on the neck with the little whip he had asked Uncle Oscar for. He *knew* the horse could take him to where there was luck, if only he forced it. So he would mount again and start on his furious ride, hoping at last to get there. He knew he could get there.

'You'll break your horse, Paul!' said the nurse.

'He's always riding like that! I wish he'd leave off!' said his elder sister Joan.

But he only glared down on them in silence. Nurse gave him up. She could make nothing of him. Anyhow, he was growing beyond her.

One day his mother and his Uncle Oscar came in when he was on one of his furious rides. He did not speak to them.

'Hallo, you young jockey! Riding a winner?' said his uncle.

'Aren't you growing too big for a rocking-horse? You're not a very little boy any longer, you know,' said his mother.

But Paul only gave a blue glare from his big, rather close-set eyes. He would speak to nobody when he was in full tilt. His mother watched him with an anxious expression on her face.

At last he suddenly stopped forcing his horse into the mechanical gallop and slid down.

'Well, I got there!' he announced fiercely, his blue eyes still flaring, and his sturdy long legs straddling apart.

'Where did you get to?' asked his mother.

'Where I wanted to go,' he flared back at her.

'That's right, son!' said Uncle Oscar. 'Don't you stop till you get there. What's the horse's name?'

'He doesn't have a name,' said the boy.

'Gets on without all right?' asked the uncle.

'Well, he has different names. He was called Sansovino last week.'

'Sansovino, eh? Won the Ascot. How did you know this name?'

'He always talks about horse-races with Bassett,' said Joan.

The uncle was delighted to find that his small nephew was posted with all the racing news. Bassett, the young gardener, who had been wounded in the left foot in the war and had got his present job through Oscar Cresswell, whose batman he had been, was a perfect blade of the 'turf'. He lived in the racing events, and the small boy lived with him.

Oscar Cresswell got it all from Bassett.

'Master Paul comes and asks me, so I can't do more than tell him, sir,' said Bassett, his face terribly serious, as if he were speaking of religious matters.

'And does he ever put anything on a horse he fancies?'

'Well—I don't want to give him away—he's a young sport, a fine sport, sir. Would you mind asking him himself? He sort of takes a pleasure in it, and perhaps he'd feel I was giving him away, sir, if you don't mind.'

Bassett was serious as a church.

The uncle went back to his nephew and took him off for a ride in the car.

'Say, Paul, old man, do you ever put anything on a horse?' the uncle asked.

The boy watched the handsome man closely.

'Why, do you think I oughtn't to?' he parried.

'Not a bit of it! I thought perhaps you might give me a tip for the Lincoln.'

The car sped on into the country, going down to Uncle Oscar's place in Hampshire.

'Honour bright?' said the nephew.

'Honour bright, son!' said the uncle.

'Well, then, Daffodil.'

'Daffodil! I doubt it, sonny. What about Mirza?'

'I only know the winner,' said the boy. 'That's Daffodil.'

'Daffodil, eh?'

There was a pause. Daffodil was an obscure horse comparatively.

'Uncle!'

'Yes, son?'

'You won't let it go any further, will you? I promised Bassett.'

'Bassett be damned, old man! What's he got to do with it?'

'We're partners. We've been partners from the first. Uncle, he lent me my first five shillings, which I lost. I promised him, honour bright, it was only between me and him; only you gave me that ten-shilling note I started winning with, so I thought you were lucky. You won't let it go any further, will you?'

The boy gazed at his uncle from those big, hot, blue eyes, set rather close together. The uncle stirred and laughed uneasily.

'Right you are, son! I'll keep your tip private. Daffodil, eh? How much are you putting on him?'

'All except twenty pounds,' said the boy. 'I keep that in reserve.'

The uncle thought it a good joke.

'You keep twenty pounds in reserve, do you, you young romancer? What are you betting, then?'

'I'm betting three hundred,' said the boy gravely. 'But it's between you and me, Uncle Oscar! Honour bright?'

The uncle burst into a roar of laughter.

'It's between you and me all right, you young Nat Gould,' he said, laughing. 'But where's your three hundred?'

'Bassett keeps it for me. We're partners.'

'You are, are you! And what is Bassett putting on Daffodil?'

'He won't go quite as high as I do, I expect. Perhaps he'll go a hundred and fifty.'

'What, pennies?' laughed the uncle.

'Pounds,' said the child, with a surprised look at his uncle. 'Bassett keeps a bigger reserve than I do.'

Between wonder and amusement Uncle Oscar was silent. He pursued the matter no further, but he determined to take his nephew with him to the Lincoln races.

'Now, son,' he said, 'I'm putting twenty on Mirza, and I'll put five on for you on any horse you fancy. What's your pick?'

'Daffodil, uncle.'

'No, not the fiver on Daffodil!'

'I should if it was my own fiver,' said the child.

'Good! Good! Right you are! A fiver for me and a fiver for you on Daffodil.'

The child had never been to a race-meeting before, and his eyes were blue fire. He pursed his mouth tight and watched. A Frenchman just in front had put his money on Lancelot. Wild with excitement, he flayed his arms up and down, yelling *'Lancelot! Lancelot!'* in his French accent.

Daffodil came in first, Lancelot second, Mirza third. The child, flushed and with eyes blazing, was curiously serene. His uncle brought him four five-pound notes, four to one.

'What am I to do with these?' he cried, waving them before the boy's eyes.

'I suppose we'll talk to Bassett,' said the boy. 'I expect I have fifteen hundred now; and twenty in reserve; and this twenty.'

His uncle studied him for some moments.

'Look here, son!' he said. 'You're not serious about Bassett and that fifteen hundred, are you?'

'Yes, I am. But it's between you and me, uncle. Honour bright?'

'Honour bright all right, son! But I must talk to Bassett.'

'If you'd like to be a partner, uncle, with Bassett and me, we could all be partners. Only, you'd have to promise, honour bright, uncle, not to let it go beyond us three. Bassett and I are lucky, and you must be lucky, because it was your ten shillings I started winning with . . .'

Uncle Oscar took both Bassett and Paul into Richmond Park for an afternoon, and there they talked.

'It's like this, you see, sir,' Bassett said. 'Master Paul would get me talking about racing events, spinning yarns, you know, sir. And he was always keen on knowing if I'd made or if I'd lost. It's about a year since, now, that I put five shillings on Blush of Dawn for him: and we lost. Then the luck turned, with that ten shillings he had from you: that we put on Singhalese. And since that time, it's been pretty steady, all things considering. What do you say, Master Paul?'

'We're all right when we're sure,' said Paul. 'It's when we're not quite sure that we go down.'

'Oh, but we're careful then,' said Bassett.

'But when are you *sure?*' smiled Uncle Oscar.

'It's Master Paul, sir,' said Bassett in a secret, religious voice. 'It's as if he had it from heaven. Like Daffodil, now, for the Lincoln. That was as sure as eggs.'

'Did you put anything on Daffodil?' asked Oscar Cresswell.

'Yes, sir. I made my bit.'

'And my nephew?'

Bassett was obstinately silent, looking at Paul.

'I made twelve hundred, didn't I, Bassett? I told uncle I was putting three hundred on Daffodil.'

'That's right,' said Bassett, nodding.

'But where's the money?' asked the uncle.

'I keep it safe locked up, sir. Master Paul he can have it any minute he likes to ask for it.'

'What, fifteen hundred pounds?'

'And twenty! And *forty*, that is, with the twenty he made on the course.'

'It's amazing!' said the uncle.

'If Master Paul offers you to be partners, sir, I would, if I were you: if you'll excuse me,' said Bassett.

Oscar Cresswell thought about it.

'I'll see the money,' he said.

They drove home again, and, sure enough, Bassett came round to the garden-house with fifteen hundred pounds in notes. The twenty pounds reserve was left with Joe Glee, in the Turf Commission deposit.

'You see, it's all right, uncle, when I'm *sure!* Then we go strong, for all we're worth. Don't we, Bassett?'

'We do that, Master Paul.'

'And when are you sure?' said the uncle, laughing.

'Oh, well, sometimes I'm *absolutely* sure, like about Daffodil,' said the boy; 'and sometimes I have an idea; and sometimes I haven't even an idea, have I, Bassett? Then we're careful, because we mostly go down.'

'You do, do you! And when you're sure, like about Daffodil, what makes you sure, sonny?'

'Oh, well, I don't know,' said the boy uneasily. 'I'm sure, you know, uncle; that's all.'

'It's as if he had it from heaven, sir,' Bassett reiterated.

'I should say so!' said the uncle.

But he became a partner. And when the Leger was coming on Paul was 'sure' about Lively Spark, which was a quite inconsiderable horse. The boy insisted on putting a thousand on the horse, Bassett went for five hundred, and Oscar Cresswell two hundred. Lively Spark came in first, and the betting had been ten to one against him Paul had made ten thousand.

'You see,' he said, 'I was absolutely sure of him.'

Even Oscar Cresswell had cleared two thousand.

'Look here, son,' he said, 'this sort of thing makes me nervous.'

'It needn't, uncle! Perhaps I shan't be sure again for a long time.'

'But what are you going to do with your money?' asked the uncle.

'Of course,' said the boy, 'I started it for mother. She said she had no luck, because father is unlucky, so I thought if *I* was lucky, it might stop whispering.'

'What might stop whispering?'

'Our house. I *hate* our house for whispering.'

'What does it whisper?'

'Why—why'—the boy fidgeted—'why, I don't know. But it's always short of money, you know, uncle.'

'I know it, son, I know it.'

'You know people send mother writs, don't you, uncle?'

'I'm afraid I do,' said the uncle.

'And then the house whispers, like people laughing at you behind your back. It's awful, that is! I thought if I was lucky—'

'You might stop it,' added the uncle.

The boy watched him with big blue eyes, that had an uncanny cold fire in them, and he said never a word.

'Well, then!' said the uncle. 'What are we doing?'

'I shouldn't like mother to know I was lucky,' said the boy.

'Why not, son?'

'She'd stop me.'

'I don't think she would.'

'Oh!'—and the boy writhed in an odd way—'I *don't* want her to know, uncle.'

'All right, son! We'll manage it without her knowing.'

They managed it very easily. Paul, at the other's suggestion, handed over five thousand pounds to his uncle, who deposited it with the family lawyer, who was then to inform Paul's mother that a relative had put five thousand pounds into his hands, which sum was to be paid out a thousand pounds at a time, on the mother's birthday, for the next five years.

'So she'll have a birthday present of a thousand pounds for five successive years,' said Uncle Oscar. 'I hope it won't make it all the harder for her later.'

Paul's mother had her birthday in November. The house had been 'whispering' worse than ever lately, and, even in spite of his luck, Paul could not bear up against it. He was very anxious to see the effect of the birthday letter, telling his mother about the thousand pounds.

When there were no visitors, Paul now took his meals with his parents, as he was beyond the nursery control. His mother went into town nearly every day. She had discovered that she had an odd knack of sketching furs and dress materials, so she worked secretly in the studio of a friend who was the chief 'artist' for the leading drapers. She drew the figures of ladies in furs and ladies in silk and sequins for the newspaper advertisements. This young woman artist earned several thousand pounds a year, but Paul's mother only made several hundreds, and she was again dissatisfied. She so wanted to be first in something, and she did not succeed, even in making sketches for drapery advertisements.

She was down to breakfast on the morning of her birthday. Paul watched her face as she read her letters. He knew the lawyer's letter. As his mother read it, her face hardened and became more expressionless. Then a cold, determined look came on her mouth. She hid the letter under the pile of others, and said not a word about it.

'Didn't you have anything nice in the post for your birthday, mother?' said Paul.

'Quite moderately nice,' she said, her voice cold and absent.

She went away to town without saying more.

But in the afternoon Uncle Oscar appeared. He said Paul's mother had had a long interview with the lawyer, asking if the whole five thousand could not be advanced at once, as she was in debt.

'What do you think, uncle?' said the boy.

'I leave it to you, son.'

'Oh, let her have it, then! We can get some more with the other,' said the boy.

'A bird in the hand is worth two in the bush, laddie!' said Uncle Oscar.

'But I'm sure to *know* for the Grand National; or the Lincolnshire; or else the Derby. I'm sure to know for *one* of them,' said Paul.

So Uncle Oscar signed the agreement, and Paul's mother touched the whole five thousand. Then something very curious happened. The voices in the house suddenly went mad, like a chorus of frogs on a spring evening. There were certain new furnishings, and Paul had a tutor. He was *really* going to Eton, his father's school, in the following autumn. There were flowers in the winter, and a blossoming of the luxury Paul's mother had been used to. And yet the voices in the house, behind the sprays of mimosa and almond-blossom, and from under the piles of iridescent cushions, simply trilled and screamed in a sort of ecstasy: 'There *must* be more money! Oh-h-h; there *must* be more money. Oh, now, now-w! Now-w-w—there *must* be more money!—more than ever! More than ever!'

It frightened Paul terribly. He studied away at his Latin and Greek with his tutor. But his intense hours were spent with Bassett. The Grand National had gone by; he had not 'known', and had lost a hundred pounds. Summer was at hand. He was in agony for the Lincoln. But even for the Lincoln he didn't 'know', and he lost fifty pounds. He became wild-eyed and strange, as if something were going to explode in him.

'Let it alone, son! Don't you bother about it!' urged Uncle Oscar. But it was as if the boy couldn't really hear what his uncle was saying.

'I've got to know for the Derby! I've got to know for the Derby!' the child reiterated, his big blue eyes blazing with a sort of madness.

His mother noticed how overwrought he was.

'You'd better go to the seaside. Wouldn't you like to go now to the seaside, instead of waiting? I think you'd better,' she said, looking down at him anxiously, her heart curiously heavy because of him.

But the child lifted his uncanny blue eyes.

'I couldn't possibly go before the Derby, mother!' he said. 'I couldn't possibly!'

'Why not?' she said, her voice becoming heavy when she was opposed. 'Why not? You can still go from the seaside to see the Derby with your Uncle Oscar, if that's what you wish. No need for you to wait here. Besides, I think you care too much about these races. It's a bad sign. My family has been a gambling family, and you won't know till you grow up how much damage it has done. But it has done damage. I shall have to send Bassett away, and ask Uncle Oscar not to talk racing to you, unless you promise to be reasonable about it: go away to the seaside and forget it. You're all nerves!'

'I'll do what you like, mother, so long as you don't send me away till after the Derby,' the boy said.

'Send you away from where? Just from this house?'

'Yes,' he said, gazing at her.

'Why, you curious child, what makes you care about this house so much, suddenly? I never knew you loved it.'

He gazed at her without speaking. He had a secret within a secret, something he had not divulged, even to Bassett or to his Uncle Oscar.

But his mother, after standing undecided and a little bit sullen for some moments, said:

'Very well, then! Don't go to the seaside till after the Derby, if you don't wish it. But promise me you won't let your nerves go to pieces. Promise you won't think so much about horse-racing, and *events,* as you call them!'

'Oh no,' said the boy casually. 'I won't think much about them, mother. You needn't worry. I wouldn't worry, mother, if I were you.'

'If you were me and I were you,' said his mother, 'I wonder what we *should* do!'

'But you know you needn't worry, mother, don't you?' the boy repeated.

'I should be awfully glad to know it,' she said wearily.

'Oh, well, you *can,* you know. I mean, you *ought* to know you needn't worry,' he insisted.

'Ought I? Then I'll see about it,' she said.

Paul's secret of secrets was his wooden horse, that which had no name. Since he was emancipated from a nurse and a nursery-governess, he had had his rocking-horse removed to his own bedroom at the top of the house.

'Surely you're too big for a rocking-horse!' his mother had remonstrated.

'Well, you see, mother, till I can have a *real* horse, I like to have *some* sort of animal about,' had been his quaint answer.

'Do you feel he keeps you company?' she laughed.

'Oh yes! He's very good, he always keeps me company, when I'm there,' said Paul.

So the horse, rather shabby, stood in an arrested prance in the boy's bedroom.

The Derby was drawing near, and the boy grew more and more tense. He hardly heard what was spoken to him, he was very frail, and his eyes were really uncanny. His mother had sudden strange seizures of uneasiness about him. Sometimes, for half an hour, she would feel a sudden anxiety about him that was almost anguish. She wanted to rush to him at once, and know he was safe.

Two nights before the Derby, she was at a big party in town, when one of her rushes of anxiety about her boy, her first-born, gripped her heart till she could hardly speak. She fought with the feeling, might and main, for she believed in common sense. But it was too strong. She had to leave the dance and go downstairs to telephone to the country. The children's nursery-governess was terribly surprised and startled at being rung up in the night.

'Are the children all right, Miss Wilmot?'

'Oh yes, they are quite all right.'

'Master Paul? Is he all right?'

'He went to bed as right as a trivet. Shall I run up and look at him?'

'No,' said Paul's mother reluctantly. 'No! Don't trouble. It's all right. Don't sit up. We shall be home fairly soon.' She did not want her son's privacy intruded upon.

'Very good,' said the governess.

It was about one o'clock when Paul's mother and father drove up to their house. All was still. Paul's mother went to her room and slipped off her white fur cloak. She had told her maid not to wait up for her. She heard her husband downstairs, mixing a whisky and soda.

And then, because of the strange anxiety at her heart, she stole upstairs to her son's room. Noiselessly she went along the upper corridor. Was there a faint noise? What was it?

She stood, with arrested muscles, outside his door, listening. There was a strange, heavy, and yet not loud noise. Her heart stood still. It was a soundless noise, yet rushing and powerful. Something huge, in violent, hushed motion. What was it? What in God's name was it? She ought to know. She felt that she knew the noise. She knew what it was.

Yet she could not place it. She couldn't say what it was. And on and on it went, like a madness.

Softly, frozen with anxiety and fear, she turned the doorhandle.

The room was dark. Yet in the space near the window, she heard and saw something plunging to and fro. She gazed in fear and amazement.

Then suddenly she switched on the light, and saw her son, in his green pyjamas, madly surging on the rocking-horse. The blaze of light suddenly lit him up, as he urged the wooden horse, and lit her up, as she stood, blonde, in her dress of pale green and crystal, in the doorway.

'Paul!' she cried. 'Whatever are you doing?'

'It's Malabar!' he screamed in a powerful, strange voice. 'It's Malabar!'

His eyes blazed at her for one strange and senseless second, as he ceased urging his wooden horse. Then he fell with a crash to the ground, and she, all her tormented motherhood flooding upon her, rushed to gather him up.

But he was unconscious, and unconscious he remained, with some brain-fever. He talked and tossed, and his mother sat stonily by his side.

'Malabar! It's Malabar! Bassett, Bassett, I *know*! It's Malabar!'

So the child cried, trying to get up and urge the rocking-horse that gave him his inspiration.

'What does he mean by Malabar?' asked the heart-frozen mother.

·'I don't know,' said the father stonily.

'What does he mean by Malabar?' she asked her brother Oscar.

'It's one of the horses running for the Derby,' was the answer.

And, in spite of himself, Oscar Cresswell spoke to Bassett, and himself put a thousand on Malabar: at fourteen to one.

The third day of the illness was critical: they were waiting for a change. The boy, with his rather long, curly hair, was tossing ceaselessly on the pillow. He neither slept nor regained consciousness, and his eyes were like blue stones. His mother sat, feeling her heart had gone, turned actually into a stone.

In the evening, Oscar Cresswell did not come, but Bassett sent a message, saying could he come up for one moment, just one moment? Paul's mother was very angry at the intrusion, but on second thoughts she agreed. The boy was the same. Perhaps Bassett might bring him to consciousness.

The gardener, a shortish fellow with a little brown moustache and sharp little brown eyes, tiptoed into the room, touched his imaginary cap to Paul's mother, and stole to the bedside, staring with glittering, smallish eyes at the tossing, dying child.

'Master Paul!' he whispered. 'Master Paul! Malabar came in first all right, a clean win. I did as you told me. You've made over seventy thousand pounds, you have; you've got over eighty thousand. Malabar came in all right, Master Paul.'

'Malabar! Malabar! Did I say Malabar, mother? Did I say Malabar? Do you think I'm lucky, mother? I knew Malabar, didn't I? Over eighty thousand pounds! I call that lucky, don't you, mother? Over eighty thousand pounds! I knew, didn't I know I knew? Malabar came in all right. If I ride my horse till I'm sure, then I tell you, Bassett, you can go as high as you like. Did you go for all you were worth, Bassett?'

'I went a thousand on it, Master Paul.'

'I never told you, mother, that if I can ride my horse, and *get there*, then I'm absolutely sure—oh, absolutely! Mother, did I ever tell you? I *am* lucky!'

'No, you never did,' said his mother.

But the boy died in the night.

And even as he lay dead, his mother heard her brother's voice saying to her: 'My God, Hester, you're eighty-odd thousand to the good, and a poor devil of a son to the bad. But, poor devil, poor devil, he's best gone out of a life where he rides his rocking-horse to find a winner.'

Jon L. Breen

TEA AND 'BISCUIT

Do have a cup of tea, and I'll tell you a story.

My nephew Jerry Brogan sometimes accuses me of trying to escape reality. That is, of course, absurd. No one my age would think such a thing possible. Reality will always come after you, whether in the form of the unavoidable processes of aging or the more dramatic form of finding a dead body on the grounds of your own home, as I did some years ago when jockey Hector Gates was murdered there. I solved that one, with some help from Jerry, and yet when he has become involved in other puzzles of a criminal nature, he has never called on me, despite my deep knowledge of detection from a lifetime of reading about it. Am I trying to evade reality or is Jerry trying to shield me from it?

I should introduce myself before I go on. My name is Olivia Barchester, widow these many years of the late Colonel Glyndon Barchester, who campaigned Vengeful and other fine thoroughbreds on California tracks. I myself raced Vicar's Roses, among others, after my husband's death.

Odd to say I raced them. I never saw any of my own horses in person, since I never went to the track after the Colonel died, but they ran in my colors. So if a trainer or a jockey's agent can say, "I hooked the favorite at the head of the stretch and beat him a nose at the wire," I suppose I can say I raced Vicar's Roses.

While I won't admit to evading reality, I do take the prerogative of one who is fairly advanced in years and comfortably off (say old and rich if you must) and control my environment to the greatest extent possible. I don't consider myself a recluse, but I see little need to leave my home and my books. After my husband's death, I decided to follow racing to the extent possible on television. More recently, I decided not to watch live races on television. That decision came after Go for Wand's tragic death in the Belmont stretch the day of the 1990 Breeder's Cup. Now I videotape the races on my VCR and watch them at my leisure the evening of the day they are run, relying on Jerry to let me know if anything tragic occurred that I can shield myself from seeing. Self-indulgent, I'll admit, but I can enjoy a race so much more when I know all the runners and their jockeys will reach home safely.

Now I must introduce you to my black cat Seabiscuit, a handsome fellow from a rather distinguished litter who has been my companion for the past fifteen years. All of Seabiscuit's siblings were named for notable one-word racehorses—Stymie, Citation, Equipoise, Swaps, Nashua, Regret. They were born on the backstretch to a stable pet from the barn of an English trainer who insisted, contrary to American superstition, black cats were *good* luck.

There are many cats in racetrack stable areas, though most of them are strays, semi-wild. They are seldom pets for racehorses. Goats are more often cast in that role, for their calming effect on the highstrung thoroughbred.

Thus it is hardly surprising that, while most of Seabiscuit's litter found homes with persons connected to racing, only one followed in his mother's footsteps as a stable mascot. That brings me, you'll be relieved, to the subject of my story.

On a coolish fall evening, toward the end of the annual Surfside Meadows meeting where my nephew Jerry works as track announcer, I was visited by an old acquaintance, trainer Walter Cribbage. I brought him into my library, where Seabiscuit was lying by the fire and I had been engrossed in a vintage Agatha Christie novel from my extensive collection. I offered Walter a choice of beverage. I was sipping tea, but he opted for a straight bourbon, an indication of his troubled state of mind.

Walter is of my generation, thus nearing eighty, but he still has a trim figure and an erect, almost military carriage, and he still is up early mornings seeing to his string of horses. On this particular evening, we began by exchanging good-natured banter in the old way, but it seemed a bit forced on his part. He was clearly worried about something, and I was relieved when he got to the point of his visit.

"Olivia, Exterminator died this morning."

Remembering the post-World War I gelding, I said, "I should think he died years ago."

"Not the horse. The cat. He lived in my stable all these years. He came from the same litter as Seabiscuit. Remember?"

"Oh, of course. I am sorry to hear it. Still, fifteen is a good age for a cat, and one cannot hope—"

"That litter is notably long-lived, Olivia. Citation and Stymie are both still around. And he didn't die of old age, Olivia. He was murdered. Poisoned."

"Oh, dear. But why? Some superstitious backstretch worker, I suppose."

"He survived fifteen years without superstition getting the better of him. I think I know why he was killed. I have a horse in my barn named Band Wagon."

"Walter, as I think you know very well, that was one of the last horses I bred. Odd to say I bred him—I wasn't there in the shed after all—but I did plan the mating of his parents, Red Band and Hay Ride."

"I thought you'd be concerned about his welfare."

"Most certainly. You're doing very well with him, I understand. Jerry tells me he may be favored for the Surfside Handicap. But I'm sorry he doesn't belong to my friends the Burnsides any more."

Walter made a face. "As one who has to deal with the current owners, Mr. and Mrs. Preston Fremont and son, I sometimes share your sorrow. Still, if the Burnsides still had him, I wouldn't have got the chance to train him, would I? I got him just over a year ago. He was a bad actor and had never run up to his potential. Since I've had him, he's gotten better and better, and I don't take a smidgen of the credit. He fell in love with Exterminator. As long as that black cat was around the barn, he was as calm and as kind as can be. He started training well and racing better. That black cat made him a stakes horse. Now he's gone into a tailspin, not eating well, acting up. In the state he's in now, I don't think he'd win a ten-thousand-dollar claimer, let alone the Surfside Handicap."

Very sad, of course, for my last good horse to fall on bad days, but how could I help? After considerable hemming and hawing, Walter finally got to the point.

"Olivia, I have a big favor to ask of you. I want to borrow Seabiscuit."

"Borrow Seabiscuit? You must be joking."

Hearing his name twice in quick succession, Seabiscuit woke from his slumber and strolled over to sit by my chair, happily oblivious to the significance of our conversation.

"He and Exterminator are virtually identical," Walter continued. "Maybe having him around the barn would bring Band Wagon back into form."

I shook my head. "Walter, I'd like to help you, but I can't believe you'd ask me that. To begin with, cats, even much younger ones than Seabiscuit, don't always adjust well to new surroundings. He has grown accustomed to this house and these grounds, a quiet and predictable environment." I reached down to scratch Seabiscuit's ear, and he appreciatively rubbed his head against my palm. "Put him in the middle of the furor of the backstretch at his age, and who knows how he would react? Second, cats as much as horses have very distinct personalities. There is no reason to think Seabiscuit could establish that same special bond with Band Wagon simply because he and Exterminator are closely related. And finally, Walter, you are asking Seabiscuit to fill in where his brother has already been poisoned. You think I would consider putting him in that situation?"

Walter looked crestfallen. "You're quite right, of course. I never should have asked. But I don't know what else to do."

It was at that moment that Jerry phoned to assure me that the day's racing at Surfside, as well as ESPN's coverage of a midwestern stake, had passed without a hitch and was safe for me to watch. Not sharing my nephew's tendency to keep a mystery to himself, I invited him to join Walter and me for a discussion of the problem. He seemed to treat it as a command appearance, though of course it was nothing of the kind. He turned up at my door within minutes.

When he had settled his considerable bulk into an easy chair and accepted a cup of tea and a scone, Jerry listened closely to Walter's story and said rather archly, "It reminds me of the curious incident of Barnbuster's goat."

Walter seemed to brighten slightly. "Barnbuster had no goat."

"That was the curious incident."

"Really," I said, "while nothing delights me more than Sherlockian allusions, I haven't any idea what you two are talking about."

"Don't you remember a horse called Barnbuster a few years ago? He only lived up to his name when his pet goat Mary Poppins wasn't around. The owner-trainer was down on his luck and forced to sell the horse. He got a good price based on the horse's record, but he cleverly withheld Mary P. Barnbuster proved unmanageable for his new owner, and the original owner was able to buy him back for considerably less than he'd been paid for him. Reunited with his nanny, Barnbuster resumed his winning ways."

Walter chuckled at what was obviously a familiar story, then turned grim again. "Doesn't apply to my situation."

"Not exactly, no, but I wouldn't rule out the former owners. Could they be looking for a way to get Band Wagon back cheap? Or maybe seeking revenge against the new owners?"

I was scandalized. "Jerry, what a suggestion! You've known Matthew and Helen Burnside all your life."

"A lot of people probably knew Jack the Ripper all *his* life, too."

"Do be serious! He's just talking this way to irritate me, Walter."

"All right, all right. I don't really suspect the Burnsides, okay?"

"Besides, they've been living on Maui for over a year," I had to add.

"Then let's see what else we can figure out," Jerry said, truly applying himself to the problem for the first time. "How do you know Exterminator was poisoned?"

"The vet recognized the symptoms," Walter said, "and it wasn't the first time someone had tried to kill him. A week or two before, I discovered someone had put a rubber band around the poor cat's stomach. It was eating into his flesh, and there was nothing he could have done about it. It surely would have killed him eventually, and very painfully. I got it off him, and saved his life."

"What a terrible thing to do to an innocent animal," I said, more thankful than ever I had declined to loan Seabiscuit. He cooperated reluctantly as I protectively gathered him into my lap.

"Any new stable employees?" Jerry asked.

"They've all worked for me for years."

"Any of them unusually superstitious?"

"Perhaps, but not about black cats."

Annoyingly, Jerry resumed his anecdotal posture. "It's not always just black cats. I once knew a hotwalker who was heavily into numerology. To him, *any* cat was bad luck in a barn. You take a horse's four legs and add them to a cat's nine lives, and what do you have? Thirteen."

Walter seemed as impatient with Jerry's digression as I was. "Everybody who works for me loved the cat," he insisted.

"Do the owners of Band Wagon visit the backstretch often?"

Walter nodded. "What a bunch. If I didn't like their horse so much, I'd dump them in a minute. Old Preston Fremont is a mean bastard with a short temper and no real regard for horses. He'd run them into the ground if I'd let him. He's smart enough not to even try to do that to Band Wagon, though, and he certainly wouldn't have harmed the cat no matter how angry he was. He loves the money Band Wagon makes him too much.

"Then there's Millicent Fremont, his wife. Kids herself she can dress like a woman half her age, and every time she comes to the stable she seems to resent those filthy things you have to have around a barn— you know, dirt, dung, people. Imagines herself a horse-lover, though. Makes a big deal of feeding her horses carrots. I wonder how'd she'd react if one of them bit her polished nails!

"And the son is the prize of the lot. Young Delbert. Twenty-five and never did an honest day's work. Doesn't know one end of the horse from another but always has big plans for the stable. A terrible snob with all his other sterling qualities. It was his bright idea Band Wagon should prove his worth by racing in Europe next spring. Even had his old man half convinced it was a good plan. I told them it was impossible, and Preston understood, but the kid practically threw a tantrum."

"What relationship did the three owners have to the late Exterminator?" Jerry asked.

"Relationship with the cat? None at all, really. Preston understood why we had to keep him around, but I don't remember he ever came near him. Millicent would make a big fuss over him until he got pawprints over one of her thousand-dollar dresses one morning. Since then, she's kept her distance. Delbert's gone on record as hating all domestic animals, and I guess that includes horses as well as cats, though money-makers like Band Wagon he manages to take some interest in."

"Are any of *them* superstitious?"

"Just the opposite, if anything. You have to understand, Jerry, the role of Exterminator in that barn was not a matter of superstition. It was just the relationship he had with Band Wagon. They were pals. Mr. and Mrs. Fremont accepted that, but the son always figured it *was* superstition, and the idea drove him nuts."

"How frequently do you see the owners, Walter?"

"More than I want to. I sometimes think they're there every day, but it probably just seems that way."

Jerry nodded. "I think I know who killed the cat," he said, with the offhand casualness appropriate to a brilliant amateur. I'm sure he puts that on for my benefit. "Not that it will do you much good. Killing a domestic animal isn't nearly as serious a criminal offense as it ought to be, and knowing who did it won't help your problem with Band Wagon . . ."

Jerry shook his head solemnly and stared into the fire, letting his dramatic pause lengthen intolerably.

I cleared my throat. "Jerry, if you'll permit me, whodunits form a large part of my recreation. I still might like to know who the killer was."

"So would I," Walter said.

"Sure," Jerry said obligingly. "It has to be the son."

Walter wagged his head. "How on earth did you figure that out?"

"Go back a minute, Walter. You didn't say racing Band Wagon in Europe would be just a bad idea because he didn't like to run on grass or something. You said it would be impossible. Why impossible?"

Before Walter could answer, I belatedly caught on to Jerry's line of reasoning. "The quarantine! A domestic cat would probably have to be quarantined for months before he would be permitted in a European country. It wouldn't be possible for Band Wagon to travel with his pal. And without Exterminator's companionship, Band Wagon would have been useless on the track. So the idea really was impossible from your point of view, Walter."

Jerry nodded. "But young Delbert thought Exterminator's role was just superstitious nonsense. He thought if he killed the cat, and if Band Wagon then carried on his winning ways as before, his scenario of campaigning the horse over European tracks could be realized."

"I ought to have known!" Walter Cribbage exclaimed. "The last time Delbert visited the stable area he had a scratch on his face."

"Probably he got that on his first attempt, when he put the rubber band on Exterminator," Jerry said. He reached down to stroke Seabiscuit, who had fled my lap when the thrill of detection made me too animated.

So among the four of us we seemed to have solved the whodunit. But what good did that do Walter Cribbage, you ask, in his effort to restore Band Wagon to form? Jerry was able to offer him a small ray of hope. One of Regret's offspring, thus a nephew of Exterminator, was a backstretch resident at Santa Anita and might conceivably be available as a new companion for Band Wagon. If bloodlines meant anything at all, Jerry argued, why not give him a try?

I remained dubious about the probable success of a surrogate, but when I heard the cat's name, I felt it was a good omen. It was Vengeful, after my late husband's best runner.

Band Wagon did win the Surfside Handicap, but Delbert Fremont wasn't around to see it. Died of an infected cat scratch, poor lad.

Well, I wouldn't have told you the story if it didn't have a happy ending.

Mary O'Hara

MY FRIEND FLICKA

When Ken opened his eyes next
morning and looked out he saw that the house was wrapped in fog. There
had been no rain at all since the day a week ago when the wind had torn
the "sprinkling system" to pieces and blown all the tattered clouds away.
That was the day he had found Flicka. And it had been terribly hot since
then. They had hardly been able to stand the sun out on the terrace. They
had gone swimming in the pool every day. On the hills, the grass was
turning to soft tan.

Now there were clouds and they had closed down. After a severe hot
spell there often came a heavy fog, or hail, or even snow.

Standing at the window, Ken could hardly see the pines on the Hill opposite. He wondered if his father would go after the yearlings in such a fog as this—they wouldn't be able to see them; but at breakfast McLaughlin said there would be no change of plans. It was just a big cloud that had settled down over the ranch—it would lift and fall—perhaps up on Saddle Back it would be clear.

They mounted and rode out.

The fog lay in the folds of the hills. Here and there a bare summit was in sunshine, then a little farther on came a smother of cottony white that soaked the four riders to the skin and hung rows of moonstones on the whiskers of the horses.

It was hard to keep track of each other. Suddenly Ken was lost—the others had vanished. He reined in Shorty and sat listening. The clouds and mist rolled around him. He felt as if he were alone in the world.

A bluebird, color of the deep blue wild delphinium that dots the plains, became interested in him, and perched on a bush nearby; and as he started Shorty forward again, the bluebird followed along, hopping from bush to bush.

The boy rode slowly, not knowing in which direction to go. Then, hearing shouts, he touched heels to Shorty and cantered, and suddenly came out of the fog and saw his father and Tim and Ross.

"There they are!" said McLaughlin, pointing down over the curve of the hill. They rode forward, and Ken could see the yearlings standing bunched at the bottom, looking up, wondering who was coming. Then a huge coil of fog swirled over them and they were lost to sight again.

McLaughlin told them to circle around, spread out fanwise on the far side of the colts, and then gently bear down on them so they would start toward the ranch. If the colts once got running in this fog, he said, there'd be no chance of catching them.

The plan worked well; the yearlings were not so frisky as usual and allowed themselves to be driven in the right direction. It was only when they were on the County Road, and near the gate where Howard was watching, that Ken, whose eyes had been scanning the bunch, as they appeared and disappeared in the fog, realized that Flicka was missing.

McLaughlin noticed it at the same moment, and as Ken rode toward his father, McLaughlin turned to him and said, "She's not in the bunch."

They sat in silence a few moments while McLaughlin planned the next step. The yearlings, dispirited by the fog, nibbled languidly at the grass by the roadside. McLaughlin looked at the Saddle Back and Ken looked too, the passionate desire in his heart reaching out to pierce the fog and the hillside and see where Flicka had hidden herself away. Had she been with the bunch when they first were found? Had she stolen away through the fog? Or hadn't she been there in the beginning? Had she run away from the ranch entirely, after her bad experience a week ago? Or— and this thought made his heart drop sickeningly—had she perhaps died of the hurts she had received when she broke out of the corral and was lying stark and riddled with ants and crawling things on the breast of one of those hills?

McLaughlin looked grim. "Lone wolf—like her mother," he said. "Never with the gang. I might have known it."

Ken remembered what the Colonel had said about the Lone Wolf type—it wasn't good to be that way.

"Well, we'll drive the yearlings back up," said Rob finally. "No chance of finding her alone. If they happen to pass anywhere near her she's likely to join them."

They drove the yearlings back. Once over the first hill, the colts got running and soon were out of sight. The fog closed down again so that Ken pulled up, unable to see where he was going, unable to see his father, or Ross or Tim.

He sat listening, astonished that the sound of their hooves had been wiped out so completely. Again he seemed alone in the world.

The fog lifted in front of him and showed him that he stood at the brink of a sharp drop, almost a precipice, though not very deep. It led down into a semicircular pocket on the hillside which was fed by a spring; there was a clump of young cottonwoods and a great bank of clover dotted with small yellow blossoms.

In the midst of the clover stood Flicka, quietly feasting. She had seen him before he saw her and was watching him, her head up, clover sticking out of both sides of her mouth, her jaws going busily.

At sight of her, Ken was incapable of either thought or action.

Suddenly from behind him in the fog, he heard his father's low voice, "Don't move—"

"How'd she get in there?" said Tim.

"She scrambled down this bank. And she could scramble up again, if we weren't here. I think we've got her," said McLaughlin.

"Other side of that pocket the ground drops twenty feet sheer," said Tim. "She can't go down there."

Flicka had stopped chewing. There were still stalks of clover sticking out between her jaws, but her head was up and her ears pricked, listening, and there was a tautness and tension in her whole body.

Ken found himself trembling too.

"How're you going to catch her, Dad?" he asked in a low voice.

"I kin snag her from here," said Ross, and in the same breath McLaughlin answered, "Ross can rope her. Might as well rope her here as in the corral. We'll spread out in a semicircle above this bank. She can't get up past us, and she can't get down."

They took their positions and Ross lifted his rope off the horn of his saddle.

Ahead of them, far down below the pocket, the yearlings were running. A whinny or two drifted up, and the sound of their hooves, muffled by the fog.

Flicka heard them too. Suddenly she was aware of danger. She leaped out of the clover to the edge of the precipice which fell away down the mountainside toward where the yearlings were running. But it was too steep and too high. She came straight up on her hind legs with a neigh of terror, and whirled back toward the bank down which she had slid to reach the pocket. But on the crest of it, looming uncannily in the fog, were four black figures—she screamed, and ran around the base of the bank.

Ken heard Ross's rope sing. It snaked out just as Flicka dived into the bank of clover. Stumbling she went down and for a moment was lost to view.

"Goldarn—" said Ross, hauling in his rope, while Flicka floundered up and again circled her small prison, hurling herself at every point, only to realize that there was no way out.

She stood over the precipice, poised in despair and frantic longing. There drifted up the sound of the colts running below. Flicka trembled and strained over the brink—a perfect target for Ross, and he whirled his lariat again. It made a vicious whine.

Ken longed for the filly to escape the noose—yet he longed for her capture. Flicka reared up, her delicate forefeet beat the air, then she leaped out; and Ross's rope fell short again as McLaughlin said, "I expected that. She's like all the rest of them."

Flicka went down like a diver. She hit the ground with her legs folded under her, then rolled and bounced the rest of the way. It was exactly like the bronco that had climbed over the side of the truck and rolled down the forty-foot bank; and in silence the four watchers sat in their saddles waiting to see what would happen when she hit bottom— Ken already thinking of the Winchester, and the way the crack of it had echoed back from the hills.

Flicka lit, it seemed, on four steel springs that tossed her up and sent her flying down the mountainside—perfection of speed and power and action. A hot sweat bathed Ken from head to foot, and he began to laugh, half choking—

The wind roared down and swept up the fog, and it went bounding away over the hills, leaving trailing streamers of white in the gullies, and coverlets of cotton around the bushes. Way below, they could see Flicka galloping toward the yearlings. In a moment she joined them, and then there was just a many-colored blur of moving shapes, with a fierce sun blazing down, striking sparks of light off their glossy coats.

"Get going!" shouted McLaughlin. "Get around behind them. They're on the run now, and it's cleared—keep them running, and we may get them all in together before they stop. Tim, you take the short way back to the gate and help Howard turn them and get them through."

Tim shot off toward the County Road, and the other three riders galloped down and around the mountain until they were at the back of the band of yearlings. Shouting and yelling and spurring their mounts, they kept the colts running, circling them around toward the ranch until they had them on the County Road.

Way ahead, Ken could see Tim and Howard at the gate, blocking the road. The yearlings were bearing down on them. Now McLaughlin slowed up and began to call, "Whoa, whoa—" and the pace decreased. Often enough the yearlings had swept down that road and through the gate and down to the corrals. It was the pathway to oats, and hay, and shelter from winter storms—would they take it now? Flicka was with them—right in the middle—if they went, would she go too?

It was all over almost before Ken could draw a breath. The yearlings turned at the gate, swept through, went down to the corrals on a dead run, and through the gates that Gus had opened.

Flicka was caught again.

Mindful that she had clawed her way out when she was corralled before, McLaughlin determined to keep her in the main corral into which the stable door opened. It had eight-foot walls of aspen poles. The rest of the yearlings must be maneuvered away from her.

Now that the fog had gone, the sun was scorching, and horses and men alike were soaked with sweat before the chasing was over, and, one after the other, the yearlings had been driven into the other corral, and Flicka was alone.

She knew that her solitude meant danger, and that she was singled out for some special disaster. She ran frantically to the high fence through which she could see the other ponies standing, and reared and clawed at the poles; she screamed, whirled, circled the corral first in one direction, and then the other. And while McLaughlin and Ross were discussing the advisability of roping her, she suddenly spied the dark hole which was the open upper half of the stable door, and dived through it. McLaughlin rushed to close it, and she was caught—safely imprisoned in the stable.

The rest of the colts were driven away, and Ken stood outside the stable, listening to the wild hooves beating, the screams, the crashes. His Flicka within there—close at hand—imprisoned. He was shaking. He felt a desperate desire to quiet her somehow, to *tell her*. If she only knew how he loved her, that there was nothing to be afraid of, that they were going to be friends—

Ross shook his head with a one-sided grin. "Sure a wild one," he said, coiling his lariat.

"Plumb loco," said Tim briefly.

McLaughlin said, "We'll leave her to think it over. After dinner we'll come up and feed and water her and do a little work with her."

But when they went up after dinner there was no Flicka in the barn. One of the windows above the manger was broken, and the manger was full of pieces of glass.

Staring at it, McLaughlin gave a short laugh. He looked at Ken. "She climbed into the manger—see? Stood on the feed box, beat the glass out with her front hooves, and climbed through."

The window opened into the Six Foot Pasture. Near it was a wagonload of hay. When they went around the back of the stable to see where she had gone they found her between the stable and the hay wagon, eating.

At their approach, she leaped away, then headed east across the pasture.

"If she's like her mother," said Rob, "she'll go right through the wire."

"Ay bet she'll go over," said Gus. "She yumps like a deer."

"No horse can jump that," said McLaughlin.

Ken said nothing because he could not speak. It was the most terrible moment of his life. He watched Flicka racing toward the eastern wire.

A few rods from it, she swerved, turned, and raced diagonally south.

"It turned her! It turned her!" cried Ken, almost sobbing. It was the first sign of hope for Flicka. "Oh, Dad, she has got sense, she has! She has!"

Flicka turned again as she met the southern boundary of the pasture, again at the northern; she avoided the barn. Without abating anything of her whirlwind speed, following a precise, accurate calculation, and turning each time on a dime, she investigated every possibility. Then, seeing that there was no hope, she raced south toward the range where she had spent her life, gathered herself, and rose to the impossible leap.

Each of the men watching had the impulse to cover his eyes, and Ken gave a howl of despair.

Twenty yards of fence came down with her as she hurled herself through. Caught on the upper strands, she turned a complete somersault, landing on her back, her four legs dragging the wires down on top of her, and tangling herself in them beyond hope of escape.

"Damn the wire!" cursed McLaughlin. "If I could afford decent fences—"

Ken followed the men miserably as they walked to the filly. They stood in a circle watching while she kicked and fought and thrashed until the wire was tightly wound and tangled about her, piercing and tearing her flesh and hide. At last she was unconscious, streams of blood running on her golden coat, and pools of crimson widening on the grass beneath her.

With the wire cutters which Gus always carried in the hip pocket of his overalls, he cut the wire away; and they drew her into the pasture, repaired the fence, placed hay, a box of oats, and a tub of water near her, and called it a day.

"I doubt if she pulls out of it," said McLaughlin briefly. "But it's just as well. If it hadn't been this way it would have been another. A loco horse isn't worth a damn."

Ken lay on the grass behind Flicka. One little brown hand was on her back, smoothing it, pressing softly, caressing. The other hand supported his head. His face hung over her.

His throat felt dry; his lips were like paper.

After a long while he whispered, "I didn't mean to kill you, Flicka—"

Howard came to sit with him, quiet and respectful as is proper in the presence of grief or mourning.

Ken's eyes were on Flicka, watching her slow breathing. He had often seen horses down and unconscious. Badly cut with wire, too—they got well. Flicka could get well.

"Gosh! She's about as bad as Rocket," said Howard cheerfully.

Ken raised his head scowling. "Rocket! That old black hellion!"

"Well, Flicka's her child, isn't she?"

"She's Banner's child too—"

There were many airtight compartments in Ken's mind. Rocket—now that she had come to a bad end—had conveniently gone into one of them.

After a moment Howard said,

"We haven't given our colts their workout today." He pulled up his knees and clasped his hands around them.

Ken said nothing.

"We're supposed to, you know—we gotta," said Howard. "Dad'll be sore at us if we don't."

"I don't want to leave her," said Ken, and his voice was strange and thin.

Howard was sympathetically silent. Then he said, "I could do your two for you, Ken—"

Ken looked up gratefully. "Would you, Howard? Gee—that'd be keen—"

"Sure I'll do all of 'em, and you can stay here with Flicka."

"Thanks." Ken put his head down on his hand again, and the other hand smoothed and patted the filly's neck.

"Gee, she was pretty," said Howard, sighing.

"What d'ya mean—*was!*" snapped Ken. "You mean she *is*—she's beautiful."

"I meant when she was running back there," said Howard hastily.

Ken made no reply. It was true. Flicka floating across the ravines was something quite different from the inert mass lying on the ground, her belly rounded up into a mound, her neck weak and collapsed on the grass, her head stretched out, homely and senseless.

"Just think," said Howard, "you could have had any one of the other yearlings. And I guess by this time, it would have been half-tamed down there in the corral—probably tied to the post."

As Ken still kept silent, Howard got slowly to his feet. "Well, I guess I might as well go and do the colts," he said, and walked away. At a little distance he turned. "If Mother goes for the mail, do you want to go along?"

Ken shook his head.

When Howard was out of sight, Ken kneeled up and looked Flicka all over. He had never thought that, as soon as this, he would have been close enough to pat her, to caress her, to hold and examine her. He felt a passion of possession. Sick and half-destroyed as she was, she was his own, and his heart was bursting with love of her. He smoothed her all over. He arranged her mane in more orderly fashion; he tried to straighten her head.

"You're mine now, Flicka," he whispered.

He counted her wounds. The two worst were a deep cut above the right rear hock and a long gash in her chest that ran down into the muscle of the foreleg. Besides those, she was snagged with three-cornered tears through which the flesh pushed out, and laced with cuts and scratches with blood drying on them in rows of little black beads.

Ken wondered if the two bad cuts ought to be sewn up. He thought of Doc Hicks, and then remembered what his Dad had said: "You cost me money every time you turn around." No—Gus might do it—Gus was pretty good at sewing up animals. But Dad said best thing of all is usually to let them alone. They heal up. There was Sultan, hit by an automobile out on the highway; it knocked him down and took a big piece of flesh out of his chest and left the flap of skin hanging loose—and it all healed up of itself and you could only tell where the wound had been by the hair's being a different length.

The cut in Flicka's hind leg was awfully deep—

He put his head down against her and whispered again "Oh, Flicka—I didn't mean to kill you."

After a few moments, "Oh, get well—get well—*get well*—"

And again, "Flicka, don't be so wild. *Be all right,* Flicka—"

Gus came out to him carrying a can of black grease.

"De Boss tole me to put some of dis grease on de filly's cuts, Ken—it helps heal 'em up."

Together they went over her carefully, putting a smear of the grease wherever they could reach a wound.

Gus stood looking down at the boy.

"D'you think she'll get well, Gus?"

"She might, Ken. I seen plenty horses hurt as bad as dot, and dey yust as good as ever."

"Dad said—" But Ken's voice failed him when he remembered that his father had said she might as well die, because she was loco anyway.

The Swede stood a moment, his pale blue eyes, transparent and spiritual, looking kindly down at the boy; then he went on down to the barn.

Every trace of fog and mist had vanished, and the sun was blazing hot. Sweltering, Ken got up to take a drink of water from the bucket left for Flicka. Then, carrying handfuls of water in his small cupped hands, he poured it on her mouth. Flicka did not move, and once again Ken took his place behind her, his hand on her neck, his lips whispering to her.

After a while his head sank in exhaustion to the ground. . . .

A roaring gale roused him, and he looked up to see racing black clouds forming into a line. Blasts of cold wind struck down at the earth and sucked up leaves, twigs, tumbleweeds, in whorls like small cyclones.

From the black line in the sky, a fine icy mist sheeted down, and suddenly there came an appalling explosion of thunder. The world blazed and shuddered with lightning. High overhead was a noise like the shrieking of trumpets and trombones. The particles of fine icy mist beating down grew larger; they began to dance and bounce on the ground like little peas—like marbles—like Ping-Pong balls—

They beat upon Ken through his thin shirt and whipped his bare head and face. He kneeled up, leaning over Flicka, protecting her head with his folded arms. The hailstones were like ping-pong balls—like billiard balls—like little hard apples—like bigger apples—and suddenly, here and there, they fell as big as tennis balls, bouncing on the ground, rolling along, splitting on the rocks.

One hit Ken on the side of the face and a thin line of blood slid down his cheek with the water.

Running like a hare, under a pall of darkness, the storm fled eastward, beating the grass flat upon the hills. Then, in the wake of the darkness and the screaming wind and hail, a clear silver light shone out, and the grass rose up again, every blade shimmering.

Watching Flicka, Ken sat back on his heels and sighed. She had not moved.

A rainbow, like a giant compass, drew a half circle of bright color around the ranch. And off to one side, there was a vertical blur of fire hanging, left over from the storm.

Ken lay down again close behind Flicka and put his cheek against the soft tangle of her mane.

When evening came, and Nell had called Ken and had taken him by the hand and led him away, Flicka still lay without moving. Gently the darkness folded down over her. She was alone, except for the creatures of the sky—the heavenly bodies that wheeled over her; the two Bears, circling around the North Star; the cluster of little Sisters clinging together as if they held their arms wrapped around each other; the eagle, Aquila, that waited till nearly midnight before his great hidden wings lifted him above the horizon; and right overhead, an eye as bright as a blue diamond beaming down, the beautiful star Vega.

Less alive than they, and dark under their brilliance, the motionless body of Flicka lay on the bloodstained grass, earthbound and fatal, every breath she drew a costly victory.

Toward morning, a half moon rode in the zenith.

A single, sharp, yapping bark broke the silence. Another answered, then another and another—tentative, questioning cries that presently became long quavering howls. The sharp pixie faces of a pack of coyotes pointed at the moon, and the howls trembled up through their long, tight-stretched throats and open, pulsating jaws. Each little prairie-wolf was allowed a solo, at first timid and wondering, then gathering force and impudence. Then they joined with each other, and at last the troop was in full, yammering chorus, capering and malicious and thumbing noses and filling the air with sounds that raise the hair on human heads and put every animal on the alert.

Flicka came back to consciousness with a deep, shuddering sigh. She lifted her head and rolled over on her belly, drawing her legs under her a little. Resting so, she turned her head and listened. The yammer rose and fell. It was a familiar sound, she had heard it since she was born. The pack was across the stream on the edge of the woods beyond.

All at once, Flicka gathered herself, made a sudden, plunging effort, and gained her feet. It was not good for a filly to be helpless on the ground with a pack of coyotes near by. She stood swaying, her legs splayed out weakly, her head low and dizzy. It was minutes before balance came to her, and while she waited for it her nostrils flared, smelling water. *Water!* How near was it? Could she get to it?

She saw the tub and presently walked unsteadily over to it, put her lips in and drank. New life and strength poured into her. She paused, lifting her muzzle and mouthed the cold water, freshening her tongue and throat. She drank deeply again, then raised her head higher and stood with her neck turned, listening to the coyotes, until the sounds subsided, hesitated, died away.

She stood over the tub a long time. The pack yammered again, but the sound was like an echo, artless and hollow with distance, a mile away. They had gone across the valley for hunting.

A faint luminousness appeared over the earth and a lemon-colored light in the east. One by one the stars drew back, and the pale, innocent blue of the early-morning sky closed over them.

By the time Ken reached Flicka in the morning, she had finished the water, eaten some of the oats, and was standing broadside to the level sunlight, gathering in every ultraviolet ray, every infrared, for the healing and the recreation her battered body needed.

Anna Sewell

BLACK BEAUTY

I must now say a little about Reuben Smith, who was left in charge of the stables when York, the head groom, went to London. No one more thoroughly understood his business than he did, and when he was all right, there could not be a more faithful or valuable man. He was gentle and very clever in his management of horses, and could doctor them almost as well as a farrier, for he had lived two years with a veterinary surgeon. He was a first-rate driver; he could take a four-in-hand, or a tandem, as easily as a pair. He was a handsome man, a good scholar, and had very pleasant manners. I believe everybody liked him; certainly the horses did; the only wonder was that he should be in an under situation, and not in the place of a head coachman like York: but he had one great fault, and that was the love of drink. He was not like some men, always at it; he used to keep steady for weeks or months together; and then he would break out and have a "bout" of it, as York called it, and be a disgrace to himself, a terror to his wife, and a nuisance to all that had to do with him. He was, however, so useful, that two or three times York had hushed the matter up, and kept it from the Earl's knowledge; but one night, when Reuben had to drive a party home from a ball, he was so drunk that he could not hold the reins, and a gentleman of the party had to mount the box and drive the ladies home. Of course this could not be hidden, and Reuben was at once dismissed; his poor wife and little children had to turn out of the pretty cottage by the Park gate and go where they could. But shortly before Ginger and I came Smith had been taken back again. York had interceded for him with the Earl, who was very kindhearted, and the man had promised faithfully that he would never taste another drop as long as he lived there. He had kept this promise so well that York thought he might be safely trusted to fill his place while he was away, and he was so clever and honest that no one else seemed so well fitted for it.

It was now early in April, and the family was expected home some time in May. The light brougham was to be freshly done up, and as Colonel Blantyre was obliged to return to his regiment, it was arranged that Smith should drive him to the town in it, and ride back; for this purpose he took the saddle with him, and I was chosen for the journey. At the station the Colonel put some money into Smith's hand and bid him good-bye, saying, "Take care of your young mistress, Reuben, and don't let Black Auster be hacked about by any random young prig that wants to ride him—keep him for the lady."

We left the carriage at the maker's, and Smith rode me to the White Lion, and ordered the ostler to feed me well and have me ready for him at four o'clock. A nail in one of my front shoes had started as I came along, but the ostler did not notice it till just about four o'clock. Smith did not come into the yard till five, and then he said he should not leave till six, as he had met with some old friends. The man then told him of the nail, and asked if he should have the shoe looked to.

"No," said Smith, "that will be all right till we get home."

He spoke in a very loud offhand way and I thought it very unlike him, not to see about loose nails in our shoes. He did not come at six, nor seven, nor eight, and it was nearly nine o'clock before he called for me, and then it was in a loud rough voice. He seemed in a very bad temper, and abused the ostler, though I could not tell what for.

The landlord stood at the door and said, "Have a care, Mr. Smith!" but he answered angrily with an oath; and almost before he was out of the town he began to gallop, frequently giving me a sharp cut with his whip, though I was going at full speed. The moon had not yet risen, and it was very dark. The roads were stony, having been recently mended; going over them at this pace my shoe became looser, and when we were near the turnpike gate it came off.

If Smith had been in his right senses, he would have been sensible of something wrong in my pace; but he was too madly drunk to notice anything.

Beyond the turnpike was a long piece of road, upon which fresh stones had just been laid; large sharp stones, over which no horse could be driven quickly without risk of danger. Over this road, with one shoe gone, I was forced to gallop at my utmost speed, my rider meanwhile cutting into me with his whip, and with wild curses urging me to go still faster. Of course my shoeless foot suffered dreadfully; the hoof was broken and split down to the very quick, and the inside was terribly cut by the sharpness of the stones.

This could not go on; no horse could keep his footing under such circumstances, the pain was too great. I stumbled, and fell with violence on both my knees. Smith was flung off by my fall, and owing to the speed I was going at, he must have fallen with great force. I soon recovered my feet and limped to the side of the road, where it was free from stones. The moon had just risen above the hedge, and by its light I could see Smith lying a few yards beyond me. He did not rise, he made one slight effort to do so, and then there was a heavy groan. I could have groaned too, for I was suffering intense pain both from my foot and knees; but horses are used to bearing their pain in silence. I uttered no sound, but I stood there and listened. One more heavy groan from Smith; but though he now lay in the full moonlight, I could see no motion. I could do nothing for him nor myself, but, oh! how I listened for the sound of horse, or wheels, or footsteps. The road was not much frequented, and at this time of the night we might stay for hours before help came to us. I stood watching and listening. It was a calm sweet April night; there were no sounds but a few low notes of a nightingale, and nothing moved but the white clouds near the moon, and a brown owl that flitted over the hedge. It made me think of the summer nights long ago, when I used to lie beside my mother in the green pleasant meadow at Farmer Grey's.

It must have been nearly midnight when I heard at a great distance the sound of a horse's feet. Sometimes the sound died away, then it grew clearer again and nearer. The road to Earlshall led through plantations that belonged to the Earl: the sound came in that direction, and I hoped it might be someone coming in search of us. As the sound came nearer and nearer, I was almost sure I could distinguish Ginger's step; a little nearer still, and I could tell she was in the dog cart. I neighed loudly, and was overjoyed to hear an answering neigh from Ginger, and men's voices. They came slowly over the stones, and stopped at the dark figure that lay upon the ground.

One of the men jumped out, and stooped down over it. "It is Reuben!" he said, "and he does not stir."

The other man followed and bent over him. "He's dead," he said; "feel how cold his hands are."

They raised him up, but there was no life, and his hair was soaked with blood. They laid him down again, and came and looked at me. They soon saw my cut knees.

"Why, the horse has been down and thrown him! Who would have thought the black horse would have done that? Nobody thought he could fall. Reuben must have been lying here for hours! Odd, too, that the horse has not moved from the place."

Robert then attempted to lead me forward. I made a step, but almost fell again.

"Hallo! He's bad in his foot as well as his knees; look here—his hoof is cut all to pieces, he might well come down, poor fellow! I tell you what, Ned, I'm afraid it hasn't been all right with Reuben! Just think of him riding a horse over these stones without a shoe! Why, if he had been in his right senses, he would just as soon have tried to ride him over the moon. I'm afraid it has been the old thing over again. Poor Susan! She looked awfully pale when she came to my house to ask if he had not come home. She made believe she was not a bit anxious, and talked of a lot of things that might have kept him. But for all that she begged me to go and meet him—but what must we do? There's the horse to get home as well as the body—and that will be no easy matter."

Then followed a conversation between them, till it was agreed that Robert as the groom should lead me, and that Ned must take the body. It was a hard job to get it into the dog cart, for there was no one to hold Ginger; but she knew as well as I did what was going on, and stood as still as a stone. I noticed that, because, if she had a fault, it was that she was impatient in standing.

Ned started off very slowly with his sad load, and Robert came and looked at my foot again; then he took his handkerchief and bound it closely around, and so he led me home. I shall never forget that night walk; it was more than three miles. Robert led me on very slowly, and I limped and hobbled on as well as I could with great pain. I am sure he was sorry for me, for he often patted and encouraged me, talking to me in a pleasant voice.

At last I reached my own box, and had some corn, and after Robert had wrapped up my knees in wet cloths, he tied up my foot in a bran poultice to draw out the heat, and cleanse it before the horse doctor saw it in the morning, and I managed to get myself down on the straw, and slept in spite of the pain.

The next day, after the farrier had examined my wounds, he said he hoped the joint was not injured, and if so, I should not be spoiled for work, but I should never lose the blemish. I believe they did the best to make a good cure, but it was a long and painful one; proud flesh, as they called it, came up in my knees, and was burnt out with caustic, and when at last it was healed, they put a blistering fluid over the front of both knees to bring all the hair off: they had some reason for this, and I suppose it was all right.

As Smith's death had been so sudden, and no one was there to see it, there was an inquest held. The landlord and ostler at the White Lion, with several other people, gave evidence that he was intoxicated when he started from the inn. The keeper of the tollgate said he rode at a hard gallop through the gate; and my shoe was picked up amongst the stones, so that the case was quite plain to them, and I was cleared of all blame.

Everybody pitied Susan; she was nearly out of her mind; she kept saying over and over again, "Oh! He was so good—so good! It was all that cursed drink; why will they sell that cursed drink? Oh, Reuben, Reuben!" So she went on till after he was buried, and then, as she had no home or relations, she, with her six little children, was obliged once more to leave the pleasant home by the tall oak trees, and go into that great gloomy Union House.

Leo Tolstoy

STRIDER: THE STORY OF A HORSE

Nester mounted the gelding by the short stirrup, unwound his long whip, straightened his coat out from under his knee, seated himself in the manner peculiar to coachmen, huntsmen, and horsemen, and jerked the reins. The gelding lifted his head to show his readiness to go where ordered, but did not move. He knew that before starting there would be much shouting, and that Nester, from the seat on his back, would give many orders to Váska, the other groom, and to the horses. And Nester did shout: "Váska! Hello, Váska! Have you let out the brood mares? Where are you going, you devil? Now then! Are you asleep . . . . Open the gate! Let the brood mares get out first!"—and so on.

The gate creaked. Váska, cross and sleepy, stood at the gatepost holding his horse by the bridle and letting the other horses pass out. The horses followed one another and stepped carefully over the straw, smelling at it: fillies, yearling colts with their manes and tails cut, suckling foals, and mares in foal carrying their burden heedfully, passed one by one through the gateway. The fillies sometimes crowded together in twos and threes, throwing their heads across one another's backs and hitting their hooves against the gate, for which they received a rebuke from the grooms every time. The foals sometimes darted under the legs of the wrong mares and neighed loudly in response to the short whinny of their own mothers.

Having driven the horses to the riverside where they were to graze, Nester dismounted and unsaddled. Meanwhile the herd had begun gradually to spread over the untrampled meadow, covered with dew and by the mist that rose from it and the encircling river.

When he had taken the bridle off the piebald gelding, Nester scratched him under the neck, in response to which the gelding expressed his gratitude and satisfaction by closing his eyes. "He likes it, the old dog!" muttered Nester. The gelding, however, did not really care for the scratching at all, and pretended that it was agreeable merely out of courtesy. He nodded his head in assent to Nester's words; but suddenly Nester quite unexpectedly and without any reason, perhaps imagining that too much familiarity might give the gelding a wrong idea of his importance, pushed the gelding's head away from himself without any warning and, swinging the bridle, struck him painfully with the buckle on his lean leg, and then without saying a word went up the hillock to a tree stump, beside which he generally seated himself.

Old age is sometimes majestic, sometimes ugly, and sometimes pathetic. But old age can be both ugly and majestic, and the gelding's old age was just of that kind.

He was tall, something over 15 hands high. His spots were black, or, rather, they had been black, but had now turned a dirty brown. He had three spots, one on his head, starting from a crooked bald patch on the side of his nose and reaching halfway down his neck. His long mane, filled with burrs, was white in some places and brownish in others. Another spot extended down his off side to the middle of his belly, the third, on his croup, touched part of his tail and went halfway down his quarters. The rest of the tail was whitish and speckled. The big bony head, with deep hollows over the eyes and a black hanging lip that had been torn at some time, hung low and heavily on his neck, which was so lean that it looked as though it were carved of wood. The pendant lip revealed a blackish, bitten tongue and the yellow stumps of the worn lower teeth. The ears, one of which was slit, hung low on either side, and only occasionally moved lazily to drive away the pestering flies.

The expression on his face was one of stern patience, thoughtfulness, and suffering.

His forelegs were crooked to a bow at the knees; there were swelling over both hooves, and on one leg, on which the piebald spot reached halfway down, there was a swelling at the knee as big as a fist. The hind legs were in better condition, but apparently long ago his haunches had been so rubbed that in places the hair would not grow again. The leanness of his body made all four legs look disproportionately long.

There was really something majestic in that horse's figure and in the terrible union in him of repulsive indications of decrepitude, emphasized by the motley color of his hair, and his manner, which expressed the self-confidence and calm assurance, that go with beauty and strength. Like a living ruin, he stood alone in the midst of the dewy meadow, while not far from him could be heard the tramping, snorting, and youthful neighing and whinnying of the scattered herd.

That evening, as Nester drove the horses past the huts of the domestic serfs, he noticed a peasant horse and cart tethered to his porch: some friends had come to see him. When driving the horses in, he was in such a hurry that he let the gelding in without unsaddling him and, shouting to Váska to do it, shut the gate and went to his friends. Whether because the gelding, with his high saddle and without a rider, presented a strangely fantastic spectacle to the horses, or for some other reason, at any rate something quite unusual occurred that night in the paddock. All the horses, young and old, ran after the gelding, showing their teeth and driving him all around the yard; one heard the sound of hooves striking against his bare ribs, and his deep groaning. He could no longer endure this, nor could he avoid the blows. He stopped in the middle of the paddock, his face expressing first the repulsive, weak malevolence of helpless old age, and then despair: he dropped his ears, and then something happened that caused all the horses to quiet down. The oldest of the mares, Vyazapúrikha, went up to the gelding, sniffed at him and sighed. The gelding sighed too . . . .

In the middle of the moonlit paddock stood the tall, gaunt figure of the gelding, still wearing the high saddle with its prominent peak at the bow. The horses stood motionless and in deep silence around him as if they were learning something new and unexpected. And they had learned something new and unexpected.

First Night

Yes, I am the son of Affable I and of Bába. My pedigree name is Muzhík, and I was nicknamed Strider by the crowd because of my long and sweeping strides, the like of which was nowhere to be found in all Russia. There is no more thoroughbred horse in the world. I should never have told you this. What good would it have done? You would never have recognized me: even Vyazapúrikha, who was with me in Khrénovo, did not recognize me till now. You would not have believed me if Vyazapúrikha were not here to be my witness, and I should never have told you this. I don't need equine sympathy. But you wished it. Yes, I am that Strider whom connoisseurs are looking for and cannot find—that Strider whom the count himself knew and got rid of from his stud because I outran Swan, his favorite.

When I was born I did not know what piebald meant—I thought I was just a horse. I remember that the first remark we heard about my color struck my mother and me deeply.

I suppose I was born in the night; by the morning, having been licked over by my mother, I already stood on my feet. I remember I kept wanting something, and that everything seemed very surprising and yet very simple. Our stalls opened into a long warm passage and had latticed doors through which everything could be seen.

My mother offered me her teats, but I was still so innocent that I poked my nose now between her forelegs and now under her udder. Suddenly she glanced at the latticed door and, lifting her leg over me, stepped aside. The groom on duty was looking into our stall through the lattice.

"Why, Bába has foaled!" he said, and began to draw the bolt. He came in over the fresh bedding and put his arms around me. "Just look, Tarás!" he shouted, "what a piebald he is—a regular magpie!"

I darted away from him and fell on my knees.

"Look at him—the little devil!"

My mother became disquieted, but did not take my part, she only stepped a little to one side with a very deep sigh. Other grooms came to look at me, and one of them ran to tell the stud groom.

Everybody laughed when they looked at my spots, and they gave me all kinds of strange names, but neither I nor my mother understood those words. Till then there had been no piebalds among all my relatives. We did not think there was anything bad in it. Everybody even then praised my strength and my form.

"See what a frisky fellow!" said the groom. "There's no holding him."

Before long the stud groom came and began to express astonishment at my color; he even seemed aggrieved.

"And who does the little monster take after?" he said. "The general won't keep him in the stud. Oh, Bába, you have played me a trick!" he addressed my mother. "You might at least have dropped one with just a star—but this one is all piebald!"

My mother did not reply, but as usual drew a sigh.

"And what devil does he take after—he's just like a peasant horse!" he continued. "He can't be left in the stud—he'd shame us. But he's well built—very well!" said he, and so did everyone who saw me.

A few days later the general himself came and looked at me, and again everyone seemed horrified at something, and abused me and my mother for the color of my hair. "But he's a fine colt—very fine!" said all who saw me.

Until spring we all lived separately in the brood mares' stable, each with our mother, and only occasionally, when the snow on the stable roofs began to melt in the sun, were we let out with our mothers into the large paddock strewn with fresh straw. There I first came to know all my near and my distant relations. Here I saw all the famous mares of the day coming out from different doors. They all gathered together with their foals, walking around in the sunshine, rolling on the fresh straw, and sniffing at one another like ordinary horses. I have never forgotten the sight of that paddock, full of the beauties of that day. It seems strange to you to think, and hard to believe, that I was ever young and frisky, but it was so. This same Vyazapúrikha was then a yearling filly whose mane had just been cut; a dear, merry, lively little thing, but—and I do not say it to offend her, although among you she is now considered a remarkable thoroughbred—she was then among the poorest horses in the stud. She will herself confirm this.

My mottled appearance, which humans so disliked, was very attractive to all the horses; they all came around me, admired me, and frisked around with me. I began to forget what people said about my mottled appearance, and felt happy. But I soon experienced the first sorrow of my life, and the cause of it was my mother. When the thaw had set in, the sparrows twittered under the eaves, spring was felt more strongly in the air, and my mother's treatment of me changed.

Her whole disposition changed: she would frisk about without any reason to run around the yard, which did not at all accord with her dignified age; then she would consider and begin to neigh, and would bite and kick her sister mares, and then begin to sniff at me and snort discontentedly; then, on going out into the sun, she would lay her head across the shoulder of her cousin, Lady Merchant, dreamily rub her back and push me away from her teats.

One day the stud groom came and had a halter put on her, and she was led out of the stall. She neighed, and I answered and rushed after her, but she did not even look back at me. The strapper, Tarás, seized me in his arms while they were closing the door after my mother had been led out.

I bolted and upset the strapper on the straw, but the door was shut and I could only hear the receding sound of my mother's neighing; and that neigh did not sound like a call to me but had another expression. Her voice was answered from afar by a powerful voice—that of Dóbry I, as I learned later, who was being led by two grooms, one on each side, to meet my mother.

I don't remember how Tarás got out of my stall: I felt too sad, for I knew that I had lost my mother's love forever. "And it's all because I am piebald!" I thought, remembering what people said about my color, and such passionate anger overcame me that I began to beat my head and knees against the walls of the stall and continued till I was sweating all over and quite exhausted.

After a while my mother came back to me. I heard her run up the passage at a trot and with an unusual gait. They opened the door for her and I hardly knew her—she had grown so much younger and more beautiful. She sniffed at me, snorted, and began to whinny. Her whole demeanor showed that she no longer loved me.

She told me of Dóbry's beauty and her love of him. Those meetings continued, and the relations between my mother and me grew colder and colder.

Soon after that we were let out to pasture. I now discovered new joys which made up to me for the loss of my mother's love. I had friends and companions. Together we learned to eat grass, to neigh like the grown-ups, and to gallop around our mothers with lifted tails. That was a happy time. Everything was forgiven me, everybody loved me, admired me, and looked indulgently at anything I did. But that did not last long.

Soon afterward something dreadful happened to me . . . .

The gelding heaved a deep sigh and walked away.

The dawn had broken long before. The gates creaked. Nester came in, and the horses separated. The keeper straightened the saddle on the gelding's back and drove the horses out.

Second Night

In August they separated me from my mother, and I did not feel particularly grieved. I saw that she was again heavy (with my brother, the famous Usán), and that I could no longer be to her what I had been. I was not jealous, but felt that I had become indifferent to her. Besides I knew that, having left my mother, I should be put in the general division of foals, where we were kept two or three together and were every day let out in a crowd into the open. I was in the same stall with Darling. Darling was a saddle horse, who was subsequently ridden by the Emperor and portrayed in pictures and sculpture. At that time he was a mere foal, with soft, glossy coat, a swanlike neck, and straight, slender legs, taut as the strings of an instrument. He was always lively, good-tempered, and amiable, always ready to gambol, exchange licks, and play tricks on horse or man. Living together as we did, we involuntarily made friends, and our friendship lasted the whole of our youth. He was merry and giddy. Even then he began to make love, courted the fillies, and laughed at my guilelessness. To my misfortune, vanity led me to imitate him, and I was soon carried away and fell in love. And this early tendency of mine was the cause of the greatest change in my fate. It happened that I was carried away . . . . Vyazapúrikha was a year older than I, and we were special friends, but toward the autumn I noticed that she began to be shy with me . . .

But I will not speak of that unfortunate period of my first love; she herself remembers my mad passion, which ended for me in the most important change of my life.

The strappers rushed to drive her away and to beat me. That evening I was shut up in a special stall where I neighed all night as if foreseeing what was to happen next.

In the morning the general, the stud groom, the stablemen, and the strappers came into the passage where my stall was, and there was a terrible hubbub. The general shouted at the stud groom, who tried to justify himself by saying that he had not told them to let me out but that the grooms had done it of their own accord. The general said that he would have everybody flogged, and that it would not do to keep young stallions. The stud groom promised that he would have everything attended to. They grew quiet and went away. I did not understand anything, but could see that they were planning something concerning me.

The day after that I ceased neighing forever. I became what I am now. The whole world was changed in my eyes. Nothing mattered any more; I became self-absorbed and began to brood. At first everything seemed repulsive to me. I even ceased to eat, drink, or walk, and there was no idea of playing. Now and then it occurred to me to give a kick, to gallop, or to start neighing, but immediately came the question: Why? What for? and all my energy died away . . . .

Already before that I had shown a tendency toward gravity and thoughtfulness, but now a decided change came over me. My being piebald, which aroused such curious contempt in humans, my terrible and unexpected misfortune, and also my peculiar position in the stud farm, which I felt but was unable to explain, made me retire into myself. I pondered over the injustice of men, who blamed me for being piebald; I pondered on the inconstancy of mother love and feminine love in general and on its dependence on physical condition; and above all I pondered on the characteristics of that strange race of animals with whom we are so closely connected, and whom we call men—those characteristics which were the source of my own peculiar position in the stud farm, which I felt but could not understand.

The meaning of this peculiarity in people and the characteristic on which it is based was shown me later.

It was in winter at holiday time. I had not been fed or watered all day. As I learned later, this happened because the lad who fed us was drunk. That day the stud groom came in, saw that I had no food, began to use bad language about the missing lad, and then went away.

Next day the lad came into our stable with another groom to give us hay. I noticed that he was particularly pale and sad, and that in the expression of his long back especially there was something significant which evoked compassion.

He threw the hay angrily over the grating. I made a move to put my head over his shoulder, but he struck me such a painful blow on the nose with his fist that I started back. Then he kicked me in the belly with his boot.

"If it hadn't been for this scurvy beast," he said, "nothing would have happened!"

"How's that?" inquired the other groom.

"You see, he doesn't go to look after the count's horses, but visits his own twice a day."

"What, have they given him the piebald?" asked the other.

"Given it, or sold it—the devil only knows! The count's horses might all starve—he wouldn't care—but just dare to leave his colt without food! 'Lie down!' he says, and they begin walloping me! No Christianity in it. He has more pity on a beast than on a man. He must be an infidel—he counted the strokes himself, the barbarian! The general never flogged like that! My whole back is covered with weals. There's no Christian soul in him!"

What they said about flogging and Christianity I understood well enough, but I was quite in the dark as to what they meant by the words "his colt," from which I perceived that people considered that there was some connection between me and the head groom. What that connection was I could not at all understand then. Only much later, when they separated me from the other horses, did I learn what it meant. At that time I could not at all understand what they meant by speaking of me as being a man's property. The words "my horse" applied to me, a live horse, seemed to me as strange as to say "my land," "my air," or "my water". . . .

I was thrice unfortunate: I was piebald, I was a gelding, and people considered that I did not belong to God and to myself, as is natural to all living creatures, but that I belonged to the stud groom.

Their thinking this about me had many consequences. The first was that I was kept apart from the other horses, was better fed, oftener taken out on the line, and was broken in at an earlier age. I was first harnessed in my third year. I remember how the stud groom, who imagined I was his, himself began to harness me with a crowd of other grooms, expecting me to prove unruly or to resist. They put ropes around me to lead me into the shafts; put a cross of broad straps on my back and fastened it to shafts so that I could not kick, while I was only awaiting an opportunity to show my readiness and love of work.

They were surprised that I started like an old horse. They began to break me and I began to practice trotting. Every day I made greater and greater progress, so that after three months the general himself and many others approved of my pace. But strange to say, just because they considered me not as their own, but as belonging to the head groom, they regarded my paces quite differently.

The stallions who were my brothers were raced, their records were kept, people went to look at them and drove them in gilt sulkies, and expensive horse cloths were thrown over them. I was driven in a common sulky to Chesménka and other farms, on the head groom's business. All this was the result of my being piebald, and especially of my being, in their opinion, not the count's but the head groom's property.

Tomorrow, if we are alive, I will tell you the chief consequence for me of this right of property the head groom considered himself to have.

All that day the horses treated Strider respectfully, but Nester's treatment of him was as rough as ever.

Third Night

For me the most surprising consequence of my not being the count's, or God's, but the head groom's, was that the very thing that constitutes our chief merit—a fast pace—was the cause of my banishment. They were driving Swan around the track, and the head groom, returning from Chesménka, drove me up and stopped there. Swan went past. He went well, but all the same he was showing off and had not the exactitude I had developed in myself—so that directly one foot touched the ground another instantaneously lifted, and not the slightest effort was lost, but every atom of exertion carried me forward. Swan went by us. I pulled toward the ring, and the head groom did not check me. "Here, shall I try my piebald?" he shouted, and when next Swan came abreast of us he let me go. Swan was already going fast, and so I was left behind during the first round, but in the second I began to gain on him, drew near to his sulky, drew level—and passed him. They tried us again—it was the same thing. I was the faster. And this dismayed everybody. The general asked that I be sold at once to some distant place, so that nothing more should be heard of me: "Or else the count will get to know of it and there will be trouble!" So they sold me to a horse dealer as a shafthorse. I did not remain with him long. A hussar who came to buy remounts bought me. All this was so unfair, so cruel, that I was glad when they took me away from Khrénovo and parted me forever from all that had been familiar and dear to me. It was too painful for me among them. They had love, honor, freedom, before them; I had labor, humiliation, humiliation, labor, to the end of my life. And why? Because I was piebald, and because of that had to become somebody's horse . . . .

Fourth Night

I have had opportunity to make many observations both of men and of horses during the time I passed from hand to hand.

I stayed longest of all with two masters: a prince (an officer of hussars), and later with an old lady who lived near the church of St. Nicholas the Wonder Worker.

The happiest years of my life I spent with the officer of hussars.

Though he was the cause of my ruin, and though he never loved anything or anyone, I loved and still love him for that very reason.

What I like about him was that he was handsome, happy, rich, and therefore never loved anybody.

You understand that lofty equine feeling of ours. His coldness and my dependence on him gave special strength to my love for him. "Kill me, drive me till my wind is broken!" I used to think in our good days, "and I shall be all the happier."

He bought me from an agent to whom the head groom had sold me for eight hundred rubles, and he did so just because no one else had piebald horses. That was my best time. He had a mistress. I knew this because I took him to her every day, and sometimes took them both out.

His mistress was a handsome woman, and he was handsome, and his coachman was handsome, and I loved them all because they were. Life was worth living then. This was how our time was spent: in the morning the groom came to rub me down—not the coachman himself but the groom. The groom was a lad from among the peasants. He would open the door, let out the steam from the horses, throw out the droppings, take off our rugs, and begin to fidget over our bodies with a brush, and lay whitish streaks of dandruff from a currycomb on the boards of the floor that was dented by our rough horseshoes. I would playfully nip his sleeve and paw the ground. Then we were led out one after another to the trough filled with cold water, and the lad would admire the smoothness of my spotted coat which he had polished, my foot with its broad hoof, my legs straight as an arrow, my glossy quarters, and my back wide enough to sleep on. Hay was piled onto the high racks, and the oak cribs were filled with oats. Then Feofán, the head coachman, would come in.

Master and coachman resembled one another. Neither of them was afraid of anything or cared for anyone but himself, and for that reason everybody liked them. Feofán wore a red shirt, black velveteen knicker-bockers, and a sleeveless coat. I like it on a holiday when he would come into the stable, his hair pomaded, and wearing his sleeveless coat, and would shout:

"Now then, beastie, have you forgotten?" and push me with the handle of the stable fork, never so as to hurt me but just as a joke. I immediately knew that it was a joke, and laid back an ear, making my teeth click.

We had a black stallion, who drove in a pair. At night they used to put me in harness with him. That Polkán, as he was called, did not understand a joke but was simply vicious as the devil. I was in the stall next to his and sometimes we bit one another seriously. Feofán was not afraid of him. He would come up and give a shout: it looked as if Polkán would kill him, but no, he'd miss, and Feofán would put the harness on him.

Once he and I bolted down Smiths Bridge Street. Neither my master nor the coachman was frightened; they laughed, shouted at the people, checked us, and turned so that no one was run over.

In their service I lost my best qualities and half my life. They ruined me by watering me wrongly, and they foundered me . . . . Still for all that it was the best time of my life. At twelve o'clock they would come to harness me, black my hooves, moisten my forelock and mane, and put me in the shafts.

The sleigh was of woven cane, upholstered with velvet; the reins were of silk, the harness had silver buckles, sometimes there was a cover of silken fly net, and altogether it was such that when all the traces and straps were fastened it was difficult to say where the harness ended and the horse began. We were harnessed at ease in the stable. Feofán would come, broader at his hips than at the shoulders, his red belt up under his arms: he would examine the harness, take his seat, wrap his coat around him, put his foot into the sleigh stirrup, let off some joke, and for appearance's sake always hang a whip over his arm, though he hardly ever hit me, and would say "Let go!" and playfully stepping from foot to foot I would move out of the gate, and the cook who had come out to empty the slops would stop on the threshold and the peasant who had brought wood into the yard would open his eyes wide. We would come out, go a little way, and stop. Footmen would come out and other coachmen, and a chatter would begin. Everybody would wait: sometimes we had to stand for three hours at the entrance, moving a little way, turning back, and standing again.

At last there would be a stir in the hall: old Tíkhon with his paunch would rush out in his dress coat and cry "Drive up!" (In those days there was not that stupid way of saying "Forward!" as if one did not know that we moved forward and not back.) Feofán would cluck, drive up, and the prince would hurry out carelessly, as though there were nothing remarkable about the sleigh, or the horse, or Feofán—who bent his back and stretched out his arms so that it seemed it would be impossible for him to keep them long in that position. The prince would have a shako on his head and wear a fur coat with a gray beaver collar hiding his rosy, black-browed, handsome face, which should never have been concealed. He would come out clattering his saber, his spurs, and the brass backs of the heels of his overshoes, stepping over the carpet as if in a hurry and taking no notice of me or Feofán, whom everybody but he looked at and admired. Feofán would cluck, I would tug at the reins, and respectably, at a foot pace, we would draw up to the entrance and stop. I would turn my eyes on the prince and jerk my thoroughbred head with its delicate forelock . . . . The prince would be in good spirits and would sometimes jest with Feofán. Feofán would reply, half turning his handsome head, and without lowering his arms would make a perceptible movement with the reins which I understand: and then one, two, three . . . with ever wider and wider strides, every muscle quivering, and sending the muddy snow against the front of the sleigh, I would go. In those days, too, there was none of the present-day stupid habit of crying "Oh!" as if the coachman were in pain, instead of the sensible "Be off! Take care!" Feofán would shout "Be off! Look out there!" and the people would step aside and stand craning their necks to see the handsome gelding, the handsome coachman, and the handsome gentleman . . . .

I was particularly fond of passing a trotter. When Feofán and I saw at a distance a turnout worthy of the effort, we would fly like a whirlwind and gradually gain on it. Now, throwing the dirt right to the back of the sleigh, I would draw level with the occupant of the vehicle and snort above his head: then I would reach the horse's harness and the arch of his troika, and then would no longer see it but only hear its sounds in the distance behind. And the prince, Feofán, and I would all be silent, and pretend to be merely going on our own business and not even to notice those with slow horses whom we happened to meet on our way. I liked to pass another horse, but also liked to meet a good trotter. An instant, a sound, a glance, and we had passed each other and were flying in opposite directions.

The gate creaked and the voices of Nester and Váska were heard.

Fifth Night

The weather began to break up. It had been dull since morning and there was no dew, but it was warm and the mosquitoes were troublesome. As soon as the horses were driven in they collected around the piebald, and he finished his story as follows:

The happy period of my life was soon over. I lived in that way only two years. Toward the end of the second winter the happiest event of my life occurred, and following it came my greatest misfortune. It was during carnival week. I took the prince to the races. Glossy and Bull were running. I don't know what people were doing in the pavilion, but I know the prince came out and ordered Feofán to drive onto the track. I remember how they took me in and placed me beside Glossy. He was harnessed to a racing sulky and I, just as I was, to a town sleigh. I outstripped him at the turn. Roars of laughter and howls of delight greeted me.

When I was led in, a crowd followed me, and five or six people offered the prince thousands for me. He only laughed, showing his white teeth.

"No," he said, "this isn't a horse, but a friend. I wouldn't sell him for mountains of gold. Au revoir, gentlemen!"

He unfastened the sleigh apron and got in.

"To Ostózhenka Street!"

That was where his mistress lived, and off we flew . . . .

That was our last happy day. We reached her home. He spoke of her as his, but she loved someone else and had run away with him. The prince learned this at her lodgings. It was five o'clock, and without unharnessing me he started in pursuit of her. They did what had never been done to me before, struck me with the whip and made me gallop. For the first time I felt out of step and felt ashamed and wished to correct it, but suddenly I heard the prince shout in an unnatural voice: "Get on!" The whip whistled through the air and cut me, and I galloped, striking my foot against the iron front of the sleigh. We overtook her after going sixteen miles. I got him there, but trembled all night long and could not eat anything. In the morning they gave me water. I drank it and after that was never again the horse that I had been. I was ill, and they tormented me and maimed me—doctoring me, as people call it. My hooves came off, I had swellings, and my legs grew bent; my chest sank in and I became altogether limp and weak. I was sold to a horse dealer, who fed me on carrots and something else and made something of me quite unlike myself, though good enough to deceive one who did not know. My strength and my pace were gone.

When purchasers came, the dealer also tormented me by coming into my stall and beating me with a heavy whip to frighten and madden me. Then he would rub down the stripes on my coat and lead me out.

An old woman bought me off him. She always drove to the Church of St. Nicholas the Wonder Worker, and she used to have her coachman flogged. He used to weep in my stall, and I learned that tears have a pleasant, salty taste. Then the old woman died. Her steward took me to the country and sold me to a hawker. Then I overate myself with wheat and grew still worse. They sold me to a peasant. There I plowed, had hardly anything to eat, my foot got cut by a plowshare and I again became ill. Then a gypsy took me in exchange for something. He tormented me terribly and finally sold me to the steward here. And here I am.

All were silent. A sprinkling of rain began to fall.

C. S. Lewis

A WAYSIDE ADVENTURE

It was nearly noon when Shasta was wakened by something warm and soft moving over his face. He opened his eyes and found himself staring into the long face of a horse; its nose and lips were almost touching his. He remembered the exciting events of the previous night and sat up. But as he did so he groaned.

"Ow, Bree," he gasped. "I'm so sore. All over. I can hardly move."

"Good morning, small one," said Bree, "I was afraid you might feel a bit stiff. It can't be the falls. You didn't have more than a dozen or so, and it was all lovely, soft springy turf that must have been almost a pleasure to fall on. And the only one that might have been nasty was broken by that gorse bush. No: it's the riding itself that comes hard at first. What about breakfast? I've had mine."

"Oh bother breakfast. Bother everything," said Shasta. "I tell you I can't move." But the horse nuzzled at him with its nose and pawed him gently with a hoof till he had to get up. And then he looked about him and saw where they were. Behind them lay a little copse. Before them the turf, dotted with white flowers, sloped down to the brow of a cliff. Far below them, so that the sound of the breaking waves was very faint, lay the sea. Shasta had never seen it from such a height and never seen so much of it before, nor dreamed how many colors it had. On either hand the coast stretched away; headland after headland, and at the points you could see the white foam running up the rocks but making no noise because it was so far off. There were gulls flying overhead and the heat shivered on the ground; it was a blazing day. But what Shasta chiefly noticed was the air. He couldn't think what was missing, until at last he realized that there was no smell of fish in it. For of course, neither in the cottage nor among the nets, had he ever been away from that smell in his life. And this new air was so delicious, and all his old life seemed so far away that he forgot for a moment about his bruises and his aching muscles and said:

"I say, Bree, didn't you say something about breakfast?"

"Yes, I did," answered Bree. "I think you'll find something in the saddlebags. They're over there on that tree where you hung them up last night—or early this morning, rather."

They investigated the saddlebags, and the results were cheering—a meat pasty, only slightly stale, a lump of dried figs and another lump of green cheese, a little flask of wine, and some money; about forty crescents in all, which was more than Shasta had ever seen.

While Shasta sat down—painfully and cautiously—with his back against a tree and started on the pasty, Bree had a few more mouthfuls of grass to keep him company.

"Won't it be stealing to use the money?" asked Shasta.

"Oh," said the Horse, looking up with its mouth full of grass, "I never thought of that. A free horse and a talking horse mustn't steal, of course. But I think it's all right. We're prisoners and captives in enemy country. That money is booty, spoil. Besides, how are we to get any food for you without it? I suppose, like all humans, you won't eat natural food like grass and oats."

"I can't."

"Ever tried?"

"Yes, I have. I can't get it down at all. You couldn't either if you were me."

"You're odd little creatures, you humans," remarked Bree.

When Shasta had finished his breakfast (which was by far the nicest he had ever eaten), Bree said, "I think I'll have a nice roll before we put on that saddle again." And he proceeded to do so. "That's good. That's very good," he said, rubbing his back on the turf and waving all four legs in the air. "You ought to have one too, Shasta," he snorted. "It's most refreshing."

But Shasta burst out laughing and said, "You do look funny when you're on your back!"

"I look nothing of the sort," said Bree. But then suddenly he rolled around on his side, raised his head, and looked hard at Shasta, blowing a little.

"Does it really look funny?" he asked in an anxious voice.

"Yes, it does," replied Shasta. "But what does it matter?"

"You don't think, do you," said Bree, "that it might be a thing *talking* horses never do—a silly, clownish trick I've learned from the dumb ones? It would be dreadful to find, when I get back to Narnia, that I've picked up a lot of low, bad habits. What do you think, Shasta? Honestly, now. Don't spare my feelings. Should you think the real, free horses—the talking kind—do roll?"

"How should I know? Anyway I don't think I should bother about it if I were you. We've got to get there first. Do you know the way?"

"I know my way to Tashbaan. After that comes the desert. Oh, we'll manage the desert somehow, never fear. Why, we'll be in sight of the Northern mountains then. Think of it! To Narnia and the North! Nothing will stop us then. But I'd be glad to be past Tashbaan. You and I are safer away from cities."

"Can't we avoid it?"

"Not without going a long way inland, and that would take us into cultivated land and main roads; and I wouldn't know the way. No, we'll just have to creep along the coast. Up here on the downs we'll meet nothing but sheep and rabbits and gulls and a few shepherds. And by the way, what about starting?"

Shasta's legs ached terribly as he saddled Bree and climbed into the saddle, but the Horse was kindly to him and went at a soft pace all afternoon. When evening twilight came they dropped by steep tracks into a valley and found a village. Before they got into it Shasta dismounted and entered it on foot to buy a loaf and some onions and radishes. The Horse trotted around by the fields in the dusk and met Shasta at the far side. This became their regular plan every second night.

These were great days for Shasta, and every day better than the last as his muscles hardened and he fell less often. Even at the end of his training, Bree still said he sat like a bag of flour in the saddle. "And even if it was safe, young 'un, I'd be ashamed to be seen with you on the main road." But in spite of his rude words Bree was a patient teacher. No one can teach riding so well as a horse. Shasta learned to trot, to canter, to jump, and to keep his seat even when Bree pulled up suddenly or swung unexpectedly to the left or the right—which, as Bree told him, was a thing you might have to do at any moment in a battle. And then, of course, Shasta begged to be told of the battles and wars in which Bree had carried the Tarkaan. And Bree would tell of forced marches and the fording of swift rivers, of charges and of fierce fights between cavalry and cavalry when the war horses fought as well as the men, being all fierce stallions, trained to bite and kick, and to rear at the right moment so that the horse's weight as well as the rider's would come down on an enemy's crest in the stroke of sword or battle-ax. But Bree did not want to talk about the wars as often as Shasta wanted to hear about them. "Don't speak of them, youngster," he would say. "They were only the Tisroc's wars and I fought in them as a slave and a dumb beast. Give me the Narnian wars where I shall fight as a free Horse among my own people! Those will be wars worth talking about. Narnia and the North! Bra-ha-ha! Broo hoo!"

Shasta soon learned, when he heard Bree talking like that, to prepare for a gallop.

After they had traveled on for weeks and weeks past more bays and headlands and rivers and villages than Shasta could remember, there came a moonlit night when they started their journey at evening, having slept during the day. They had left the downs behind them and were crossing a wide plain with a forest about half a mile away on their left. The sea, hidden by low sandhills, was about the same distance on their right. They had jogged along for about an hour, sometimes trotting and sometimes walking, when Bree suddenly stopped.

"What's up?" said Shasta.

"S-s-ssh!" said Bree, craning his neck around and twitching his ears. "Did you hear something! Listen."

"It sounds like another horse—between us and the woods," said Shasta after he had listened for about a minute.

"It is another horse," said Bree. "And that's what I don't like."

"Isn't it probably just a farmer riding home late?" said Shasta with a yawn.

"Don't tell me!" said Bree. *"That's* not a farmer's riding. Nor a farmer's horse either. Can't you tell by the sound? That's quality, that horse is. And it's being ridden by a real horseman. I tell you what it is, Shasta. There's a Tarkaan under the edge of that wood. Not on his war horse—it's too light for that. On a fine blood mare, I should say."

"Well, it's stopped now, whatever it is," said Shasta.

"You're right," said Bree. "And why should he stop just when we do? Shasta, my boy, I do believe there's someone shadowing us at last."

"What shall we do?" said Shasta in a lower whisper than before. "Do you think he can see us as well as hear us?"

"Not in this light so long as we stay quite still," answered Bree. "But look! There's a cloud coming up. I'll wait till that gets over the moon. Then we'll get off to our right as quietly as we can, down to the shore. We can hide among the sandhills if the worst comes to the worst."

They waited till the cloud covered the moon and then, first, at a walking pace and afterward at a gentle trot, made for the shore.

The cloud was bigger and thicker than it had looked at first, and soon the night grew very dark. Just as Shasta was saying to himself, "We must be nearly at those sandhills by now," his heart leaped into his mouth because an appalling noise had suddenly risen up out of the darkness ahead; a long snarling roar, melancholy and utterly savage. Instantly Bree swerved around and began galloping inland again as fast as he could gallop.

"What is it?" gasped Shasta.

"Lions!" said Bree, without checking his pace or turning his head.

After that there was nothing but sheer galloping for some time. At last they splashed across a wide, shallow stream, and Bree came to a stop on the far side. Shasta noticed that he was trembling and sweating all over.

"That water may have thrown the brute off our scent," panted Bree when he had partly got his breath again. "We can walk for a bit now."

As they walked Bree said, "Shasta, I'm ashamed of myself. I'm just as frightened as a common, dumb Calormene horse. I am really. I don't feel like a Talking Horse at all. I don't mind swords and lances and arrows, but I can't bear—those creatures. I think I'll trot for a bit."

About a minute later, however, he broke into a gallop again, and no wonder. For the roar broke out again, this time on their left from the direction of the forest.

"Two of them," moaned Bree.

When they had galloped for several minutes without any further noise from the lions Shasta said, "I say! That other horse is galloping beside us now. Only a stone's throw away."

"All the b-better," panted Bree. "Tarkaan on it—will have a sword—protect us all."

"But, Bree!" said Shasta. "We might just as well be killed by lions as caught. Or *I* might. They'll hang me for horse-stealing." He was feeling less frightened of lions than Bree because he had never met a lion; Bree had.

Bree only snorted in answer, but he did sheer away to his right. Oddly enough the other horse seemed also to be sheering away to the left, so that in a few seconds the space between them had widened a good deal.

But as soon as it did so there came two more lions' roars, immediately after one another, one on the right and the other on the left, and the horses began drawing nearer together. So, apparently, did the lions. The roaring of the brutes on each side was horribly close, and they seemed to be keeping up with the galloping horses quite easily. Then the cloud rolled away. The moonlight, astonishingly, showed up everything almost as if it were broad day. The two horses and the two riders were galloping neck to neck and knee to knee just as if they were in a race. Indeed Bree said (afterward) that a finer race had never been seen in Calormen.

Shasta now gave himself up for lost and began to wonder whether lions killed you quickly or played with you as a cat plays with a mouse and how much it would hurt. At the same time (one sometimes does this at the most frightful moments) he noticed everything. He saw that the other rider was a very small, slender person, mail-clad (the moon shone on the mail) and riding magnificently. He had no beard.

Something flat and shining was spread out before them. Before Shasta had time even to guess what it was, there was a great splash and he found his mouth half full of saltwater. The shining thing had been a long inlet of the sea. Both horses were swimming and the water was up to Shasta's knees. There was an angry roaring behind them, and looking back, Shasta saw a great, shaggy, and terrible shape crouched on the water's edge: but only one. "We must have shaken off the other lion," he thought.

The lion apparently did not think its prey worth a wetting; at any rate it made no attempt to take the water in pursuit. The two horses, side by side, were now well out into the middle of the creek, and the opposite shore could be clearly seen. The Tarkaan had not yet spoken a word. "But he will," thought Shasta. "As soon as we have landed. What am I to say? I must begin thinking out a story."

Then, suddenly, two voices spoke at his side.

"Oh, I *am* so tired," said the one.

"Hold your tongue, Hwin, and don't be a fool," said the other.

"I'm dreaming," thought Shasta. "I could have sworn that other horse spoke."

Soon the horses were no longer swimming but walking and soon with a great sound of water running off their sides and tails and with a great crunching of pebbles under eight hooves, they came out on the farther beach of the inlet. The Tarkaan, to Shasta's surprise, showed no wish to ask questions. He did not even look at Shasta but seemed anxious to urge his horse straight on. Bree, however, at once shouldered himself in the other horse's way.

"Broo-hoo-hah!" he snorted. "Steady there! I *heard* you, I did. There's no good pretending, ma'am. I heard you. You're a Talking Horse, a Narnian horse just like me."

"What's it got to do with you if she is?" said the strange rider fiercely, laying hand on sword hilt. But the voice in which the words were spoken had already told Shasta something.

"Why, it's only a girl!" he exclaimed.

"And what business is it of yours if I am *only* a girl?" snapped the stranger. "You're only a boy: a rude, common little boy—a slave probably, who's stolen his master's horse."

"That's all *you* know," said Shasta.

"He's not a thief, little Tarkheena," said Bree. "At least if there's been any stealing, you might just as well say I stole *him*. And as for its not being my business, you wouldn't expect me to pass a lady of my own race in this strange country without speaking to her? It's only natural I should."

"I think it's very natural too," said the mare.

"I wish you'd held your tongue, Hwin," said the girl. "Look at the trouble you've got us into."

"I don't know about trouble," said Shasta. "You can clear off as soon as you like. We shan't keep you."

"No, you shan't," said the girl.

"What quarrelsome creatures these humans are," said Bree to the mare. "They're as bad as mules. Let's try to talk a little sense. I take it, ma'am, your story is the same as mine? Captured in early youth—years of slavery among the Calormenes?"

"Too true, sir," said the mare with a melancholy whinny.

"And now, perhaps—escape?"

"Tell him to mind his own business, Hwin," said the girl.

"No, I won't, Aravis," said the mare, putting her ears back. "This is my escape just as much as yours. And I'm sure a noble war horse like this is not going to betray us. We are trying to escape, to get to Narnia."

"And so, of course, are we," said Bree. "Of course you guessed that at once. A little boy in rags riding (or trying to ride) a war horse at dead of night couldn't mean anything but an escape of some sort. And, if I may say so, a highborn Tarkheena riding alone at night—dressed up in her brother's armor—and very anxious for everyone to mind their own business and ask her no questions—well, if that's not fishy, call me a cob!"

"All right then," said Aravis. "You've guessed it. Hwin and I are running away. We are trying to get to Narnia. And now, what about it?"

"Why, in that case, what is to prevent us all going together?" said Bree. "I trust, Madam Hwin, you will accept such assistance and protection as I may be able to give you on the journey?"

"Why do you keep on talking to my horse instead of to me?" asked the girl.

"Excuse me, Tarkheena," said Bree (with just the slightest backward tilt of his ears), "but that's Calormene talk. We're free Narnians, Hwin and I, and I suppose, if you're running away to Narnia, you want to be one too. In that case Hwin isn't *your* horse any longer. One might just as well say you're *her* human."

The girl opened her mouth to speak and then stopped. Obviously she had not quite seen it in that light before.

"Still," she said after a moment's pause, "I don't know that there's so much point in all going together. Aren't we more likely to be noticed?"

"Less," said Bree; and the mare said, "Oh do let's. I should feel much more comfortable. We're not even certain of the way. I'm sure a great charger like this knows far more than we do."

"Oh come on, Bree," said Shasta, "and let them go their own way. Can't you see they don't want us?"

"We do," said Hwin.

"Look here," said the girl. "I don't mind going with *you*, Mr. War Horse, but what about this boy? How do I know he's not a spy?"

"Why don't you say at once that you think I'm not good enough for you?" said Shasta.

"Be quiet, Shasta," said Bree. "The Tarkheena's question is quite reasonable. I'll vouch for the boy, Tarkheena. He's been true to me and a good friend. And he's certainly either a Narnian or an Archenlander."

"All right, then. Let's go together." But she didn't say anything to Shasta and it was obvious that she wanted Bree, not him.

"Splendid!" said Bree. "And now that we've got the water between us and those dreadful animals, what about you two humans taking off our saddles and our all having a rest and hearing one another's stories."

Both the children unsaddled their horses, and the horses had a little grass and Aravis produced rather nice things to eat from her saddlebag. But Shasta sulked and said no thanks, and that he wasn't hungry. And he tried to put on what he thought very grand and stiff manners, but as a fisherman's hut is not usually a good place for learning grand manners, the result was dreadful. And he half knew that it wasn't a success, and then became sulkier and more awkward than ever. Meanwhile the two horses were getting on splendidly. They remembered the very same places in Narnia—"the grasslands up above Beaversdam"—and found that they were some sort of second cousins once removed. This made things more and more uncomfortable for the humans until at last Bree said, "And now, Tarkheena, tell us your story. And don't hurry it—I'm feeling comfortable now."

Aravis immediately began, sitting quite still and using a rather different tone and style from her usual one. For in Calormen, storytelling (whether the stories are true or made up) is a thing you're taught, just as English boys and girls are taught essay-writing. The difference is that people want to hear the stories, whereas I never heard of anyone who wanted to read the essays.

Walter Farley

RESCUE

Alec's eyes blurred; he couldn't see. He stumbled and fell and then clambered to his feet. Again he rushed forward. Then they had their arms around him.

"For the love of St. Patrick," the man called Pat groaned, "he's just a boy!"

Words jumbled together and stuck in Alec's throat as he looked into the five pairs of eyes staring at him. Then he found his voice. "We're saved!" he yelled. "We're saved, Black, we're saved!"

The sailors looked at him—he was a strange sight! His red hair was long and disheveled, his face and body so brown that they would have taken him for a native if it hadn't been for the torn remnants of his clothing which hung loosely on him.

One of the men stepped forward. From his uniform he was obviously the captain of the ship. "Everything is going to be all right, son," he said as he placed an arm around Alec and steadied him.

Slowly Alec gained control of himself. "I'm OK now, sir," he said.

The sailors gathered around him. "Is there someone else with you on this island?" the captain asked.

"Only the Black, sir."

The men looked at one another, and then the captain spoke again, "Who's the Black, son?" he asked.

"He's a horse, sir," Alec answered.

And then he told them his story—of the storm and the shipwreck, the hours spent in the raging sea holding desperately to the rope tied to the stallion's neck, their fight against starvation on the island, his conquest of the Black, and the fire which that night had reduced his shelter to ashes. Sweat broke out upon his forehead as in the vivid word pictures he once again lived the twenty days of hardships and suffering since the *Drake* had gone down.

When he finished there was a moment of silence, and then one of the men spoke. "This lad is imagining things, Captain. What he needs is some hot food and a good bed!"

Alec looked from one face to another and saw that they didn't believe him. Rage filled him. Why should they be so stupid? Was his story so fantastic? He'd prove it to them, then—he'd call the Black.

He raised his fingers to his lips and whistled. "Listen," he shouted. "Listen!" The men stood still. A minute passed, and then another—only the waves lapping on the beach could be heard in the terrifying stillness of the island.

Then the captain's voice came to him. "We have to go now, son. We're off our course and away behind schedule."

Dazed, Alec's eyes turned from the island to the freighter lying at anchor, smoke belching from its two stacks. It was larger than the *Drake.*

The captain's voice again broke through his thoughts. "We're bound for South America—Rio de Janeiro is our first stop. We can take you there and wire your parents from the ship that you're alive!"

The captain and Pat had him by the arms; the others were in the boat ready to shove off. Desperately Alec tried to collect his thoughts. He was leaving the island. He was leaving the Black. The Black—who had saved his life! He jerked himself free, he was running up the beach.

Their mouths wide open, the sailors watched him as he stumbled up the hill. They saw him reach the top and raise his fingers to his lips. His whistle reached them—then there was silence.

Suddenly, an inhuman scream shattered the stillness—a wild, terrifying call! Stunned, they stood still and the hairs on the back of their necks seemed to curl. Then as if by magic, a giant black horse, his mane waving like flame, appeared beside the boy. The horse screamed again, his head raised high, his ears pricked forward. Even at this distance they could see that he was a tremendous horse—a wild stallion.

Alec flung his arms around the Black's neck and buried his head in the long mane. "We're leaving together, Black—together," he said. Soothingly he talked to the stallion, steadying him. After a few minutes he descended the hill and the horse hesitatingly followed. He reared as they approached the sailors, his legs pawing in the air. The men scrambled into the boat: only Pat and the captain stood their ground. Fearfully they watched the Black as he strode toward them. He drew back; his black eyes glanced nervously from Alec to the group of men. Alec patted him, coaxed him. His action was beautiful and every few steps he would jump swiftly to one side.

Approximately thirty yards away, Alec came to a halt.

"You just have to take us both, Captain! I can't leave him!" he yelled.

"He's too wild. We couldn't take him, we couldn't handle him!" came the answer.

"I can handle him. Look at him now!"

The Black was still, his head turned toward the freighter as if he understood what actually was going on. Alec's arm was around his neck. "He saved my life, Captain. I can't leave him!"

The captain turned, spoke with the men in the boat. Then he shouted, "There isn't any possible way of getting that devil on board, anyway!" He paused. "How're you going to get him out there!" The captain pointed to the ship.

"He can swim," answered Alec.

There was another discussion between captain and crew. When he turned, the captain's heavily-lined face was more grim than ever. He doffed his cap and ran a large hand through his gray hair. "OK, son," he said, "you win—but you'll have to get him out there!"

Alec's heart beat heavily and he gazed at the stallion. "Come on, Black," he said. He walked forward a few steps. The Black hesitated and then followed. Again Alec moved ahead. Slowly they approached the group. Then the Black halted, his nostrils quivered and he reared.

"Get in the boat, Captain," Alec shouted. "Move up to the bow. I'm going to get in the stern when you get her in the water."

The captain ordered his men to shove off, and he and Pat climbed in; then they waited for Alec.

Alec turned to the Black. "This is our chance, Black," he said. "Don't let me down!" He could see the stallion was nervous; the horse had learned to trust him, but his natural instincts still warned him against the others. Soothingly Alec spoke to him. Slowly he backed away—the Black raised his head nervously, then followed. As the boy neared the boat, the stallion stopped. Alec kept backing up and climbed into the boat. "Row slowly," he said, without turning his eyes away from the horse.

As they moved away from the beach Alec called, "Come on, Black-boy!" The stallion pranced, his head and tail erect, his ears forward. He half-reared and then stepped into the water. Like a flash he was back on the beach; his foreleg pawing into the sand and sending it flying. His black eyes never left the boat as it moved slowly out into the water. He ran a short way down the beach, and then back again.

Alec realised the terrific fight that the stallion was waging with himself. He whistled. The Black stopped in his tracks and answered. Slowly the boat moved farther away.

Suddenly the stallion rose high into the air on his hind legs, and then plunged into the water. "Come on, Black," shouted Alec. "Come on!"

The Black was in water up to his big chest now—then he was swimming and coming swiftly toward the boat.

"Row for the ship, Captain," yelled Alec.

The black head rose in the water behind them, the eyes fearfully following Alec as he half-hung out of the boat and called to the stallion. The large, black body slid through the water, his legs working like pistons.

Soon they reached the freighter. The captain and three men sprang up the ladder. Only Pat remained behind with Alec. "Keep him there for two minutes!" the captain yelled over his shoulder.

The Black reached the rowboat and Alec managed to get his hand on the stallion's head. "Good boy!" he murmured proudly. Then he heard the captain's hail from on top of the deck. He looked up and saw the cargo hoist being lowered; on the end was a belly band to go around the Black so that he could be lifted up. He had to get that band around the stallion's stomach!

Alec saw the Black's eyes leave him and gaze fearfully at the line descending over his head. Suddenly he swam away from the boat. Frantically Alec called to him.

As the band came within reach, Pat grabbed it—his fingers tore at the straps and buckles. "We've got to get this around him somehow!" he shouted to Alec. "It's the only way!"

Alec tried desperately to think. Certainly there must be some way! The stallion had turned and once again was looking in their direction. If he could only get close to him. "Let me have the band, Pat, and more line," he said.

Pat handed it to him and signaled above. "And what are you going to do?" he asked.

But Alec didn't seem to hear his query. He gripped the straps of the band tightly. "We've come this far," he said to himself. He climbed over the side and lowered himself into the water; Pat was too astonished to speak. Alec swam a few yards towards the Black, the band stretched out behind him; then he stopped and trod water. He called softly and the stallion swam toward him.

He came within an arm's reach and Alec touched him, keeping his body far enough away to avoid the driving legs. How could he get the band around the stallion? Pat was yelling suggestions, but Alec could think of only one way that might be successful.

He sank lower in the water, his hand gradually sliding down the Black's neck; he held the straps of the belt tightly in the other. He took a deep·breath and filled his lungs with air; then he dived sideways and felt the waters close over his head. Down he went, striving desperately to get enough depth to clear the stallion's legs. He swam directly beneath the Black's belly; the water churned white above his head and he caught a glimpse of striking hoofs. When he felt sure that he was on the other side, he started up, his fingers still tightly closed upon the straps and the band dragging behind.

When he reached the surface, he found the stallion in the same position, his eyes searching for him. Now the band was directly below the Black! He signaled for Pat to pull up the slack between the boat and the horse. All that he had to do now was to tighten the band around the stallion by getting these straps through the buckles on the other side! Alec moved closer to the Black. He would have to take the chance of being kicked. He kept as close to the middle of the stallion as possible. Then he was beside him. He felt the waters swirling on both sides. The line was taut now, ascending in the air to the top of the hoist on the freighter.

The Black became uneasy. Alec reached over his back and desperately tried to pull the straps through the buckles. A searing pain went through his leg as one of the Black's hoofs struck him. His leg went limp. Minutes passed as his fingers worked frantically. Then he had the straps through and began pulling the band tighter. The stallion went wild with rage as he felt it tighten around him. Alec pulled harder. Once again he felt the Black's hoof strike his leg—but there was no pain. He had the straps through the buckles as far as they would go; he made sure they were securely fastened, and then wearily pushed himself away from the Black.

A safe distance away, Alec signaled the men on the freighter to hoist. He heard the starting of a motor and the chain line became more taut. Then the stallion was dragged through the water until he was beside the ship, his teeth were bared, his eyes were filled with hate! Then the hoist started lifting him up. Slowly the Black moved out of the water—up, up in the air he ascended, his legs pawing madly!

Alec swam towards the rowboat, his leg hanging limp behind him. When he reached it, Pat hung over the side and helped him up into the boat. "Good boy," he said.

The pain in his leg made Alec's head whirl. Blackness seemed to be settling down upon him—he shook his head. Then he felt Pat's big arm around his waist and he went limp.

When Alec regained consciousness, he found himself in bed. Beside him sat Pat—a large grin on his face, his blue eyes crinkling in the corners. "For the love of St. Patrick," he exclaimed, "I thought you were going to sleep forever!"

"What time is it, Pat?" Alec asked. "Have I been sleeping long?"

Pat ran a large, gnarled hand through his black hair. "Well, not so long, son—you were pretty tired, y'know." He paused. "Let's see, we picked you up Tuesday morning and now it's Wednesday night."

"Whew!" said Alec, "that's some sleeping!"

"Well, we did wake you up a couple of times to give you some soup, but I guess you wouldn't be remembering now."

Alec moved slightly and felt a pain go through his leg. His eyes turned to Pat. "Did I get hurt bad?" he asked.

"The Doc says not—went to the bone, but it's healing nicely. You'll be all right in a few days."

"And the Black—what happened?"

"Lad, never in my life did I ever expect to see the like of him! What a fight he put up—he almost tore the boat apart!" Pat's blue eyes flashed. "Lord, what a devil! The moment his hoofs touched the deck he wanted to fight. If we hadn't still had the band around him, he would have killed us all! He plunged and struck his legs out like I've never seen before. He wouldn't stand still. You could have helped us, son. We hoisted him in the air again, off his feet. I thought he had gone crazy, his face was something terrible to see—and those screams, I'll hear them till my dying day!"

Pat stopped and moved uneasily in his seat. Then he continued, "It was when one of the boys got a little too close, and that black devil struck him in the side and he fell at our feet, that we decided there was nothing else to do but choke him! We got our lassoes around his neck and pulled until we had him pretty near gone. It was tough on him, but there was no other way. When he was almost unconscious, we let him down once again and somehow managed to lower him below.

"It was a job, lad, that I hope I'll never have to be in on again. We have some other horses and cattle in the hold, too, and they're all scared to death of him. It's a regular bedlam down there now, and I hate to think what might happen when that horse is himself again! We've got him in the strongest stall, but I'm wondering whether even that'll hold him!"

Pat rose from his chair and walked to the other side of the cabin.

Alec was silent, then he spoke slowly, "I'm sorry I've caused you all so much trouble. If only I'd been able to—"

"I didn't aim to make you feel like that, lad," Pat interrupted. "I guess we knew what we were doing, and from the looks of that animal he's worth it. Only we all realise now that he needs you to handle him—the Lord help anyone else that tries to!"

"Tell the captain I'll repay him and you fellows, too, Pat, somehow."

"Sure, lad, and now I have some work to do. You try and get some more sleep, and tomorrow or the next day you'll be on your feet again." He paused on his way to the door. "If you give me your address, we can wire your parents that you are safe, and tell them where we're bound for."

Alec smiled and wrote his address on the piece of paper Pat handed him. "Tell them I'll be with them—soon," he said as he finished.

R. D. Blackmore

A MAN JUSTLY POPULAR

It happened upon a November evening (when I was about fifteen years old, and outgrowing my strength very rapidly, my sister Annie being turned thirteen, and a deal of rain having fallen, and all the troughs in the yard being flooded) that the ducks in the court made a terrible quacking, instead of marching off to their pen, one behind another. Thereupon Annie and I ran out to see what might be the sense of it and when we got down to the foot of the courtyard where the two great ash trees stand by the side of the little water, we found good reason for the urgence and melancholy of the duck-birds. Lo! The old white drake, the father of all, a bird of high manners and chivalry was now in a sad predicament, yet quacking very stoutly.

For the brook was coming down in a great brown flood, as if the banks never belonged to it. The foaming of it, and the noise, and the cresting of the corners, and the up and down, like a wave of the sea, were enough to frighten any duck, though bred upon stormy waters, which our ducks never had been.

There is always a hurdle, nine feet long and four and a half in depth, swung by a chain at either end from an oak laid across the channel. But now this hurdle, which hung in the summer a foot above the trickle, would have been dipped more than two feet deep but for the power against it. For the torrent came down so vehemently that the chains at full stretch were creaking, and the hurdle buffeted almost flat. But saddest to see was between two bars, our venerable mallard jammed in by the joint of his shoulder, speaking aloud as he rose and fell, with his topknot full of water, unable to comprehend it, with his tail washed far away from him, but often compelled to be silent, being ducked very harshly against his will by the choking fall-to of the hurdle.

Annie was crying, and wringing her hands, and I was about to rush into the water, although I liked not the look of it, but hoped to hold on by the hurdle, when a man on horseback came suddenly around the corner of the great ash hedge on the other side of the stream, and his horse's feet were in the water.

"Ho, there," he cried. "Get thee back, boy. The flood will carry thee down like a straw. I will do it for thee, and no trouble."

With that he leaned forward, and spoke to his mare—she was just of the tint of a strawberry, a young thing, very beautiful—and she arched up her neck, as misliking the job; yet, trusting him, would attempt it. She entered the flood, with her dainty forelegs sloped farther and farther in front of her, and her delicate ears pricked forward, and the size of her great eyes increasing; but he kept her straight in the turbid rush, by the pressure of his knee on her. Then she looked back, and wondered at him, as the force of the torrent grew stronger, but he bade her go on; and on she went, and it foamed up over her shoulders; and she tossed up her lip and scorned it, for now her courage was waking. Then as the rush of it swept her away, and she struck with her forefeet down the stream, he leaned from his saddle in a manner which I never could have thought possible, and caught up the old drake with his left hand, and set him between his holsters, and smiled at his faint quack of gratitude. In a moment all three were carried downstream, and the rider lay flat on his horse, and tossed the hurdle clear from him, and made for the bend of smooth water.

They landed, some thirty or forty yards lower, in the midst of our kitchen garden, where the winter cabbage was; but though Annie and I crept in through the hedge, and were full of our thanks and admiring him, he would answer us never a word, until he had spoken in full to the mare, as if explaining the whole to her. She answered him kindly with her soft eyes, and sniffed at him very lovingly, and they understood one another. Then he took from his waistcoat two peppercorns, and made the old drake swallow them, and tried him softly upon his legs, where the leading gap in the hedge was.

The gentleman turned around to us with a pleasant smile on his face, as if he were lightly amused with himself; and we came up and looked at him. He was rather short, but very strongly built and springy, as his gait at every step showed plainly, although his legs were bowed with much riding, and he looked as if he lived on horseback. To a boy like me he seemed very old, being over twenty, and well-found in beard; but he was not more than four-and-twenty, fresh and ruddy-looking, with a short nose, and keen blue eyes, and a merry waggish jerk about him, as if the world were not in earnest. Yet he had a sharp, stern way, like the crack of a pistol, if anything misliked him; and we knew (for children see such things) that it was safer to tickle than buffet him.

"Well, young uns, what be gaping at?" He gave pretty Annie a chuck on the chin, and took me all in without winking. "I am thy mother's cousin, boy, and am going up to house. Tom Faggus is my name, as everybody knows; and this is my young mare, Winnie."

What a fool I must have been not to know it at once! Tom Faggus, the great highwayman, and his young blood-mare, the strawberry! Already her fame was noised abroad, nearly as much as her master's, especially as there were rumors that she was not a mare after all, but a witch. However, she looked like a filly all over, and wonderfully beautiful, with her supple stride, and soft slope of shoulder, and glossy coat beaded with water, and prominent eyes full of docile fire.

Tom Faggus stopped to sup that night with us, and having changed his wet things first, he seemed to be in fair appetite, and praised Annie's cooking mightily, with a kind of noise like a smack of his lips, and a rubbing of his hands together, whenever he could spare them.

Tom Faggus was a jovial soul, if ever there has been one, not making bones of little things, nor caring to seek evil. There was about him such a love of genuine human nature, that if a traveler said a good thing, he would give him back his purse again. It is true that he took people's money more by force than fraud; and the law (being used to the inverse method) was bitterly moved against him, although he could quote precedent.

"Now let us go and see Winnie, Jack," he said to me after supper. "She must be grieving for me, and I never let her grieve long." I was too glad to go with him, and Annie came slyly after us. The filly was walking to and fro on the naked floor of the stable and without so much as a headstall on, for he would not have her fastened.

"Hit me, Jack, and see what she will do. I will not let her hurt thee." He was rubbing her ears all the time he spoke, and she was leaning against him. Then I made believe to strike him, and in a moment she caught me by the waistband, and lifted me clean from the ground, and was casting me down to trample upon me, when he stopped her suddenly.

"What think you of that, boy? Have you horse, or dog, that would do that for you? Ay, and more than that she will do. If I were to whistle, by and by, in the tone that tells my danger, she would break this stable door down, and rush into the room to me. Nothing will keep her from me then, stone wall, or church tower. Ah, Winnie, Winnie, you little witch, we shall die together."

Now although Mr. Faggus was so clever, and generous and celebrated, I know not whether, upon the whole, we were rather proud of him as a member of our family, or inclined to be ashamed of him. And sure, I should pity, as well as condemn him, though our ways in the world were so different, knowing as I do his story. Much cause he had to be harsh with the world; and yet all acknowledged him very pleasant, when a man gave up his money. And often and often he paid the toll for the carriage coming after him, because he had emptied their pockets, and would not add inconvenience. By trade he had been a blacksmith, in the town of Northmolton, in Devonshire, a rough rude place at the end of Exmoor; so that many people marveled if such a man was bred there. Not only could he read and write, but he had solid substance; a piece of land worth a hundred pounds, and right of common for two hundred sheep, and a score and a half of beasts, lifting up or lying down. And being left an orphan (with all these cares upon him) he began to work right early, and made such a fame at the shoeing of horses, that the farriers of Barum were like to lose their custom.

When his trade was growing upon him, and his sweetheart ready to marry him (for he loved a maid of Southmolton), suddenly, like a thunderbolt, a lawyer's writ fell upon him.

This was the beginning of a lawsuit with Sir Robert Bampfylde, a gentleman of the neighborhood, who tried to oust him from his common, and drove his cattle and harassed them. And by that suit of law poor Tom was ruined altogether, for Sir Robert could pay for much swearing; and then all his goods and his farm were sold up, and even his smithery taken. But he saddled his horse, before they could catch him, and rode away to Southmolton, looking more like a madman than a good farrier, as the people said who saw him. But when he arrived there, instead of comfort, they showed him the face of the door alone and, a month after, his sweetheart married another.

All this was very sore upon Tom; and he took it to heart so grievously, that he said, as a better man might have said, being loose of mind and property, "The world hath preyed on me, like a wolf. God help me now to prey on the world."

And in sooth it did seem, for a while, as if Providence were with him; for he took rare toll on the highway, and his name was soon as good as gold anywhere this side of Bristowe. He studied his business by night and by day, with three horses all in hard work, until he had made a fine reputation.

One of his earliest meetings was with Sir Robert Bampfylde himself, who was riding along the Barum road, with only one serving-man after him. Tom Faggus put a pistol to his head, being then obliged to be violent, through want of reputation; while the serving-man pretended to be a long way around the corner. Then the baronet pulled out his purse, quite trembling in the hurry of his politeness. Tom took the purse, and his ring, and timepiece, and then handed them back with a very low bow, saying that it was against all usage for him to rob a robber. Then he turned to the unfaithful knave, and trounced him right well for his cowardice, and stripped him of all his property.

But now Mr. Faggus kept only one horse, lest the Government should steal them; and that one was the young mare Winnie. When I have added that Faggus as yet had never been guilty of bloodshed (for his eyes, and the click of his pistol at first, and now his high reputation made all his wishes respected), and that he never robbed a poor man, neither insulted a woman, but was very good to the Church, and of hot patriotic opinions, and full of jest and jollity, I have said as much as is fair for him, and shown why he was so popular. All good people liked Mr. Faggus— when he had not robbed them—and many a poor sick man or woman blessed him for other people's money; and all the hostlers, stable boys, and tapsters entirely worshiped him.

Saki

THE BROGUE

The hunting season had come to an end, and the Mullets had not succeeded in selling the Brogue. There had been a kind of tradition in the family for the past three or four years, a sort of fatalistic hope, that the Brogue would find a purchaser before the hunting was over; but seasons came and went without anything happening to justify such ill-founded optimism. The animal had been named Berserker in the earlier stages of its career; it had been rechristened the Brogue later on, in recognition of the fact that, once acquired, it was extremely difficult to get rid of. The unkinder wits of the neighborhood had been known to suggest that the first letter of its name was superfluous. The Brogue had been variously described in sale catalogues as a lightweight hunter, a lady's hack, and, more simply, but still with a touch of imagination, as a useful brown gelding, standing 15.1 hands. Toby Mullet had ridden him for four seasons with the West Wessex; you can ride almost any sort of horse with the West Wessex as long as it is an animal that knows the country. The Brogue knew the country intimately, having personally created most of the gaps that were to be met with in banks and hedges for many miles around. His manners and characteristics were not ideal in the hunting field, but he was probably safer to ride to hounds than he was as a hack on country roads. According to the Mullet family, he was not really road-shy, but there were one or two objects of dislike that brought on sudden attacks of what Toby called swerving sickness. Cars and cycles he treated with tolerant disregard, but pigs, wheelbarrows, piles of stones by the roadside, perambulators in a village street, gates painted too aggressively white, and sometimes, but not always, the newer kind of beehives, turned him aside from his tracks in vivid imitation of the zigzag course of forked lightning. If a pheasant rose noisily from the other side of the hedgerow the Brogue would spring into the air at the same moment, but this may have been due to a desire to be companionable. The Mullet family contradicted the widely prevalent report that the horse was a confirmed crib-biter.

It was about the third week in May that Mrs. Mullet, relict of the late Sylvester Mullet, and mother of Toby and a bunch of daughters, assailed Clovis Sangrail on the outskirts of the village with a breathless catalogue of local happenings.

"You know our new neighbor, Mr. Penricarde?" she vociferated; "awfully rich, owns tin mines in Cornwall, middle-aged and rather quiet. He's taken the Red House on a long lease and spent a lot of money on alterations and improvements. Well, Toby's sold him the Brogue!"

Clovis spent a moment or two in assimilating the astonishing news; then he broke out into unstinted congratulation. If he had belonged to a more emotional race he would probably have kissed Mrs. Mullet.

"How wonderful lucky to have pulled it off at last! Now you can buy a decent animal. I've always said that Toby was clever. Ever so many congratulations."

"Don't congratulate me. It's the most unfortunate thing that could have happened!" said Mrs. Mullet dramatically.

Clovis stared at her in amazement.

"Mr. Penricarde," said Mrs. Mullet, sinking her voice to what she imagined to be an impressive whisper, though it rather resembled a hoarse, excited squeak, "Mr. Penricarde has just begun to pay attentions to Jessie. Slight at first, but now unmistakable. I was a fool not to have seen it sooner. Yesterday, at the Rectory garden party, he asked her what her favorite flowers were, and she told him carnations, and today a whole stack of carnations has arrived, clove and malmaison and lovely dark red ones, regular exhibition blooms, and a box of chocolates that he must have got on purpose from London. And he's asked her to go around the links with him tomorrow. And now, just at this critical moment, Toby has sold him that animal. It's a calamity!"

"But you've been trying to get the horse off your hands for years," said Clovis.

"I've got a houseful of daughters," said Mrs. Mullet, "and I've been trying—well, not to get them off my hands, of course, but a husband or two wouldn't be amiss among the lot of them; there are six of them, you know."

"I don't know," said Clovis, "I've never counted, but I expect you're right as to the number; mothers generally know these things."

"And now," continued Mrs. Mullet, in her tragic whisper, "when there's a rich husband-in-prospect imminent on the horizon Toby goes and sells him that miserable animal. It will probably kill him if he tries to ride it; anyway it will kill any affection he might have felt toward any member of our family. What is to be done? We can't very well ask to have the horse back; you see; we praised it up like anything when we thought there was a chance of his buying it, and said it was just the animal to suit him."

"Couldn't you steal it out of his stable and send it to grass at some farm miles away?" suggested Clovis. "Write 'Votes for Women' on the stable door, and the thing would pass for a Suffragette outrage. No one who knew the horse could possibly suspect you of wanting to get it back again."

"Every newspaper in the country would ring with the affair," said Mrs. Mullet; "can't you imagine the headline, 'Valuable Hunter Stolen by Suffragettes'? The police would scour the countryside till they found the animal."

"Well, Jessie must try and get it back from Penricarde on the plea that it's an old favorite. She can say it was only sold because the stable had to be pulled down under the terms of an old repairing lease, and that now it has been arranged that the stable is to stand for a couple of years longer."

"It sounds a queer proceeding to ask for a horse back when you've just sold him," said Mrs. Mullet, "but something must be done, and done at once. The man is not used to horses, and I believe I told him it was as quiet as a lamb. After all, lambs go kicking and twisting about as if they were demented, don't they?"

"The lamb has an entirely unmerited character for sedateness," agreed Clovis.

Jessie came back from the golf links next day in a state of mingled elation and concern.

"It's all right about the proposal," she announced, "he came out with it at the sixth hole. I said I must have time to think it over. I accepted him at the seventh."

"My dear," said her mother, "I think a little more maidenly reserve and hesitation would have been advisable, as you've known him so short a time. You might have waited until the ninth hole."

"The seventh is a very long hole," said Jessie; "besides, the tension was putting us both off our game. By the time we'd got to the ninth hole we'd settled lots of things. The honeymoon is to be spent in Corsica, with perhaps a flying visit to Naples if we feel like it, and a week in London to wind up with. Two of his nieces are to be asked to be bridesmaids, so with our lot there will be seven, which is rather a lucky number. You're to wear your pearl gray, with any amount of Honiton lace jabbed into it. By the way, he's coming over this evening to ask your consent to the whole affair. So far all's well, but about the Brogue it's a different matter. I told him the legend about the stable, and how keen we were about buying the horse back, but he seems equally keen on keeping it. He said he must have horse exercise now that he's living in the country, and he's going to start riding tomorrow. He's ridden a few times in the Row on an animal that was accustomed to carry octogenarians and people undergoing rest cures, and that's about all his experience in the saddle—oh, and he rode a pony once in Norfolk, when he was fifteen and the pony twenty-four; and tomorrow he's going to ride the Brogue! I shall be a widow before I'm married, and I do so want to see what Corsica's like; it looks so silly on the map."

Clovis was sent for in haste, and the developments of the situation put before him.

"Nobody can ride that animal with any safety," said Mrs. Mullet, "except Toby, and he knows by long experience what it is going to shy at, and manages to swerve at the same time."

"I did hint to Mr. Penricarde—to Vincent, I should say—that the Brogue didn't like white gates," said Jessie.

"White gates!" exclaimed Mrs. Mullet; "did you mention what effect a pig has on him! He'll have to go past Lockyer's farm to get to the high road, and there's sure to be a pig or two grunting about in the lane."

"He's taken rather a dislike to turkeys lately," said Toby.

"It's obvious that Penricarde mustn't be allowed to go out on that animal," said Clovis, "at least not till Jessie has married him, and tired of him. I tell you what: ask him to a picnic tomorrow, starting at an early hour; he's not the sort to go out for a ride before breakfast. The day after I'll get the rector to drive him over to Crowleigh before lunch, to see the new cottage hospital they're building there. The Brogue will be standing idle in the stable and Toby can offer to exercise it; then it can pick up a stone or something of the sort and go conveniently lame. If you hurry on the wedding a bit the lameness fiction can be kept up till the ceremony is safely over."

Mrs. Mullet belonged to an emotional race, and she kissed Clovis.

It was nobody's fault that the rain came down in torrents the next morning, making a picnic a fantastic impossibility. It was also nobody's fault, but sheer ill luck, that the weather cleared up sufficiently in the afternoon to tempt Mr. Penricarde to make his first essay with the Brogue. They did not get as far as the pigs at Lockyer's farm; the rectory gate was painted a dull unobtrusive green, but it had been white a year or two ago, and the Brogue never forgot that he had been in the habit of making a violent curtsey, a backpedal, and a swerve at this particular point of the road. Subsequently, there being apparently no further call on his services, he broke his way into the rectory orchard, where he found a hen turkey in a coop; later visitors to the orchard found the coop almost intact, but very little left of the turkey.

Mr. Penricarde, a little stunned and shaken, and suffering from a bruised knee and some minor damages, good-naturedly ascribed the accident to his own inexperience with horses and country roads, and allowed Jessie to nurse him back into complete recovery and golf-fitness within something less than a week.

In the list of wedding presents which the local newspapers published a fortnight or so later appeared the following item:

"Brown saddle horse, 'The Brogue,' bridegroom's gift to bride."

"Which shows," said Toby Mullet, "that he knew nothing."

"Or else," said Clovis, "that he had a very pleasing wit."

Molly Gloss

THE BLUE ROAN

As soon as they had the cast on my leg I loaded the mare in the trailer and drove down to Jim's place in the Indian Valley. I was overnight getting there, on account of my leg would swell up every little while, working that stiff clutch, and I'd have to pull the truck over to the shoulder of the road and prop the cast up on the windowsill or the dashboard and let the ache ease out of it for an hour or two. In the morning, in the town, I asked an old man standing in front of a store if he knew where the Longanecker farm was and I went where he said.

The house I took to be Jim's stood most of the way up a hillside, above a flat, milky creek. There was a long slope of plowed ground between the creek and the house, and a woman working an old tractor across the field, towing a harrow. I don't think she could have heard the truck over the tractor noise, but maybe she saw the dust we raised going up her road because she looked around sudden from under the brim of her hat and then shut the tractor off and stood down from it and walked up across the plowed ground toward the house. It wasn't much of a house. The porch was rotted so it leaned downhill, and the roof had club moss along the eave edges. There was no barn, just a cow shed with manure piled up under it, and a lean-to at the end where she stood her tools. There was a post and wire fence that went around a couple of acres of grass and weed. An old pickup with a fender gone stood in the yard under the only tree.

There wasn't any bridge going over the creek. I had to ford the truck across. I took it slow on account of the trailer and the blue roan, but it was a shallow crossing and the rocks were cleared out of it so the trailer didn't buck too much getting over. The woman had beat me to the house and she was waiting for me when I got up the hill. She had her sleeves rolled up and was hugging herself so I could see she had rough red hands and rough red elbows, but her face under the hat-shadow looked smooth and fine-skinned, only a couple of pinch marks where the corners of her mouth tucked in. She had her hair drawn back in a knot but there was a thick bang of fuzz just under the edge of the hat and more of it leaking out at the neck. She maybe cussed that hair every day, too much of it and all frizzed like that, but it was a good color, gold-brown as wheat, and I can't say I minded the way it made a sort of halo around her face. She had on filthy jeans that fit poor, but I could see why Jim would have married her.

I stayed in the truck. "I'm after Jim Longanecker's place," I said across the windowsill. "I wonder if this is it." I was pretty sure it was, and as soon as I spoke his name those little tucks by her mouth squeezed in.

"Jim's gone rodeoing," she said, in a short way.

I had to ask her, I didn't want to tell it to the wrong woman. "Are you Mrs. Longanecker?"

She watched me, holding her head straight and keeping her arms folded up on her chest. "I'm Irene Longanecker," she said. "Who are you?"

"I'm a friend of Jim's. I've brought down some news."

Her mouth flattened out a little. It wasn't a frown, but as if she had got tired suddenly, and she spoke like that, too, with a flatness. "Where's he at now? Lakeview?"

There was a big ark of cloud sculling across the sky above the ridge beam of the house and I looked at that while I took off my hat and sleeved the sweat-edge on my forehead. "The news I've got isn't good," I said. I had quit watching her, but I could see from the tail of my eye she had raised her head back a little out of the shadow of the hat and now she had one hand flat above her eyes to shade against the glare. "Jim's dead," I said. I had meant to say, *Your husband Jim has been taken from you*—I had planned it, wooly and formal and old-fashioned like that. But I didn't remember until right afterward, so it came out straight and maybe sounding a little hard-boiled, though I wasn't feeling that way at all.

In the three years I'd known Jim he'd only come down to this place maybe a dozen different times, two or three weeks at a stretch during the off seasons. But he would get a letter now and then with his name spelled out in a spiky woman's hand, spelled all the way out, James Thomas Longanecker, like there might be more than one Jim Longanecker anywhere. And Jim used to speak of his wife like he spoke of his good bird gun or his handmade saddle, like she was something he had that he was proud of. So when I told her he was dead, I didn't know what I ought to expect.

She watched me a minute without moving, with the edge of her hand against her bangs to shade out the sun, and then her mouth moved again, slipping down in that tired way, but there wasn't any sound out of her and the face she made wasn't grief. She began to shake her head like she couldn't believe it. She didn't say anything to me, she just shook her head half a dozen times and then turned around and went up onto the leaning porch and cracked the screen door back and went inside.

I sat quite a while after that, creasing the edge of my hat with my thumbs, and then I eased my cast out of the truck and set it down on the dirt and stood up. I held on to the door of the truck and stood there looking across the plowed hill to where the tractor waited in front of the harrow.

The boy came from behind the hill, driving the cow and calf ahead of him. I could see him watching me while he switched the cow into her little shed, and for a while after that he stood by the buildings just looking down the hill at me. I thought the woman might come out to talk to him but she didn't. Finally he drifted down and stood at the edge of the field, watching me fight the tractor across those furrows, but he tired of that pretty quick and began to sidle up to the mare where I had let her out into the fenced pasture. She was soft-gaited, that horse, and light in the mouth, sweet-tempered and willing as any horse I'd seen. And she had that pretty roan color, that dark charcoal hide veined with white so it showed up blue, like the bluing on a new gun, and where the boy stroked her long stretched-down neck there was a shine I could see sometimes, bright as metal. Jim was killed on account of I loved that horse too much, I guess. So after a while I couldn't watch the boy with her anymore and I called to him, "She's testy. She's been known to bite," and heard it come out hard-boiled again. The sun was high up and hot and the sweat was itching over my ribs and my leg was aching all the way up to the hip. I don't know if he heard me over the tractor, but he gave me a look and went back up to the cow shed. He was maybe seven or eight years old. There was a ditch in his chin, just like Jim had.

Before too long, the woman came out and she said something to the boy and then came downhill to where I was. She had her sleeves rolled down now and her hat was gone so the sun lit up her hair like it was burning along the scalp.

"Dinner," she said. "You'd better come in." She didn't come any closer than the edge of the furrows. She just shouted it out so I'd hear her.

The boy and I took turns at the outside faucet. I didn't know what his mother had said to him and I was afraid he might ask me something about Jim, but he just washed his hands real slow, looking at me side-long, and then went ahead into the house. I stayed out a while, wetting my hair and combing it back smooth, and I left my hat in the truck when

I went inside. The woman was already sitting, spooning food onto the boy's plate, and it felt like quite a while before she looked up and saw me standing in the door.

"Sit down," she said, and that was the last thing anybody said until the meal was done, though the boy kept sneaking looks in my direction. When the woman began to clear the plates, the boy pitched right in. That left me sitting there, so I made as if to help too. She said, "You can go on out and sit in the shade. I'll be out in a minute," and stuck her chin toward the door. So I went outside. I stood a while. Then I walked back down to the tractor and started in at the harrowing again.

After a while the woman came out. She walked down to the edge of the field and said something. I couldn't hear what it was so I shut off the tractor, and she walked across the plowed ground, then, until she was standing right next to me.

"Thank you for the harrowing. Most cowboys don't like to do that work at all." Maybe she meant it as a complaint against Jim but if she did I couldn't hear the sourness in it.

I said, "My folks were farmers. I used to know my way around a tractor pretty well."

She nodded, as if there was a meaning in it. "Well, I can finish it now. I appreciate you helping out."

There was a little speech I had readied while I was driving down here overnight. I said it now. "I'd help you out a while, if you want. I can finish up this field, get it put to seed. Or whatever else you need done. I can't rodeo much with this broken leg but I can do a little farming, I guess. I don't mind working for bed and board. I expect there's room for me to sleep in your tool shed, and I eat about anything."

She gave me a look, like she was hunting for something in my face. Maybe she was just making sure it was a true offer. Then she ducked her head and said, "I guess you're Glenn." That caught me short and I must have looked it. In a minute, watching me, she said, "Jim wrote that you were his friend." I'd seen Jim sweating out a few letters all right, but I'd never figured he would put me in one. I wondered what he had written. I don't know why it made me feel itchy.

"What killed him?" she said, so it came straight out without a warning, and I was caught short again.

I bent my broken leg up and rubbed the knee above the cast. I looked at my hand, my fingers working at the knee. "A horse kicked him," I said. "I guess he didn't feel it. At least that's what they said." She didn't say anything to that, so after a while I let out a little more: "I couldn't make it here right away but I came as soon as I was able. It happened Wednesday night. You don't have a telephone and I didn't think the news ought to be put in a letter if it could be otherwise." I thought it over and then I said, "I can drive you up there tomorrow if you want. Or tonight."

Finally she looked off, away from me, off toward her old house. "I appreciate you coming so far." I couldn't hear grief in it, just that same flat tone, like she was worn out, worn down.

I thought about it. "Jim would've done the same for me," I said.

She raised her head without looking around. "Yes. I guess that's so," she said. "Jim always set his friends high." She said it like she faulted him for it, and there was a look in her face, somewhat of bitterness. After a silence she said, "Were you with him?"

I had to think a minute what she was getting at, and then when it came clear I began to knead my leg again, working my knuckles at the knee. "Yes. I was there."

She nodded in that way she had, as if it meant something serious. Then finally she looked at me again, a straight look. "I want to hear about it."

I had thought I might get away with just telling her he had been kicked by a horse. But she stood there waiting for the rest, so I told her more or less what happened, though I hadn't got myself ready to tell it.

I told her we had got drunk after the rodeo in Sprague and Jim had started in teasing me about that blue roan I loved so much. Actually, I never did tell her it was the roan. I just said it was a mare Jim had, which I had taken a liking to. She had lately come into heat and every stallion who stood within half a mile of her was probably rubbing himself against a post that night. Jim was kidding me about it, asking if I was man enough to service her myself, and so on. But after a while things took a turn and he started talking in a serious way, as if we weren't both drunk, sitting on our butts under the dark bleachers in the rain.

"Female needs offspring," he said solemnly. "She won't be happy until she throws a colt. I ought to put her in with that good-looking red stud belongs to Chip Lister. She'll get herself a little red roan baby to keep her happy."

"The hell," I believe I said, and kept drinking my beer.

In a while he made a thoughtful sound and stood up. He walked off, dragging his boot heels in the mud in a lazy, strutting way. It was a while before I got up to follow him. I was pretty drunk. By the time I caught up to him, he had the mare in with Chip's stallion and was leaning on the rail watching them.

"Hey," I said. "Hey. What the hell are you doing?"

"If you weren't so blind-drunk you'd see what I'm doing."

I took off my hat and waved it. I don't know what good I thought that would do. "Jim, damn you, this ain't funny."

Jim clapped me on the shoulder. He was grinning. "The hell it ain't," he said.

The stud was driving the mare just ahead of him around the edge of the corral. In the rain and the darkness the mare looked black, the stallion dark red, the color of old blood. I flapped my hat again. "Get away from her you big bastard."

Jim laughed. "That old boy's going to make her a baby."

I stood holding my hat. Then I said, "The hell he is," and I went over the fence. Chip's horse had her pushed up against the rails by then and he was trying to work around behind her. I went up and just hit him in the muzzle with my fist. I was drunk. I should have got a stick of wood or something but I didn't. I just pushed in between them and started hitting.

I don't know what happened. I guess I got bumped. I was sitting in the mud, all at once, and they were stepping on me. I heard Jim yelling, I still don't know if it was at me or at those horses, but a big drunk yell, and then he came wading in, beating at the stallion like I'd done, with his knuckles. The horse got up on his hind legs, squealing, I saw his big chest and his mane swinging loose, and then I heard the sound the iron shoe made against the solid bone of Jim's head. That was all there was, just that sound, because Jim never made any, just fell back straight as a tree and heavy.

I got up from under him and got hold of a two-by-four and beat hell out of that stallion. I felt bad about it afterward, it wasn't the damn horse's fault. But I beat him off the mare and ran the mare outside, and then I went back and sat down next to Jim, with the rain falling on us in the dark. One of the horses had broken my shinbone and my boot was filled up with blood, but there was no pain there, just the sticky wetness, and I didn't know I was hurt until somebody told me afterward.

Jim's wife never said a word while I told her how Jim had got killed. When I was done she just stood there looking out at the sky edge. Finally she said, "Well, I'll think about the work you offered," and she looked down at her feet and then walked back up the hill to the house. She had a deliberate way of walking, even across the soft field. I'd noticed it before. She walked like somebody who has a long way ahead and has set herself a pace to get there.

By the time I had got the harrowing done, the sun was low. I gave the mare what feed I had from the back of the truck and was doling out the woman's hay to her cow when the boy walked out to me.

"I'm supposed to do that," he said, mumbling, pointing the words somewhere to the left of where I was.

"Okay," I said, and stood off and watched him do it.

"You're supposed to come in for supper," he said, when he had finished with the cow. "We're both supposed to."

I followed him up to the faucet and we took turns again.

"Did you get bucked off?" he asked me, sideways eyeing the dirty cast.

"Got stepped on," was all I said.

He nodded like his mother, in a solemn way. "Oh."

The woman had brought out a bit of a cold supper and we ate as before, silently, in the high-ceilinged kitchen. She didn't turn on a lamp, but the daylight began to fail fast while we were sitting there, and when she stood to do up the dishes she pointed with her chin and the boy pulled the chain on the ceiling light without being told. I didn't wait for her to point her chin at the door. I went on outside.

I'd been hoarding the few cigarettes I had left, but I was needing one pretty bad tonight and, hell, that's what they were for, so I got one out. I went partway down the hill and sat down on the grass in the darkness with my cast stuck straight out in front of me while I smoked, I watched the mare grazing on the poor grass in that fenced field. I could hear her ripping the tough stalks with her teeth.

After a while I heard the screen door crack. I kept on sitting there, sucking up the last of my smoke, staring off at the mare like I didn't know, but I could feel the woman's eyes on me—I knew she was standing back there, watching me. I was about to get onto my feet again when she came down from the house and sat a couple of yards away, with her knees pulled up in front of her and her arms clasped around them.

In a bit she said, "Jim never could stay put. I guess you know that, you'd be like that yourself. So the boy and me, we've been alone half his life, and sometimes we get pretty hungry for a man's voice. Both of us do, I won't deny it; we get pretty lonesome." There was a silence. Then she said, "If I was looking for somebody to wear the edge off my lonesomeness, I guess you'd do; you have a kind face, as far as that goes."

I felt a heat start up from my neck. I took a long stem of grass and began to split it down the middle with my thumbnail. I guess I had known all along she might take my offer that way. Afterward, when I thought about it, I wondered if I might even have meant her to take it that way. I don't know. I sat there on the grass in the dark, looking at my hands.

"The truth is, I could use the help," she said. "There's more work than I can do, and no money to pay anybody." She waited again. "But the boy sees you with that good-looking horse, looking like you do, dressing like you do, just smelling of places a long way from here. And I can see his eyes going away from me." I didn't know what she meant, not then, but I figured it out later. She said, "Jim's eyes used to do that," and there was tenderness in it, or pain, the first I'd heard since telling her Jim was dead.

She didn't say anything else for a while. I wondered if she had started to cry. Then she said, "I guess I'm stupid, turning you away when you offer your help. I could use it, that's for sure. But it wasn't your fault, what happened; you don't owe Jim anything. And my saying no doesn't have anything much to do with you." She lifted her chin a little and gave a straight look and then I saw her eyes were tearless. "It's just a lonesome woman isn't any mare in heat," she said in a level voice. I looked away. I looked down at my hands. "I'm just trying to hold on to my son," she said after a wait. Her voice had dropped lower. "I appreciate your harrowing the field. And coming down here with the news. If you don't mind sleeping in the shed, I'll see you get a good breakfast in the morning before you leave."

She stood up without waiting for me to say anything else and walked back up the short hill to the house. I kept sitting where I was for a while. I watched the blue roan, the shadow of her, in that field.

She and the boy made a space for me under the eaves of the lean-to, amid the stacked-up tools, and it was snug there; I'd slept in worse places. But after a while I just gave it up. There was a pretty good wind shaking the tree and my leg was aching and I blamed it on those things. In the dark I had to watch out not to kick over a rake or something, feeling careful with my boot and my cast until I was out in the open, where the moon gave some light to see what I was doing. I sat down and wrote on a scrap of paper the name of the mortuary where Jim's body was, in Sprague, and below that I wrote, *His horse and gear was sold, this is the sum of what it came to. The truck was his too.* Jim had had a little money and I put it with my own money, all I had, in a stack on the piece of paper, and I folded it so it was a flat packet. Then I went up and set it under a rock on the porch, where she would find it. I lugged the saddle out of the truck and put it on the mare. I had a hell of a time getting her saddled and a worse time getting myself up on her with that damn cast. I had to lead her up next to the house so I could stand on the porch and clamber up. I was afraid maybe the woman would hear me bumping around, but if she heard, she didn't come out to see what it was.

I left her the truck sitting there with the keys in it. It was a better one than she had, and the trailer was damn near new. Half of the rig was Jim's anyway, and I didn't have the money to buy him out, after giving her the money for the horse. Driving up here, I had thought I would give her the blue roan too, but I could see, now, she wouldn't have wanted it there, around the boy. So that was the only thing of Jim's I held on to.

Laura Frankos

THE NJUGGLE

Rasmus Harraldsoun shoveled stew into his mouth as fast as he could, so eager was he to head for the boat. His father, Einar, was less enthusiastic about the start of the deep-sea fishing season, with its many dangers and long, grueling hours away from their home in Shetland. Father ate slowly, holding his bowl out to Rasmus's mother for another helping. Mother served him in equally grim silence.

Rasmus's grandfather, Olav Larsen, however, talked loudly and often enough for all of them. "Look at Rasmus eating like there's no tomorrow! So you think you can pull oars on a háf-boat, lad?" "Háf" is the ancient Shetlandic word for the ocean, and Grandfather Olav constantly peppered his conversation with old words and phrases. He talked more of ancient legends than of the real people who lived in the sea town of Norwick. Some, like Cousin Magnus, found Grandfather a bore, but Rasmus liked the old stories.

"I did well enough last year, Grandfather," he said between spoonfuls. "I'm sixteen now and much stronger."

"Aye, your father said you pulled your weight, and your help made all the difference after we lost your brothers, with me laid up all those months. A bad year, that was. I thank God that 1876 has been better."

"May it continue to be," said Mother, whose eyes still filled with tears at the memory of the great storm that took her older sons. Grandfather Olav had nearly joined them and had spent months regaining his health. Rasmus was not surprised that Grandfather Olav was itching to return to the háf at last.

Einar Harraldsoun shoved his bowl aside and drank the rest of his tea. "It's time," he said in a low voice. "The others will be waiting for us."

Rasmus held his tongue, though he knew perfectly well Father was the slow one.

"Run ahead, Rasmus, and get the lines from the shed and into the boat," said Father.

Rasmus gave Mother a quick embrace and a wide smile, hoping to ease those worried lines from her brow. It didn't work. She always worried during the háf-season, and even more after last year's storm.

He pelted down the path to the beach, Grandfather Olav and Father following more slowly. He could see Cousin Magnus at the shed bringing out the baited lines, and Magnus's older brothers, Cousins Donald and Johnny, readying the square sail of the sixern.

Magnus waved him over, a broad grin on his freckled face. "So, Rasmus, Grandfather's ready to join us again? I'm glad he's well, but I'll tell you true: It was restful on my ears not to have him in the sixern with us last year. All those endless tales of trolls and monsters! And whacking my cheek with a wet mitten if ever I uttered an unlucky word at sea. As if it made any difference to the fish what fishermen say! Silly superstitions!"

Rasmus shrugged. "I like Grandfather's stories. They help pass the time. You shouldn't complain or tease him, Magnus; he's an old man, so give him respect."

"Och, aye, that I do," said Magnus, but he did not sound at all respectful. "How mad he was when I put a dead mouse in his fish basket years ago! He swore it would bring bad luck, but it didn't, except to my backside." He grinned impishly as Grandfather Olav and Einar approached. "Welcome back, Grandfather!"

"Thank you, lad. Let's see what the waters hold for us this season." Grandfather knelt on the rocky beach, picked up a stone, and addressed the heavens. "Lord, bring us back safe where this stone came from." He chucked the stone into the bottom of the sixern and climbed in after it, taking his place at one of the six oars that gave the little craft its name.

Einar, Donald, and Johnny said nothing as they followed Grandfather, but Magnus made a face at the old man's lucky stone. When Rasmus was certain Magnus was not watching, he slipped a rock into his pocket and muttered the same prayer. Rasmus approved of Grandfather's ways. Even if they were just superstitions, how could they hurt?

To Rasmus's disappointment, Grandfather Olav said little as they rowed thirty miles to the open sea. The old man was pale and perspiring, despite the biting wind. He sighed in relief when Einar signaled for them to stop.

Rasmus handed Grandfather a bottle of water, which he took gratefully. "Ah, that's better! It was a long haul, but I made it! Let's set out the lines."

The six fishermen worked quickly. Though late evening, the sun still shone bright because they were so far north, closer to the Arctic Circle than to London. In a few weeks' time, at the summer solstice, it would be dark for just three or four hours. The Shetlanders made the most of those long, bright nights, fishing for cod, mackerel, and ling.

When the miles of lines were cast, Grandfather shouted to the waves, "Roll, roll, rise, and wait! Nibble, nibble, take the bait!"

Magnus ducked his head so Grandfather Olav wouldn't see him laughing at the charm to increase the catch.

They chewed on oatcakes and drank water, waiting for the fish to begin biting. Grandfather was telling the famous story of the two giants tricked by a mermaid when he stopped abruptly and pointed to the east. "Look there, lads! A Sifan! Haven't seen one in years!"

Rasmus looked east. He thought he saw a dark shape moving through the waves far in the distance. Magnus looked, too, and made another sour face.

"Watch the Sifan carefully, Rasmus," said Grandfather Olav, "for if it jumps out of the water and falls to the left, it means death to the fishes and a good catch for us. But if it jumps to the right, it means death to a man. You can see it has the shape of a coffin. Ah, it's swimming away."

"I can't see a thing," complained Johnny. "My eyes are best for close work."

"Do you really believe in such sea monsters?" asked Magnus, this time not hiding the scorn in his voice.

Donald, who never said much, shrugged, but Johnny nodded. "There's all manner of monsters in the world."

"Are you doubting my word, Grandson?" Grandfather Olav thundered.

"Yes," Magnus said bluntly. "There's no such thing as a Sifan. It's probably just a whale. Sometimes whales jump like that."

Grandfather Olav, instead of arguing, shook his gray head and sighed. "I fear for you, lad. It's folk like you that are easiest fooled by the devil's creatures, because you deny they're there. Beware especially the shape changers, like the Njuggle. You'll fall for its tricks, like my friend Andrew Grott, back when we were lads."

Magnus snorted. "I can't keep all your tales straight, Grandfather. What dreadful beastie is the Njuggle? Will he bite my toes off while I sleep?"

Johnny kicked Magnus in the shins, reminding him he owed Grandfather respect.

Grandfather nodded approvingly to Johnny. "The Njuggle is a freshwater demon. He can take many shapes, most often that of a stick of wood or a handsome pony. While he waits for his victim, he roars in anticipation—a sure sign someone will drown that night, when the Njuggle's powers are strongest."

"What happened to your friend Andrew, Grandfather?" asked Rasmus, though he had heard the story many times.

"We were walking home over the hills in the west, not far from Loch Brekkan, when we suddenly saw a pony where nothing had been a moment before! I was wary, but Andrew ran forward and stroked its mane, saying what a fine beast it was and wondering who owned it. The creature never moved, save to raise its head and look at me. Och, those eyes! They shone with hell's fires, they did!

"I told Andrew to stay away, but he laughed at my fears and jumped on its back. The beast galloped off like a Derby winner, with Andrew clinging to it in terror. It vanished over the hill with him. I followed, but there was nothing I could do: That Njuggle had taken Andrew into the loch and drowned him. They found his body next morning. I've carried a charm against the Njuggle ever since; gave one to Rasmus, too, when he asked me for one."

Clearly unimpressed, Magnus was about to retort when Einar jerked a thumb at the lines. "They're biting well. Haul them in fast, and we may have time for a second cast tonight." The dreary work of removing the fish from hundreds of hooks and baiting them again drove away all thoughts of monsters.

The háf-season had gone well by late July. The weather was decent and the catches enough to pay the laird his due and then some. Grandfather Olav entertained them with tales of the Stoor Worm, the Fin Folk, the trolls, and the fierce Brigdi, a sea monster so vast he could eat a sixern in one gulp. Even Magnus listened quietly, though sullenly; Rasmus learned Johnny had boxed his ears for his rudeness to Grandfather.

But fortunes change rapidly, as Rasmus's family knew too well. While they were far at sea one night, dark storm clouds began forming in the distance. Not taking any chances, Einar decided to cut the lines and head for home. Donald and Johnny grumbled about his caution, but he snapped, "Better to lose lines than to lose lives."

They rowed like men possessed and beat the storm by a wide margin. Exhausted by the effort, Grandfather Olav coughed and wheezed his way to the croft. Mother was alarmed at their early and empty-handed return but quickly bundled the old man into bed. She searched the kitchen in vain for the cough elixir.

"Rasmus, be a good lad and run over to Auntie Sinnie's for some medicine for that cough, or he'll get no rest tonight."

Rasmus yearned for his bed but did as she asked. Auntie Sinnie's croft was seven miles inland, past the "bachelors' croft" where his three cousins lived. Magnus threw open the door as Rasmus strode by. "Where you off to this hour, Ras?"

"Auntie Sinnie's, for cough liquor."

"I'll come with you," Magnus offered. "I pulled my back rowing and can't sleep. All that hurry, and it's barely drizzling!"

"Aye, but who knows how much rain is falling out at sea?" Rasmus defended his father's decision to turn back early.

As if to prove his point, the rain began pelting down. Magnus grimaced at the sky. Thunder boomed in the distance, followed by a deep roar. The winds playing over the sea caves sometimes sounded like that, but those were miles away. Rasmus thought it peculiar, but Magnus ignored it, pulling his hood over his head. The two young men walked in silence, using Rasmus's lantern to guide their feet.

"Must be around nine o'clock," said Magnus. "Just about sundown, though the clouds are so thick, you'd never know it."

Rasmus nodded, his eyes looking ahead to where the path broadened into the road that led to Loch Brekkan. There was something long and white at the side of the road—a piece of driftwood, he thought. Then his boot caught in the mud, distracting him.

Magnus suddenly exclaimed, "Well, look there!"

Rasmus glanced up from his boot, and there, where he thought he had seen the driftwood, was a dark brown pony, its coat glistening in the rain. Grandfather Olav's story of the Njuggle flashed through his mind. "Don't go near it, Magnus!" he shouted, his throat tightening with fear. Of itself, his hand crept into his coat and reassuringly touched Grandfather's charm.

His cousin stared at him in surprise. "Whatever's the matter? He's a fine gentle pony and doesn't deserve to be left in the rain. We may get a reward for finding him, and if no one claims him, we've a grand little animal for ourselves. Hello, fella! What are you doing out in the wet?" He patted the pony's flanks and walked all around him, admiring. "A good strong back, no marks of ill-treatment. A bit thin, perhaps."

"Magnus, listen," Rasmus pleaded. "Do you remember Grandfather's story of the Njuggle? Just before we saw the pony, I saw a piece of wood lying there. And earlier, I heard a roar or a bellow."

"What of it?" Magnus stroked the pony, which stood calmly in the driving rain. "You're not thinking this splendid little fellow is some weird water demon? Ras, you're getting as daft as Grandfather!"

"He's not daft! Some of his notions are a bit odd. . . ." Rasmus's voice trailed off. It did seem a ridiculous story. The lantern light flickered on a perfectly ordinary-looking pony. Rasmus kicked at the ground. "Maybe we should wait until daylight, or else use this charm Grandfather gave me."

"Ah, you're a frightened baby, just like him. I'm not afraid of this pony!" Magnus vaulted onto its back as a bolt of lightning ripped across the sky. At once, the creature sprang forward, its eyes wide and glowing eerily, its long tail whirling in a circle like a windmill. A peal of thunder nearly drowned out Magnus's terrified scream. The Njuggle galloped down the road some fifty feet, then stopped and tossed its head, taunting Rasmus. It howled triumphantly, knowing it had outwitted a man who recognized it.

"Jump, Magnus!" Rasmus yelled, but Magnus couldn't let go. Rasmus was too far away to pull his cousin from the Njuggle's back, too far to use the charm Grandfather Olav had given him. In rage, he heaved the lucky stone he'd carried all háf-season at the monster. It bounced off the Njuggle's hindquarters, a poor throw that would have barely bruised an ordinary horse. But the lucky stone pained the Njuggle like a hornet's sting. It bucked and for a moment lost its power over Magnus, who fell heavily to the ground and scrambled off the road toward the safety of a stone wall. The Njuggle looked at him. Its eyes were peaceful and dark once more, its ears pricked forward, its posture friendly, not menacing.

Rasmus grabbed the lantern and ran to Magnus's side. The other youth was bruised but not badly hurt.

"Well, Cousin," Magnus gasped, "I admit when I'm wrong: That's no horse. Hey! Keep away from it, Ras!"

Rasmus cautiously approached the monster, Grandfather's charm tightly bundled in his hand. "We've got to capture it, so it won't kill again. After Grandfather's friend drowned, he always carried this with him for protection." He uncoiled a lasso of thin, plaited rawhide, decorated on both sides with small iron studs.

Magnus snorted. "It's too thin to hold him. He may look small, but there's more power in those bones than in any beast I've ever ridden." He shuddered at the memory of the brief ride. "You can't make him come with you using that puny thing."

"It's strong enough because of those studs. Grandfather taught me demons hate one thing: iron. Let's see how the Njuggle likes it!" He tossed the lasso over the monster's neck and braced himself for the reaction.

The Njuggle once again went from gentle pony to a wild-eyed creature of evil. It shied away from Rasmus, bellowing in fury, then halted abruptly when it pulled against the rawhide rope. It threw back its head and screamed in pain. In the faint light of the lantern, Rasmus could see a clear, slimy liquid oozing from sores where the iron studs touched the njuggle's flesh. Rasmus stood his ground, holding firm to his end of the rope. The Njuggle strained and screamed, realizing it was helpless against the iron. Its tail whirled round and round, creating more wind than the storm.

Magnus leaped up to help Rasmus. "I never would have believed it! We've got it! But what do we do with it?"

"The standing stones by Nilsen's beach. It's but another mile, and there are good, stout chains anchored to the stones. Iron chains," Rasmus added.

The mile to the standing stones (which Grandfather Olav claimed were placed there by feuding giants, who tossed them at each other) took nearly an hour to travel. The Njuggle fought every inch of the way, sometimes trying to bite or kick, but always yielding when they pulled on the rope and the studs burned its monstrous flesh.

"Why doesn't it turn back into a stick or something?" Magnus gasped as they tied the lasso to the heavy chains of the stones. "Then it could get away from us."

"Must be the iron," Rasmus said. "Grandfather would know."

"Aye, that he would," said Magnus, with a new note of respect in his voice.

The job done, they stepped away from the creature. The rain tapered off; the moon broke through the clouds, though the wind still blew fiercely. The Njuggle tugged at the rope again, clanking the chains. It glanced toward the east, something like desperation filling its luminous eyes. It pulled harder, ignoring the wounds made by the iron.

"Maybe we should go home before it breaks loose," Magnus said. "It won't be very pleased with us, you know."

Rasmus watched the monster struggle. "Grandfather said its powers were greatest at night. I think it's afraid of being chained when the sun rises. I wish I could stay to see what happens, but I must get that cough liquor to Mother. She'll be worrying after me."

As they hurried back to the road, they could still hear the chains clanking and the Njuggle snorting in frustration. They did not tell Auntie Sinnie of their encounter with the demon; she was too sleepy to understand anything more than that they needed the medicine for Grandfather.

In their haste to return, they did not go back to Nilsen's beach but headed straight for their homes. Magnus paused before entering his croft. "Rasmus, if you don't mind, I'd like to tell Grandfather Olav about the Njuggle myself. I think I owe him an apology."

Rasmus nodded and hurried home to find everyone asleep—Grandfather's cough had quieted without the medicine. He pulled on some dry clothes and staggered into his own cot but soon found he was too tense to sleep; his memory kept reliving the encounter with the Njuggle. He tossed and turned until the faint glow of dawn appeared in his window. He could wait no longer. He had to find out what had happened to the monster. He crept out of bed, grabbed his coat, and went outside.

A brisk wind was blowing in a clear sky as he approached the beach, but all was silent save the pounding of the surf and the cries of the seabirds. Had the Njuggle escaped? As he drew closer, he saw the chains hanging limp and empty, and his heart fell. He ran to the boulders for a better look. The stones were chipped and scarred in many places where the Njuggle had thrashed against the iron that bound him. Shimmering gobs of slime showed where the demon had bled in its efforts to escape.

Crestfallen, Rasmus began to walk back home when a shout came from the west. Magnus ran toward him, crowing gleefully, twirling his hat in his hand in a motion that reminded Rasmus of the Njuggle's whirligig tail.

"Stop your cheering," Rasmus said. "It got away."

"It did not! Come see! I thought the same as you when I got here not long after dawn, but then I found its trail." Magnus grabbed Rasmus by the arm and led him off the gravel beach. "You can see it better on the grass. I think it was trying to get back to its home in the loch; at least, it was headed west when it died."

A few yards up the muddy and grassy slope, Magnus pointed out the demon's spoor: more of the transparent, gooey slime that Rasmus had seen smeared on the standing stones. "Like the world's biggest slug trail," Magnus said. "Follow it for a few paces, Ras, but don't touch it. It burns the skin."

Rasmus did, and once again he met the Njuggle—or what was left of it. Tangled in the rawhide rope was a gelatinous blob, something like a jellyfish but much larger.

Magnus poked it with a stick. It didn't move. "It's well and truly gone, Rasmus. There's less of it now than there was ten minutes ago. You can see it shriveling up under the sun."

The two young men stood together and watched the Njuggle disappear, never to claim another victim in its loch. "I'll have to get another rope with those iron studs," Rasmus said.

"I want one, too," Magnus said.

That night, the fishing was extremely good, and the baskets were full of mackerel and ling. Grandfather Olav was in a jovial mood, never stopping his tale telling while they hauled in the heavy lines. Rasmus and Johnny, as usual, were his most interested listeners, but Grandfather Olav noticed a new attentiveness in Magnus.

"By thunder, Magnus, you almost look like you enjoyed that yarn," said Grandfather. "What's got into you, lad?"

Magnus blushed nearly as red as his hair. "Well, Grandfather, it wasn't so much what's got *into* me as what got *under* me." He glanced at his brothers, who were looking at him curiously, and at Rasmus, who was trying not to laugh. "If you don't mind too much, I'll tell you about it later."

Julian Symons

MURDER ON THE RACE COURSE

"With my son up he can do it," Sir Reginald Bartley said emphatically. "There's no better amateur in the country than Harry. I tell you I'm not sorry Baker can't ride him."

There was something challenging in his tone. Trainer Norman Johnson, wooden-faced, bowlegged, said noncommittally, "He can ride, your son, I'm not denying it."

"And Lucky Charm's a fine horse."

"Ay, there's nothing against the horse," Johnson said.

"Then what's the matter with you, man? A few days ago you were keen as mustard, telling me I had a chance of leading in my first Grand National winner. Today you're as enthusiastic as the cat who started lapping a saucer of cream and found it was sour milk."

"I wouldn't want to raise false hopes, Sir Reginald, that's all. Here comes Lucky Charm."

"And here comes Harry."

Private detective Francis Quarles stood with them in the paddock at Aintree and listened to this conversation with interest. Horse racing was one of the few subjects about which he had no specialized knowledge, and he was here only because he had been tracking down the man who later became known as the Liverpool Forger.

Quarles had once cleared up a troublesome series of robberies committed in the chain of department stores owned by Sir Reginald, and when they met again in the Adelphi Hotel the business magnate had invited the private detective to be his guest at Aintree.

In the hotel that morning Quarles had learned that Lucky Charm was a 40-to-1 outsider in this year's Grand National, that his jockey Baker had fallen and thrown out his shoulder on the previous day, and that Lucky Charm would now be ridden by Sir Reginald's son, Harry.

Now he looked at the big-shouldered powerful-looking black horse, with the number 8 on his saddle cloth, being led round by a stable boy. Then he looked at the young man who walked up to them wearing a jacket of distinctive cerise and gold hoops.

"How is it, Harry? All set?" asked Sir Reginald.

"Why not?" Harry Bartley had the kind of dark, arrogant good looks that Quarles distrusted.

"We're all ready to lead him in," Sir Reginald said, with what seemed to Quarles almost fatuous complacency. "We know we've got the horse and the jockey too, Harry my boy."

Johnson said nothing. Harry Bartley pulled a handkerchief out of his breast pocket and blew his nose.

"Got your lucky charm?" the owner persisted.

"Of course." Harry's voice was lightly blurred, as though he had just had a tooth out. From the same pocket he produced a rabbit's foot, kissed it, and put it back carefully.

"There's Mountain Pride," said Sir Reginald a little wistfully. Mountain Pride, Quarles knew, was the favorite, a bay gelding with a white star on his forehead.

"Time to go." Harry Bartley gave them a casual nod and turned away, walking a little erratically across the paddock to the place where the stable boy stood, holding Lucky Charm. Had he been drinking, Quarles wondered?

"Good luck," his father called. "Better be getting along to the stand." Sir Reginald was a choleric little man, and now his face was purple as he turned to the trainer. "You may not like the boy, but you could have wished him luck."

Johnson's wooden expression did not change. "You know I wish Lucky Charm all the luck there is, Sir Reginald."

"Trouble with Johnson is, he's sulking," Sir Reginald said when they were in the stand. "Insisted Baker should ride the horse when I wanted Harry. I gave way—after all, Baker's a professional jockey. Then, when Baker was injured, he wanted to have some stable boy and I put my foot down."

"What has he got against your son?"

Sir Reginald looked at Quarles out of the corner of one slightly bloodshot eye. "The boy's a bit wild, y'know. Nothing wrong with him, but—a bit wild. There they go."

The horses had paraded in front of the stand and now they were going down to the starting post. Bright March sunlight illuminated the course and even Francis Quarles, who was not particularly susceptible to such things, found something delightful in the scene. The men and women in the stands and the crowd chattering along the rails, the men with their raglans and mackintoshes and the patches of color in women's coats and hats, the ballet-like grace of the horses and the vivid yet melting green of the Aintree background . . .

Quarles pulled himself up on the edge of sentiment. His companion said sharply, "Harry's having trouble."

The horses were at the starting post. Quarles raised his glasses. After a moment he picked out Lucky Charm. The black horse was refusing to get into line with the rest. Three times Harry Bartley brought him up and he turned away.

Sir Reginald tapped his stick on the ground. "Come on now, Harry. Show him who's master. Never known Lucky Charm to act like this before."

"Is he used to your son?"

The question was not well received. "Harry can ride any horse," Bartley snapped. Then he drew in his breath and his voice joined with thousands of others in the cry, "They're off!"

Now in the stand a mass of binoculars was raised to follow the progress of some thirty horses over some of the most testing fences in the world. Now bookmakers looked anxious, punters let cigars go out, women twisted race cards in gloved hands. Everything depended now on the jumping skill and staying power of horses that had been trained for months in preparation for this day, and on the adeptness of the jockeys in nursing their charges and then urging them forward to moments of supreme endeavor.

The horses came up in a bunch to the first fence, rose to it, cleared it. Thousands of throats exhaled and articulated sighingly the words: "They're over."

They were not all over, Quarles saw. A jockey lay on the ground, a jockey wearing red jacket and white cap. A riderless horse ran on.

On to the second jump and the third, a six-foot ditch with a four-foot-nine fence on the other side of it. Now there was a cry: "O'Grady's down. Double or Quits is down. Bonny Dundee's down."

There were more riderless horses, more jockeys on the ground who stumbled to their feet and ran to the rails when all the horses had passed.

Past Becher's they came and round the Canal Turn and then over Valentine's, the field beginning to string out.

"There's Mountain Pride in front," Sir Reginald cried. "And Johnny Come Lately and Lost Horizon. And Lucky Charm's with them." Almost under his breath he muttered, "But I don't like the way the boy's handling him."

The horses came round toward the stand. Quarles watched the cerise and gold jacket take the fourteenth fence, and it seemed to him that Harry Bartley was not so much riding as desperately clinging to the horse.

They came to the fifteenth fence, the Chair, which is one of the most awkward at Aintree—a six-foot ditch and then a fence five-foot-two in height which rises roughly in a chair's shape.

Mountain Pride soared over, and so did the two horses that followed. Then came the cerise and gold jacket. Lucky Charm rose to the fence and went over beautifully, but as he landed the jockey seemed simply to slip off and lay prone on the turf.

Lucky Charm ran on, the rest of the field thundered by.

Sir Reginald lowered his glasses slowly. "That's that. Not my Grand National, I'm afraid."

Quarles waited for the figure on the turf to get up, but it did not move. Ambulance men beside the jump ran onto the course with a stretcher and bent over the jockey. Still he did not move as they lifted him onto the stretcher.

They watched in stupefaction as the ambulance men carried him away. Then Sir Reginald, his usually ruddy face white as milk, said, "Come on, man, come on."

"What about the race?"

"To hell with the race," Sir Reginald cried. "I want to know what's happened to my son."

The limp body of Harry Bartley was carried round to the course hospital, in the administrative block. Doctor Ferguson, the local doctor, had just begun his examination when the door of the ward was pushed open and a handsome gray-haired man, with a pair of binoculars slung round his neck, came in.

"Ferguson? My name's Ramsay, I'm Harry's doctor. We've met before, up here last year. Is the boy badly hurt?"

"As far as I can see he's received no injury at all. There's something very wrong though—his pulse is feeble and irregular. Was he subject to any kind of fits, do you know?"

"Harry? Not to my knowledge." Ferguson made way as Doctor Ramsay approached the body and bent over it. He straightened up with a puzzled frown. "Have you smelled round the nose and mouth?"

"No, I haven't. I'd only begun to examine him." Ferguson bent over too and caught the odor of bitter almonds. "My God, he's taken poison!"

"Taken it—or it's been administered to him." Ramsay's face was grave. "The question is what, and how? It's not cyanide, obviously, or he wouldn't be alive now."

"I must telephone—" Doctor Ferguson broke off as Sir Reginald and Francis Quarles, followed by trainer Norman Johnson, came into the room. Ramsay went over to Sir Reginald and placed a hand on his arm.

"Bartley, I won't mince words. You must be prepared for a shock. Harry has been poisoned in some way, and there's very little we can do for him."

"He'll be all right?"

"It's touch and go," Ramsay said evasively. He watched Francis Quarles approach the body. "Who's that?"

Sir Reginald told him.

Quarles bent over the unconscious figure, looked at its pale face and purple lips and nose, sniffed the scent of bitter almonds. He came over to Ramsay, who had now been joined by Ferguson. Sir Reginald introduced the detective.

"Have you gentlemen made up your minds about this case?" Quarles asked. He spoke in a faintly languid manner which made Ramsay, who was brisk and soldierly, bristle slightly.

"Not yet. In your superior wisdom I suppose you have done so."

"Have you considered nitrobenzene?"

"Nitrobenzene," Doctor Ferguson said thoughtfully. "Yes, that would explain the prussic acid symptoms, but I don't see why it should have occurred to you."

"I know little about horse racing, but something about poisoning," Quarles said. "And I had the opportunity of seeing Harry Bartley just before the race. His appearance then seemed to me very strange. His speech was blurred and he walked unsteadily. The thought crossed my mind that he might be drunk, but as you know such an appearance of drunkenness is a common symptom in nitrobenzene poisoning."

There was silence. Ramsay shifted uncomfortably. Sir Reginald said, "What are we waiting for? If there's no ambulance let's get him in to Liverpool in my car."

Ferguson crossed over to Harry Bartley again, felt pulse and heart, and then drew a sheet up over the face.

Ramsay said to Sir Reginald, "He's gone. I wanted to break it gently. There was never any chance."

"But when we came in Ferguson here was telephoning—"

"I was telephoning the police superintendent on the course," Ferguson said. "There'll need to be an investigation. This is a bad business."

Francis Quarles took no part in the flurry of conversation that followed the arrival of the police superintendent and the other officers with him. Instead, he went over to the wooden-faced trainer, Norman Johnson, and took him outside. They paced up and down in hearing of the excited crowds who were cheering the victory of Mountain Pride, and Quarles asked questions.

"Harry Bartley may have died by accident, but I would bet a hundred pounds that he was murdered. Now there's one obvious question I should like to have answered by a racing expert. Is it likely that he was killed to prevent Lucky Charm winning the National?"

Johnson paused for an appreciable time before he said bluntly, "No."

"It's unlikely?"

"You can put it out of your mind. I'm not saying horse racing's pure as snow, Mr. Quarles. Far from it. Horses have been nobbled before now, horses have been doped. But favorites, not forty-to-one outsiders. And horses, not men."

"You mean—?"

"If anyone wanted to stop Lucky Charm they'd go for the horse, not the man. Kill a horse and get caught, you may go to prison. Kill a man— well, it's murder."

"Sir Reginald seemed very optimistic about his horse's chances in the National. What did you feel?"

The trainer rubbed his chin, making a sound like a saw cutting wood. "With Baker up, he was a good outsider, a nice each-way bet. Hadn't quite the class for it, but you never can tell. He liked Baker, did Lucky Charm."

"And he didn't like Harry Bartley?"

"Hated him. Bartley used the whip more than he needed to. Lucky Charm wasn't a horse you could treat that way. I tried to persuade Sir Reginald to give the ride to another jockey, but it was no good."

"You shared the horse's dislike of Harry Bartley, I gather."

The trainer said nothing. His faded blue eyes stared into the distance, and the Red Indian impassiveness of his features did not change. "Was there a special reason for that?"

Slowly and without passion, Norman Johnson said, "Sir Reginald Bartley is a man I respect and like, none more so. I don't know how he came to have such a son. He couldn't be trusted with a woman, he couldn't be trusted to pay his debts, he was a good rider but he couldn't be trusted to treat a horse decently."

"But there's something personal in your dislike," Quarles insisted.

Johnson brought his blue eyes out of the middle distance and focused them on Quarles. "You'll learn about it soon enough. It might as well be from me. I had a daughter named Mary. She was a good girl until she took up with Harry Bartley. He was always around the stables, every day for weeks, and I was fool enough not to realize what he was after— until Mary went away with him and left me a note. I understood it then well enough. That was six months ago. He walked out on her after a few weeks. She put her head in a gas oven."

"I see."

"When I've worked out my contract with Sir Reginald, I'm asking him to take his horses away."

Quarles said softly, "Some people might call that a motive for murder."

"I don't deny it, Mr. Quarles. It happens that I didn't kill him, that's all." Johnson drove the fist of one hand into the palm of the other, and his voice for the first time vibrated with excitement. "But if you ever find his murderer you'll find he has a personal reason, a reason like mine.

For me, I hope you never find him. I say good luck to the man or woman who killed Harry Bartley."

Back in the course hospital Quarles met young Inspector Makepeace, who had been working with him in running down the Liverpool Forger.

Makepeace looked at the private detective with a wry smile. "You seem to manage to be where things happen, Mr. Quarles. I understand you saw young Bartley before the race."

Quarles told him the impression he had formed that Bartley might be drunk, and the outcome of his conversation with Johnson. The Inspector listened with interest.

"I should say Johnson's right, and this was almost certainly the working out of a private enmity. As you say, he's got a motive himself, although I'm keeping an open mind about that. In return I don't mind telling you that we've got a pretty good idea of how the poison was administered. Miss Moore here has been very helpful about that. She was engaged to Harry Bartley."

Miss Jennifer Moore had a round innocent face and dark hair. She had been crying. "But Inspector, I only said—"

"Bear with me a moment," Inspector Makepeace asked. Quarles, whose own sense of modesty was conspicuous by its absence, noted mentally that Makepeace had a good opinion of himself. "I don't know whether you know much about nitrobenzene poisoning, Mr. Quarles?"

"I know that nitrobenzene is comparatively easy to make," Quarles answered. "It is generally taken in the form of a liquid although it is equally poisonous as a vapor. I remember the case of a young man who spilled nitrobenzene on his clothes, became stupefied, finally collapsed in coma and died. But the most interesting thing about it is that there is an interval between taking the poison and its effects appearing, which can vary from a quarter of an hour to three hours, or longer in the case of vapor. Is that what you were going to tell me?"

The Inspector laughed a little uncomfortably. "You're a bit of a walking encyclopedia, aren't you? That's pretty much what I was going to say, yes. You see, if we can trace the course of Bartley's eating and drinking today we should be able to see when he took the poison. Now it so happens that we can do just that. Doctor Ramsay, would you come over here, please?"

The poker-backed doctor came forward.

"I understand Harry Bartley came to see you this morning."

Ramsay nodded. "I'm staying with friends a couple of miles outside Liverpool. Harry rang me up this morning before nine o'clock. He was pretty jittery, wanted something to pep him up. He was out at the place I'm staying before half-past nine and I gave him a couple of pills, and put two more in a box for him in case he needed to take them before the race."

"They were in his clothes in the changing room," Makepeace said to Quarles with a smile. "I can see your eyes fixed thoughtfully on Doctor Ramsay, but Ferguson here assures me that any pills taken at half-past nine must have had effect well before the time of the race. Now, follow the course of events, Quarles. Bartley returned to the hotel by ten o'clock, met Miss Moore in the lobby, and said that he was going up to his room to write some letters. She arranged to pick him up at about twelve, because they were going to a cocktail party. She picked him up then.and they went to the party, which was given by a friend of theirs named Lapetaine. There, Miss Moore can testify, Harry Bartley drank just one glass of orange juice."

"What about lunch?" Quarles asked the girl.

She shook her head. "Harry was worried about making the weight. He came and watched Bill and me eat lunch and didn't touch anything, not so much as a piece of toast or a glass of water."

"Bill?"

She colored slightly. "Doctor Ramsay and I have known each other for years. He can bear out what I say. We had lunch on the course, and after it Harry went off to the changing room. Of course he may have drunk something after that."

"Most unlikely," Ferguson said. "Particularly if he was worried about making the weight."

"So you see we're down to the one glass of orange juice." The Inspector smoothed his fair hair with some complacency.

"Apparently," Quarles agreed. "At lunch, did he show any sign of confusion, blurred speech, unsteady walk—anything like that?"

Both Ramsay and Jennifer Moore returned decided negatives.

"Come on now, Mr. Quarles," Makepeace said with a smile. "The fact is you're reluctant to admit that the police are ever quick off the mark, and this time we've surprised you."

"It isn't that, my dear Inspector. Something's worrying me, and I don't quite know what it is. Something that I've seen, or that's happened or that's been said. I shall be interested to know the result of the post-mortem."

"The P.M.?" The Inspector was startled. "Surely you don't doubt that—"

"That he died of nitrobenzene poisoning? No, I don't, but there's still something that tantalizes me about it. Ah, here are his personal possessions."

The detective paused by a table on which a number of articles lay in two separate piles. One of them contained the things Bartley had been wearing during the race, the other came from his clothes in the changing room.

In the first pile were Lucky Charm's saddle, the cerise and gold shirt and cap, and the breeches Bartley had been wearing. Here too, isolated and pathetic, was the rabbit's-foot charm he had kissed; it was neatly ticketed: *Found in pocket.*

The things in the other pile were naturally more numerous—sports jacket, vest, shirt and gray trousers, gold wrist watch, keys on a ring, silver and copper coins, a wallet with notes and other papers, three letters.

Inspector Makepeace picked up one of these letters and handed it to Quarles.

It was a letter written in a sprawling hand by a woman who had used violet ink, and it was full of bitter reproaches, in painfully familiar phrasing. "Cast me off like an old shoe . . . given you everything a woman can give . . . shan't let you get away with it . . . sooner see you dead than married to somebody else."

Why is it, Quarles wondered, that at times of strong emotion, almost all of us express ourselves in clichés? The letter began "Darling Harry" and was signed "Hilary."

"You haven't traced the writer of this letter yet?" The undercurrent of sarcasm in Quarles's voice was so faint that Inspector Makepeace missed it.

"Give us a chance, Mr. Quarles. Between you and me I'm not inclined to attach too much importance to it—shouldn't be surprised to learn that there were half a dozen women in Master Harry's life. I'm more interested in getting a complete list of guests at that cocktail party. Nothing very informative here, I'm afraid."

"On the contrary," Quarles said.

Makepeace stared. "You mean there's something I've missed—"

"You haven't missed anything, but something's missing that should be here. You should be able to deduce it yourself. Now I'm more anxious than ever to know the result of the post-mortem."

Sir Reginald Bartley paced up and down the drawing room of his suite. His voice had lost none of its vigor, but his appearance was pitiably different from that of the jaunty man who had talked about leading in the Grand National winner twenty-four hours earlier. There was an unshaved patch on his chin, his face was pallid and his hand trembled slightly.

"I want this murderer caught," he said. "I want to see him in the dock. I want to hear the judge pronounce sentence on him. That police Inspector is smart, but I believe you're smarter, Quarles. I want you to investigate this case, and if you catch the man who poisoned my son you can write your own ticket."

Quarles looked at him intently. "Why do you call it a man? There is a general belief that most poisoners are women."

"Man or woman." Sir Reginald made an impatient gesture to indicate that this was merely splitting hairs. "I want them in the dock."

"Then you'll have to be franker with me than you have been so far. You might begin by telling me what you know about Hilary."

"Hilary?" Sir Reginald's surprise seemed genuine. "That's not a name I've ever heard in relation to Harry."

"She wrote an interesting letter to your son." Quarles did not pursue the point. "Norman Johnson said that your son behaved very badly to his daughter."

Sir Reginald blew his nose emphatically. "She was a foolish girl, wouldn't leave him alone. I'm not denying that Harry was sometimes wild. But there was never any real harm to him."

"Johnson's story was that your son lured this girl away from home, lived with her for a short time, then walked out on her. Do you accept that?"

"I've really no idea. Harry was of age. I knew little about that side of his life. I don't see," he added stiffly, "that it's our place to sit in moral judgment on him."

"It's not a question of moral judgment," Quarles said patiently. "I'm trying to get at facts. What do you think of Miss Moore?"

"A very nice girl, very nice indeed," said Sir Reginald emphatically.

"She'd only recently become engaged to your son, I believe?"

"About three weeks ago, yes. She is—was—very much in love with him."

"Doctor Ramsay had known her for years?"

"Yes. Known Harry for many years too, for that matter, ever since he was a boy. Good chap, Ramsay, pulled me through a bad go of pneumonia a couple of years ago, just after my wife died."

Quarles stood up. His eyes, hard and black, stared at Sir Reginald, who bore their gaze uneasily. "I accept the commission. But you will realize, Sir Reginald, that I am no respecter of persons. You are engaging me to discover the truth, regardless of consequences."

Sir Reginald repeated after him, "Regardless of consequences."

In the hotel lobby Quarles heard himself being paged. He stopped the boy and was told that Miss Moore was in the lounge and would like to speak to him. He found her talking in a deserted corner of the room to a dark-skinned, rather too beautifully dressed young man, with a fine large nose.

"This is Jack Lapetaine, who was Harry's great friend," she said. "As a matter of fact, it was through Jack that I met Harry, and it was Jack who gave the cocktail party yesterday."

"Is that so?" Quarles looked at Lapetaine with interest, wondering about his ancestry. Indian perhaps? Turkish? "Are you a racing man, Mr. Lapetaine?"

"I am an art dealer." Lapetaine smiled, showing pointed yellowish teeth. "But I am interested in horse racing, yes. I like the excitement. I like to gamble, I was very fond of Harry. So I came up for the National. I am almost ashamed of it, but I had a good win."

"You backed Mountain Pride?"

"I did. I had just a little flier on Lucky Charm, for sentiment's sake as you might say, but I did not think he had quite—how shall I put it?— the class for the race."

"You watched it, of course?"

"No, Mr. Quarles." Lapetaine looked down at his elegant suede shoes. "I was engaged on urgent business."

Jennifer Moore said impatiently, "Look here, Mr. Quarles, there's something I want you to tell me. Has Sir Reginald asked you to investigate this case?" Quarles nodded. "I hope you won't."

"Why not?"

"It can't possibly do any good. Harry's dead, and nothing can bring him back. And it might—well, might embarrass people who haven't any connection with it."

Lapetaine listened with a malicious smile. Quarles said quietly, "I see. Your engagement is very recent, isn't it, Miss Moore?"

"Harry and I met for the first time five weeks ago. It sounds silly, I expect, but we fell in love at first sight. Within a fortnight we were engaged."

"Should I be right in thinking that Doctor Ramsay feels some affection for you, and that you are afraid my investigations may involve him?"

Still with that slightly objectionable smile, Lapetaine said, "I can tell you exactly what Jennifer is afraid of. Ramsay has been sweet on her for years. Now, you know that Harry went out to see Ramsay on the morning of the race to get some pep tablets. What was to stop Ramsay from giving him two more, one of them filled with nitrobenzene, and saying, 'Take one of these at twelve thirty, my boy, and you'll ride as you've never ridden before.' It simply happened that Harry took the poisoned tablet first. The timing would be just about right."

The girl buried her face in her hands. "You shouldn't have—"

"My dear, Mr. Quarles is an intelligent man. I should be surprised if that idea had not already occurred to him."

Quarles looked at him. "You seem to know a good deal about the operation of nitrobenzene, Mr. Lapetaine."

Unperturbed, the art dealer showed his teeth. "I trained for a medical degree in youth before I—what shall I say?—discovered my vocation."

"There are certain objections to that idea," Quarles began, when a page boy came running up.

"Mr. Quarles, sir. Telephone for you."

On the telephone Quarles heard Inspector Makepeace's voice, raw with irritation. "We've got the result of the P.M. I don't know how you guessed, but you were perfectly right."

"There was no question of guessing," Quarles said indignantly. "My suggestion was the result of deduction from observed facts."

"Anyway, it seems to leave us just where we began."

"Oh, no," Quarles said softly. "I have told you exactly what happened before and during the race. Surely it leaves only one possible explanation."

He went back to the lounge, and addressed Jennifer Moore. "You need not worry any further, Miss Moore, about Doctor Ramsay or anyone else having administered a poisonous pill to Harry Bartley. I have just learned the result of the post-mortem. There was only a trace of nitrobenzene in the stomach."

They looked at him in astonishment, Lapetaine with his mouth slightly open. "I will spell out the meaning of that for you. Harry Bartley was not poisoned by a pill or by the orange juice he drank at your cocktail party, Mr. Lapetaine. He was poisoned by nitrobenzene, yes, but in the form of vapor."

* * *

Lapetaine had been surprised by Quarles's revelation but, as the detective admitted to himself with some admiration, the art dealer was a cool card. After the initial shock he nodded.

"Will you excuse me? I must remember to make a note of an appointment." He scribbled something on a sheet of paper torn from a pocket diary and said with a smile, "I am relieved. You will no longer suspect me of poisoning my guest's orange juice, which would hardly have been playing the game, as you might say."

Jennifer Moore seemed bewildered. "I thought it must be the orange juice. If it was vapor, then—well, I simply don't understand. Perhaps it was an accident."

"It was not an accident," Francis Quarles said. "You can see that my investigations may be useful after all, Miss Moore."

"I suppose so," she said a little doubtfully. "Goodbye, Mr. Quarles."

Lapetaine held out his hand to say goodbye, and when Quarles took it he found a piece of paper in his palm. He opened it after they had turned away, and saw that it was the paper torn from Lapetaine's diary.

On it the art dealer had scribbled: *Can you meet me in ten minutes at Kismet Coffee House, down the street?*

Ten minutes later Quarles pushed open the door of the Kismet Coffee House. In one of the cubicles he found the darkly handsome Lapetaine, drinking black coffee.

"Mr. Quarles, you'll think me immensely mysterious, but—"

"Not at all. It was plain enough from your note that you wanted to talk to me when Miss Moore was not present. From that I deduce that you want to talk about a woman connected with Harry Bartley, and that it would upset Miss Moore to hear about her. I admit, however, that I am making no more than an informed guess when I suggest that her name is Hilary."

Lapetaine looked at Quarles with his mouth open, then laughed unconvincingly. "My word, Mr. Quarles, it's not much use trying to keep secrets from you. I didn't know you'd ever heard of Hilary Hall."

"I didn't say that I had. But now that you have told me her full name, you may as well go on with the story. I take it that she was a friend of Harry Bartley's."

"She certainly was. Hilary's a night-club singer, the star at the Lady Love, which is a newish club just off Piccadilly. She's a red-head with a tremendous temper. When she heard that Harry was engaged to be married, she really hit the roof. Harry had played around with a lot of girls in his time, you know."

Quarles nodded. "I do know. But about Miss Hall."

Lapetaine leaned forward. "This I'll bet you *don't* know, Mr. Quarles, and neither does anybody else. Hilary Hall came up here the day before the race, and she came to make trouble. She telephoned Harry that evening and he went to see her, tried to quiet her down, but without much effect. She rang Harry again at the cocktail party I gave the morning before the race, but I spoke to her. I spent the afternoon of the race arguing with her." Lapetaine smiled. "She finally agreed that a thousand pounds might help to soothe her injured feelings. I think you should talk to her."

"I think so too. Why didn't you give this information to the police, Mr. Lapetaine?"

The art dealer looked down at his shoes. "I didn't think Hilary could be involved, but after what you tell me about vapor—I don't know. If I'm going to get into any trouble myself, then with me it's strictly Number One. Hilary's gone back to London. You'll find her at the Lady Love night-club."

Francis Quarles talked on the telephone to the owner of the Lady Love, then took a plane from Liverpool to London. He arrived at the night-club, caught a glimpse of a cabaret-turn ending, and pushed his way backstage among a crowd of blondes and brunettes, wondering as he had often done before why a dozen half-dressed girls should be so much less attractive than one.

He tapped on the door of a room that was labeled *Miss Hall.* A deep, harsh voice said "All right."

Hilary Hall was sitting in front of a looking glass and her reflection frowned out at him. Her beauty was like a physical blow after the commonplace prettiness of the dancing girls outside. Yet on a second look it was not really beauty, Quarles saw, but simply the combination of flaming red hair, a milk-white skin, and certain unusual physical features— the thick brows that almost met in the middle, the jutting red underlip, the powerful shoulders.

This was a woman whom you could imagine as a murderess, although such an exercise of the imagination, as Quarles well knew, could easily be misleading.

"I was told you were coming," she said in that rusty, attractive voice. "And I've seen your picture in the papers. What do you want?"

"I would like you to answer some questions."

"I'm on in ten minutes. You've got till then." She had not turned round.

Quarles said, "I can put it simply. You were in love with Harry Bartley. You wrote him a threatening letter after his engagement. You went up to Liverpool to cause trouble."

Her thick brows were drawn together. "So what? He's dead now. I never went near the course, Mr. Detective."

Quarles said softly, "He came to see you the night before the race."

She swung round now and faced him. Her eyes were snapping with temper. She looked magnificent. "Of course he did, after I'd rung him up. He came to pour out all his troubles and say how sorry he was it had to be goodbye. He didn't want to marry that silly little bit he'd got engaged to. She had money, that was all. Can you imagine any man preferring her to me?"

She paused and Quarles, although not particularly susceptible, felt a kind of shiver run down his back.

"He had other troubles too," she said. "A frightful cold that he was afraid might develop into flu and make it difficult for him to ride that damned horse. Said he'd have to do something about it. Altogether, he was pretty low."

"You were very much in love with him?"

Looking down at her scarlet fingernails she said, "He was a man."

With a deprecating cough Quarles said, "But you were prepared to accept a thousand pounds to soothe your feelings."

She struck the dressing table sharply with a clenched fist. "That filthy Paul Lapetaine's been talking to you. He was after me himself, but he never got to first base. I like men, not dressed-up dolls. Yes, I said I'd take the money. I need it. I knew Harry would never put a ring on my finger. You can think what you like about it."

"What I think," Quarles said abruptly, "is that you're an honest woman."

Her heavy frown changed into a smile. "You're all right."

A head poked through the door and a voice said, "On in two minutes, Miss Hall."

"Look here," she said, "I'm on now, but why don't you stay here? We'll talk afterwards, have a drink. I want to find Harry's murderer as much as you do."

"I should be delighted to have a drink, and honored if you would allow me to take you out to supper," Francis Quarles said. "But we don't have to talk about the case. The case is solved."

Quarles's secretary, Molly Player, was a neatly attractive—but not too attractive—blonde. He had told her something about the people involved in the case, and now as the suspects arrived and she took them all in to Quarles's office overlooking Trafalgar Square, she found some amusement in comparing the detective's remarks with the reality.

Sir Reginald came first, pale and anxious ("self-made man, vulgar and cocky, but really cut to pieces by his son's death," Quarles had said), and he was closely followed by Doctor Ramsay ("every inch a soldier, so military he seems phoney, but in fact he was an army doctor, and a good one").

Then came Jennifer Moore wearing a becoming amount of black, accompanied by elegant Paul Lapetaine. "She looks and talks like a mouse, but that doesn't mean she *is* a mouse," Quarles had said thoughtfully of Miss Moore. Lapetaine he had dismissed briskly. "One of nature's spivs."

Then, on her own, in a glory of furs and radiating bright sex, Hilary Hall. "You can't miss *her,* Molly, any more than you can miss the sun coming out," Quarles said. "An orange sun," he added as an afterthought. "High in the sky, a scorcher."

Last of all, Norman Johnson, the brown-faced bow-legged trainer of Lucky Charm. About him Quarles's comment had been tersest of all. "Poker face."

Molly Player let them all in. Then she sat down and tried to type a report, but found herself making a number of mistakes. She remembered Quarles's last words to her: "One of these six, Molly, is a murderer."

Francis Quarles sat back in the big chair behind his desk, and said pleasantly to the six people, "One of you is a murderer."

His office was large, but it had only four chairs for visitors, so that Paul Lapetaine stretched his elegant legs from a stool, and Doctor Ramsay sat in a window-seat from which he could look down on the square far below with its pigeons, its children, and its lions. Jennifer Moore sat next to Ramsay, as far away as possible from Hilary Hall.

"It may be of interest to you all," Quarles continued didactically, "to know how I discovered the murderer, after Sir Reginald had engaged me to investigate.

"I considered first the question of motive, and I found that five of you had motives for killing Harry Bartley. Johnson, trainer of the horse he rode, hated him because Bartley had treated his daughter badly. Miss Hall had been thrown over by Bartley, and had written him a threatening letter.

"Miss Moore might have discovered that Bartley went to see Miss Hall on the night before the race. She looks like a quiet young lady, but quiet young ladies have been known to poison through jealousy.

"Paul Lapetaine, I should judge, was jealous of Bartley's success with women, and especially with Hilary Hall. Doctor Ramsay was obviously fond of Miss Moore, and had been for years. He must have had bitter feelings when he learned that she was going to marry a man like Harry Bartley."

Ramsay on his window-seat made a motion of protest. Sir Reginald said, "You have no right to talk about my son like that."

Quarles's voice was harsh. "I'm sorry, Sir Reginald. I told you that this inquiry might be disagreeable for you. I don't condone murder, but I must admit that your son strikes me as an unpleasant character.

"Let us move on from motive to opportunity. Bartley was killed by nitrobenzene, and it was thought at first that he had drunk the poison in a glass of orange juice, or perhaps taken it in the form of a pill. There was a thought in Miss Moore's mind, or perhaps Lapetaine put it there, that Doctor Ramsay might have given Bartley a tablet filled with nitrobenzene when Bartley came to see him early on the morning of the race.

"The post-mortem proved conclusively that this idea was mistaken. Dr. Ramsay's pills were perfectly harmless. Bartley had not been killed by nitrobenzene introduced into his stomach. He had been poisoned by it in the form of vapor.

"This was the essential feature of the crime. The last vital clue, however, was provided by Miss Hall. She told me that on the night before the race, when Bartley came to see her, he complained of a bad cold that he feared might develop into influenza."

There was silence in the room. Then Jennifer Moore said timidly, "I suppose I knew that too. I mean, I knew Harry was sniffing a lot and had a bit of a cold, but I still don't understand why it should be important— vital, you said."

"Quite early in the case I said that I remembered an affair in which a young man spilled nitrobenzene on his clothes, became stupefied, collapsed in coma, and died. Something like that happened to Harry Bartley."

"His clothes weren't poisoned." That was Johnson, speaking for the first time.

"No. He was killed by a handkerchief impregnated with nitrobenzene, which he used frequently because he had a cold."

Hilary Hall objected, in her rusty voice, "I don't believe that that points to anybody in particular."

"There are two other things I should tell you. When I met Harry Bartley in the paddock I noticed that he used a handkerchief to wipe his nose. After the race, when his things were laid out on a table, the handkerchief was no longer there."

"It came out when he fell from the horse," Ramsay suggested.

"No. Because the rabbit's foot which he had tucked into his pocket at the same time was still there. The handkerchief had been taken away—stolen."

Sir Reginald rubbed his chin. "I may be slow, but I simply don't see how that can be possible. Nobody came near Harry's body—" He stopped.

"That isn't true," Quarles said. "But it is true that only one person fulfills all *five* of our murderer's qualifications. He had to be a person who disliked Harry Bartley. He had to possess some knowledge of the properties of nitrobenzene. He had to know that Bartley had a cold, and would frequently wipe his nose with a handkerchief. He had to be a person from whom Bartley would have accepted a handkerchief—having been told that it was impregnated with what our murderer might have said was oil of eucalyptus, good for a cold. Finally he had to be a person who had access to Harry Bartley very soon after he collapsed. He was able to bend over the body—making an examination, shall we say?—and steal the handkerchief.

"The police are outside, Doctor Ramsay. It's no good trying to use that gun in your hip pocket."

Doctor Ramsay was on his feet now, and the gun was in his hand. "I'm not sorry for what I did," he said. "Not in the least. Harry was a dirty little devil with girls, had been since he was a boy. I'd always loved you, Jennifer, although I've never said it. In the wrong age group, I know. When I heard he'd got hold of you I just couldn't stand it. Don't come near me, now. I don't want to hurt anybody else."

"Bill." Jennifer Moore held out a hand to him. "Please don't—"

Ramsay flung up the window. "You don't think I'm going to endure the farce of a trial, do you? It's better this way, for me and for everybody else."

He stepped out onto the ledge, and looked for a moment at the pigeons and the children, the placid lions and Nelson on his pillar.

Then he jumped.

William Saroyan

THE SUMMER OF THE BEAUTIFUL WHITE HORSE

One day back there in the good old days when I was nine and the world was full of every imaginable kind of magnificence, and life was still a delightful and mysterious dream, my cousin Mourad, who was considered crazy by everybody who knew him except me, came to my house at four in the morning and woke me up by tapping on the window of my room.

Aram, he said.

I jumped out of bed and looked out the window.

I couldn't believe what I saw.

It wasn't morning yet, but it was summer and with daybreak not many minutes around the corner of the world it was light enough for me to know I wasn't dreaming.

My cousin Mourad was sitting on a beautiful white horse.

I stuck my head out of the window and rubbed my eyes.

Yes, he said in Armenian. It's a horse. You're not dreaming. Make it quick if you want a ride.

I knew my cousin Mourad enjoyed being alive more than anybody else who had ever fallen into the world by mistake, but this was more than even I could believe.

In the first place, my earliest memories had been memories of horses and my first longings had been longings to ride.

This was the wonderful part.

In the second place, we were poor.

This was the part that wouldn't permit me to believe what I saw.

We were poor. We had no money. Our whole tribe was poverty-stricken. Every branch of the Garoghlanian family was living in the most amazing and comical poverty in the world. Nobody could understand where we ever got money enough to keep us with food in our bellies, not even the old men of the family. Most important of all, though, we were famous for our honesty. We had been famous for our honesty for something like eleven centuries, even when we had been the wealthiest family in what we liked to think was the world. We were proud first, honest next, and after that we believed in right and wrong. None of us would take advantage of anybody in the world, let alone steal.

Consequently, even though I could see the horse, so magnificent; even though I could *smell* it, so lovely; even though I could *hear* it breathing, so exciting; I couldn't *believe* the horse had anything to do with my cousin Mourad or with me or with any of the other members of our family, asleep or awake, because I *knew* my cousin Mourad couldn't have *bought* the horse, and if he couldn't have bought it he must have *stolen* it, and I refused to believe he had stolen it.

No member of the Garoghlanian family could be a thief.

I stared first at my cousin and then at the horse. There was a pious stillness and humor in each of them which on the one hand delighted me and on the other frightened me.

Mourad, I said, where did you steal this horse?

Leap out of the window, he said, if you want a ride.

It was true, then. He *had* stolen the horse. There was no question about it. He had come to invite me to ride or not, as I chose.

Well, it seemed to me stealing a horse for a ride was not the same thing as stealing something else, such as money. For all I knew, maybe it wasn't stealing at all. If you were crazy about horses the way my cousin Mourad and I were, it wasn't stealing. It wouldn't become stealing until we offered to sell the horse, which of course I knew we would never do.

Let me put on some clothes, I said.

All right, he said, but hurry.

I leaped into my clothes.

I jumped down to the yard from the window and leaped up onto the horse behind my cousin Mourad.

That year we lived at the edge of town, on Walnut Avenue. Behind our house was the country: vineyards, orchards, irrigation ditches, and country roads. In less than three minutes we were on Olive Avenue, and then the horse began to trot. The air was new and lovely to breathe. The feel of the horse running was wonderful. My cousin Mourad who was considered one of the craziest members of our family began to sing. I mean, he began to roar.

Every family has a crazy streak in it somewhere, and my cousin Mourad was considered the natural descendant of the crazy streak in our tribe. Before him was our uncle Khosrove, an enormous man with a powerful head of black hair and the largest mustache in the San Joaquin Valley, a man so furious in temper, so irritable, so impatient that he stopped anyone from talking by roaring, *It is no harm; pay no attention to it.*

That was all, no matter what anybody happened to be talking about. Once it was his own son Arak running eight blocks to the barber shop where his father was having his mustache trimmed to tell him their house was on fire. The man Khosrove sat up in the chair and roared, It is no harm; pay no attention to it. The barber said, But the boy says your house is on fire. So Khosrove roared, Enough, it is no harm, I say.

My cousin Mourad was considered the natural descendant of this man, although Mourad's father was Zorab, who was practical and nothing else. That's how it was in our tribe. A man could be the father of his son's flesh, but that did not mean that he was also the father of his spirit. The distribution of the various kinds of spirit of our tribe had been from the beginning capricious and vagrant.

We rode and my cousin Mourad sang. For all anybody knew we were still in the old country where, at least according to our neighbors, we belonged. We let the horse run as long as it felt like running.

At last my cousin Mourad said, Get down. I want to ride alone.

Will you let me ride alone? I said.

That is up to the horse, my cousin said. Get down.

The *horse* will let me ride, I said.

We shall see, he said. Don't forget that I have a way with a horse.

Well, I said, any way you have with a horse, I have also.

For the sake of your safety, he said, let us hope so. Get down.

All right, I said, but remember you've got to let me try to ride alone.

I got down and my cousin Mourad kicked his heels into the horse and shouted, *Vazire,* run. The horse stood on its hind legs, snorted, and burst into a fury of speed that was the loveliest thing I had ever seen. My cousin Mourad raced the horse across a field of dry grass to an irrigation ditch, crossed the ditch on the horse, and five minutes later returned, dripping wet.

The sun was coming up.

Now it's my turn to ride, I said.

My cousin Mourad got off the horse.

Ride, he said.

I leaped to the back of the horse and for a moment knew the awfulest fear imaginable. The horse did not move.

Kick into his muscles, my cousin Mourad said. What are you waiting for? We've got to take him back before everybody in the world is up and about.

I kicked into the muscles of the horse. Once again it reared and snorted. Then it began to run. I didn't know what to do. Instead of running across the field to the irrigation ditch the horse ran down the road to the vineyard of Dikran Halabian where it began to leap over vines. The horse leaped over seven vines before I fell. Then it continued running.

My cousin Mourad came running down the road.

I'm not worried about you, he shouted. We've got to get that horse. You go this way and I'll go this way. If you come upon him, be kindly. I'll be near.

I continued down the road and my cousin Mourad went across the field toward the irrigation ditch.

It took him half an hour to find the horse and bring him back.

All right, he said, jump on. The whole world is awake now.

What will we do? I said.

Well, he said, we'll either take him back or hide him until tomorrow morning.

He didn't sound worried and I knew he'd hide him and not take him back. Not for a while, at any rate.

Where will you hide him? I said.

I know a place, he said.

How long ago did you steal this horse? I said.

It suddenly dawned on me that he had been taking these early morning rides for some time and had come for me this morning only because he knew how much I longed to ride.

Who said anything about stealing a horse? he said.

Anyhow, I said, how long ago did you begin riding every morning?

Not until this morning, he said.

Are you telling the truth? I said.

Of course not, he said, but if we are found out, that's what you're to say. I don't want both of us to be liars. All you know is that we started riding this morning.

All right, I said.

He walked the horse quietly to the barn of a deserted vineyard which at one time had been the pride of a farmer named Fetvajian. There were some oats and dry alfalfa in the barn.

We began walking home.

It wasn't easy, he said, to get the horse to behave so nicely. At first it wanted to run wild, but as I've told you, I have a way with a horse. I can get it to want to do anything *I* want it to do. Horses understand me.

How do you do it? I said.

I have an understanding with a horse, he said.

Yes, but what sort of an understanding? I said.

A simple and honest one, he said.

Well, I said, I wish I knew how to reach an understanding like that with a horse.

You're still a small boy, he said. When you get to be thirteen you'll know how to do it.

I went home and ate a hearty breakfast.

That afternoon my uncle Khosrove came to our house for coffee and cigarettes. He sat in the parlor, sipping and smoking and remembering the old country. Then another visitor arrived, a farmer named John Byro, an Assyrian who, out of loneliness, had learned to speak Armenian. My mother brought the lonely visitor coffee and tobacco and he rolled a cigarette and sipped and smoked, and then at last, sighing sadly, he said, My white horse which was stolen last month is still gone. I cannot understand it.

My uncle Khosrove became very irritated and shouted, It's no harm. What is the loss of a horse? Haven't we all lost the homeland? What is this crying over a horse?

That may be all right for you, a city dweller, to say, John Byro said, but what of my surrey? What good is a surrey without a horse?

Pay no attention to it, my uncle Khosrove roared.

I walked ten miles to get here, John Byro said.

You have legs, my uncle Khosrove shouted.

My left leg pains me, the farmer said.

Pay no attention to it, my uncle Khosrove roared.

That horse cost me sixty dollars, the farmer said.

I spit on money, my uncle Khosrove said.

He got up and stalked out of the house, slamming the screen door.

My mother explained.

He has a gentle heart, she said. It is simply that he is homesick and such a large man.

The farmer went away and I ran over to my cousin Mourad's house.

He was sitting under a peach tree, trying to repair the hurt wing of a young robin which could not fly. He was talking to the bird.

What is it? he said.

The farmer, John Byro, I said. He visited our house. He wants his horse. You've had it a month. I want you to promise not to take it back until I learn to ride.

It will take you a *year* to learn to ride, my cousin Mourad said.

We could keep the horse a year, I said.

My cousin Mourad leaped to his feet.

What? he roared. Are you inviting a member of the Garoghlanian family to steal? The horse must go back to its true owner.

When? I said.

In six months at the latest, he said.

He threw the bird into the air. The bird tried hard, almost fell twice, but at last flew away, high and straight.

Early every morning for two weeks my cousin Mourad and I took the horse out of the barn of the deserted vineyard where we were hiding it and rode it, and every morning the horse, when it was my turn to ride alone, leaped over grapevines and small trees and threw me and ran away. Nevertheless, I hoped in time to learn to ride the way my cousin Mourad rode.

One morning on the way to Fetvajian's deserted vineyard we ran into the farmer John Byro who was on his way to town.

Let me do the talking, my cousin Mourad said. I have a way with farmers.

Good morning, John Byro, my cousin Mourad said to the farmer.

The farmer studied the horse eagerly.

Good morning, sons of my friends, he said. What is the name of your horse?

My Heart, my cousin Mourad said in Armenian.

A lovely name, John Byro said, for a lovely horse. I could swear it is the horse that was stolen from me many weeks ago. May I look into its mouth?

Of course, Mourad said.

The farmer looked into the mouth of the horse.

Tooth for tooth, he said. I would swear it *is* my horse if I didn't know your parents. The fame of your family for honesty is well known to me. Yet the horse is the twin of my horse. A suspicious man would believe his eyes instead of his heart. Good day, my young friends.

Good day, John Byro, my cousin Mourad said.

Early the following morning we took the horse to John Byro's vineyard and put it in the barn. The dogs followed us around without making a sound.

The dogs, I whispered to my cousin Mourad. I thought they would bark.

They would at somebody else, he said. I have a way with dogs.

My cousin Mourad put his arms around the horse, pressed his nose into the horse's nose, patted it, and then we went away.

That afternoon John Byro came to our house in his surrey and showed my mother the horse that had been stolen and returned.

I do not know what to think, he said. The horse is stronger than ever. Better-tempered, too. I thank God.

My uncle Khosrove, who was in the parlor, became irritated and shouted, Quiet, man, quiet. Your horse has been returned. Pay no attention to it.

Hamlin Garland

OWEN RIDES AT THE COUNTY FAIR

The one break in the monotony of the farm's fall work was the County Fair, which usually came about the 20th of September. Toward this, Lincoln and his mates looked longingly. By this time they were inexpressibly weary of the ploughing and cattle-tending, and longed for a visit to the town. There were always three days of the Fair, but only two were of any amusement to the boys. The first day was always taken up in preparation, getting the stock housed and the like; the fun came on the last day with the races, though Lincoln was always mildly interested in the speechmaking on the second day.

The older boys planned to take their sweethearts, just as on the Fourth of July, and the wives and mothers baked up dozens of biscuits, and baked chicken, and made pies and cake for dinner on the grounds. The country was new, and the show was not great, but it called the people together, and that was something. So most of the threshing-machines fell silent for a single day, the ploughs rested in the furrow, and the men put on clean shirts. The women, however, kept on working up to the very hour of starting for the grounds. Their work was never done. After getting everything and everybody else ready they took scant time to get themselves ready—all the others clamoring to be off. The weather was usually clear and dry, cool of a morning, becoming hot and windless at noon, but on this particular day it was cold and cloudy, making overcoats necessary at the start.

The four inseparable boys rode away together, their horses shining with the extra brushing they had endured. Rance was mounted on "Ivanhoe," Lincoln rode "Rob Roy," Milton "Mark," while Owen rode a four-year-old colt which he called "Toot," for some curious reason, while the rest of the family generally spoke of her as "Kitty." She was almost pure blood Morgan, a bright bay, very intelligent, and for a short dash very swift. Owen was entered for "The Boys' Riding Contest"; the other three boys were all too old to come in, but were going down with him as body-guard. It was a goodly land to look at; trim stacks of wheat stood four and four about the fields. The corn was heavy with ears, and the sound of the threshing-machine came into hearing each mile or two. Only the homes showed poverty.

The boys did not stop in town—merely rode through the street and on down toward the Fair Grounds. At the gate, where two very important keepers stood at guard, the boys halted, and Rance, after collecting quarters from his fellows, bought the four tickets; the keepers fell back appeased, and the boys rode in, their fine horses causing people to remark, "There are some boys for the races, I guess."

The boys were all very proud of these remarks, and galloped around the track to show off their horses and to get the lay of the land.

"We mustn't wind our nags," said Rance, after making the circuit once or twice. "Let's tie up."

While the people were pouring in at the gates, the boys rode slowly round the grounds to see what was displayed; on past fat sheep and blooded stallions and prize cows and Poland-China pigs; on past new-fangled sulky ploughs, "Vibrator" threshing-machines, and so on. The stock didn't interest them so much as the whirligig and the candy-puller, and the man who twisted copper wire into "Mamie" and "Arthur" for "the small sum of twenty-five cents, or a quarter of a dollar."

One or two enormous Norman horses, being a new importation, commanded their attention, and they joined the crowd around them and listened to the comments with interest; but the crowd, after all, was the wonder. The swarming of so many people, all strangers, was sufficient, of its own motion, to keep the open-eyed boys busy. They were there, not to see hogs and cattle, but the strange fakirs and the curious machines, and the alien industries. A deft and glib seller of collar-buttons and lamp-chimney wipers enthralled them, and a girl, playing a piano in "Horticultural Hall," entranced them; at least, she so appealed to Lincoln and to Rance—her playing had the vim and steady clatter of a barrel piano, but it stood for music in absence of anything better.

Hitching their horses to the family wagons, which had by this time arrived, the boys wandered about afoot. Lincoln and Owen had on new suits. The Fair was the time set apart for the one suit they were able to afford each year. Sometimes it was bought on Fair day, but usually a little before, so that the great day should be free for other pleasures. Their suits never fitted, of course, and Owen's was always of the same goods precisely as Lincoln's, differing in size merely. They were of thick woollen goods of strange checks and stripes, the shoddy refuse of city shops which the local dealers bought cheap and sold dear—being good enough for country folks. As they were intended for all the year round, they were naturally uncomfortable in the middle of September and intolerable in July. Even on this windy day, the boys sweated their paper collars into pulp before they concluded to lay off their coats and go about in their shirt-sleeves. As it was one of the few occasions when they could reasonably be dressed up, they were willing to suffer a little martyrdom for pride's sake.

Lincoln's heart was full of bitterness as he saw the town boys go by in well-fitting garments, looking comfortable even while in dressed-up conditions. His hat troubled him also, for it was of a shape entirely unlike anything else on the grounds. The other boys were almost all wearing a hat with a tall crown and a narrow rim, but his hat, and Owen's as well, was a flat-crowned structure, heavy and thick, and to make matters worse, it was too large, and Owen's, especially, came down and rested against his ears.

Another cause of shame to Lincoln was the cut on his hair. Up to this time he had never enjoyed a "real barber cut." Mr. Stewart generally detailed one of the hired men to the duty, and the boys were, in very truth, "shingled." Both had heavy heads of brown hair, and after Jim Beane got done with them they had ruffles like a pineapple, or a girl's nightgown. Rance and Milton had long ago rebelled against this kind of torture, and employed the barber at least twice each year. Milton declared on his thirteenth birthday, "No hired man shall chaw my hair off again, and don't you forget it."

This Fair day marked another great advance in Lincoln's life. He ate no candy or peanuts, and by his advice Owen limited himself to "home-made candy" and a banana, which he allowed Lincoln to taste. Neither of them had ever seen one before. "If you want to scoop in that saddle, Owen, you keep well," Lincoln said, every time Owen suggested trying some new drink or confection.

Rance was bitterly disappointed when he found himself shut out of the contest for the saddle, and was very glum all the forenoon. Lincoln shared his disappointment, although he cared very little about his own part in it. He believed Rance to be the best rider in the county, but did not expect to win a prize himself.

One by one they met all their friends from Sun Prairie and Burr Oak, and once they met "Freckles," the town bully, face to face. He made furious signs of battle, and dared them to go over to the back fence with him, to which Owen replied by putting his thumb to his nose, and waving his fingers like a flag. "Freckles" was visibly enraged by this, but as the Sun Prairie boys were in full force, and confident, he withdrew, uttering threats.

Wonderful to say, the boys were able to share in the jolly dinner which their mothers arranged on the grass between the wagons, over on the south side of the grounds. The wagon-seats were taken off to serve as chairs: a snowy-white cloth was spread as neatly as on a table, and the entire Jennings family joined in the feast of cold chicken, jelly, pickles, "riz" biscuits, dried beef, apple pie, cake, and cheese. Lincoln had never felt so well on a holiday, and his spirits rose instead of sinking as the day wore on. Owen was fed with anxious care by his mother. He was even allowed to drink a cup of coffee as a special tonic.

Mr. Stewart declined to take the contest seriously, but Mr. Jennings agreed that some provision should be made for the older boys.

"I'll see the President of the Day," he said, "and see if a special contest can't be arranged to follow the boys' race."

The idea pleased everybody, and spread from lip to lip, till it became a definite announcement.

Meanwhile various unimportant matters, like displaying sheep and cattle, and beets and honey, for prizes, were going on, when Mr. Stewart came back where Lincoln was observing the candy-puller for the twentieth time. He said, "Lincoln, go get the team; I've entered you for the pulling match."

Lincoln's heart suddenly failed him, "Oh, I can't do that before all these people."

"Yes, you can. Go hitch up."

As he drove his team through the crowd, with alternate traces unhooked to drag the double tree, Lincoln felt just as he used to feel when rising to recite a piece in school on a holiday. He was queer and sick at his heart, but something nerved him to the trial.

The crowd opened, and he swung the horses to the stone-boat walled in by spectators. Dan and Jule were not large, but they were broad in the chest, and loyal to the centre of each brown eye, and they knew him. He had the opinion that they could pull anything they set their shoulders to, and as he gathered up the reins his eyes cleared. He climbed upon the load. The Judge said:—

"Keep quiet, everybody. All ready, my boy."

Lincoln's voice was calm as he said: "Steady now, Jule. Chk-chk, Dan, steady now." The noble animals settled to the load, obeying every word. Dan was a little in advance, a few inches, with his legs set. "Get down there, Jule," called the boy. The old mare squatted, set her shoulders to the collar, lifting like a trained athlete, and the stone-boat slid half its length. The crowd applauded. "Bully boy!"

"All right," said the Judge, "take 'em off for a minute. Anderson, it's your turn again."

Anderson, a Norwegian, with a fine showy team, hitched on, but could not move it; not because his horses were not strong enough, but because they were nervous and tricky. The audience jeered at him—"Take 'em off; they're no good."

Lime Gilman came next, and Lincoln lost his exultation as the big fellow winked at him. His team were brown Morgan grades, as responsive to his voice as dogs. They were the lightest of all the teams, but they were beautiful to see as they swung to place. Their harnesses were covered with costly ivory rings, and as they wore no blinders, they eyed their master in love, not fear. The crowd uttered a cheer of genuine admiration as Lime heaved two extra rocks upon the load.

As he took the reins in one hand Lime began uttering a pleasant, bird-like, chirping sound. Slowly, softly, the superbly intelligent creatures squared and squatted together, setting their feet fairly, flatly, and carefully on the sod.

"Dexter, boy!" said Lime, and at the soft word the load slid nearly a yard.

"Ho! that'll do, boys," called Lime, and said with a smile, as he turned to Lincoln, "Try again, Link."

"It's yours," shouted the crowd.

"Oh, no it isn't," said Lime. "I know this boy and his team!"

A big, long-legged gray team took a second trial, but though they tugged furiously, could not move the extra weight. "They're up too high upon legs," said the Judge, critically.

Anderson was out of the contest, so that Lincoln was Lime's only rival. The boy had forgotten all his shyness. He threw off his coat and hat, and said to the Judge,—

"Pile on two more stones."

"Good for you, sonny!" someone said as Lime threw on one of the big flat limestone slabs. Again Lincoln swung his faithful team in and hooked the traces. As he climbed on the load and took the reins in hand, he was tense with excitement; he saw only Lime's pleasant face and his father's anxious smile.

"Stiddy, Dan. Take hold of it; w-o-oo-p, stiddy!" Again they settled to the task, their great muscles rolling, their ears pointing, their eyes quiet. For a few moments they hung poised—

"*Now, Jule!*" shouted Lincoln, and the mare lifted, strained to her almost best, but the load did not move.

"Ho!" shouted Lincoln, checking them so that they would not become discouraged.

"Give it up. Take off a stone," cried a friendly voice.

"Not much," said Lincoln.

Springing from the load, he drew the reins over Jule's back, and again called on Dan to take his position, and just as they settled to their work, Lincoln brought his hand with a sharp slap under Jule's belly.

"*Jule!*"

With a tremendous effort the grand brute lifted the boat six good inches, and the crowd clapped hands heartily.

"That's enough. Unhitch," called the Judge.

It was now Lime's turn to swing into place.

"Good boy, Link," he said as he passed.

Once more he swung his horses to the load, but this time he looped the reins over Dexter's brass-bound harness, and took his place nearer his side.

Chirp, chirp, chirp!

Again the brown team settled into place.

"Easy now, Dexter. Easy, Dave. Now then, boys, all together. *Get down, boy!*" With the simultaneous action of shadows, the beautiful horses squatted and lifted, guided only by their master's words. For nearly half a minute they held to the work, their necks outthrust, their feet clutching the earth, steady, loyal, bright-eyed, unwavering, pulling every pound that was in them. Such action had never been seen on the Fair Grounds, but they were defeated,—they had not the weight necessary; the task was too great.

They released their hold only when Lime spoke the word, and the crowd was vociferous with admiration.

"That's what ye might call pullin'.'"

"Call it a draw, Judge."

"I'm willing," said Lincoln, who had expected the browns to move the load, for he knew Lime's wonderful horsemanship.

Mr. Stewart came forward, "We'll divide the honors, Lime."

And the Judge so decided, while the spectators pressed close around the brown horses, to feel of their sleek coats and to look at their sturdy legs. In looks and character no team on the grounds approached them.

As Lincoln rejoined the boys, they received him with a touch of awe, because of his honorable public exhibition of skill and the prize he had won.

"I knew old Jule would lift it," said Lincoln. "But Lime's team scared me. I knew they could pull. I've seen 'em dig down on a load while Lime lit his pipe."

The ringing of the signal bell broke in upon the talk, and a crier galloped through the grounds shouting, "Get ready for 'the Boys' Contest.' "

"That's you, Owen," said Lincoln.

Owen stripped as for battle. He could not ride in his lumpy, heavy coat, and his hat was also an incumbrance. With hands trembling with excitement, Lincoln helped him set the saddle on Kitty, and wipe from her limbs all dust and sweat. She shone like a red bottle when the youngster clambered to his seat.

"Don't touch her with the whip," said Lincoln.

"Look out for the crowd at the home-stretch," said Rance; but Owen was as calm as a clam, and rode forth in silence, accompanied by his body-guard. Kitty danced and flung her head, as though she knew some test of her quality was about to be made. At the entrance to the track Lincoln and Rance halted, and Owen rode into the track alone, his head bare, his shirt-sleeves gleaming.

Five or six boys, on all kinds of ponies, were already riding aimlessly up and down before the judges' stand. Four of them were town boys, who wore white-visored caps and well-fitting jackets. The fifth was a tall, sandy-haired lad in brown overalls and a checked shirt. He rode a "gauming" sorrel colt, with a bewildering series of gaits, and he was followed up and down the track by a tall, roughly dressed man and a slatternly girl of thirteen or fourteen, who repeated each of the old man's orders.

"HOLD HIM UP A LITTLE!" shouted the father.

"Hold him up a little," repeated the girl.

"LET HIM OUT A GRAIN!"

"Let him out a grain."

"SET UP A LITTLE."

"Set up a little."

This was immensely entertaining to the crowd, but interfered with the race, so the Marshal was forced to come down and order them both from the track. This was a grateful relief to the boy, who was already hot with rebellion.

The bell's clangor called all the boys before the grand stand, and the Judge said:—

"Now, boys, we want you to ride up and down past us, for a few turns. Don't crowd each other, and don't hurry, and do your prettiest."

A single tap of the bell, and the boys were off at a gallop. The town boys, on their fat little ponies, cantered along smoothly, but Kitty, excited by the noise and the people, forced Owen to lay his weight against the bit, which didn't look well. Sandy was all over the track with his colt, pounding up and down like a dollar's worth of tenpenny nails in a wheelbarrow. He could ride, all the same, and his face was resolute and alert.

As they turned to come back, Kitty took the bit in her teeth and went round the other horses with a wild dash, and the swing of Owen's body at this moment betrayed the natural rider; but he was only a bareheaded farmer's son, and the judges were looking at Frank Simpson, the banker's boy, and Ned Baker, Dr. Baker's handsome nephew. Their ponies were accustomed to crowds and to the track and to each other, while everything was strange to Sandy's colt and to fiery little Kitty.

Owen did not see his father and mother, but Lincoln and Rance kept near the entrance, and each time he came to the turn they had a word of encouragement.

As the boys came under the wire the third time, the Judge said:—

"When you turn again, go round the track—and don't race," he said as an afterthought.

At every turn Kitty whirled in ahead as if rounding a herd, swift as a wolf, a bright gleam in her eye, her ears pointing. What all this see-sawing back and forth meant, she could not tell, but she was ready for anything whatever.

The town boys came about in a bunch, with Owen close behind and Sandy over at one side, sawing at his colt's open jaw, while his father yelled instructions over the fence.

"LET HIM GO, SON!"

"*Let him go, son,*" repeated the girl.

As they passed under the wire, some wag on the stand tapped the bell, and hundreds of voices yelled,—

"Go!"

The boys forgot previous warnings. Plying whip and spur, they swept down the track, all in a bunch, except Sandy, who was a length behind.

"Where's Owen?" asked Rance.

"Wait a minute," replied Lincoln. "He'll show up soon." As he spoke, the white sleeves of Owen's shirt flashed into sight ahead of the crowd. The bay mare was a beautiful sight then. She ran low like a wolf. Her long tail streamed in the air, and her abundant mane, rising in waves, almost hid the boy's face. He no longer leaned ungracefully. Erect and at his ease, he seemed to float on the air, and when at intervals he looked back to see where his rivals were, Lincoln laughed.

"Oh, catch him, will you? Let's see you do it. *Now* where are your fancy riders?"

The slick ponies fell behind, and Sandy, yelling and plying the "bud," came on, the only possible competitor. He gained on Kitty, for Owen had not yet urged her to her best. As he rounded the turn and saw that the colt was gaining, he brought the flat of his hand down on Kitty's shoulder with a shrill whoop,—and the colt gained no more! As he swept under the wire at full speed, the boy had on his face the look of a Cheyenne lad, a look of calm exultation, and his seat in the saddle was that of the born horseman. Lincoln's heart was big with pride.

"He's won it! He's won it sure!"

When the red ribbon was put to Simpson's bridle, a groan went up from hundreds of spectators.

"Aw, no. The other one—the bare-headed boy!"

"Stewart!"

"Sandy!"

A crowd gathered around the Judges, and Mr. Stewart and Mr. Jennings joined it. Talk was plainly in Owen's favor.

"This is favoritism," protested Mr. Jennings. "Anybody can ride those trained town ponies. The decision lies between MacElroy's son and Owen Stewart. Put your slick little gentlemen on those two horses, and see how they will go through."

The crowd grew denser each moment, and Kitty was led through up to the Judges as they stood arguing. Owen did not know what it was all about, except that he had not won the prize.

The Judge argued: "We were not deciding a race. The specifications were 'displaying most grace and skill at horsemanship.' "

"How you going to decide? You can't do it without a change of horses. Owen will ride any horse you bring him. Will your natty little men ride the bay mare and the sorrel colt?"

MacElroy and his daughter, by this time, had fought their way through the crowd.

"This ain't no fair shake. I wouldn't a minded your givin' it to the feller on the bay mare, but them little rockin'-horse ponies—why, a suckin' goose can ride one of them."

"Now this is my opinion," said one of the Judges. "I voted for the first prize to go to Stewart, the second prize to MacElroy, and let 'em change horses and see what they can do."

"That's fair. That's right," said several bystanders.

The third Judge went on: "*But,* I was out-voted. Mine is a minority report, and can't stand."

The Chairman remained firm, notwithstanding all protests, but the second Judge, who was a candidate for election to the position of County Treasurer, became alarmed. He called Beeman aside, and after a moment's talk the Chairman said:—

"Mr. Middleton, having decided to vote with Mr. Scott, we have to announce that the first prize will go as before to Master Simpson, the second to Master Stewart, and the third to Master MacElroy, and this is final."

Returning to his stand, he rang the bell sharply, and again announced the decision, which was cheered in a mild sort of way.

"Clear the track for the Free-for-all running race—best two in three."

Lincoln helped Owen put the fine new bridle on Kitty without joy, for young Simpson was riding about the grounds on the saddle which almost every one said should be Owen's.

Sandy rode up, the white ribbon tied to his sorrel's bridle, a friendly grin on his face.

"I say, your horse can run five or six a minute, can't she?"

And Owen, who counted the bridle clear gain, and held no malice, said:—

"I was scared one while, when I saw your old Sorrel a-comin'. I'm dry. Le's go have some lemonade. Link, hold our horses."

And they drank, Owen standing treat with all the airs of a successful candidate for senatorial honors.

"Get out your horses for the four-year-old sweepstakes," shouted the Marshal as he rode down the track. "Bring out your horses."

The boys put down their glasses hastily. "Oh, let's see that," said Owen.

"Let's climb the fence," suggested Rance, indicating the high board fence which enclosed the ground, on whose perilous edge rows of boys were already sitting like blackbirds. From this coign of vantage they could "sass" anybody going, even the Marshal, for at last extremity it was possible to fall off the fence on the outside and escape. Here all the loud-voiced wags were stationed, and their comical phrases called forth hearty laughter from time to time, though they became a nuisance before the races were over. They reached the top of the fence by two convenient knot-holes, which formed toe-holes, and the big fellows then pulled the smaller ones after them.

It was a hard seat, but the race-course was entirely under the eye, and no one grumbled.

The boys were no sooner perched in readiness for the race than the Marshal came riding down the track, shouting. As he drew near, Owen heard his name called.

"Is Owen Stewart here?"

"Yes!" shouted Lincoln, for Owen was too much astonished to reply.

"Here he is," called a dozen voices.

The Marshal rode up: "You're wanted at the Judges' Stand," he said. "Come along."

"Go ahead," said Lincoln, and as Owen hesitated, he climbed down himself. "Come on, I'll go with you. It's something more about the prize."

Owen sprang from the fence like a cat, at the thought that perhaps the Judges had reconsidered their verdict, and were going to give him the saddle, after all.

The other boys, seeing Owen going up the track beside the Marshal, also became excited, and a comical craning of necks took place all along the fence.

"Here's your boy," said the Marshal, as he reached the Judges' Stand.

"Come up here, son," called the Judge, and Owen climbed up readily, for he saw his father up there beside the Judge.

A tall and much excited man took him by the shoulders and hustled him before a long-whiskered man, who seemed to be boss of the whole Fair.

"Will this boy answer?"

The Judge looked Owen over slowly, and finally lifted him by putting his hands under his arms, then he asked his weight of Mr. Stewart. The answer was satisfactory.

"Now, my boy, you are to ride this man's horse in the race, because his own boy is too light. Do you think you can handle a race-horse?"

"Yes, sir," replied Owen, sturdily.

"All right, sir, if his father is willing, I can mount your horse."

As they went down the stairs, Mr. Mills, the owner of the running horse "Gypsy," said: "You needn't be afraid. When once she's off, 'Gyp' is perfectly safe."

"I don't think he's afraid," remarked Mr. Stewart, quietly. "You tell him what you want him to do, and he'll do it."

"Now there are two horses," Mills explained as he got opportunity. "The bald-faced sorrel don't cut any figger—but the black, the Ansgor horse, is sure to get away first—for Gypsy is freaky at the wire. You will get away a couple of lengths behind, but don't worry about that—don't force the mare till you come around the last turn."

At the barn Owen took off his coat and hat while they led out the horse, a beautiful little bay mare, with delicate, slender legs, and a brown eye full of fire. The saddle was a low racing pad, and as they swung the boy to his seat, the mare began to rear and dance, as if she were a piece of watch-spring.

A thrill of joy and of mastery swept over the boy as he grasped the reins in his strong brown hands. It was worthwhile to feel such a horse under him.

"Let down my stirrups," he commanded. "I can't ride with my knees up there."

They let down his stirrups, and then with Mills holding the excited colt by the bit, he rode down the wire.

Gypsy's peculiarity was that she could be started at the wire only by facing her the other way, and it took both Mills and the hostler to hold her. At the tap of the bell, each time, the mare reared and whirled like a mad horse, and Mrs. Stewart trembled with fear of her son's life. Lincoln was near her, and said, "Don't worry, mother; he's all right."

Twice a false start was made, and the horses were called back. The third time they were off, the black in the lead, the sorrel next, the bay last. As Gypsy settled smoothly to her work, Owen had time to think of his instructions. Just before him was the black, running swiftly and easily, and he felt that Gypsy could pass him. At the turn he loosened the reins and leaned to the outside, intending to pass, but the jockey on the black pulled in front of him. He then swung the bay to the left to pass on the inside of the track, but again the jockey cut in ahead, and looking back with a vicious smile said, "No, you don't!" It was "Freckles," and the recognition took the resolution out of Owen, and before he could devise a plan to pass they rushed under the wire, Gypsy a length behind.

Mills was much excited and threatened to break the jockey's head,—and asked that he be taken off the track,—but the Judges decided that Gypsy had not been fouled. Mills then filled Owen's ears with advice, but all the boy said was: "He won't do that again. Don't you worry." He was angry, too.

At the second start they got away as before, except the sorrel ran for a long time side by side with Gypsy. The two boys could talk quite easily as the horses ran smoothly, steadily, and the jockey on the sorrel said:—

"Don't let him jockey you. Pass him on the back stretch, when he ain't lookin'."

Owen again loosened the rein, and the bay mare shot by the sorrel and abreast of the black. Again the jockey cut him off, but Owen pulled sharply to the left, intending to pass next the pole. For the first time he struck the mare, and she leaped like a wolf to a position at the flank of the black. Freckles pulled viciously in crowding his horse against the mare, intending to force Owen against the fence and throw him; but the boy held his mare strongly by the right rein, and threw himself over on his saddle with his right knee on the horse's back, uttering a shrill cry as he did so. In first leap the mare was clear of the black, and went sailing down the track, an easy winner—without another stroke of the whip.

He now had a clear idea of his horse's powers, and though he got away last, as before, he put Gypsy to her best and passed the black at once, and taking the pole, he held it without striking a blow or uttering a word, though the black tried twice to pass. The spectators roared with delight, to see the round-faced boy sitting erect, with the reins in his left hand, his shirtsleeves fluttering, come sweeping down the inside course, the black far behind and laboring hard.

There was something distinctly comic in Owen's way of looking behind him to see where his rival was.

Mills pulled him from the horse in his delight, and put an extra five dollars in his hand. "I'll give you ten dollars to ride Gypsy at Independence," he said.

"All right," said Owen.

But his parents firmly said, "No, this ends it. We don't want him to do any more of this kind of work."

Swiftly the sun fell to the west, and while the dealers and showmen redoubled their outcries in hopes to close out their stocks, the boys began to think of going home. Out along the fences where the men were hitching up the farm-teams, the women stood in groups for a last exchange of greetings. The children, tired, dusty, sticky with candies, pulled at their skirts. The horses, eager to be off, pranced under the tightening reins. The dust rose under their hoofs, whips cracked, goodbys passed from lip to lip, and so, in a continuous stream the farm-wagons passed out of the gate, to diverge like the lines of a spider's web, rolling on in the cool, red sunset, on through the dusk, on under the luminous half-moon, till silent houses in every part of the country bloomed with light and stirred with the bustle of home-comers from a day's vacation at the Fair.

Lincoln and Owen slipped off their new suits and resumed their hickory shirts and overalls and went out to milk the cows and feed the pigs, while Mrs. Stewart skimmed the milk and made tea for supper. The boys had no holiday to look forward to till Thanksgiving came, and that was not really a holiday, for it came after the beginning of school.

Next morning, long before light, they rose to milk cows and curry horses again, and at sunrise the boys went forth upon the land to plough.

Will James

FOR A HORSE

Dusty Knight was a bronc peeler (bronco buster), and when that's said about him there's nothing to be took back, for he was at the top at the rough game. Dusty was most always horse-poor, meaning that he always had more horses than he could use; he kept 'em in fine shape, and on one of his horses he could of rode anywhere with the best of 'em and felt proud. If he come across a horse that was an exception and to his taste, he'd dicker for him or work out the money in breaking other horses for him, but some way or another he'd get that horse. It was very seldom that he was left with only two saddle horses, as he was now, but them two was his picked best, and few could touch them for looks, speed, and knowledge with rope and cow work. The other horses he'd let go, as good as they was, wasn't quite perfect to Dusty, and of course whatever little flaws they had wasn't found out till they was worked with a herd, maybe a week after he'd dickered for 'em.

Since his dad had took him on his first ride and before Dusty could walk, he'd rode hundreds of different horses, and always at the back of his head, seems like since he was born, there was the picture of one horse he had there, and with the many horses he rode and the thousands he seen he'd kept alooking and watching for that one perfect horse. He hadn't found him as yet; there'd been a little flaw that went against the mind picture he had in all of the best ones he'd picked on.

He was a couple of days' ride out of town, in the thick of good horse range, where he was always bound to be, and while riding through, going no place in particular, he zig-zagged around quite a bit to always look over this and that bunch of range horses he passed near. Sometime soon he'd strike an outfit that wanted some horses broke; such a job was never hard to get, not for such a hand as Dusty was. He could prove his hand quick, too, by just watching him handle and ride one green bronc, just one; after that the job was his.

A job was his on his third day out. He'd struck a big horse outfit and where a man who could break horses well could always get a job. That outfit had plenty of horses to break, tough good ones, and it sure took a bronc-riding fool to line 'em out, because they was the kind that was born with a snort and raised with a buck.

Dusty done his usual fine work of lining out the first bunch, and then, when he run a second bunch in to start breaking, there was one horse in that bunch that come near taking his breath away. It was the horse he'd always had the picture of at the back of his head—the perfect one. The color of him was blood bay, black mane and tail, the blackest that Dusty had ever seen, and that horse's hide shined to the sun the same as dark blood that'd been polished on redwood. It was sure a pretty color. But that wasn't the only thing that agreed with Dusty's taste about that horse. There was the perfect build of him, from his little intelligent-looking head to his little hard hoofs. There was plenty of good body in between, about eleven hundred pounds of it, and all a proportion to what Dusty thought a horse should be.

"That's him, sure enough," says Dusty as he watched the horse snort and run around the corral, "and you just wait till I get his round back shaped to my saddle and his neck working to the rein, I'll be mounted like no king ever was."

Dusty was about right. But as perfect as the horse seemed to be, there was something about him that wasn't cleared yet. That was the brand on him; that brand showed that he belonged to another outfit than the one he was working for, to a horseman by the name of Bill Huff, and Dusty figured he might have a little trouble fixing things so he could call that horse his own.

He was more than aching to start breaking him and see how he'd turn out, but breaking him would only raise the value in the horse, and so Dusty just broke him to lead, because now he was going to ride over and see the owner of that horse, Bill Huff.

He found out from the riders at the ranch that the horse had strayed. It was a good two days' ride to Huff's ranch, and Dusty, being wise to men's weaknesses for good horses, didn't take the horse with him as he saddled up one of his own and started over to see Huff.

Bill Huff had many horses; about half of 'em he would recognize by description; but when Dusty gave as poor a description as he could of that blood bay, he of a sudden perked his ears and didn't finish rolling his cigarette before he asked:

"Where did you see him?"

"Oh, about a hundred miles east of here. He's running with a bunch of wild horses and I'm thinking he'll be hard to get. I just happened to be riding this way," Dusty went on, "and being I'm circling back now I could maybe catch the horse if you'll sell him cheap enough. I need a pack horse pretty bad."

"Pack horse!" snorted Huff. "Why, man, you'll never find the makings of a better saddle horse in your life. I'll give you fifty dollars to get him and bring him here to me."

That last gave Dusty something to think about. He seen that Bill Huff sure had no intentions of parting with that animal; he also seen how glad he'd been to learn the horse's whereabouts and the relief that he hadn't been stole. It'd been near a year since he'd strayed away.

"Why, I wouldn't take five hundred dollars for that horse," says Huff, "even if he is wild and unbroke."

But Dusty had nowheres near given up the idea of getting that horse. He wasn't built that way. And it was while he was thinking hard and heard Huff say "unbroke" that he thought of a way.

"Have you any horses here you'd want broke?" he asks.

"Yes," says Huff, "quite a few, and the blood bay is one of 'em. Are you out for a job breaking horses?"

"If I can get enough horses to make the job worth while."

"I can rake up about thirty head easy, and if you're good enough hand I'll pay you extra for breaking the blood bay."

That went well with Dusty. With the scheme he had in mind, even though it would take time to put it through, he seen where sooner or later the bay horse would be his. He loped back to the outfit where he'd been working, drawed what money he had coming, caught his other horse and the blood bay, and in five days' time was back to Bill Huff's outfit.

There he went to work on the first ten head of broncs that was run in, and keeping in mind that he had to prove himself a good hand before he could get the blood bay to break, he brought out all his art at the game. The first few he started got the benefit of that, and in a easy way that made Bill Huff wonder, it seemed to him that them fighting broncs was no more than run in when the rough seemed to be took off of 'em overnight and a little girl could ride 'em. After a few days of watching such goings on, Bill decided that Dusty would sure do in handling his prize blood bay.

And Bill wasn't disappointed. Dusty took that horse, right away gave him the high-sounding name of Capitan before Huff could give him one, and was as careful of his hide as though it was made of diamond-inlaid gold lace. Capitan behaved fine for a green, high-strung bronc and bowed his head to buck only at the first few saddlings. He was quick to learn to turn at the feel of the hackamore rein, and his little chin quivered with nothing, seemed like, only by being anxious to tell ahead of time what was wanted of him and before the mecate knot touched the nerves of his jaws. His little pin ears worked back and forth as alive as his flashing eyes to what all was around him. Dusty still felt him to be the perfect horse, and to Bill Huff he was a dream that'd come to life.

All went fine for a week or so. Dusty rode the other broncs as their turns come, along with Capitan. And then, being Capitan was coming along so good, Dusty told Huff that he was going to turn him loose for a few days, that it would do the horse good and give him time to think things over; besides, he wanted more time to line out the other broncs so he would be done with 'em quicker.

Capitan run loose in a meadow of tall grass for a whole week, and, as Dusty expected and hoped for, that horse had accumulated a lot of kinks in that time. If that pony thought things over, it was towards how to buck good and nothing else.

It seemed that way to Bill, anyway. He was there when Dusty rode him time and again, and there hadn't been a one saddling when the horse didn't buck, and harder every time.

"Take it out of him, Dusty!" Bill Huff would holler, as Capitan would buck and beller around the corral. "Take it out of him, or, by gad, I'll kill him!"

That last would make Dusty grin to himself. He was now getting the horse to act the way he wanted him and so that Bill Huff wouldn't want him. Dusty would let on that he was also disappointed in the horse and act for all the world as though he was trying his best to take the buck out of him. He'd pull on the reins and slap with the quirt, and the pulls was easy and so was the slaps, and, at the side where Bill wouldn't see, Dusty was only encouraging the horse to buck a little harder.

Capitan didn't need much encouraging; it was in his system to buck anyway, and he always felt like he had something off his chest when he done a good job at it. He'd been just as good in other ways and as a cow horse if that bucking instinct had been left to sleep, as it had before he'd been turned loose for a week; but after that week, and with Dusty giving him his head to do as he pleased while Bill Huff wasn't watching, he'd humped up and bucked a little. Dusty could of easy broke him off of that right then, but it was part of his scheme to have him buck, and when Capitan didn't see no objections coming from his rider he fell into bucking in great style. Now it would take a heap of convincing by a mighty good rider to make him quit.

The horse was acting in great shape for Dusty, and Bill Huff had stopped coming to the corral when he was being rode. Bill had wanted that horse for himself, but he was too old to ride such as he'd turned out to be, and he was fast losing hope of his ever being of any use to him.

"He'll always buck," he says to Dusty one day.

Dusty had walked away and grinned. A few more days now and maybe Bill could be talked into selling the horse to him.

All was going fine, and then one day, before Dusty got to dickering for Capitan, a hammer-headed fifteen-dollar bronc bucked too high, and his feet wasn't under him when he hit the ground, but Dusty was. The horse had turned plumb over while in the air and come down on his back.

Dusty didn't come to his senses soon enough to talk to Bill about Capitan. When he come to he was stretched out in the back of an automobile and headed for town and hospital.

He laid in the hospital for a few months, wabbled around town for one or two more, and when he was able to ride again he hit for Bill Huff's.

Capitan wasn't there no more, and Bill Huff went on to tell how it come about. When Dusty was laid up in the hospital he hired another bronc fighter to take his place and finish up on the batch of broncs that he'd started. That new feller was a pretty fair hand and he handled the broncs all right, all but Capitan. That horse had been loose for a couple of weeks and when he caught him he soon found he couldn't ride him. Capitan had kept agetting worse every time he was rode at. Other riders had tried him with no better luck than the first, and when there came rumors of a rodeo being pulled off in town, one of the boys was for taking that horse to it and let him buck there. He was entered as a tryout bucking horse, and he'd bucked so well that before the contest was over that horse had been promoted to a final horse, amongst the hardest of the buckers. Then Bill Huff had sold him as a bucker for two hundred dollars.

Well, it seemed like Dusty had sure done a good job in giving Capitan the free rein. He'd given him so much free rein that it now looked like he'd never catch up with him. But Dusty had nowheres near given up the chase. Capitan was the one horse in a lifetime to him, the one perfect horse, and of the kind he'd sort of lost hope of ever running across.

If he hadn't had the bad luck of a knot-headed bronc falling on him and laying him flat, Capitan would now be his instead of belonging to somebody else and being shipped from one rodeo to another as a bucking horse. It didn't matter to Dusty if Capitan had turned bucker; he was a young horse and he'd get over that. The main thing that worried him was if the new owner would part with him.

It wasn't many days later when he seen that new owner and found out he wouldn't part with Capitan for no love nor money. It was while a rodeo was going on, and when Dusty seen that horse buck he seen plenty of reasons why he couldn't be bought. Capitan had sure turned wicked.

Dusty was in a worse fix than ever towards getting that horse now. But he didn't lose sight of him. He followed him to two more rodeos, and his heart sort of bled every time he seen him buck out into the arena. That horse, he felt, was too much horse to be no more than just a bucker. It had been his intentions to take that out of him soon as he got him away from Bill Huff and make a top cow horse out of him; he had the brains and Dusty knowed he'd of made a dandy.

Being he hadn't as yet got over his injuries, Dusty didn't compete in the rodeos. He just stuck around. And one day it came to him to ask Tom Griffin, the owner of the bucking stock, for a job helping in the shipping and taking care of the bucking horses. He had to follow along to two more rodeos before he got that job, and by the time he worked at it for a month or so, Griffin was so pleased with Dusty that after the last rodeo of the season was pulled off he gave him the job of taking care of the bucking horses for the whole winter and till the season opened up again next early summer. Dusty was happy and felt he now had a mane holt towards what he was after.

Dusty was alone at a camp that winter. He had charge of sixty head of bucking horses and fifty head of Mexico longhorns that was used for bucking, roping, and bulldogging. The stock run out on good range, and in case of bad weather there was hay by the corrals for him to feed to 'em. He had plenty of grub and smoking and he was all set.

It was during that winter that Dusty went to doing something that made him feel sort of guilty. He was in good shape to ride again by then, and it would of struck anybody queer that knowed the bucking horses, more so Griffin, if they'd seen him pick on the worst one in the string, Capitan, and go to riding that horse.

But Dusty wasn't out for the fun of riding a bucker when he straddled Capitan; he was out to make that horse quit being a bucker and make him worthless as such, and that's what made him feel guilty. He was spoiling his boss' best bucking horse by taking the buck out of him.

The only consolation Dusty had was by repeating to himself that there was lots of good bucking horses and that Capitan was too good to be one, and when the thought came to him that that horse would most likely be his after the first rodeo was pulled off, that sort of washed away all the guilty feelings he might of had.

Dusty about earned that horse before the hard bucking jumps at every saddling dwindled down to crow hops. Spring was breaking and Capitan still had plenty of buck in him, and any rider that could of went so far with such a horse was sure worth a heap of consideration, because few of 'em ever stayed over a few jumps while that horse bucked in the arenas. Of course there the riders had to ride by rules, and it's harder to sit a bucking horse that way than it is when there's no rules and all you have to do is stay on top.

By the time the snow all went away and the grass got tall and green, Dusty was using Capitan for a saddle horse, and what a saddle horse he turned out to be! As good as he'd been a bucking horse, and that's saying something. And now the only thing that worried Dusty was how Griffin was going to take it when he seen that horse come out of the chute and not buck, or would he go to bucking again? If he did there'd be no hope of Dusty ever owning him.

The day came when all the stock was gathered and preparations was made for the first rodeo of the year. Capitan didn't look like he'd ever had a saddle on that winter, and with the care that Dusty gave him—extra feeds of grain and all—he was as round and fat as a seal. Griffin looked at him and smiled.

But that smile faded when that horse came out of the chute on that first rodeo, for Capitan just crow-hopped a couple of jumps and trotted around like the broke saddle horse he was. The cowboy hooked him a couple of times and all he could get out of him was a couple more gentle crow hops. That cowboy had to get a reride on another bucking horse so he could qualify. Dusty was just as happy as Griffin was surprised and disappointed. Griffin couldn't figure out how that horse quit bucking, for he'd expected him to be a top at that for quite a few years. He couldn't suspicion Dusty of having anything to do with it; he'd never seen Dusty ride and it would never come to his mind that any cowboy could take the buck out of such a horse, not when that horse had it in him so natural.

But Griffin wasn't going to lose hope of that horse ever bucking again. He put him in the tryouts twice a day. Capitan didn't at all do at first, but before the last day of the contest came it looked like he was beginning to turn loose and go to bucking again. Griffin begin to smile and Dusty begin to worry.

It was two weeks before time for another rodeo. In that time Dusty took charge of the horses again and held 'em in a pasture not far out of town. It was there that Dusty took the buck out of Capitan once more. It was easier this time because he hadn't accumulated much.

The same thing happened at the second rodeo as with the first. Capitan wouldn't buck, and every cowboy that came out on him wanted a reride, "on a bucking horse," they said, "not a saddle horse."

Capitan began to loosen up some more before the end of that second rodeo; but by the time Dusty got through with him in the three weeks before the next rodeo that horse was scared to buck, and when that third contest did open up and Capitan couldn't be made to buck was when Griffin sort of lost his temper. The cowboys had been digging into him about bringing in gentle horses and trying to make bucking horses out of 'em, remarking that they was tired of asking for rerides and so on, till finally, when Capitan came out of the chute once more and only humped up as a cowboy hooked him, he lost his temper for good and passed the remark that he'd take two bits for that horse.

Dusty was standing close by, expecting him to say such a thing.

"I'll do better than that, Tom," he says. "I've got fifty dollars in wages coming that I'll give you for him."

Tom hardly looked at him. He scribbled out a bill of sale and passed it to Dusty. Dusty folded the bill of sale, stuck it in a good safe pocket of his vest, and started to walk away. Tom sort of star-gazed at him as he did, still dazed by the way Capitan quit bucking after every rodeo. Then, as he watched Dusty walk away so spry, the whole conglomeration came to him as clear as day. He was the one that wanted the horse.

"Hey, Dusty!" he hollered. Dusty stopped and looked back. "You're fired," he says.

"I know it," says Dusty, grinning, and walked on.

Capitan was led out of the bucking string of horses, saddled, and peacefully rode out of town. When the lanes was left behind and open country was all around, Dusty ran his fingers through the silky mane of the bay and says:

"All is fair in love as in war."

Will James

ONCE A COWBOY

It was a mean fall, and on that account the round-up wagons was late with the works, and later getting in at the winter quarters. The cold raw winds of the early mornings wasn't at all agreeable to get up in, and I'd just about got so I could choke the cook when he hollered "Come and get it, you rannies, before I throw it out." We'd hear that holler long before daybreak, and sticking our heads out from under our tarps we'd greet the new day with a cuss word and a snort.

A wet snow would be falling and laying heavy on our beds, and feeling around between the tarp and blankets for socks we'd took off wet the night before, we'd find 'em froze stiff, but by the time they was pulled on and made to fit again and the boots over 'em, buckled on chaps and all what we could find to keep a feller warm, we wasn't holding no grudge against the cook, we just wanted a lot of that strong steaming hot coffee he'd just made and had waiting for us.

The bunch of us would amble up and around the fire like a pack of wolves, only there was no growling done; instead there'd be remarks passed around such as, "This is what makes a cowboy wonder what he done with his summer's wages." There'd be a whoop and a holler and a bucking cowhand would clatter up near top of the pots by the fire, "Make room, you waddies, Ise frizzed from my brisket both ways," and slapping his hands to his sides would edge in on the circle and grin at the bunch there before him.

The lids of the big dutch ovens was lifted, steaks, spuds and biscuits begin to disappear, but tracks was made most often toward the big coffeepot, and when the bait is washed down and the blood begins to circulate freer there was signs of daybreak, and rolling a cigarette we'd head for the muddy rope corral.

Our ropes would be stiff as cables, and it was hard to make a good catch. The particular pony you'd be wanting would most generally stick his head in the ground like a ostrich, and mixed in with about two hundred head of his kind and all a milling around steady, he'd be mighty hard to find again in case you missed your first throw.

Daylight being yet far off at that time, there's no way to identify any of the ten or twelve horses in your string only by the outline of their heads against the sky or by the white there may be on their foreheads. You throwed your rope but you couldn't see it sail and you didn't know you'd caught your horse till you felt the rope tighten up, and sometimes when you'd led out the horse you'd caught and got close to him it'd be another horse—the one you'd throwed the rope at had heard it coming and ducked.

Turning that horse back in the corral, you'd make another loop and try to get another sight of the horse you wanted; when you did, and the rope settled on him this time and let him out—if he didn't have to be drug out by a saddle horse—to your saddle, then's when the fun most generally did begin.

The snow and sleet and cold wind made the ponies, young or old, mighty sensitive to whatever touched 'em; they'd kick, and buck, and strike then, no matter how gentle some of 'em might of been when the nice weather was on. The cowboy, all bundled up on account of the cold, his feet wet and in the slippery mud the wet snow had made, finds it all a big drawback in handling himself when saddling and a flying hoof comes.

The shivering pony don't at all welcome the frozen and stiff saddle blanket, and it might have to be put on the second time; getting a short hold and hanging on to the hackamore rope the cowboy then picks up the saddle and eases it on that pony's back, and before that pony can buck it off, a reach is made for the cinch, the latigo put through the cinch ring and drawed up. If you work fast enough and know how, all that can be done, and you don't have to pick up your saddle and blanket out of the mud.

I've seen it on many a morning of that kind and you'd just about have your pony half in the humor of being good, when some roman-nosed lantern-jawed bronc would go to acting up, jerk away from a rider and try to kick him at the same time and go to bucking and a bawling, and with an empty saddle on his back, hackamore rope a dragging, would make a circle of the rope corral where all the boys would be saddling up.

The ponies led out and shivering under the cold saddle that put a hump in their backs would just be a waiting for such an excuse as that loose hunk of tornado to start 'em, and with a loud snort and a buck half of 'em would jerk away. The cowboy had no chance holding 'em, for nine times out of ten that loose bronc would stampede past between him and the horse he was trying to hold, the hackamore rope would hook on the saddle of that bronc and it'd be jerked out of his hands.

Those folks who've seen rodeos from the grand stand most likely remember the last event of each day's doings; it's the wild-horse race, and maybe it'll be recollected how the track gets tore up by them wild ponies and how if one horse jerks loose he'll most likely make a few others break away. At them rodeos there's two men handling each horse, where with the round-up wagon on the range each man handles his horse alone.

And just picture for yourself the same happenings as you seen in the wild-horse race at the rodeo, only just add on to the picture that it's not near daylight, that instead of good sunshine and dry dirt to step on there's mud or gumbo six inches deep with snow and slush on top, the cowboy's cold wet feet, heavy wet chaps and coat that ties him down—a black cloudy sky, and with the cold raw wind comes a wet stinging snow to blind him.

That gives you a kind of an idea of how things may be along with the round-up wagon certain times of the year. Montana and Wyoming are real popular for rough weather as I've just described, and you can look for it there most every spring till late and sometimes in the fall starting early. I've seen that kind of weather last for two weeks at the time, clear up for one day and it was good to last for two weeks more.

It was no country for a tenderfoot to go playing cowboy in, besides the ponies of them countries wouldn't allow him to. It took nothing short of a long lean cowboy raised in the cow country to ride in it, and even though he'd cuss the weather, the country, and everything in general, there was a feeling back of them cuss words that brought a loving grin for the whole and the same that he was cussing.

Getting back to where a cowboy was saddling his horse and the stampeding bronc started the rumpus, I'll make it more natural and tell of how one little horse of that kind and on them cold mornings can just set the whole remuda saddled ponies and all to stampeding and leave near all the cowboys afoot.

Yessir, I remember well one cold drizzly morning that same fall, the wind was blowing at sixty per, the saddle blanket and saddle had to be put on at the same time or it'd blow out of the country. My horse was saddled and ready to top off, and pulling my hat down as far as I could get it I proceeds to do that. I'm getting a handful of mane along with a short holt on my reins and am just easing up in the saddle. When I gets up about half ways I meets up with the shadow of another horse trying to climb up on the other side of my horse. Me being only about a thousand pounds lighter than that shadow I'm knocked out of the way pronto, my horse goes down on part of me and that shadow keeps on a going as though there'd been nothing in its road.

That seemed to start things, and the wind that was blowing plenty strong already got a heap stronger, and all at once.

There was a racket of tearing canvas down by the chuck wagon and soon enough the big white tarpaulin that was covering that wagon breaks loose, comes a skipping over the brush, and then sails right up and amongst the two hundred saddle horses in the rope corral.

Them ponies sure didn't wait to see how and where it was going to light, they just picked up and flew, taking rope corral and everything right with 'em. A couple of the boys that was already mounted had to go too or else quit the pony they was riding, and they didn't have time to do that.

My horse being down for just the second he was knocked that way was up and gone, and I sure has to do some tall scrambling when the remuda broke out of the corral. I could near touch 'em as they went by and I'm drawing a long breath for the narrow escape I just had, when that same long breath is knocked out of me and I sails a ways, then lands in a heap. There must of been one horse I hadn't accounted for.

It's about daylight when I comes to enough to realize that I should pick myself up and get out of that brush I'd lit into. I'm gazing around kind of light-headed and wonders where everybody went, and finally, figgering that they'd be by the fire at the chuck wagon, makes my way that direction.

It's broad daylight by the time we hears the bells of the remuda coming back to the corral, some of the boys had put it up again while I was asleep in the brush, and the two riders what stampeded away when the remuda did was hazing the spooky ponies in again.

"Well, boys, we'll try it again," says the wagon boss as he dabs his rope on a big brown horse that was tearing around the corral.

Most of our ponies being already saddled it don't take us long to get lined out again. The boss is up on his horse, taking a silent count to see if any of his men are missing, while waiting for everybody to be on their horses and ready to follow him.

Our horses was all spooked up from that stampede, and when we started away from camp that morning it was a wild bunch for fair. I was trying to ease my pony into a lope without him breaking in two with me, and I just about had him out of the notion when there's a beller alongside of me, and I turns to see a bucking streak of horseflesh with a scratching cowboy atop of it headed straight my way.

It's a good thing I was ready to ride, 'cause my horse had been aching to act up from the start, and that example headed our way more than agreed with his spirits at that time. He went from there and started to wipe up the earth, and every time he'd hit the ground he'd beller, "I'll get you!"

At first I was satisfied to just be able to keep my saddle under me, but come a time when as my blood started circulating and getting warmed up on the subject that my spirits also answered the call and agreed with the goings on; then's when I begins to reefing him, and my own special war whoop sure tallied up with the bellering of that active volcano under me.

A glance to one side, and I notice that I'm not the only one who's putting up a ride, the rain and snow mixed kept me from seeing very far, but I could see far enough to tell that at least half the riders was busy on the same engagement that drawed my attention just then; one of the ponies had took a dislike for the cook and, tearing up everything as he went, was chasing him over pots and pans and finally under the wagon. The cowboy on top of that bronc was near losing his seat for laughing; he'd never seen the cook move that fast before.

We're out of camp a couple of miles before the usual rumpus quiets down, and stringing out on a high lope we all heads for a high point we don't see but know of, and some ten miles away. From that point the boss scatters the riders, and in pairs we branch out to circle and comb the country on the way back, running all the stock we see to the cutting grounds.

I'm riding along, trying to look through the steady-falling drizzle snow for stock; it seemed to me that I was born and raised under a slicker, on a wet saddle, riding a kinky bronc, going through slush and snow, and facing cold winds. It struck me as a coon's age since I seen good old sunshine, and for the first time I begins to wonder if a cow-puncher ain't just a plain locoed critter for sticking along with the roundup wagons as he does; it's most all knocks, and starting from his pony's hoofs on up to the long sharp horns of the ornery critters he's handling, along with the varieties the universe hands him in weather—twelve to sixteen hours in the saddle, three to four changes of horses a day, covering from seventy-five to a hundred miles, then there's one to two hours night guard to break the only few hours left to get rest in.

We was moving camp for the last time that year, the next stop was the home ranch, and when we hooked up the cook's six-horse team and handed him the ribbons we all let out a war whoop that started the team that direction on a high lope. The cook wasn't holding 'em back any, and hitting it down a draw to the river bottoms the flying chuck wagon swayed out of sight.

Us riders was bringing in upwards of a thousand head of weaners and we didn't reach the big fields till late that day, when we finally got sight of the big cottonwoods near hiding the long log building of the home ranch; that, along with the high pole corrals, the sheds and stables, all looked mighty good to me again.

The stock turned loose, we all amble towards the corrals to unsaddle; I tries to lead my horse in the dry stable, but him being suspicious of anything with a roof on won't have it that way. "All right, little horse," I says to him, "if you're happier to be out like you've always been used to, I'm not going to try to spoil you," and pulling off my wet saddle I hangs it where it's dry for once. The pony trots off a ways, takes a good roll and, shaking himself afterwards, lets out a nicker and lopes out to join the remuda.

"Just like us punchers," I remarks, watching him; "don't know no better."

Over eight months had passed since I'd opened a door and set my feet on a wooden floor, and when I walks in the bunk house and at one end sees a big long table loaded down with hot victuals, and chairs to set on, I don't feel at all natural, but I'm mighty pleased at the change.

The ranch cook is packing in more platters, and watching him making tracks around the table, looking comfortable and not at all worried of what it may be like outside, I'll be daggone if I didn't catch myself wishing I was in his warm moccasins.

The meal over with, I drags a bench over by one of the windows and, listening some to the boys what was going over the events that happened on the range that summer, I finds myself getting a lot of satisfaction from just a-setting there and looking out of the window; it was great to see bum weather and still feel warm and comfortable. I gets to stargazing and thinking, so that I plum forgets that there's twenty cowboys carrying on a lot of conversation in the same big room.

I'd just about come to the conclusion I was through punching cows when one of the boys digs me in the ribs and hollers, "Wake up, Bill! Time for second guard."

I did wake up, and them familiar words I'd heard every night for the last eight months struck me right where I lived; they was said as a joke, but right there and then I was sure I'd never want to stand no more of them midnight guards.

The work was over, and all but a few of the old hands was through. The superintendent gave us to understand as a parting word that any or all of us are welcome to stay at the ranch and make ourselves to home for the winter. "You can keep your private saddle horses in the barn and feed 'em hay. The cow foreman tells me," he goes on, "that you've all been mighty good cowboys, and I'm with him in hoping to see you all back with the outfit in time for the spring works."

A couple of days later finds me in town, my own top horse in the livery stable and me in a hotel. I makes a start to be anything but a cowboy by buying me a suit, a cap, shoes, and the whole outfit that goes with the town man. I then visits the barber and the bathtub, and in an hour I steps out thinking that outside my complexion and the way I walks I looks about the same as everybody else I see on the street.

I takes it easy for a few days, then gradually I tries to break myself to looking for a job where there's no ponies or bellering critters to contend with. I wanted an inside job where the howling blizzard wouldn't reach me and where I could have a roof over my head at night instead of a tarpaulin.

Time goes on, and it seems like my education is lacking considerable to qualify for the job I set out to get; you had to know as much as a schoolma'am to even get a look in. I made a circle every day and run in all the likely places I'd see.

I'm some leg weary as I makes my way back to the hotel one night, and going to my room I stretches out on the bed to rest up a little before I go out to eat. I have a feeling that all ain't well with me as I lays there thinking.

I don't want to think that I'm hankering to get back to the range, so blames it to the new ways of everything in general what comes with town life, and I tries to cheer myself up with the idea that I'll soon get used to it and in time like it.

"I got to like it," I says to myself, "and I'm going to stay with it till I do, 'cause I'm through with punching cows"; and getting up real determined I goes out to hunt a restaurant.

I'd been feeding up on ham and eggs and hamburger steak with onions ever since I hit town, and this night I thought I'd change my order to something more natural and what I'd been used to on the range.

"Bring me a rib steak about an inch thick," I says to the waiter. "Don't cook it too much, but just cripple the critter and drag 'er in."

I kept a waiting for the order to come, and about concluded he must of had to wait for the calf to grow some, when here he comes finally. I tackles the bait on the platter, and I was surprised to see a piece so much like beef, and still taste so different from any I'd ever et before. With a lot of work I managed to get away with half of it, and then my appetite, game as it was, had to leave me.

The waiter comes up smiling as he sees I'm about through, and hands me the bill. "I don't want to spread it around," I says as I picks up the bill and goes to leave, "but between you and me, I'll bet you that steak you brought me has been cooked in the same grease that's been cooking my ham and eggs these last two weeks. I can taste 'em."

The weather had been good and stayed clear ever since I hit town, but as I walks out of the restaurant I notice a breeze had sprung up, and snow was starting to fall. I finds myself taking long whiffs of air that was sure refreshing after stepping out of that grub-smelling emporium.

Feeling rested up some, I faces the breeze for a walk and to no place in particular. I'm walking along, thinking as I go, when looking around to get the lay of my whereabouts I notices that right across the street from where I'm standing is the livery stable where I'd left my horse, and being that I'd only been over to see him once since I'd rode in, thinks I'd enjoy the feel of his hide once more.

The stable man walks in on us as we're getting real sociable, and with a "Howdy" asks if I may be looking for a job. "Man named Whitney, got a ranch down the river about fifty miles, asked me to look out for a man who'd want a job breaking horses on contract, and I thought maybe you'd be wanting to take it."

"Not me," I says, feeling tempted and refusing before considering. "I'm not riding any more, and I been looking for work in town."

"Did you try the Hay and Grain Market next block up the street?" he asks. "They was looking for a man some time back."

No, I hadn't tried it, but the next day bright and early I was on the grounds and looking for the major-domo of that outfit.

At noon that day I'd changed my suit, and putting on a suit of Mexican serge I went to work. My job was clerking, and on the retail end of the business, filling in orders and help load the stuff on the wagon of the customers.

And that night, when the place closed up and I walks to my hotel I felt a heap better than any time since I'd hit town. Of course I wasn't in love with the job, it was quite a change and mighty tame compared to punching cows, but then I figgered a feller had to allow some so's to get what he's after.

I gets along fine with everybody around, and it ain't long before I'm invited to different gatherings that's pulled off now and again. I gets acquainted more as I stays on, and comes a time when if feeling sort of lonesome I know where to go and spend my evenings.

I'd manage to stop in at the stable and say "Hello" to my gray horse most every night when the work was through, and with everything in general going smooth I thought it wasn't so bad.

There was times though when coming to my room I'd find myself staring at my chaps and boots with the spurs still on and where I'd put 'em in the corner. They got to drawing my attention so that I had to hide 'em in the closet where I couldn't see 'em, and then I thinks, "What about my horse and saddle? A town man don't have no need for anything like that."

But somehow I didn't want to think on that subject none at all right then, and I drops it, allowing that a feller can't break away from what all he's been raised with or at in too short a time.

That winter was a mean one, just as mean as the fall before, I still remembered; the snow was piled up heavy on the hills around town and every once in a while there'd be another storm adding on a few inches. The sight of it and the cold winds a howling by on the streets kept me contented some, and it all helped break me in to the new ways of living I'd picked on.

I'd been on the job a month or so when I notice that my appetite begins to leave me. I changes eating places often, but they all seemed to have the same smell as you walked in, and there was times when I felt like taking the decorated platter and all outside and eating it there.

And what's more, my complexion was getting light, too light.

January and February had come and went, the cold spell broke up some, and then March set in wild and wicked. I'm still at my job at the Feed Market and my wages being raised once along with promises of another raise soon, proves that I'm doing well. What's more, my time had been took up considerable on account of me meeting up with a young lady what put my gray horse a far second in my thoughts, and when I'd walk past the stable I'd most generally be in too big a hurry to stop and see him. One day the stable man stops me as I'm hurrying by and tells me that he has a chance to sell that little horse for me for a hundred dollars.

That was a call for a show-down to myself, and of a sudden I realized that parting with that horse I was parting with the big open range I'd been born and raised into. I studies it over for quite a spell and finds the more I thinks the more my heart lays the ways of where that horse can take me, and my mind all a milling I can't decide.

I walks away, telling the stable man I'd let him know later.

I does a lot of comparing between the range and the town, and finds that both has qualities and drawbacks, only in town it was easier living, maybe too easy, but I figgered that here was more of a future.

Just the other day I was told by the main owner at the market that they was figgering on quitting the business and retiring, and that there'd be a good opportunity for a serious-thinking man like myself to grab. It was suggested that I could let my wages ride and buy shares with 'em as I worked till there'd come a time as I kept at it when I'd find myself part owner of a good business and a steady income.

That night I went to see the young lady, who by this time had a lot to say as to my actions. I didn't let her know what was going on in my think tank, 'cause I wanted to fight it out by myself; besides I'd come to conclusions, and long before I left her to go back to my hotel.

The next morning I stops by and tells the stable man that if he can get a hundred dollars for that little horse of mine, to take it. But it hit me pretty hard and I didn't go by the stable any more after that, not for a long time.

April come, and with the warm weather that came with it the snow started to melting, the streets was muddy, and the gutters was running full; it was spring, and even with all the resolutions I'd made, I didn't feel any too strong right then.

I was afraid to give my imagination full swing and think of the home ranch on the Big Dry; I knew the boys that came back for the spring works would be out on the horse round-up and getting ready to pull out with the wagons.

Each cowboy would be topping off his string about now, the bronc peeler would be picking out a bunch of green colts from the stock horses and start in breaking, the cook would be a cleaning up the chuck box on the back end of that wagon, and the cow foreman, glancing often on the road that leads from town to the ranch, would be looking for any of the missing cowboys what was with him the year before.

I found it mighty hard to walk away from that spring sunshine into the building where I was working. There was orders on the desk waiting for me to fill, and picking 'em up I walks among high walls of grain and baled hay.

Everybody I'd see would remark how great it was outside in the spring air, and rubbing their hands would get to work at the desk and typewriter, and forget all about it the minute they set down.

I felt sorry for 'em in a way, 'cause it struck me as though they'd never had a chance to really appreciate springtime—or was it that their years in captivity that way had learnt 'em better than to hanker for such?

Anyway, I sure didn't seem to be able to dodge how I felt. My girl and everybody else noticed it, and even though I'd try to laugh it off I'd soon find myself picturing little white-faced calves scattered out either playing or sunning themselves while their mammies was feeding on the new green grass.

I could near feel the slick shiny hide of the ponies after their long winter hair had just fell off. And dag-gone it, it was getting the best of me.

I'd catch myself sneaking glances at the green hills around the town and feeling as though I had no right to. And once in a while in the evening as I'd be walking to my room and I'd hear a meadow lark a-singing way off in the distance, I'd look at the buildings, the sidewalks and streets as though they was a scab on this earth. I wanted my horse under me and lope out away from it.

I'd done a heap of reasoning with myself, and kept a pointing out all the whys I should forget the range and get used to the town, and I'd pretty near give in as long as I was in my room and couldn't feel the breeze, but once outside again and a meadow lark sang out, my heart would choke out all what the town offered and leave breath only for the blue ridges and the big stretches that layed past 'em.

Then came a day when my hide got too thick to feel the reasoning spur I was giving it. Something way deep inside of me took charge of things and I finds myself making tracks towards the stable.

I sneaks in, and I had to rub my eyes considerable to make sure that there in the same box stall was my little gray horse, fat as a seal and a snorting like a steam engine.

"Dag-gone your hide!" I says, and I makes a grab for him, he's pawing the air snorting and a rearing, but I'm hanging on to his neck with a death grip and hands him all the pet cuss words I can think of.

The stable man runs up to see what's making all the rumpus, and his expression tell me plain he thinks I'm drunk and celebrating. I was drunk all right, but not on the same stuff that's handed over the bar.

"Sorry I couldn't sell him for you," I hear him say as I let go of my horse and walks up to him, "but the fellow what wanted him came over one day to try the horse out and the little son of a gun throwed him off as fast as he'd get on; he brought another feller over the next day and the same thing happened. Too bad he acts that way," he goes on, " 'cause he's a right pretty horse."

"You're dag-gone right he's a pretty horse," I says; "the prettiest horse I ever seen."

It's three days later when I gets sight of the Triangle F main herd, then the remuda, and down in a creek bottom by a bunch of willows is the chuck wagon.

There's war whoops from the bunch as I lopes into sight, and the wagon boss comes up to meet me. "I knowed you'd be back, Bill," he says, smiling, "and I got your string of ponies a waiting for you, twelve of 'em."

And on guard that night, riding around the bedded herd, I was singing a song of the trail herd, happy again, and just a cowboy.

Clarence Day

MOTHER AND OUR WICKED MARE

Mother never thought of the horse as the friend and companion of man. She looked at all horses suspiciously. Perhaps they were not wild animals, in the sense in which lions and zebras were wild, but still there was something strange about them. They weren't really tame, like our dogs. She loved dogs. She liked ponies too, they were more our own size, but horses were too large to be trusted, and they had ironshod feet.

Once in a while she grew fond of some special horse after she had watched it for years, but even then she never undertook to drive it herself. Driving was a man's job. That didn't mean that she thought men in general were good drivers, however. Mother hadn't any more confidence in men in general than she had in horses. Men were always assuring her that they knew how to do this or that, when they didn't at all. If it had been safe to do so, she would have liked to trust herself in their hands, it would have been so convenient, for as she was a woman she felt that she had to have certain things done for her. But men, although stronger, were childish. They greatly over-estimated their ability as drivers, for instance. All of them firmly believed that they understood horses, whereas Mother knew better. When she saw a horse and a man having trouble, she privately bet on the horse.

In the nineties everybody used horses—if in no other way at least in horse-cars and buses. Our family needed several every summer when we lived in the country. One was reserved solely as a saddle-horse for Father to ride. Father rode early every morning before breakfast and then took a train to the city. The other horses were used for all sorts of things. What with catching trains, mornings, and meeting them again, afternoons, and going for the mail, or taking some of us down to the beach, or trotting along the dusty country roads with Mother when she paid an afternoon call on some friend three or four miles away, or when she went to the village to shop, our horses were kept pretty busy, and when one of them had to be turned out to rest, it was hard on the others.

Mother at last went to Father about it. She said that things had come to a point where we had to have one more horse.

Father said, "The trouble with you, Vinnie, is that you don't use enough forethought. You don't plan these things out. With a little careful management you can get along with what we have now."

Mother replied that there wasn't a woman on earth who could plan every minute, and she'd like to see forethought pull the station-wagon when Brownie went lame, but if we used Father's saddle-horse in the dog-cart perhaps that would do.

From Father's point of view this was blasphemous. "Any time that I can't have even one horse in condition to ride," he told Mother, "I'll sell the whole lot of them, hide and hair, and the family can walk. Do 'em good."

He got thinking things over after this conversation however, and made up his mind that he'd better do something about it and look around for some decent animal that could be got cheap. He heard of one soon at the club, a dark brown, muscular mare.

The member of the club who owned her had gone abroad and couldn't be reached. He had posted the mare for sale with the cryptic phrase, "Warranted sound." The usual guarantee, when there was any, was "Warranted sound, kind and willing," but we thought that perhaps the omission was inadvertent. The price was low. Father bought her.

This mare's name was Uarda, a strange name, but somehow it fitted her. We heard later that an Egyptian princess named Uarda, of evil repute, had lived a bad life in some dynasty centuries back. Whether Uarda the mare had come from Egypt too, nobody knew. She looked it, however. She looked like the horse of some genie in the *Arabian Nights*. She was slithery, bony and lean, and her coat had a glitter, and her eyes were unnaturally greenish and wild and unfathomable.

There was plenty of work in her. She never went lame or got tired. She seemed made of steel. Sudden sights or sounds that made other horses shy, Uarda ignored. She was wholly without fear, and there wasn't an ounce of love in her either. She was oblivious of the Day family, and not interested in her surroundings.

O'Dowd the coachman was frankly afraid of her. "She's always brooding, sir," he whispered to Father, as though she could understand what he said and revenge herself on him. She certainly had a remote and contemptuous look.

Uarda's contempt could be seen in her eye. Her hatred she expressed with her tail. All carriage horses were docked in those days, many of them too much, but Uarda from O'Dowd's point of view hadn't been docked enough. She had an extra long bone in her tail, he explained, and it had only been shortened a trifle. And the muscle in her tail, which was strong as steel, hadn't been nicked. The purpose of nicking the under muscle was to weaken it, so that a horse's little bobbed tail would stand cocked up and look stylish, and aside from looks there was a practical advantage to this, because it prevented a horse from catching a rein under his tail and clamping it down. When that happened, he couldn't be reined in or guided, and now and then that led to a runaway or some bad collision.

Humanitarians were always denouncing men who docked horses' tails. A horse with a docked tail was helpless in fly-time, they argued, and when it was chopped off it hurt. Father pished at those arguments. He said that it wasn't his fault if there were flies in the world, and that nobody wept over him when his teeth were chopped by the dentist.

He wouldn't have a horse docked himself though. He simply bought them that way. When O'Dowd wanted Uarda's tail shortened, Father wouldn't allow it. O'Dowd shook his head over this. He said we'd live to regret it.

We came to see what he meant. As Uarda sullenly trotted along, thinking of sin, or black magic, she would flail her tail round and round powerfully, like a propeller. Sooner or later, no matter how careful O'Dowd was, she'd catch a rein under it, and hold that rein tight as a vise. With some horses you could watch till the muscle relaxed for a moment and then vigorously yank the rein out, but no one could do this with Uarda. The only thing to do was to reach over the dashboard and yank at her tail, and yank hard with all your strength too, and yank over and over, hoping that she wouldn't lash out and kick you before you got the rein loose. This was an undignified performance to go through, and O'Dowd felt it shamed him in public.

What mortified him still more was the way Mother behaved at such moments. At the very first sign of trouble Mother's one idea was to get out of the carriage just as quick as she could. She couldn't jump, her skirts were too long and voluminous and there were too many petticoats under them, but she could and did shout to O'Dowd to stop, at the top of her voice, and then gather up her dress in one hand and clutch at the arm of the seat and feel around with her foot for the inadequate little round metal steps, which always seemed so high from the ground when she hadn't any horse-block to step out onto, and then while the springy surrey was shaking, and giving a bit on one side, she would precariously descend in a hurry, getting dust or mud on her skirts from the wheel, and more on her high buttoned shoes in the old-fashioned dirt road.

Standing there in safety she would stare at O'Dowd while he yanked. She would also make comments. When this happened way off on some deserted road it wasn't so bad, but sometimes it happened on Purchase Street in Rye, where other coachmen were watching, or outside old Mr. Raser's store opposite the station in Harrison. "Mercy on us, what takes you so *long,* O'Dowd?" Mother would cry. "If you can't drive any better than that, why don't you say so?"

O'Dowd was a good-natured soul, but he knew he could drive as well as most coachmen, and he used to get silently exasperated on these occasions. It was useless for him, though, to attempt to lay the blame upon Uarda, or to say he had never seen such a horse in all his born days. "Never mind about all your born days, O'Dowd," Mother would tell him impatiently. "That horse knows more than you do, this minute, and I should think that you'd be ashamed to sit there and admit it."

As O'Dowd had never even dreamt of admitting it, this kind of attack used to stagger him. "I know as much as any horse in the stable, Mum," he would begin, in confusion.

"But you ought to know *more* than an animal!" Mother would interrupt swiftly. "That's what we pay you your wages for, O'Dowd. You're a *man,* not a horse. If you don't know any more than our horses you ought not to be driving them. It really isn't safe for me to go out with you."

"Not an accident have I ever had on my soul, Mrs. Day, in all the twenty years that—"

"You'll have one this very minute if you can't get that rein out," Mother would interrupt sharply.

As O'Dowd knew that this was highly probable he would concentrate upon Uarda, and when he had got her under control again Mother would climb back into the carriage, still talking, and off they would go.

Somehow O'Dowd never seemed to feel any resentment toward Mother, after a scene of this sort. He understood Mother. His hostility was all toward that mare. On Uarda's bad days he got into such a bitter state, as he drove her about, that he used to carry on a one-sided conversation with her, in a low growling mutter. "Oho! That's the way of it, is it? Trying it on me again! Ye black-hearted Eye-gyptian! Bad scran to ye, ye limb of the Divil, ye!"

After a while he invented an arrangement of buckles and straps, which moored Uarda's tail to the shafts. This contraption left her tail just leeway enough for her to arch it but kept her from flailing it around or getting it over the reins. She was in a cold fury about it. O'Dowd wore a broad grin.

These moorings were so elaborate that they were unsightly, however. They looked very odd. Mother complained that everyone stared at them, which was perfectly true. People even asked questions. Mr. Read, who was a judge at the horseshow, and who had supposed himself to be familiar with every kind of harness there was, couldn't get his eyes off them when Mother went to call on his wife and when he came forward to help her get out at his door. "Ah," he said, staring fixedly at the bright silver buckle in the middle of Uarda's slick tail, and the leather shrouds and stays that led down from it to either shaft, "Ah! May I ask what this—er—? Why this—?"

"Oh, don't pay any attention to that, Mr. Read," Mother answered. "Our coachman seems to feel he can't drive without it. It's just some idea of O'Dowd's." And she hurried up the piazza steps, leaving O'Dowd red and speechless, and taking Mr. Read with her, so mystified by what he had seen and so baffled for the moment by Mother that he became speechless too.

As for Father, he said it was a disgusting arrangement, the first time he saw it, and he ordered O'Dowd to "remove that infernal rigging at once." But the fact remained that when we used them those straps were effective, and every time we went out without them, we got into trouble. Uarda never actually ran away when she got a rein under her tail, but she never would quite admit that she wasn't going to bolt, and she had such a wicked look about her that we knew things were dangerous. We all gradually came to tolerate letting O'Dowd strap her up, even Father. There was really only one safe alternative, when he left O'Dowd home and drove us around in the low surrey himself, and that was to hold the reins up very high, at the level almost of his nose. Father couldn't and wouldn't do that.

One day Father and Mother and George and I were out in the surrey. Father was driving of course, and I was sitting beside him on the front seat. Uarda was in a vile mood. Her tail strained at O'Dowd's straps and buckles. It writhed like a snake. Two or three miles from home she triumphantly tore it loose. "Oh, oh!" Mother wailed.

"Be quiet, confound it," said Father. "Clarence, can you strap it down again?"

I got out and tried but I couldn't strap it securely enough. Only O'Dowd knew the secret. No matter how I adjusted the buckles and hauled on the straps, Uarda contemptuously flicked her tail out. "Take it off altogether," Father ordered. "We'll never get home at this rate."

"I want to get out then," said Mother. "I'd much rather walk."

Father gritted his teeth. "Sit still," he said sharply. "I've driven horses since I was a boy."

Back-seat driving was invented long before motors, and when Mother was nervous she had a really deadly gift for this art. She tried to control herself that afternoon, at Father's repeated requests, but she couldn't. Uarda's tail was too much for her.

"I only bought this horse to please your mother," Father said in a loud, oratorical tone, as though he were making a speech, addressing his sons and the landscape in general as Uarda trotted along, "and if I ever saw any animal that came straight from hell—"

"She's swishing it, Clare," Mother called to him.

"She can swish and be hanged," Father said, feeling that he had his hands full, fore and aft, with these two unmanageable females who were spoiling his drive.

"Look out! Look out, Clare dear!"

"Vinnie, will you keep still!"

"I'm trying to, darling," screamed Mother, "but that awful horse— Oh! Oh! Look *out!*"

Father cut at Uarda's flanks with the whip.

"Clare! *Do* please be careful!"

"I *am* being careful. Be quiet."

"There she goes again! Oh Clare, let me out!"

"See here," Father said to her sternly, turning half-around in his seat, "if you cannot control yourself—"

Swish! Uarda's tail caught the rein.

Father swore and leaned forward and pulled on it. Uarda came to a stop. We were on our way up a long hill at the moment, and Father had just begun walking her. Luckily for us, she now decided it was a good place to rest.

Father jerked at the rein twice more—once cautiously, and once with more force. Uarda held it clamped tight to her rump. Her ears went back. She snorted.

"Oh mercy! Let me get out of this!" Mother shrieked, and climbed down onto the road. "Come on, Georgie!"

George jumped out beside her. It was a narrow road with a ditch on each side. She scrambled across the ditch to safety, and stood on the steep, grassy bank.

Father felt deeply insulted at this lack of confidence in him. His blood surged to his face, his eyes popped with passion. He stood up, facing a little sidewise, took the rein in both hands, set his jaws, and gave one mighty yank. At that very instant Uarda, with the skill of a demon, let go. Father fell over backward out of the surrey and crashed into the ditch.

Mother screamed.

I leaned over the dashboard and got the reins. George ran to help Father. Uarda tossed her head and stood still.

Father rose from the ditch, muddy yet somehow majestic, and said to us, "It was your mother."

"Why, *Clare!*" Mother shouted indignantly from the opposite bank.

Cleveland Amory

OF HORSES AND THEIR HISTORY—WILD, DIVING, DOMESTIC, AND OTHERWISE

A ranch bearing the name Black Beauty could hardly be without horses. Our Ranch may not have started out to have been, first and foremost, a place for horses—that position was reserved, as befitting our most famous rescue, for burros. Nonetheless, from the beginning, our horses were, in the minds and hearts of all of us who had developed the Ranch, second only to our burros and came indeed not only to outnumber them but also to outnumber any other animal on the Ranch. From the beginning, too, we either attracted or rescued a truly extraordinary variety of horses—thoroughbreds and plough horses, racehorses and show horses, Arabians and Appaloosas, Morgans and miniatures, ponies and paints.

They came in every conceivable color—blacks and whites, grays and bays, chestnuts and pintos, sorrels and strawberry roans. One thing, however, almost all of them had in common—by the time they came to us they were, as were the other animals, either old and infirm, lost or abandoned, abused or misused. And every single one of them would learn, as the horse Black Beauty had put it in the last lines of the book, that, when they came to the Black Beauty Ranch, they had found a home which would be theirs for the rest of their lives.

The history of the horse in North America is a fascinating one. In the first place, all modern horses are believed to be linear descendants of the original horse, *Eohippus,* whose bones have been found in both Great Britain and America. In the second place, although the bones of *Eohippus* existed almost fifty million years ago, they were fairly recently discovered in, of all places, the Texas Panhandle. In the third place, although *Eohippus* was only ten hands tall—too small to defend himself and not fast enough to escape his enemies—he nonetheless managed, somehow or other, to exist for fifty million years. In the fourth and final place, after existing for all those years all of a sudden, like the dinosaurs, the horses disappeared. Furthermore, they disappeared along with the very companions with which they had lived—animals that ranged from dinosaurs to camels.

As in the case of the dinosaurs, historians have never been able to come up with a reason for this disappearance—with the single exception that, generally speaking, they believe Man was the culprit. Whether *Eohippus* and his ill-fated companions were hunted to death, raced to death, or eaten to death is not known, but the probability is that all three of these possibilities played a large part in their demises. In any case, what is known is that all of a sudden, and as suddenly as the horse disappeared, he and his companions reappeared—8,000 years after their disappearance.

Furthermore, the horse reappeared, at least in America, under the aegis of no less a renowned figure than the explorer Hernando Cortés. In 1519, on his first voyage to Mexico, Cortés brought horses with him, if for no other reason because, as he himself put it, he valued the life of a horse more than the lives of twenty of his men. When Cortés left Mexico for Seville he took what horses he had left with him—all except the foal of one mare who escaped and went wild. In 8,000 years she may conceivably have been, in all senses of the word—with the presumed aid of the stallion of some follower of Cortés—the founding mother of America's first wild horse dynasty.

Unfortunately the wild horses, or mustangs as they had come to be called, would undoubtedly have been better off if they had never reappeared, at least in North America. Although in time they grew far taller than their ancestors had been in the latters' previous existence, and although they were at least at first regarded as a vital and interesting phenomenon of the Old West, that feeling was all too short-lived. Indeed as the nineteenth century went on, and the cattlemen and sheepmen became more and more powerful, they decided that the wild horses were predators, if not of the cattle and sheep themselves, then at least of their grazings. In time these cattlemen and sheepmen used every means possible to exterminate the wild horses, even though, ironically, one of the main reasons for the increasing numbers of these horses was that in bad times, the cattlemen and sheepmen often simply released their own horses to fend for themselves and these, joining up with wild horse bands, became wild themselves.

No method was too cruel for the ranchers to use in their zeal to exterminate the wild horses—from poisoning their watering holes to blinding lead stallions by shooting their eyes out or just by running them to death, off and over cliffs. Not the least cruel method of wild horse capture was taking a group of already captured mustangs, sewing their nostrils together with rawhide so that they could barely breathe, and then returning them to another band. Here, since they could only run slowly, particularly in the heat, they would slow down the entire new band and make the new band's capture that much easier. As if all this was not enough, finally, in 1897, the Nevada legislature passed a law allowing wild horses to be shot on sight by any citizen.

The twentieth century was no better for the wild horse than the nineteenth. The cruelties were still inflicted on them, perhaps most memorably in the famous movie *The Misfits*. Ironically this movie, Clark Gable's last as well as that of Marilyn Monroe, befitted its title all too well since both stars, at least when they were working together, were so obviously miscast. Nonetheless, the portrayal of the mustangers and their brutality was unforgettable—except, of course, to the western ranchers, who dismissed it as being exaggerated and of course did nothing to address the problem.

One Nevada housewife, however, who had married a rancher, did do something about it. Her name was Velma Johnston. Small in stature, weighing less than a hundred pounds, she was a woman who had as a child suffered a severe case of polio which left much of her body and even part of her face misshapen. Nonetheless she also had had from childhood a remarkable combination of persistence and courage, and these traits were combined with a blazingly deep hatred of cruelty, all of which made her, from the moment she saw her first wild horse, one of the greatest animal friends ever.

When I first met her, she told me that although she had lived almost all her life in Nevada, where there are more wild horses than in any other state, it was relatively late in her life when she first saw one. "The fact that I never saw one," she said, her eyes sparkling with irony, "shows how much trouble to the ranchers they really were." Nonetheless, from the day she saw her first wild horse she never gave up her fight for them—even though, ironically, she saw that first wild horse purely by chance. What had happened was she was driving one day when she noticed in front of her car a truck carrying what she assumed to be a load of animals of some kind. But what she also noticed about this truck was that it was leaving a trail of blood.

That was enough for Mrs. Johnston. She followed the truck and, when it finally stopped, got out and demanded from the driver that she be allowed to look inside. The truck was literally crammed with what the driver told her, in a relatively unconcerned fashion, were wild horses. To her dying day Velma Johnston never forgot what sight greeted her eyes in that truck. One little foal had actually been trampled to death in the crowding of the animals. Another had no hooves at all. Where the hooves should have been had been worn down to bloody stumps. A stallion stood motionless, looking toward her, except that his eyes were shot out—he was totally blind. When she had seen all she could stand, Mrs. Johnston turned to the driver and asked him what had happened to the horses. He told her they had been "run down," as he put it, by airplanes.

Mrs. Johnston's next stop was at the district office of the Bureau of Land Management, the agency supposed to "look after" the wild horses and also the office from which permits were issued to "run" them, as it was called, from planes. All too typically Mrs. Johnston would later learn the Bureau director was very pleased to see her. He was also certain that she had come to praise his work. "By letting these profiteers run the horses," he told her, "we've been able to get them off the ranges to make more land available for your cattle and sheep." Mrs. Johnston could hardly believe his words, but the director went on. "It's all done without any expense to the taxpayer," he concluded proudly. "You see," he said, "everybody profits."

Mrs. Johnston didn't answer the man, but she had a special look for people like that. She also told me that she never forgot what that director said. Later, when she told her father what she was going to do, and how determined she was to fight for the wild horses, he did not try to stop her but asked only that she remember four things. "Dress like a lady," he said, "act like a lady, talk like a lady, but think like a man."

Such advice may seem not only old-fashioned but on the Neanderthal side today, but the fact is for that time, in that state, in that particular fight, it was good advice. And Mrs. Johnston abided by it, even when her fellow ranchers refused to call her by her real name but instead mocked her with the nickname they made up for her—"Wild Horse Annie." Tirelessly, with facts and figures and pictures and statistics about the cruelty, she went from legislator to legislator to ask that something be done about the horses. At first she had only one supporter, a state legislator named James Slattery. But on a memorable day in 1955 a so-called pro-wild horse bill, dubbed the "Wild Horse Annie Law," was adopted by the legislature.

Basically what the bill provided was the banning of the use of aircraft to round up or hunt wild horses, and also the prohibiting of the poisoning or pollution of watering holes. Remarkably, the ranchers and Annie's other opponents hardly bothered to fight her law. Their reason was a simple one. In their opinion, and accurately, Annie had spent four years fighting for virtually nothing. The law affected just state-owned land, and since 86 percent of Nevada was Federal land, what it amounted to was that Annie had been able to stop the cruelty in just 14 percent of the state.

By ignoring her law, however, the ranchers had underestimated Annie. She knew full well that her law affected only 14 percent of Nevada, and she also knew full well just how she would make use of that fact. Hardly was the ink dry on Nevada's "Wild Horse Annie Law" when Wild Horse Annie, who now proudly called herself by that name only, was on her way to Washington, D.C., fighting for a Federal law. "Look," she told every Senator and Congressman who would listen, "the poor people of Nevada are trying to protect their wild horses even though they know they can only protect them on just 14 percent of their land. Now they are begging you to allow them to protect those horses on the other 86 percent of their land."

This was actually, of course, some distance from the way all too many people in Nevada felt about wild horses, but Annie was at her persistent best in seeing that the people in Washington got the message anyway. Soon she was proving herself as adept at handling Federal legislators as she had been handling those at the state level. Again she had the facts and the figures, the pictures and the statistics. Besides this, she took advantage of every possibility that came her way.

The most remarkable of these was when a class of nine-year-old schoolchildren from Roseburg, Oregon, under the direction of their teacher, Ms. Joan Bolsinger, wrote to Annie in Washington, D.C., on behalf of the wild horses. Annie saw this as a very special opportunity. Soon she had children in other states also writing. First there was a trickle, then a river, finally a flood—actually, the largest amount of mail from children in Congressional history up to that time.

But Annie did not stop with just letters. She undertook to see that as many children as possible actually followed their letters and went to Washington, D.C., in person, with their mothers with them. She also saw to it that as many children and their families as possible not only personally visited the offices of Senators and Congressmen but also visited them in their homes, where they could personally talk with the legislators' children and get them also to plead for the wild horses. Since it is a bold legislator who will vote against his or her children's wishes, not long after the children descended on the Capitol, Annie had her Federal law. It was called the Wild and Free-Roaming Horses and Burros Act:

"Be it enacted by the Senate and House of Representatives of the United States of America in Congress assembled," the bill declared in ringing language, "That it is the sense of the Congress that free-roaming horses and burros are living symbols of the historic and pioneer spirit of the West, that they contribute to the diversity of life-forms within the Nation, and they enrich the lives of the American people, and that all free-roaming horses and burros shall be protected from capture, branding, harassment, or death. . . ." There was even an amendment that included, also in two ringing prohibitions, the following:

> *(a) Whoever uses an aircraft or a motor vehicle to hunt, for the purpose of capturing or killing, any wild unbranded horse, mare, colt, or burro running at large on any of the public land or ranges shall be fined not more than $500, or imprisoned not more than six months, or both.*

> *(b) Whoever pollutes or causes the pollution of any watering hole on any of the public land or ranges for the purpose of trapping, killing, wounding, or maiming any of the animals referred to in subsection (a) of this section shall be fined not more than $500, or imprisoned not more than six months, or both.*

Sadly, even with all Annie's work the wild horses and burros were not yet really protected. The law was basically a "no-chasing" law, and even that was flawed. The mustangs could still be chased to private land where they were not protected, and no one could prove where the chase had started. They obviously needed much stronger protection, but such was the hold of the ranchers and wildlife management people that more protection looked impossible to achieve.

Indeed, up until the "Wild Horse Annie" law the Federal Government did not even have a category for wild horses and burros. The Federal Government, in fact, had just four categories of animals: (1) predators, like the wolf and mountain lion, virtually all of which have been hunted or trapped to near extinction; (2) target—i.e., "game"—animals, deer, antelope, bears, etc., which are hunted in regular seasons; (3) "varmints"—coyotes, foxes, raccoons, skunks, etc., which are killed all year 'round, by day and night, by hunting, trapping, poisoning, and every other way; and finally (4) endangered species—animals whose whole population is so low that, under certain conditions, they are protected. Not so much as a word about wild horses and burros.

At least after Annie there were, at long last, two categories of animals who finally did have Federal protection, the wild horse and the wild burro. But the problem was far from solved. Those of us who attempted to carry on Annie's fight for her horses and burros were often glad she had not lived to see the outrageous way both state and Federal authorities went about pretending to carry out what she had started. The Fund for Animals, for example, was during one period actually in court with the Bureau of Land Management for a dozen years—not only over the cruelty of their wild horse roundups but also over the really blatant hypocrisy of their adoption program.

Although the Bureau was, by law, supposed to allow no one person to adopt any more than four horses or burros, over and over again the Fund found out that they had permitted what often seemed like a whole herd to be adopted by just one person—a person who often, after the required one year's holding time, would then turn around and sell their animals for slaughter. On top of this, the Fund several times caught the Bureau redhanded permitting cronies of theirs to operate their holding corrals after their roundups. One such crony, we found out, received $25,000 a day of Bureau of Land Management money for operating such a corral. When I personally visited his corrals and asked to see what animals he had for adoption, he showed me a very small number of reasonably well cared-for animals. After inspecting these, I looked him in the eye and told him I wished to see the cripples. "Oh," he said, "you wouldn't want to see those." I said I did, at which point he looked both surprised and obviously uneasy that I would even know there were such things. Then when he saw I meant what I said, he did everything he could to stop me from going into the cripples' corral. It was one of the saddest and most infuriating sights I have ever seen in animal work, and while looking at them I remember thinking just how Wild Horse Annie felt that day she first saw those wild horses in the truck.

In the way none of us ever forgot our first sight of Peg, the three-legged cat, our people at the Ranch would never forget their first sight of the first wild horses who came to Black Beauty. Early on everyone noticed how remarkably diverse in appearance the mustangs were, not only from other horses, but also even from one another. Many of them had a definite Indian horse look to them—around the eyes particularly. Indeed, one of the most notable of that first group was a special type of Spanish mustang who had bonnet and shield markings over their eyes and were believed, by the Cheyenne Indians, to be magical. One thing, however, was certain, and this was that to any of us who had taken part in anything having to do with mustang rescues, there was magic in all our new residents, if for no other reason than that they would no longer ever be subject to the cruel roundups and adoptions which so often ended, sooner or later, in trips to the slaughterhouse.

Chris Byrne, the longtime manager of Black Beauty, has an extraordinary knowledge of, understanding of, and ability with all kinds of horses. Born in Wimbledon, England, he never succumbed to the lure of being a tennis ball boy but instead, at the age of six, followed a Gypsy woman who carried and sold firewood in a cart pulled by a Welsh pony. Chris became so enamored of the pony that he prevailed upon the Gypsy woman to agree that if he would deliver the firewood, she would let him look after the pony. Chris went on from there to all kinds of animal work and, in the years before he came to Black Beauty, looked after not only farms full of horses but also, specifically, the horses of the Du Pont family. Like Wild Horse Annie, however, Chris had never seen a wild horse before he came to Black Beauty. But, from the moment he saw one he became just as enamored as he had been with that Gypsy woman's pony. Chris particularly loves talking to horses, and all kinds of horses seem equally to enjoy his talking to them. He tries his best not to play any favorites at the Ranch, but he has a hard time disguising that among the mustangs, his favorite is Chieftain.

Chieftain is a white stallion. Only, Chris will tell you, to horsemen there is no such thing as a white horse. There are just different colors of gray, until there is hardly any gray at all and they are what, to a horse neophyte, looks white. Chieftain is actually a dappled gray but, whatever his color, one thing is certain—he is the big chief not only of all the wild horses on the Ranch but of most of the domestic ones too. He loves best to run his herd at least once a day at full gallop, and few sights at the Ranch can compare to watching Chieftain run his herd off in the far pastures just at sunset. Sometimes after such a run Chieftain will allow Chris to approach him and have one of their man-to-man talks. I asked Chris once what they talked about, and he said what they talked about most of the time was how lucky Chieftain was to be away from the roundups and the slaughterhouses. I asked Chris if Chieftain agreed. "He does indeed," Chris said, "in so many words, you might say."

Second only as a talker to the horses was Mary Da Ros, a woman who worked at the Ranch as assistant manager for many years. Besides talking to them, however, she also wrote memorably about them. My favorite among these writings was one she wrote about one of Black Beauty's first mustang arrivals—a filly she named Missy:

OF MISSY

Wild caught by the Bureau of Land Management, Missy came to Black Beauty Ranch from Nevada. Her dark eyes, reckless mane and defiant face made her look strong and earthy, as if she had learned self-reliance while being brushed and groomed by desert wind.

Now, having just arrived at the Ranch and still in the trailer, she was breaking out in a sweat from travel and panic. It did no good to tell her we meant no harm, that this was her home now and she would be able to live out her life in spacious, peaceful pastures. She would have to learn that in time. And with all her pawing and pacing and snorting and stomping, we knew that this would be a challenge, even before we saw the gnarled limb.

When Missy backed out onto the grass we saw, on her right front leg, a knot the size of a melon where her knee should have been. As wild animals instinctively do, she pretended not to hurt, and possibly hoped we wouldn't notice as she limped out. But the deformation made the leg almost unstable as it twisted in a 45 degree angle under her. Though Missy could slowly bring up the leg from behind as she walked, it was at best awkward for her and it was certainly painful for us to watch. Now we knew why no one had wanted to adopt her, why she was here.

Because Missy was so wild and fearful, we had to have our vet anesthetize her so he could examine the knee. After looking her over, he said he could do nothing for it. There were no fluids to be drained, no foreign objects to be removed. The ball at her knee, almost 30 inches in diameter, had, over the years, hardened to a mass of solid calcium.

We considered putting her down. How could we justify her pain and suffering if she could not live a decent and comfortable life? It is not our policy to prolong the life of an animal with endless drugs and surgeries if there is no hope of a good recovery. We tried looking at other angles, but came up blank. Nothing was going to change the leg.

Except, possibly, if we could get her to lose some weight. We thought if she could shed 100 lbs, it would take pressure off the knee and make her living more comfortable. She was a bit overweight anyway, we commented, even for having survived in a barren desert.

It was then we realized the mare was in foal. For all the attention we put on her leg we had, up to now, overlooked that she was obviously well along in a pregnancy. Our vet tried to continue his examination. But Missy was getting up, albeit wobbly, and obviously wanted nothing to do with us. "Examination over!" she declared. Determining the remaining length of her term was now out of the question. She was moved to a barn where we could watch her and where she had access to a corral so she could walk around.

Several days later, in the quiet cool of the morning, Missy gave birth. When we first saw the filly, she was already up and dry, standing proud with long eager legs. She was solid black with a white star and her eyes, dark like her mother's, were as wild as wind.

Thankfully, this young horse will never have to know that threatened wilderness in which her mother had lived. She will never have to know the endless search for water in an empty pond or a blade of grass through an overgrazed field. And she will never know what it is to be hunted by those who think they have a better use for the land, or a better use for the horse.

Instead, with Missy, she will graze in our lush green pastures. With the other horses she will swim in the fresh deep ponds and run to her heart's content. And she will know what it is to sleep peacefully under the stars, wrapped in the blanket of a warm summer night.

Now we watched Missy lovingly care for her foal, and we could see that she was already moving more easily. With almost 100 lbs of weight already off, she was well on her way to an improved life. And at that moment she certainly wasn't concerned about her leg.

It would be good to know that, as time went on, things got better for the wild horses. It would, however, not be the truth. If the various Park Services with which the Fund for Animals has had the doubtful privilege of dealing over the years were not enough, the Bureau of Land Management with which the Fund had to deal over the wild horses was even worse. Indeed, comparing the two groups over the years, one with the other, I would have no hesitation in saying that while the Park Services have been, generally speaking, cowardly and cruel, the Bureau of Land Management has been crooked and cruel.

The Bureau of Land Management lost a suit brought many years ago by the Fund for Animals and the Animal Protection Institute—one that required the BLM not to adopt out more than four wild horses to a customer. Here the BLM not only failed in its appeal but also had to listen, in its failed appeal, to the Ninth Circuit Court Judge term the whole BLM adoption program a "farce." And as if this was not enough, as recently as January 1997, Martha Mendoza, of the Associated Press, wrote that more than two hundred current BLM employees had themselves adopted over six hundred wild horses and "could not account for the whereabouts of their animals." Others barefacedly acknowledged that some of their horses had been sent to slaughter. Ms. Mendoza also wrote that in the twenty-five years since the "Wild Horse Annie" law was passed, the BLM had spent $250 million rounding up 165,635 animals and went on to quote Tom Pogacnik, director of the Bureau's Wild Horse and Burro Program, who conceded that 90 percent of the animals went to slaughter each year, while another agent made what Ms. Mendoza called a "tacit admission" of backdating documents used in the Wild Horse Program.

In other words, the BLM, not satisfied with taking in multimillions of dollars in the continuation of their cruel roundup, and at the same time allowing thousands upon thousands of animals to be slaughtered, went on from these atrocities to allowing its own employees to profit from the slaughter. Even the Department of Justice got into the act, having prepared a memorandum detailing numerous deliberate acts in violation of the letter and spirit of the original injunction brought against the BLM by the Fund for Animals. As an example, the Department of Justice memorandum cited a situation in which the BLM gave title to a horse despite the fact that, before the title was transferred, the adopter told the BLM inspector that "the horse was mean," and that she "would be very scared to have it around kids or people with dark skin."

In sad summary, all that has happened in the management of a Federal program intended to protect wild horses has been for the BLM to reassign management of the program from Reno to the BLM's national headquarters in Washington, D.C. Here the new "interim director" of the BLM avowed, in a written statement, that "the animals which are under our protection are cared for properly and are treated humanely." If indeed something comes from this avowal, it will be the first time in the long, crooked, cruel history of one of the most despicable agencies in the entire history of the Federal government. In any case, to help this devoutly to be wished event come to pass, the Fund has, as this book went to press, once more taken the BLM to court.

Hard on the heels of our work for the beleaguered wild horses came our rescue of two very different equine customers. These were the last of a long line of so-called diving horses—horses that had long been part of one of the stupidest and most unfeeling animal acts ever foisted on a public which had to be equally stupid and unfeeling to watch it, let alone enjoy it. This act took place at the famous Atlantic City Steel Pier, along with a wide variety of other equally stupid acts such as trained cats boxing each other and kangaroos boxing people. This latter event, incidentally, had at least one redeeming feature—almost invariably the kangaroo promptly knocked down the human.

The diving-horse act had no such redeeming features. It began when a horse was first prodded up a long runway which led to a platform, sometimes forty-five feet in height and at other times sixty-five feet, above a tank below—one that was just a little over ten feet deep. Before the horse made the "dive," a scantily clad young woman, already having climbed a ladder to the top, reached out as the horse went by her, grabbed a bit of harness around his neck, mounted him, and then urged him to jump free of the short ramp leading down to that tank far below.

The idea for this idiocy was originated by a curious Buffalo Bill-wannabe character—a man who had, in fact, a show business acquaintanceship with the late, unlamented buffalo assassin. For years Dr. W.F. Carver, as he was known—although few people ever learned the authority for the "Dr."—had made something of a carnival name for himself by his prowess as a sharpshooter, his most memorable stunt being his ability, by his own well-trumped-up figuring, to register in skeet shooting 10,000 hits a day for six days running.

One day, on a trip to Australia, Dr. Carver persuaded two of the Buffalo Bill troupe playwrights to write a play in which the central character would be played, not by Bill, but by him. In this there was a scene in which Dr. Carver had to ride a horse over a bridge over a river. Midway in this effort he had a lever which was pulled by a stagehand which collapsed the bridge, which in turn collapsed into something looking, at least from the audience, like a river. When these collapses came, Dr. Carver jumped up and caught hold of an upright, thus masterfully upstaging—something at which he was remarkably adept—not only his rival Buffalo Bill but also his horse, who had to plunge down, and disappear, into the aforesaid river.

The only problem the playwrights faced with their absurd drama was that once a horse had to fall off the bridge and into the river, that same horse was so loath to repeat the scene the following night that each night a new horse had to be procured for the job. In short order the company ran out of horses, and the whole show would have been brought to a well-deserved final curtain had not Dr. Carver resolved to find the answer to the problem by enlisting one of his own horses, one named Silver King, who apparently did not mind being goaded into falling into the river night after night. In no time at all Dr. Carver, having gotten rid of such encumbrances as Buffalo Bill and the playwrights, was well on his way to perfecting a brand-new act—a diving horse, courtesy of Silver King and the scantily clad young woman.

Actually, as the diving-horse act grew in popularity, Dr. Carver's son, Al, soon produced a second company, which went national. From time to time both Carver and his son cut expenses by letting their horses dive without even bothering with a girl on top. In the early days, too, he occasionally ran afoul of some spoilsports who felt the act was cruel. So weak, though, were the animal groups in those days that they failed to achieve their objective to make headway against the Carvers. On one occasion, however, an animal group in California managed to take Al Carver's company to court, whereupon Al proceeded to put one of his horses in a truck which he himself drove all over town and on which was a large sign over the horse which read, "I'm Being Taken to Jail for Jumping in a Tank of Water." Afterwards, during the court hearing on the case, Al attempted to take his horse into court to show the judge what good shape he was in and was only persuaded not to do so because his crew warned him of the danger of taking a horse—which was not shod, for the diving act—up the marble steps to the courthouse. Even with the horse kept outside on the lawn, however, the Carvers won their case easily. The judge recessed the trial, came out of the courthouse himself, inspected the horse, and threw the case out of court.

Despite the "victory" for the Carvers, there was of course abundant cruelty in, if not the act itself, the whole training program for the diving horses—the same way as there almost always was in the training of so many other animals for such idiotic acts as dancing bears. There was also danger to the girl in the act. The horse had no saddle, no bridle, and no stirrups, and not even a bit in his or her teeth. Instead, the girl had to hold on to guide the horse by two leather bands—one around the horse's neck and the other around his body. Both the kick-off board at the bottom of the horse's take-off ramp and the sides of the platform from which the girl jumped on the horse were padded—the kick-off board so that the horse had something to kick from and the sides so that the girl did not get friction burns.

The diving girls learned the act on a twelve-foot platform rigged beside the real high one. They were taught that when the horse first put his hooves over the edge of the down ramp, they would have the feeling that the horse was going to somersault and that they would go off over his head. However, if, just before the horse got to that kick-off point, the girls leaned back and kept a firm hold on the harness, they would not be injured. Nonetheless, on one occasion a girl in training got so frightened she let go of the harness, and then of course shot right off the back of the horse. Going off like that, she did not even reach the tank of water—instead she landed in front of the tank on the bare floor, and was only saved from breaking her neck by the fact that she landed absolutely flat.

Actually, the landing in the tank was no walk in the park. Sonora Carver, the Carvers' most famous girl rider and the wife of Al, found this out one day when the horse she was riding made an almost straight-down nosedive. She recalled the event in her book, *A Girl and Five Brave Horses:*

> *Normally I would have ducked just before hitting the water and would have entered the tank foremost, but this time his body was in such an extremely perpendicular position that I was afraid of throwing him over on his back. Several times before on a nosedive I had struck the water in an upside-down position, a method of landing that can be both painful and dangerous, for even if a rider escapes without serious injury she gets a severe shaking up. I had to make a split-second decision, and in a desperate effort to avoid turning him over I stiffened my arms and held my weight back, hoping to maintain our balance. I was successful, but that position caused me to strike the water flat on my face instead of diving in on the top of my head. In the excitement of the moment I failed to close my eyes quickly enough, and as we hit the water I felt a dull stinging sensation.*

After the experience, Mrs. Carver first put off going to an eye doctor for some time and then only did so after another experience in which she hit the water with her eyes opened. It was then, however, too late, and she eventually went totally blind. Remarkably enough, even totally blind she kept on diving horses for eleven years, wearing a helmet with a special lens to protect her eyes. Almost equally remarkably, for the first five of those eleven years she kept the fact that she was blind from both the press and the public. During this period, however, she had many close calls with other accidents, either by missing mounting properly as the horse entered the platform preparatory to the jump, or by losing her grip on the harness and getting thrown off when the horse hit the water. Despite this she managed to get by without serious incident until she retired.

On the other hand, not so lucky were many of the other diving horse girls, some of whom were badly injured. Sonora's sister, Arnette, who also had a long career of diving, told me that it was by no means easy to grab the horse's harness from the platform. When she was learning she sometimes missed the harness entirely, after which, she remembered, the instructor made her, as well as the horse, do it again. "I noticed," she said, "it always made the horse very mad to have to do it again." Even after she learned to dive regularly, she also learned that some of the horses would roll over when they hit the water—at which time, she said, "you had to help them get right-side-up for swimming."

The horses, of course, also suffered accidents. Indeed the most tragic of these happened to the most beautiful and skillful of all diving horses— one named The Duchess of Lightning. Always trying to stretch the act to the limit, the authorities in Atlantic City decided that rather than have the horses dive into a tank, it would be more amusing to have them dive into the real ocean. Accordingly, one of the Carver contracts called for The Duchess of Lightning to do just this. The Duchess had done the ocean dive before at Atlantic City, but the new contract called for her to do it at a seaside resort in California. Here, unfortunately, the conditions were different. On her first attempt The Duchess apparently made a beautiful dive, but afterwards, turning to swim ashore, she became confused by the shore breakers and, in attempting to find an easier way, got herself turned around and headed for the open ocean. Seeing this, lifeguards jumped in a boat and started after her. The faster they went, however, the faster Duchess swam away from them until finally, with the lifeguards watching from their boat, in the words of Al Carver, "She gave up—put her head down and drowned."

That should have been enough to end the idiocy of the diving horses for good, but it was not. Year after year the act was renewed at both Atlantic City and other resorts. And although the animal groups grew stronger and stronger in opposition, they were not enough to put an end to the act until the 1980s. Even after this, and long after the diving act was stopped, the Disney studios not only did not criticize the act but instead seemed to support it with a pro-diving-act movie about the blind Sonora Carver—one which bore the curious title *Wild Hearts Can't Be Broken*. Fortunately for the by-now vast majority of anti-diving horse people, the movie was a well-deserved failure—in fact, it was one of the largest flops in Disney history.

As Fund for Animals workers as well as others will attest, not only was it difficult to stop the diving-horse act; even after it was stopped, there were still other similar acts regularly doing business. The most persistent of these was Johnny Rivers and His Diving Mules. Although they dove from a relatively low height, the mule act was particularly belittling to animals because it also involved monkeys tied on top of the mules and even monkeys tied on top of dogs who were tied on top of the mules. According to two of the longtime diving-horse trainers, Ruth and Bill Ditty, there was even for some time an act involving diving zebras. "They didn't go over too good," the Dittys reported to me. "They were awful high-strung and hard to handle." I could well understand why.

People who do not know horses think of them as big and strong and healthy. People who know them, however, quickly learn that they are extremely delicate creatures and are highly prone to disease and all kinds of accidents. At the same time, as the patient animal slaves they are to mankind they suffer all kinds of cruelties at mankind's hands. Start with the outrages in horse racing—from the racing of two-year-olds and the drugging at the racetrack, and go on to distance racing, steeplechasing, and the horrible "Grand National," not to mention such "genteel" sports as polo. In all these the horse has a grim time indeed. Outside of sports the menu of misery for horses is a long one and goes all the way from carriage horses plodding the city streets in blazing heat and traffic, to Tennessee walking horses whose training cruelties pass belief, all the way to *Sports Illustrated*'s recent report on the incredibly brutal bludgeoning of show horses for the insurance money. Placed against such examples it is not surprising that such a seemingly minor matter as diving horses should take such a long time to overcome. It received such wide publicity, however, that it became essential for something to be done about it. The Fund for Animals has always felt that not doing anything about highly publicized cruelties is wrong for many reasons, not the least of which being that, if nothing was done about them, then people would either think that the act wasn't that cruel, or perhaps even that the horses enjoyed it.

In any case, there was a strange postscript to our efforts. Out of the blue one day came a letter to the Fund from a woman who told us that Resorts International, the outfit that had bought the Steel Pier, had decided to close down the diving-horse act for good. They were going, she told us, to sell off the last three diving horses at auction. As she said this, we knew that meant they would be headed for the slaughterhouse. Again, it might seem curious, since thousands of horses go to slaughter every day, to try to stop three of them from that fate just because they were diving horses. But once more, the fact that they were going to slaughter would be a highly publicized cruelty and might ultimately affect not only the fate of those horses but perhaps help some others. In any case, almost at once we made a decision to try to get those last three horses and bring them to Black Beauty Ranch.

To achieve this objective we dispatched Cynthia Branigan, a long-time Fund for Animals field agent from New Hope, Pennsylvania, first to find where the horses were, second to stop them from going to slaughter, and third to try to get them for Black Beauty Ranch. Promptly Ms. Branigan reported first bad news, then medium news, and, third, good news. The bad news was that one of the horses, Powderface, had already been auctioned and gone to slaughter. The medium news was that, because of this, the public was already aware of the selling of Powderface to slaughter and since the Fund for Animals had now entered the picture, the second horse, a twenty-six-year-old big, dark bay named Gamal, would now go for a large price. The third, last, and good piece of news was that the third horse, a seven-year-old small chestnut filly named Shiloh, had already been bought at auction and was owned by someone, but that person was willing to sell her.

Only on very special occasions and for very good reasons does the Fund for Animals pay for animals at rescues. And on this occasion we decided that before we went after Gamal and Shiloh we would ask Resorts International if they would like to help in the rescue. At first they were happy to do so and even admitted that the reason for this was that they were tired of receiving bad publicity just for having owned the diving-horse act, even if they had now stopped it, and felt that helping with this rescue would at least counter that, and get them some good publicity. Unfortunately, just before they did so, they suddenly changed their minds and said they would not help us. When we asked their reason for this, they said they now felt that any publicity connected with the diving horses—even an attempt to rescue one—would be detrimental.

In one way this pleased us—it proved at last that by far the majority of people were that much against the diving-horse act. But in another way it did not please us, because we couldn't help wondering whether the people who didn't like the idea of Resorts International being connected to their rescue only hesitated because the diving horses were stars and they didn't like the idea of their being reduced to hamburger. Whatever the reason, the upshot left Cynthia alone to face the job of somehow getting ahold of the last two horses, at least to avert the possibility of the slaughterhouse. In the end she did it, managing to procure Gamal for the Fund for Animals for $2,600. The woman who had bought Shiloh, however, was now not willing to resell her. In view of all the publicity, she realized a good thing when she had it, and before it was all over Cynthia had to pay more than twice the price the woman had originally paid for Shiloh.

On top of all this, our plans to take both Gamal and Shiloh to Black Beauty went awry. The reason for this had nothing to do with Shiloh, who still today is an extremely happy Black Beauty horse. It had to do with Gamal, or rather Cynthia and Gamal. Cynthia, like so many women I have known, was unreliable where the first horse of her very own was concerned. In the two days she had Gamal before he was to be taken off to Black Beauty, she fell head over heels in love with him. Above all, she wanted him to stay with her and not go all the way to Texas. To build her case she foisted argument after argument upon us, claiming she would pay for every cent of his stable care and would look after him every day. She even went to such despicable lengths as persuading various horse authorities to tell us that Gamal was far too tired and sick to make the trip to Texas. As if that were not enough, even after it was obvious that Gamal was neither tired nor sick she pressured the same authorities into telling us that he was now too old to make the trip.

Actually, Gamal lived for ten years under Cynthia's faithful care. "I loved him," she told us, "not because he was a beautiful, sleek, quivering thoroughbred. He wasn't anything like that. He never quivered at anything—he was as tough as nails. In all those ten years I only rode him once, and then just because I wanted the experience. Almost every day I would go over to his pasture and walk around with him and talk to him and hug him and kiss him. I guess you could say it was just one more of that 'little girl and big horse' thing. Anyway, I know he liked me because I was a girl, and I liked him because he was a boy."

One day Cynthia and I took Gamal for a walk down to the Delaware River. Gamal went right into the water, up to his chest, and then sank down and plopped back and forth. As I watched this, a horribly disagreeable thought entered my head. "You don't suppose, do you," I said darkly to Cynthia, "he misses diving?" For some time Cynthia, too, watched what he was doing, then finally answered my question. "No," she said, "I don't. And, even if I did, I promise you my lips will be sealed."

Our domestic horses were perhaps not as exciting to other people as our wild horses or our diving horses, but they were equally exciting, and often more so, to us. Two very recent arrivals who stand out are two huge, beautiful Belgians—sister draft horses with especially beautiful fur over their huge hooves. Feathers, these are called. Told by an informant that the horses had no place to go, having first been workhorses in Amish country and later in a commune which was now about to be abandoned, we immediately offered to take them at Black Beauty.

There were, however, as occurs so often in our rescues, three difficulties. The first was that the horses needed immediate help and medical attention, the second was that they were hundreds of miles away, and the third was that the weather, typical of Texas, was a combination of driving rain and incredibly long-lasting thunderstorms. None of these matters bothered Chris Byrne in the slightest. He was off in our truck and trailer almost immediately and, when he got to where the horses were and realized that the weather had, if possible, worsened, he reacted in typical Chris Byrne rescue fashion and decided to stay overnight right with the horses in the trailer so that, as he put it, "I could get to know them better."

"I guess what I like best about horses," Chris once told me, "is just watching the way they interact with each other." And certainly that night, with those two huge horses in the trailer with him, he had plenty of opportunities to do his watching. By the time he was back at the Ranch it was clear he had a special feeling for Hobby and Polly, as the giant sisters were called. There was still much work to be done, particularly on their hooves with those beautiful feathers. All in all, because he knew they needed work but also because I had a sneaking suspicion he just liked them that much, we decided to keep Hobby and Polly right down near where we keep all our old and infirm animals, what we call our "house animals"—as near to the main ranch house door as possible, so we can keep a close weather eye on them.

Both these horses needed Chris's very firm weather eye, because in their former situation they had been both overworked and undervetted. When I spoke earlier about horses being often thought of by nonhorse people to be strong—as in the expression "strong as a horse"—Hobby and Polly clearly proved that not only was that expression generally wrong, it was even wrong when it came to two giants like Polly and Hobby. Both had in fact, before they came to us, foundered. Once a horse has foundered it can often founder again, no matter how big and strong he or she appears, and can do so even from such a simple thing as having eaten a too-rich diet. From this, indeed, it is even possible for a horse to die.

Chris was particularly concerned with the horses' hooves, which had apparently been severely neglected for years and would need much and regular attention. During this period the huge horses spent much of their time with the very smallest horse at the Ranch, a crippled miniature horse named Pee Wee. At just three feet or, in horse talk, nine hands high, Pee Wee could literally walk back and forth under Hobby and Polly. And the sight of the three of them, soon all close friends, walking around and, in Pee Wee's case, under, one another, was a very special one at the Ranch. It was particularly so because Pee Wee's crippled shoulder bothers him so badly that he is normally inordinately shy about any larger animal, be it four legged or two legged, and only made this extraordinarily large exception to his shyness because of his complete confidence in his firm friendship with Hobby and Polly. I have no doubt, however, that Pee Wee, one of the smartest horses on the Ranch, also immediately realized that his two newfound friends would also make, in time of trouble, perfect bouncers.

Looking back on all our domestic horses that have gone through the gates of Black Beauty, one that still stands out as special in the minds of all of us is a beautiful mare named Jamie. Mary Da Ros, who wrote the moving saga of Missy, also wrote the saga of Jamie:

OF JAMIE

What I remember most about Jamie were her eyes. They were graceful and brown like a deer's, only bigger. They were the kind of eyes that, when you looked into them, gave you an immediate connection to Jamie. Although, of course, they did not tell you everything—not, anyway, everything she had gone through—they did tell you what kind of a horse she was, and how, in spite of everything, she still loved people.

Jamie was a horse who did, without hesitation, all that was asked of her. She made the perfect brood mare and, for years, she delivered beautiful foals for the various people who owned her. She had the run of the pastures and she used them to raise her young—where they, like she, could run to their hearts' content.

That is, she had their run until she was crippled by a carelessly discarded piece of metal. She tripped on this and was badly cut just above her coronet band. The coronet is the growing part of the hoof and extremely sensitive—and, unless the horse has a great deal of luck, and the immediate attention of a very competent veterinarian, any horse sustaining an injury to the coronet will have a permanently injured hoof. Jamie it seems was, at the very least, out of luck.

Although she was treated and put on medication, her hoof never healed. She went lame. It would seem that this would have been a good time to retire Jamie from the horse-breeding business. But her owners thought otherwise. They kept her on heavy doses of pain medication so that she could continue to produce foals which they, in turn, could sell. That, apparently, was the important thing.

Eventually, even with all the pain medication, Jamie could no longer bear her own weight and was unable to stand for long periods of time. Her foals learned to nurse on their knees, taking milk from their mother while she was lying down. Finally she could not even do that, and that was when she came to Black Beauty Ranch—when her owners had finally sought to retire their horse and had given in to their conscience. Evidently they did have one, small as it was.

Over the phone they told us that Jamie had a leg injury and with continuing medication she would eventually heal. They wanted to send her to the Ranch so that she could, eventually, run free with our wild mustangs. "Nothing but the best," they said, for their horse. Evidently their conscience was now working overtime. Ever suspicious of people who want to retire their horse once it is no longer "useful," and unable to hear the details from Jamie's side of the story, we could only guess at how awful it really was. We said of course we would take her immediately.

When Jamie arrived at the Ranch we found her to be far worse off than we had been told. She had little to no use of her front legs and moving at all was incredibly painful for her. In fact, in order for her even to turn around she had to place all of the weight from her *front legs onto her back legs and then, picking both front legs up off the ground, used her back legs to do all the work and slide herself around. Because horses normally keep most of their weight towards the front, she had developed severe and frequent muscle spasms from all of the weight shifting she had to do. To watch her was nothing short of agonizing.*

It is customary to have all of the new horses arriving at the Ranch examined by our veterinarian and certainly there would be no exception here. When Jamie first arrived we knew that she had been living with this frightful injury for years—it was a very old injury, and a very serious one at that. This was all confirmed by Jamie's sad, tired eyes and it was reconfirmed again by our vet. But that was not all. We also found out that Jamie had developed an ulcer from all the pain medication she had had to take. And now we had to give her more drugs for the ulcer, and yet she still could not go off of the pain medication.

For months we tried to help Jamie with her condition, and with every treatment we gave, we grew more attached to and fond of her. We liked to think that because she was now at Black Beauty, where our objective is to do what we can for the horse and not what the horse can do for us—she started to relax, and she started to trust. She seemed to be trying so hard to get better and helped us to administer her treatment in every way she could, never flinching and always brave. Her big brown eyes lit up whenever we came toward her and I felt them follow us when we left. And when she saw the other horses running free in the outside pastures I was sure she wanted badly to join them. She whinnied at them often.

We tried everything short of surgery to help Jamie with her condition. Finally, after watching her remain the same, despite everything, and still being caught in a serious tangle of drugs, we decided to have surgery done to block the nerves in her front hoof. Then she could use it, but she would not feel the pain. And, if everything went well, she could come off all medication and live a somewhat normal life. Optimistically, we tried to picture the day when she would be able to run in the pastures again.

*The day before Jamie's surgery, we loaded her carefully into a
horse trailer to be driven to the vet's office. After parking, I opened one
of the trailer windows and she put her head out to get some fresh air,
and get a grip on where she was. As I walked toward the vet's office,
she whinnied. I looked back and there were those big brown eyes, soft
and trusting as always, looking into mine.*

*Although that was not the last time I saw Jamie alive, it is
that moment I will carry with me and remember always. With her
beautiful head sticking out of the trailer window and watching every
move I made. That is how I will remember Jamie.*

*The surgery did not go well and there were complications due to
the serious ulcer that had developed over the years. Upon hearing the
news we rushed over to see her. Although she was still alive, I could
see that Jamie was already gone. Lying there was an animal in so
much pain who could not possibly recognize—did not want to recognize—what was going on around her and that we were there for her,
even though we could do nothing to make it stop.*

*We rushed off for the veterinarian and had her put to sleep
immediately. I held her head and then it was over. We were so
hurried to put her out of her misery that we did not even pause to say
good-bye. But after it was over we sat quietly and softly said our
good-byes to the Jamie we remembered and the Jamie we would like to
remember—Jamie in the pasture, Jamie in the stable, Jamie running
in the field with her foals. And then there was the Jamie sticking her
head out of the trailer window—and then, finally, there were just
those eyes. There was Jamie.*

We have been lucky not to have had many, if any, horse stories as
sad as Jamie's—although the majority of our hundreds of horses were
either abused or ill-used to begin with. One horse who particularly comes
to mind in this regard was a small colt all alone in a field to whom we
were directed by someone who came upon him by accident. It was a
starvation case of which there is an inexcusably large number in Texas,
but this one was particularly inexcusable. When the rescuer first saw him
he was trying to make a pathetic little whinny. He was lying in the dirt,

cold and wet and barely alive, beside a tree. He was also, we could see from the dirt around him, trying to make his way from a lying position toward the tree.

The day we found him was, ironically, Thanksgiving. How long he had been where he was, how long without water or food, how long without his mother—where she was or even if she was—we would never know. All we did know was that someone had left this tiny little colt to die a long, lonely, painful death and we also knew that the most important thing we could do for him was to give him water and something for his Thanksgiving dinner, besides the bark of the tree he was trying to reach. We also decided, once we had him safely in a stall in the main Black Beauty barn, that we would name him, in honor of the holiday, Pilgrim.

The veterinarian gave Pilgrim less than a ten percent chance of survival. But Pilgrim was not a colt who gave up. He just, as the vet later said, refused to consider that option. Pilgrim never grew up to be a large horse, or even a medium-sized horse but, as he had already tried to prove, he did grow up to be a brave horse. And, after months of medical care on the vet's part and that special bravery on his part, he started to come around faster than anyone thought he ever had a chance of doing. And, as he did so, he began to take an interest in the other animals at the Ranch. He eventually even tried to make a four-legged friend—something, it seemed to us, he had never had before his rescuer found him. In any case, this four-legged friend turned out to be, of all the horses on the Ranch, Shiloh, the last of the diving horses. It was certainly eminently fitting, for Shiloh, in her way, was a brave horse, too. And, even more eminently fitting, a year and a half after their meeting Shiloh had a foal, and Pilgrim was a pilgrim father.

Of all the Ranch stories of man's inhumanity to horse, the story of a horse named Cody is not only, like Pilgrim's, inexcusable, it is close to infuriating even to think about. And although it started out, again like Pilgrim's story, as if it could not possibly end happily, in the end it did, or at least as happily as possible. Cody, a beautiful white or, in horse talk, gray, was owned by a doctor in Atlanta—a doctor who, one day, shot him. He shot him in the knee, the reason being that, although Cody would not come to him when he called, he would come to the young man who looked after him. The doctor, in a fit of fury over this, and jealous of the young man, was not only not content with shooting Cody in the knee, he had such a fit of fury that he fired the young man, then rigged a block and tackle with weights and left Cody so shackled with a wound so unattended that there was no hope for even partial recovery. In other words, he wanted to see that Cody would not only be crippled for life but would also be tortured for life. All for not coming when he was called.

It was not all, however, for a group of Fund for Animals volunteers in Atlanta. Learning about this story from the young man, they took the doctor to court about Cody and, although they were able to get him fined for cruelty, try as they did they were unable to get the judge to accede to their demand that Cody be taken away from the doctor and that they be given custody of him. Or, if not that, that at least he should be taken away from the doctor. As happens in all to many cruelty cases, the judge refused to do this. The volunteers did, however, succeed in making the doctor so infamous in Atlanta that in time he gave in—or, rather, gave up—and sold Cody at auction, a fate that might well have led, as the doctor might well have hoped, to the slaughterhouse. But this time the volunteers were ready for him. They not only bought Cody at auction but, besides this, also saw that he had a proper operation on his knee. In this operation—which, incidentally, took more than four hours—surgeons first removed the bullet from Cody's leg, then fused the splintered bones back together, pinned the knee with stainless steel screws, and finally implanted a metal plate to support the fractured bone. After all this, the volunteers sent Cody to our Ranch.

To this day a fragment of the bullet remains in Cody's knee, a fragment that was unreachable due to its closeness to the nerves and an artery. As I write this Cody is now twenty-seven years old and has been living at the Ranch for more than fifteen years. He is doing well and although he doesn't gallop anymore, he has been known to at least try to trot a little bit, especially if it is to the trough at feeding time. Cody's toughness earned him the respect of all the other horses, particularly in his early days, when he was lamest, when a horse named Stanley took it upon himself to stand beside him at feeding time and see that there was no nonsense about who got what, especially when the who was Cody. Our farrier made a special shoe for Cody which allows him to walk a little easier, particularly as he grows older and his bones become weaker. Just the same, to be on the safe side we have always kept Cody as near to the main Ranch house as possible, just because we want him close. And although he is always nearby, he is just a little out of reach because he remains, to this day, to most people, people-shy. He is even a little shy with those of us he has learned over the years to trust. We believe that, given his experience with people, he will always be so and we highly respect him for it.

There remains, finally, the story of Stanley, a grand sorrel gelding. Stanley has passed on now, but no animal at the Ranch was ever more loved or ever more missed. Most of his years were spent as a police horse on the streets of New York City—in the heat in the summer, in the cold in the winter, in traffic in rush hours, in unruly crowds, in crimes and on concrete. Wherever he was, and whatever he did, Stanley, always the gentleman, did his job with pride. And when his duty was finally over, and he was sent by friends to retire at Black Beauty, he saw he had a different job, but one that should be done with the same pride with which he had done his former job. This one did not involve policing a whole city, but it did involve policing a very large ranch and six hundred animals, and among these, when he was there, he made sure that there was no bullying by larger animals of smaller animals and no stealing of anyone else's food.

People remember different things about Stanley—how big and strong he was, yet how gentle and friendly, even to another animal who, at least at first, was not that way to him. But they always were that way in the end because Stanley had more friends at the Ranch than any other animal ever had before or since. His best friend was Cody. He stood by Cody's side through thick and thin, especially watching out for him against some of the other horses who, knowing Cody could not move very well, took advantage and, at least before Stanley, used to take his food. When Stanley took over no other horse, not even the wildest mustang, ever even tried to do such a thing. And when Cody was, as he was so often, sick and had to be in the barn, Stanley would wait for him outside day after day. Then finally, when Cody would emerge, they whinnied, nickered, and went off grazing together, business as usual.

Next to Cody, Stanley loved best the burros. He searched them out to stand by them, and would go to great lengths for them as he would for Cody and his other friends. He would slowly make his way from the stables, around the elephant barn and corral, and then down the lane to wait for someone to walk or drive to the gate so he could be with his burros out on the hill. Eventually he even learned to walk gingerly across the cattle guard—a difficult feat, as he grew older—so he could get to the burros on his own.

Anyone who conducted a tour of the Ranch would never forget how he or she could always count on Stanley to be so steady when children rushed him. And while it would have been a little on the dangerous side to see so many small children so close to almost any other horse, it was not that way with him. Even the most nervous mother could see immediately that her smallest child would be safe with Stanley. Indeed, when one of those very small ones would want to touch him, Stanley would put his nose way down so that that very small child could touch his soft muzzle. All the children loved Stanley very much—perhaps more than any other animal at the Ranch. But just the same, those of us who worked with him loved him the most.

Stanley is buried now—out on that hill with his burros. We believe that he will always be in their hearts, too. And one day Cody will be out there with him, and they will always be together.

Mark Twain

A MEXICAN PLUG

I resolved to have a horse to ride. I had never seen such wild, free, magnificent horsemanship outside of a circus as these picturesquely-clad Mexicans, Californians and Mexicanized Americans displayed in Carson streets everyday. How they rode! Leaning just gently forward out of the perpendicular, easy and nonchalant, with broad slouch-hat brim blown square up in front, and long *riata* swinging above the head, they swept through the town like the wind! The next minute they were only a sailing puff of dust on the far desert. If they trotted, they sat up gallantly and gracefully, and seemed part of the horse; did not go jiggering up and down after the silly Miss-Nancy fashion of the riding-schools. I had quickly learned to tell a horse from a cow, and was full of anxiety to learn more. I was resolved to buy a horse.

While the thought was rankling in my mind, the auctioneer came skurrying through the plaza on a black beast that had as many humps and corners on him as a dromedary, and was necessarily uncomely; but he was "going, going, at twenty-two!—horse, saddle and bridle at twenty-two dollars, gentlemen!" and I could hardly resist.

A man whom I did not know (he turned out to be the auctioneer's brother) noticed the wistful look in my eye, and observed that that was a very remarkable horse to be going at such a price; and added that the saddle alone was worth the money. It was a Spanish saddle, with ponderous *tapidaros,* and furnished with the ungainly sole-leather covering with the unspellable name. I said I had half a notion to bid. Then this keen-eyed person appeared to me to be "taking my measure"; but I dismissed the suspicion when he spoke, for his manner was full of guileless candor and truthfulness. Said he:

"I know that horse—know him well. You are a stranger, I take it, and so you might think he was an American horse, maybe, but I assure you he is not. He is nothing of the kind; but—excuse my speaking in a low voice, other people being near—he is, without the shadow of a doubt, a Genuine Mexican Plug!"

I did not know what a Genuine Mexican Plug was, but there was something about this man's way of saying it, that made me swear inwardly that I would own a Genuine Mexican Plug, or die.

"Has he any other—er—advantages?" I inquired, suppressing what eagerness I could.

He hooked his forefinger in the pocket of my army-shirt, led me to one side, and breathed in my ear impressively these words:

"He can out-buck anything in America!"

"Going, going, going—at *twent–ty*-four dollars and a half, gen—"

"Twenty-seven!" I shouted, in a frenzy.

"And sold!" said the auctioneer, and passed over the Genuine Mexican Plug to me.

I could scarcely contain my exultation. I paid the money, and put the animal in a neighboring livery-stable to dine and rest himself.

In the afternoon I brought that creature into the plaza, and certain citizens held him by the head, and others by the tail, while I mounted him. As soon as they let go, he placed all his feet in a bunch together, lowered his back, and then suddenly arched it upward, and shot me straight into the air a matter of three or four feet! I came as straight down again, lit in the saddle, went instantly up again, came down almost on the high pommel, shot up again, and came down on the horse's neck—all in the space of three or four seconds. Then he rose and stood almost straight up on his hind feet, and I, clasping his lean neck desperately, slid back into the saddle, and held on. He came down, and immediately hoisted his heels into the air, delivering a vicious kick at the sky, and stood on his forefeet. And then down he came once more, and began the original exercise of shooting me straight up again. The third time I went up I heard a stranger say:

"Oh, *don't* he buck, though!"

While I was up, somebody struck the horse a sounding thwack with a leathern strap, and when I arrived again the Genuine Mexican Plug was not there. A Californian youth chased him up and caught him, and asked if he might have a ride. I granted him that luxury. He mounted the Genuine, got lifted into the air once, but sent his spurs home as he descended, and the horse darted away like a telegram. He soared over three fences like a bird, and disappeared down the road toward the Washoe Valley.

I sat down on a stone, with a sigh, and by natural impulse one of my hands sought my forehead, and the other the base of my stomach. I believe I never appreciated, till then, the poverty of the human machinery—for I still needed a hand or two to place elsewhere. Pen cannot describe how I was jolted up. Imagination can not conceive how disjointed I was—how internally, externally and universally I was unsettled, mixed up and ruptured. There was a sympathetic crowd around me, though.

One elderly-looking comforter said:

"Stranger, you've been taken in. Everybody in this camp knows that horse. Any child, any Injun, could have told you that he'd buck; he is the very worst devil to buck on the continent of America. You hear *me*. I'm

Curry. *Old* Curry. Old *Abe* Curry. And moreover, he is a simon-pure-out-and-out, genuine d——d Mexican plug, and an uncommon mean one at that, too. Why, you turnip, if you had laid low and kept dark, there's chances to buy an *American* horse for mightly little more than you paid for that bloody old foreign relic."

I gave no sign; but I made up my mind that if the auctioneer's brother's funeral took place while I was in the Territory I would postpone all other recreations and attend it.

After a gallop of sixteen miles the Californian youth and the Genuine Mexican Plug came tearing into town again, shedding foam-flakes like the spume-spray that drives before a typhoon, and, with one final skip over a wheelbarrow and a Chinaman, cast anchor in front of the "ranch."

Such panting and blowing! Such spreading and contracting of the red equine nostrils, and glaring of the wild equine eye! But was the imperial beast subjugated? Indeed he was not. His lordship the Speaker of the House thought he was, and mounted him to go down to the Capitol; but the first dash the creature made was over a pile of telegraph poles half as high as a church; and his time to the Capitol—one mile and three quarters—remains unbeaten to this day. But then he took an advantage—he left out the mile, and only did the three quarters. That is to say, he made a straight cut across lots, preferring fences and ditches to a crooked road; and when the Speaker got to the Capitol he said he had been in the air so much he felt as if he had made the trip on a comet.

In the evening the Speaker came home afoot for exercise, and got the Genuine towed back behind a quartz wagon. The next day I loaned that animal to the Clerk of the House to go down to the Dana silver mine, six miles, and *he* walked back for exercise, and got the horse towed. Everybody I loaned him to always walked back; they never could get enough exercise any other way. Still, I continued to loan him to anybody who was willing to borrow him, my idea being to get him crippled, and throw him on the borrower's hands, or killed, and make the borrower pay for him. But somehow nothing ever happened to him. He took chances that no other horse ever took and survived, but he always came out safe. It was his daily habit to try experiments that had always before been considered impossible, but he always got through. Sometimes he miscalculated a little, and did not get his rider through intact, but *he* always got through himself. Of course I had tried to sell him; but that was a stretch of simplicity which met with little sympathy. The auctioneer stormed up and down the streets on him for four days, dispersing the populace, interrupting business, and destroying children, and never got a bid—at least never any but the eighteen-dollar one he hired a notoriously substanceless bummer to make. The people only smiled pleasantly, and restrained their desire to buy, if they had any. Then the auctioneer brought in his bill, and I withdrew the horse from the market. We tried to trade him off at private vendue next, offering him at a sacrifice for second-hand tombstones, old iron, temperance tracts—any kind of property. But holders were stiff, and we retired from the market again. I never tried to ride the horse any more. Walking was good enough exercise for a man like me, that had nothing the matter with him except ruptures, internal injuries, and such things. Finally I tried to *give* him away. But it was a failure. Parties said earthquakes were handy enough on the Pacific coast— they did not wish to own one. As a last resort I offered him to the Governor for the use of the "Brigade." His face lit up eagerly at first, but toned down again, and he said the thing would be too palpable.

Just then the livery stable man brought in his bill for six weeks' keeping—stall-room for the horse, fifteen dollars; hay for the horse, two hundred and fifty! The Genuine Mexican Plug had eaten a ton of the article, and the man said he would have eaten a hundred if he had let him.

I will remark here, in all seriousness, that the regular price of hay during that year and a part of the next was really two hundred and fifty dollars a ton. During a part of the previous year it had sold at five hundred a ton, in gold, and during the winter before that there was such scarcity of the article that in several instances small quantities had brought eight hundred dollars a ton in coin! The consequence might be guessed without my telling it: people turned their stock loose to starve, and before the spring arrived Carson and Eagle valleys were almost literally carpeted with their carcases! Any old settler there will verify these statements.

I managed to pay the livery bill, and that same day I gave the Genuine Mexican Plug to a passing Arkansas emigrant whom fortune delivered into my hand. If this ever meets his eye, he will doubtless remember the donation.

Now whoever has had the luck to ride a real Mexican Plug will recognize the animal depicted in this chapter, and hardly consider him exaggerated—but the uninitiated will feel justified in regarding his portrait as a fancy sketch, perhaps.

Mike Resnick

MALISH

His name was Malicious, and you can look it up in the *American Racing Manual:* from ages 2 to 4, he won 5 of his 46 starts, had seven different owners, and never changed hands for more than $800.

His method of running was simple and to the point: he was usually last out of the gate, last on the backstretch, last around the far turn, and last at the finish wire.

He didn't have a nickname back then, either. Exterminator may have been Old Bones, and Man o' War was Big Red, and of course Equipoise was the Chocolate Soldier, but Malicious was just plain Malicious.

Turns out he was pretty well-named, after all.

It was at Santa Anita in February of 1935—and *this* you can't look up in the *Racing Manual,* or the *Daily Racing Form Chart Book,* or any of the other usual sources, so you're just going to have to take my word for it—and Malicious was being rubbed down by Chancey McGregor, who had once been a jockey until he got too heavy, and had latched on as a groom because he didn't know anything but the racetrack. Chancey had been trying to supplement his income by betting on the races, but he was no better at picking horses than at riding them—he had a passion for claimers who were moving up in class, which any tout will tell you is a quick way to go broke—and old Chancey, he was getting mighty desperate, and on this particular morning he stopped rubbing Malicious and put him in his stall, and then started trading low whispers with a gnarly little man who had just appeared in the shed row with no visitor's pass or anything, and after a couple of minutes they shook hands and the gnarly little man pricked Chancey's thumb with something sharp and then held it onto a piece of paper.

Well, Chancey started winning big that very afternoon, and the next day he hit a 200-to-1 shot, and the day after that he knocked down a $768.40 daily double. And because he was a good-hearted man, he spread his money around, made a lot of girls happy, at least temporarily, and even started bringing sugar cubes to the barn with him every morning. Old Malicious, he just loved those sugar cubes, and because he was just a horse, he decided that he loved Chancey McGregor, too.

Then one hot July day that summer—Malicious had now lost 14 in a row since he upset a cheap field back in October the previous year—Chancey was rubbing him down at Hollywood Park, adjusting the bandages on his forelegs, and suddenly the gnarly little man appeared inside the stall.

"It's time," he whispered to Chancey.

Chancey dropped his sponge onto the straw that covered the floor of the stall and just kind of backed away, his eyes so wide they looked like they were going to pop out of his head.

"But it's only July," he said in a real shaky voice.

"A deal's a deal," said the gnarly man.

"But I was supposed to have two years!" whimpered Chancey.

"You've been betting at five tracks with your bookie," said the gnarly man with a grin. "You've had two years' worth of winning, and now I've come to claim what's mine."

Chancey backed away from the gnarly man, putting Malicious between them. The little man advanced toward him, and Malicious, who sensed that his source of sugar cubes was in trouble, lashed out with a forefoot and caught the gnarly little man right in the middle of the forehead. It was a blow that would have killed most normal men, but as you've probably guessed by now, this wasn't any normal man in the stall with Malicious and Chancey, and he just sat down hard.

"You can't keep away from me forever, Chancey McGregor," he hissed, pointing a skinny finger at the groom. "I'll get you for this." He turned to Malicious. "I'll get you *both* for this, horse, and you can count on it!"

And with that, there was a puff of smoke, and suddenly the gnarly little man was gone.

Well, the gnarly little man, being who he was, didn't have to wait long to catch up with Chancey. He found him cavorting with fast gamblers and loose women two nights later, and off he took him, and that was the end of Chancey McGregor.

But Malicious was another story. Three times the gnarly little man tried to approach Malicious in his stall, and three times Malicious kicked him clear out into the aisle, and finally the gnarly little man decided to change his tactics, and what he did was to wait for Malicious on the far turn with a great big stick in his hand. Being who he was, he made sure that nobody in the grandstand or the clubhouse could see him, but it wouldn't have been a proper vengeance if Malicious couldn't see him, so he made a little adjustment, and just as Malicious hit the far turn, trailing by his usual 20 lengths, up popped the gnarly little man, swinging the stick for all he was worth.

"I got you now, horse!" he screamed—but Malicious took off like the devil was after him, which was exactly the case, and won the race by seven lengths.

As he was being led to the winner's circle, Malicious looked off to his left, and there was the gnarly little man, glaring at him.

"I'll be waiting for you next time, horse," he promised, and sure enough, he was.

And Malicious won *that* race by nine lengths.

And the gnarly little man kept waiting, and Malicious kept moving into high gear every time he hit the far turn, and before long the crowds fell in love with him, and Joe Hernandez, who called just about every race ever run in California, became famous for crying ". . . and here comes Malish!"

Santa Anita started selling Malish t-shirts 30 years before t-shirts became popular, and Hollywood Park sold Malish coffee mugs, and every time old Malish won, he made the national news. At the end of his seventh year, he even led the Rose Bowl parade in Pasadena. (Don't take *my* word for it; there was a photo of it in *Time*.)

By the time he turned eight years old, Malish started slowing down, and the only thing that kept him safe was that the gnarly little man was slowing down, too, and one day he came to Malish's stall, and this time he looked more tired than angry, and Malish just stared at him without kicking or biting.

"Horse," said the gnarly little man, "you got more gumption than most people I know, and I'm here to declare a truce. What do you say to that?"

Malish whinnied, and the gnarly little man tossed him a couple of sugar cubes, and that was the last Malish ever did see of him.

He lost his next eleven races, and then they retired him, and the California crowd fell in love with Seabiscuit, and that was that.

Except that here and there, now and then, you can still find a couple of railbirds from the old days who will tell you about old Malish, the horse who ran like Satan himself was chasing him down the homestretch.

That's the story. There really was a Malicious, and he used to take off on the far turn like nobody's business, and it's all pretty much the truth, except for the parts that aren't, and they're pretty minor parts at that.

Like I said, you can look it up.

Josepha Sherman

THE CAT WHO WASN'T BLACK

Now, folks who work around a racetrack are a superstitious lot, I'm not denying that. Hell, I've got a few quirks myself. It's only when you believe, *really* believe, in superstitions that you're in trouble.

In fact, sometimes those superstitions can ruin your life.

I'm getting ahead of myself. Me? I'm a trainer, small-time, good enough to have half a barn at Union Downs, stalls occupied by solid, honest horses, even a couple of minor stakes winners. Maybe we weren't going into any record books, but they were for the most part earning their oats.

That's what I thought when I first set eyes on the colt: another good, solid wage-earner if nothing special. He was a shiny black two-year-old, that being the age at which they start racing the babies, a great-something-grandson of Gato del Sol, old Sun Cat, he who won a Kentucky Derby a good many years back. The colt's owner, tongue firmly in cheek, had named the youngster Changeable Cat, and if you know anything about horse coat color genetics, you'll get the joke.

If not, just bear with me.

Changeable Cat settled into his new life easily enough, with a good turn of foot and signs that he'd make a stayer, a long-distance runner, like old Gato. Friendly youngster, the sort who would follow you around like a pup if you'd let him. I'd sometimes put him on a lead shank and take him along on my rounds, getting him used to things. Only a few quirks to Changeable Cat, quirks being normal in a two-year-old: Took to cats as though he were one himself and *hated* anything at all like a snake. This meant he did his best to destroy lead ropes and garden hoses till we let him beat up one, sniff it, and decide it wasn't going to bite him. Real snakes were another matter. I saw him, screaming like a grown-up stallion, once mash a garden snake into a damp spot on the ground.

Not too many snakes on the racetrack. Genuine ones, I mean. As for the other kind . . . well, too bad there are always some folks not happy with a cleanly run operation. Too bad there are always some trying to change that.

One guy in particular. His name, though I doubt it would turn up on any birth certificate, was Mr. George Serpentin—yeah, suitable—and he turned up on the backstretch, the barn area, one day, smooth as you please, without so much as a trace of a visitor's pass, and asking to see me. Nothing wrong with him at first glance: nice, neat, ordinary fellow, olive-skinned and dark-haired. Not old, not young. And I won't lie and say that there was something *wrong* about the eyes either.

Still . . .

"This is a good-looking operation," he said right out, the faintest hint of some weird accent in his voice, "really good-looking."

I gave a noncommittal grunt, waiting.

Sure enough, here came the attack. "A shame if something were to—"

"Mister," I cut in before he could go on, "I don't know who you are or who's behind you, but this is Union Downs, not some bush league track. Protection rackets don't work here."

With that, I started looking around for a security guard, half-expecting to hear his oh-so-innocent protests.

What I heard instead was the softest hiss of a laugh. "Do they not?" he purred. "Wait, my honest friend. Wait."

He strolled off. I noticed he made a wide berth around a ladder leaning against a wall. And when Bill, the barn's cat, who's almost all black, meowed at him, the guy carefully avoided him, as though making *sure* Bill couldn't cross his path. Superstitious, I thought, wondering if that was a useful fact to know.

But then . . . hell, I don't know how he managed it, but Serpentin was gone between one step and the next. I blinked and rubbed my eyes, and told myself it was that old standby, a trick of the light. Main thing was, he was gone, and I'd have a little talk with Security. Mr. Serpentin, or whoever he was, was *not* going to return.

That night, we heard the one cry no one ever wants to hear at a track: "Fire!" It was in one of the storage sheds, mercifully not in the stall area, and was easily brought under control. All the hands, from hot walkers up to guards, swore they hadn't seen how it had started; all of them swore up and down that they hadn't been sneaking a smoke.

But under some tough questioning later, I got one known nicotine addict, Luis, to confess, yes, he'd been sneaking a smoke, carefully away from the horses and hay.

"But as I light up, boss, there's a, you know, snake. *Big* snake, not one of those little grass fellas. He jump at me, out of nowhere, and I, you know, get startled. Drop the match and then—whoosh."

Whoosh, indeed. There was nothing in that shed to catch fire so quickly *Serpentin*, I thought. *I don't know how he did it, I don't know how he got in, but it had to be Serpentin.*

I discarded that line about *big* snake. Probably Serpentin had thrown a grass snake at him: Any snake was going to look big if it was coming right at your face.

Serpentin. Sure enough, with the first hint of dawn, there he was, smooth and smiling. "I heard that you had a small disturbance last night," he purred.

"You try anything like that again, and I swear—"

"Tsk. Don't make threats unless you're prepared to carry them out."

"Think I'm not?" I'm not sure what I meant to do just then: charge him, punch him out. But he was staring at me, and this time I'll say his eyes did look weird, hard as two stones. Weirder, I just couldn't seem to find the energy to move.

Serpentin smiled. "And are you willing to listen to my proposition now?"

"What do you want?"

He shrugged. "This isn't a large-scale operation, but it is well-run and profitable. Half."

"Go to hell."

"Perhaps. But not just yet." He bent so suddenly I jumped, then straightened, smiling all over again. "Look."

He'd plucked a four-leaf clover from bare ground. *No mystery*, I told myself. Easy enough for a man to palm something small, then perform a bit of sleight-of-hand.

"You see?" Serpentin said. "You can't hurt me. i'm . . . let's just say that I'm lucky. But you . . . I fear that your luck is rapidly running out. And remember that misfortune comes in threes."

I was about to tell him to keep his clichés to himself when shouts told me that one of the horses, excitable My Clarion, had broken away from his handler. The fool of a colt was heading, ears flat and tail raised and trailed by frantic workers, straight for the gap between barns—the gap that led out to the road and the fast-moving traffic.

Swearing, I ran to block his path, getting there just in time, and stood semaphoring my arms to slow him down. Scary, a thousand pounds of panic-stricken equine running straight at me. If My Clarion was too panicky to even notice me, I'd have maybe a second at best to dive out of the way or be trampled into a damp spot like that garden snake Changeable Cat had stomped—

No. My Clarion stopped so suddenly he nearly went back on his haunches, snorting, eyes wild and white-rimmed. Almost, I thought, as though he'd been struck. As I got a hand on him, crooning the usual nonsense you do to calm a horse, his handler, Jim, came hurrying up, stammering apologies as he took My Clarion's lead rope from me.

"Boss, we got a snake somewhere in the barns, a big one. The damned thing struck at me just as I was leading Clary here out. Didn't give any sort of warning; just appeared out of nowhere and *wham.* Sorry, boss, you know I'd never do something so stupid as letting go of a horse, not usually, but I wasn't expecting anything like that. Nearly jumped out of my skin."

A big snake that startled Luis into dropping a match. A big snake—the same one?—that startled Jim into letting go of My Clarion.

Well, yeah, when you have grain and hay, you have mice. And snakes as well as cats hunt mice. But a snake, a big one, that specialized in startling humans? And an unwelcome visitor named Mr. Serpentin? He might just as well have left a neon business card.

Still, I had to check. We didn't have any poisonous ones in the area, far as I knew, and we certainly didn't have anything that qualified as big. What the guys had seen *could* have been merely someone's pet boa. Every now and then, the papers ran a story about lost snakes, and just maybe that's what we had.

And just maybe Changeable Cat was the son of Pegasus.

Anyhow, that last thing I wanted was for hands to start quitting because there was a "devil snake" loose. I put in a call to the zoo: sure enough, no venomous snakes native to the area. As for big snakes, no one had reported a missing pet, but they promised to send a guy around to inspect the barn, just in case.

I also got Security to agree that they'd put extra personnel on the job should Mr. Serpentin try another visit.

But of course he didn't. To sum up the events of the next couple of days, the guy from the zoo found nothing over the size of an earthworm, and the fire in the shed turned out to be nothing more drastic than the result of one match hitting one oily rag. I told myself Serpentin's cold eyes weren't surprising for a would-be shake-down artist, nothing mystic about that, and as for my sudden lack of energy—I'd been letting superstition get the better of me.

As for Changeable Cat, my equine snake hater, he remained reassuringly unalarmed and playful as a pup.

After a few of those days of ordinary backstretch life, Security decided that Mr. Serpentin, if indeed he had been associated with the incidents, had been scared off and wouldn't return.

Me, I wasn't so sure. He'd clearly been a very superstitious guy, and that "misfortunes come in threes" line that he'd thrown at me—well, almost everyone has heard about that belief. It just wasn't likely anyone so superstitious would risk leaving the triple threat unfinished. So far, his attacks—and for all the lack of proof I wasn't going to say they weren't attacks—had been relatively harmless, by chance or Serpentin's luck.

The third attack might not be harmless at all.

So I did a little research, read up on superstitions. Amazing how many of them there are, particularly those circling around snakes. Amazing how many superstitions pick up on that supposedly mystical "three" and all its forms. I did a quick calculation, and came up with the realization that tonight would be the ninth night since the first attack. Three times three: How could Serpentin resist it?

An idea began to form. I went down to the barn and took a good, hard look at Changeable Cat, who snorted at me and cocked his ears forward as though he knew what I was thinking. I ran a hand down the line of his jaw the way he liked, and he let his lower lip flop in contentment.

"Tonight, my four-legged friend," I told him, scratching his jaw, "we are going to go on our own little patrol."

The guard looked more than a little surprised to see me there that night, but, hey, I was the boss, and if I had decided that a midnight stroll was good for a colt, it wasn't for an underling to argue. I snapped a lead rope onto Changeable Cat's halter and led him out of his stall, he following along with amiable curiosity.

Now, a horse moving very slowly can be pretty quiet, as anyone who's ever been surprised by one who's gotten loose can attest. I can move pretty quietly too, a leftover skill from service days. I was planning to sneak up on Mr. Serpentin and catch him in the act of whatever he was trying to do. Nothing complex here: I just meant to play on our Mr. Serpentin's superstitious fears a little.

What I had not expected was for Changeable Cat to suddenly go from docile youngster to one of those neck-arched warhorses, charging forward with a roar that said in equine, *snake*, and nearly lifting me off my feet. I dug in my heels to slow him, but even a two-year-old colt has a hell of a lot of strength in him, and we kept going.

Sure enough, something large was moving in the shadows. *Snake!* my mind yelped even as my eyes were telling me, *Serpentin.* Couldn't really be sure which it was, a snake or a man crouching over—

Over Bill, the barn cat. The mostly black barn cat. That much I saw clearly as Changeable Cat dragged me along: Bill was definitely . . . dead, crushed, the way I'd once seen a constrictor kill its prey on TV before I could flip the channel. I found myself thinking foolishly, *Now he can't cross Serpentin's path.*

Serpentin whirled as we neared him, and so help me he was *hissing,* his eyes glinting in the dark the way nobody's eyes should glow. Nobody human.

I guess I wasn't too sane right then. A snake-man, shapeshifter, minor league demon or major con artist—whatever the hell he was, I wanted him *out of my barn,* I wanted him *away from my horses,* now!

And that's why I yelled at Serpentin like a loon, "Look what I've got! A cat—Changeable Cat's his name, and he's a *black* Changeable Cat! And he's going to cross your path but good!"

With that, I did something I wouldn't have done under sane conditions: I let Changeable Cat go.

The colt rushed straight at Serpentin like a demon himself, ears flat, teeth bared, roaring like a stallion, and Serpentin scrambled frantically to his feet. Instead of doing the sensible thing and climbing out of Changeable Cat's reach, he screeched something about, "You won't cross my path!" and ran. Of course no man can outrun a horse, and my first sane thought was that I'd just caused a murder.

No murder. Serpentin, mindless with panic, dodged and darted—and collided with the ladder that was still leaning up against a wall. He and it went down with a crash, his head caught in the rungs like a man with a wooden noose. I heard an unmistakable *crack* as he hit the ground.

Mr. Serpentin had most definitely just broken his neck.

I caught Changeable Cat before he could trample the enemy, and by that time the noise had brought everyone running so I had help holding the colt. The police arrived shortly after that, and so did an ambulance to take Serpentin away. I gave my statement to the cops: attempt by Serpentin at extortion, the criminal startled in the act, the accident with the ladder. Probably don't have to mention that I left out any trace of . . . weird.

But weird it was. I mean, here's the list of superstitions involved:

Go under a ladder and you'll end up hanged. Serpentin had hanged himself.

Kill the first snake you see, and win over a foe. Well, Changeable Cat and I had certainly won over that one.

Oh, and here's the nastiest one: If you break a snake's back, said snake can't die until the sundown of the next day. Nasty, indeed, because Mr. Serpentin lingered on throughout the whole next day. He died, the hospital records show, at the exact moment the sun set.

Coincidence. Has to be. The records apparently also showed that Serpentin registered as human, and that's good enough for me. I've got a racing operation to run, and that's a tough enough business without adding any occult stuff to it. So let's just call what happened one big mess of coincidences.

Think I left out one superstition? The one about a black cat crossing your path being bad luck? Well, here's the point of the joke I promised to tell, the one about a horse's coat color and Changeable Cat's name?

Changeable Cat isn't black at all. He's a gray. And like all gray horses, he was born dark but will shed out lighter and lighter with each season's coat. Give him a year or two, and our equine "black cat" will be almost white.

Now, if the late Mr. Serpentin had done some homework about the business he was trying to take over, he would have known that horsey fact. He wouldn't have panicked over "You won't cross my path!" or ended up killing himself—not that I'm shedding any tears over him.

It's just what I said at the beginning: Sometimes your superstitions can ruin your life.

Stephen Crane

HORSES–ONE DASH

Richardson pulled up his horse and looked back over the trail, where the crimson serape of his servant flamed amid the dusk of the mesquit. The hills in the west were carved into peaks, and were painted the most profound blue. Above them, the sky was of that marvellous tone of green—like still, sun-shot water—which people denounce in pictures.

José was muffled deep in his blanket, and his great toppling sombrero was drawn low over his brow. He shadowed his master along the dimming trail in the fashion of an assassin. A cold wind of the impending night swept over the wilderness of mesquit.

"Man," said Richardson, in lame Mexican, as the servant drew near, "I want eat! I want sleep! Understand no? Quickly! Understand?"

"Si, señor," said José, nodding. He stretched one arm out of his blanket, and pointed a yellow finger into the gloom. "Over there, small village! Si, señor."

They rode forward again. Once the American's horse shied and breathed quiveringly at something which he saw or imagined in the darkness, and the rider drew a steady, patient rein and leaned over to speak tenderly, as if he were addressing a frightened woman. The sky had faded to white over the mountains, and the plain was a vast, pointless ocean of black.

Suddenly some low houses appeared squatting amid the bushes. The horsemen rode into a hollow until the houses rose against the sombre sundown sky, and then up a small hillock, causing these habitations to sink like boats in the sea of shadow.

A beam of red firelight fell across the trail. Richardson sat sleepily on his horse while the servant quarrelled with somebody—a mere voice in the gloom—over the price of bed and board. The houses about him were for the most part like tombs in their whiteness and silence, but there were scudding black figures that seemed interested in his arrival.

José came at last to the horses' heads, and the American slid stiffly from his seat. He muttered a greeting as with his spurred feet he clicked into the adobe house that confronted him. The brown, stolid face of a woman shone in the light of the fire. He seated himself on the earthen floor, and blinked drowsily at the blaze. He was aware that the woman was clinking earthenware, and hieing here and everywhere in the manœuvres of the housewife. From a dark corner of the room there came the sound of two or three snores twining together.

The woman handed him a bowl of tortillas. She was a submissive creature, timid and large-eyed. She gazed at his enormous silver spurs, his large and impressive revolver, with the interest and admiration of the highly privileged cat of the adage. When he ate, she seemed transfixed off there in the gloom, her white teeth shining.

José entered, staggering under two Mexican saddles large enough for building-sites. Richardson decided to smoke a cigarette, and then changed his mind. It would be much finer to go to sleep. His blanket hung over his left shoulder, furled into a long pipe of cloth, according to a Mexican fashion. By doffing his sombrero, unfastening his spurs and his revolver-belt, he made himself ready for the slow, blissful twist into the blanket. Like a cautious man, he lay close to the wall, and all his property was very near his hand.

The mesquit brush burned long. José threw two gigantic wings of shadow as he flapped his blanket about him—first across his chest under his arms, and then around his neck and across his chest again, this time over his arms, with the end tossed on his right shoulder. A Mexican thus snugly enveloped can nevertheless free his fighting arm in a beautifully brisk way, mere shrugging his shoulder as he grabs for the weapon at his belt. They always wear their serapes in this manner.

The firelight smothered the rays which, streaming from a moon as large as a drum-head, were struggling at the open door. Richardson heard from the plain the fine, rhythmical trample of the hoofs of hurried horses. He went to sleep wondering who rode so fast and so late. And in the deep silence the pale rays of the moon must have prevailed against the red spears of the fire until the room was slowly flooded to its middle with a rectangle of silver light.

Richardson was awakened by the sound of a guitar. It was badly played—in this land of Mexico, from which the romance of the instrument ascends to us like a perfume. The guitar was groaning and whining like a badgered soul. A noise of scuffling feet accompanied the music. Sometimes laughter arose, and often the voices of men saying bitter things to each other; but always the guitar cried on, the treble sounding as if some one were beating iron, and the bass humming like bees.

"Damn it! They're having a dance," muttered Richardson, fretfully. He heard two men quarrelling in short, sharp words like pistol-shots; they were calling each other worse names than common people know in other countries.

He wondered why the noise was so loud. Raising his head from his saddle-pillow, he saw, with the help of the valiant moonbeams, a blanket hanging flat against the wall at the farther end of the room. Being of the opinion that it concealed a door, and remembering that Mexican drink made men very drunk, he pulled his revolver closer to him and prepared for sudden disaster.

Richardson was dreaming of his far and beloved North.

"Well, I would kill him, then!"

"No, you must not!"

"Yes, I will kill him! Listen! I will ask this American beast for his beautiful pistol and spurs and money and saddle, and if he will not give them—you will see!"

"But these Americans—they are a strange people. Look out, señor."

Then twenty voices took part in the discussion. They rose in quivering shrillness, as from men badly drunk.

Richardson felt the skin draw tight around his mouth, and his knee-joints turned to bread. He slowly came to a sitting posture, glaring at the motionless blanket at the far end of the room. This stiff and mechanical movement, accomplished entirely by the muscles of the wrist, must have looked like the rising of a corpse in the wan moonlight, which gave everything a hue of the grave.

My friend, take my advice, and never be executed by a hangman who doesn't talk the English language. It, or anything that resembles it, is the most difficult of deaths. The tumultuous emotions of Richardson's terror destroyed that slow and careful process of thought by means of which he understood Mexican. Then he used his instinctive comprehension of the first and universal language, which is tone. Still, it is disheartening not to be able to understand the detail of threats against the blood of your body.

Suddenly the clamour of voices ceased. There was a silence—a silence of decision. The blanket was flung aside, and the red light of a torch flared into the room. It was held high by a fat, round-faced Mexican, whose little snake-like moustache was as black as his eyes, and whose eyes were black as jet. He was insane with the wild rage of a man whose liquor is dully burning at his brain. Five or six of his fellows crowded after him. The guitar, which had been thrummed doggedly during the time of the high words, now suddenly stopped.

They contemplated each other. Richardson sat very straight and still, his right hand lost in the folds of his blanket. The Mexicans jostled in the light of the torch, their eyes blinking and glittering.

The fat one posed in the manner of a grandee. Presently his hand dropped to his belt, and from his lips there spun an epithet—a hideous word which often foreshadows knifeblows, a word peculiarly of Mexico, where people have to dig deep to find an insult that has not lost its savour.

The American did not move. He was staring at the fat Mexican with a strange fixedness of gaze, not fearful, not dauntless, not anything that could be interpreted; he simply stared.

The fat Mexican must have been disconcerted, for he continued to pose as a grandee with more and more sublimity, until it would have been easy for him to fall over backward. His companions were swaying in a very drunken manner. They still blinked their beady eyes at Richardson. Ah, well, sirs, here was a mystery. At the approach of their menacing company, why did not this American cry out and turn pale, or run, or pray them mercy? The animal merely sat still, and stared, and waited for them to begin. Well, evidently he was a great fighter; or perhaps he was an idiot. Indeed, this was an embarrassing situation, for who was going forward to discover whether he was a great fighter or an idiot?

To Richardson, whose nerves were tingling and twitching like live wires, and whose heart jolted inside him, this pause was a long horror; and for these men who could so frighten him there began to swell in him a fierce hatred—a hatred that made him long to be capable of fighting all of them, a hatred that made him capable of fighting all of them. A 44-caliber revolver can make a hole large enough for little boys to shoot marbles through, and there was a certain fat Mexican, with a moustache like a snake, who came extremely near to have eaten his last tamale merely because he frightened a man too much.

José had slept the first part of the night in his fashion, his body hunched into a heap, his legs crooked, his head touching his knees. Shadows had obscured him from the sight of the invaders. At this point he arose, and began to prowl quakingly over toward Richardson, as if he meant to hide behind him.

Of a sudden the fat Mexican gave a howl of glee. José had come within the torch's circle of light. With roars of singular ferocity the whole group of Mexicans pounced on the American's servant.

He shrank shuddering away from them, beseeching by every device of word and gesture. They pushed him this way and that. They beat him with their fists. They stung him with their curses. As he grovelled on his knees, the fat Mexican took him by the throat and said: "I'm going to kill you!" And continually they turned their eyes to see if they were to succeed in causing the initial demonstration by the American.

Richardson looked on impassively. Under the blanket, however, his fingers were clenched as rigidly as iron upon the handle of his revolver.

Here suddenly two brilliant clashing chords from the guitar were heard, and a woman's voice, full of laughter and confidence, cried from without: "Hello! Hello! Where are you?"

The lurching company of Mexicans instantly paused and looked at the ground. One said, as he stood with his legs wide apart in order to balance himself: "It is the girls! They have come!" He screamed in answer to the question of the woman: "Here!" And without waiting he started on a pilgrimage toward the blanket-covered door. One could now hear a number of female voices giggling and chattering.

Two other Mexicans said: "Yes; it is the girls! Yes!" They also started quietly away. Even the fat Mexican's ferocity seemed to be affected. He looked uncertainly at the still immovable American. Two of his friends grasped him gaily. "Come, the girls are here! Come!" He cast another glower at Richardson. "But this—" he began. Laughing, his comrades hustled him toward the door. On its threshold, and holding back the blanket with one hand, he turned his yellow face with a last challenging glare toward the American. José, bewailing his state in little sobs of utter despair and woe, crept to Richardson and huddled near his knee. Then the cries of the Mexicans meeting the girls were heard, and the guitar burst out in joyous humming.

The moon clouded, and but a faint square of light fell through the open main door of the house. The coals of the fire were silent save for occasional sputters. Richardson did not change his position. He remained staring at the the blanket which hid the strategic door in the far end. At his knees José was arguing, in a low, aggrieved tone, with the saints. Without, the Mexicans laughed and danced, and—it would appear from the sound—drank more.

In the stillness and night Richardson sat wondering if some serpent-like Mexican was sliding toward him in the darkness, and if the first thing he knew of it would be the deadly sting of the knife. "Sssh," he whispered to José. He drew his revolver from under the blanket and held it on his leg.

The blanket over the door fascinated him. It was a vague form, black and unmoving. Through the opening it shielded was to come, probably, menace, death. Sometimes he thought he saw it move.

As grim white sheets, the black and silver of coffins, all the panoply of death, affect us because of that which they hide, so this blanket, dangling before a hole in an adobe wall, was to Richardson a horrible emblem, and a horrible thing in itself. In his present mood Richardson could not have been brought to touch it with his finger.

The celebrating Mexicans occasionally howled in song. The guitarist played with speed and enthusiasm.

Richardson longed to run. But in this threatening gloom, his terror convinced him that a move on his part would be a signal for the pounce of death. José, crouching abjectly, occasionally mumbled. Slowly and ponderous as stars the minutes went.

Suddenly, Richardson thrilled and started. His breath, for a moment, left him. In sleep his nerveless fingers had allowed his revolver to fall and clang upon the hard floor. He grabbed it up hastily, and his glance swept apprehensively over the room.

A chill blue light of dawn was in the place. Every outline was slowly growing; detail was following detail. The dread blanket did not move. The riotous company have gone or become silent.

Richardson felt in his blood the effect of this cold dawn. The candour of breaking day brought his nerve. He touched José. "Come," he said. His servant lifted his lined, yellow face and comprehended. Richardson buckled on his spurs and strode up; José obediently lifted the two great saddles. Richardson held two bridles and a blanket on his left arm; in his right hand he held his revolver. They sneaked toward the door.

The man who said that spurs jingled was insane. Spurs have a mellow clash—clash—clash. Walking in spurs—notably Mexican spurs—you remind yourself vaguely of a telegraphic lineman. Richardson was inexpressibly shocked when he came to walk. He sounded to himself like a pair of cymbals. He would have known of this if he had reflected; but then he was escaping, not reflecting. He made a gesture of despair, and from under the two saddles José tried to make one of hopeless horror. Richardson stooped, and with shaking fingers unfastened the spurs. Taking them in his left hand, he picked up his revolver, and they slunk on toward the door.

On the threshold Richardson looked back. In a corner he saw, watching him with large eyes, the Indian man and woman who had been his hosts. Throughout the night they had made no sign, and now they neither spoke nor moved. Yet Richardson thought he detected meek satisfaction at his departure.

The street was still and deserted. In the eastern sky there was a lemon-coloured patch.

José had picketed the horses at the side of the house. As the two men came around the corner, Richardson's animal set up a whinny of welcome. The little horse had evidently heard them coming. He stood facing them, his ears cocked forward, his eyes bright with welcome.

Richardson made a frantic gesture, but the horse, in his happiness at the appearance of his friends, whinnied with enthusiasm.

The American felt at this time that he could have strangled his well-beloved steed. Upon the threshold of safety he was being betrayed by his horse, his friend. He felt the same hate for the horse that he would have felt for a dragon. And yet, as he glanced wildly about him, he could see nothing stirring in the street, nor at the doors of the tomb-like houses.

José had his own saddle-girth and both bridles buckled in a moment. He curled the picket-ropes with a few sweeps of his arm. The fingers of Richardson, however, were shaking so that he could hardly buckle the girth. His hands were in invisible mittens. He was wondering, calculating, hoping about his horse. He knew the little animal's willingness and courage under all circumstances up to this time, but then—here it was different. Who could tell if some wretched instance of equine perversity was not about to develop? Maybe the little fellow would not feel like smoking over the plain at express speed this morning, and so he would rebel and kick and be wicked. Maybe he would be without feeling of interest, and run listlessly. All men who have had to hurry in the saddle know what it is to be on a horse who does not understand the dramatic situation. Riding a lame sheep is bliss to it. Richardson, fumbling furiously at the girth, thought of these things.

Presently he had it fastened. He swung into the saddle, and as he did so his horse made a mad jump forward. The spurs of José scratched and tore the flanks of his great black animal, and side by side the two horses raced down the village street. The American heard his horse breathe a quivering sigh of excitement.

Those four feet skimmed. They were as light as fairy puff-balls. The houses of the village glided past in a moment, and the great, clear, silent plain appeared like a pale blue sea of mist and wet bushes. Above the mountains the colours of the sunlight were like the first tones, the opening chords, of the mighty hymn of the morning.

The American looked down at his horse. He felt in his heart the first thrill of confidence. The little animal, unurged and quite tranquil, moving his ears this way and that way with an air of interest in the scenery, was nevertheless bounding into the eye of the breaking day with the speed of a frightened antelope. Richardson, looking down, saw the long, fine reach of forelimb as steady as steel machinery. As the ground reeled past, the long dried grasses hissed, and cactus-plants were dull blurs. A wind whirled the horse's mane over his rider's bridle hand.

José's profile was lined against the pale sky. It was as that of a man who swims alone in an ocean. His eyes glinted like metal fastened on some unknown point ahead of him, some mystic place of safety. Occasionally his mouth puckered in a little unheard cry; and his legs, bent back, worked spasmodically as his spurred heels sliced the flanks of his charger.

Richardson consulted the gloom in the west for signs of a hard-riding, yelling cavalcade. He knew that, whereas his friends the enemy had not attacked him when he had sat still and with apparent calmness confronted them, they would certainly take furiously after him now that he had run from them—now that he had confessed to them that he was the weaker. Their valour would grow like weeds in the spring, and upon discovering his escape they would ride forth dauntless warriors.

Sometimes he was sure he saw them. Sometimes he was sure he heard them. Continually looking backward over his shoulder, he studied the purple expanses where the night was marching away. José rolled and shuddered in his saddle, persistently disturbing the stride of the black horse, fretting and worrying him until the white foam flew and the great shoulders shone like satin from the sweat.

At last Richardson drew his horse carefully down to a walk. José wished to rush insanely on, but the American spoke to him sternly. As the two paced forward side by side, Richardson's little horse thrust over his soft nose and inquired into the black's condition.

Riding with José was like riding with a corpse. His face resembled a cast in lead. Sometimes he swung forward and almost pitched from his seat. Richardson was too frightened himself to do anything but hate this man for his fear. Finally he issued a mandate which nearly caused José's eyes to slide out of his head and fall to the ground like two silver coins.

"Ride behind me—about fifty paces."

"Señor—" stuttered the servant.

"Go!" cried the American, furiously. He glared at the other and laid his hand on his revolver. José looked at his master wildly. He made a piteous gesture. Then slowly he fell back, watching the hard face of the American for a sign of mercy.

Richardson had resolved in his rage that at any rate he was going to use the eyes and ears of extreme fear to detect the approach of danger; and so he established his servant as a sort of outpost.

As they proceeded he was obliged to watch sharply to see that the servant did not slink forward and join him. When José made beseeching circles in the air with his arm he replied by menacingly gripping his revolver.

José had a revolver, too; nevertheless it was very clear in his mind that the revolver was distinctly an American weapon. He had been educated in the Rio Grande country.

Richardson lost the trail once. He was recalled to it by the loud sobs of his servant.

Then at last José came clattering forward, gesticulating and wailing. The little horse sprang to the shoulder of the black. They were off.

Richardson, again looking backward, could see a slanting flare of dust on the whitening plain. He thought that he could detect small moving figures in it.

José's moans and cries amounted to a university course in theology. They broke continually from his quivering lips. His spurs were as motors. They forced the black horse over the plain in great headlong leaps.

But under Richardson there was a little, insignificant, rat-coloured beast who was running apparently with almost as much effort as it requires for a bronze statue to stand still. As a matter of truth, the ground seemed merely something to be touched from time to time with hoofs that were as light as blown leaves. Occasionally Richardson lay back and pulled stoutly at his bridle to keep from abandoning his servant.

José harried at his horse's mouth, flopped around in the saddle, and made his two heels beat like flails. The black ran like a horse in despair.

Crimson serapes in the distance resembled drops of blood on the great cloth of plain.

Richardson began to dream of all possible chances. Although quite a humane man, he did not once think of his servant. José being a Mexican, it was natural that he should be killed in Mexico; but for himself, a New Yorker—

He remembered all the tales of such races for life, and he thought them badly written.

The great black horse was growing indifferent. The jabs of José's spurs no longer caused him to bound forward in wild leaps of pain. José had at last succeeded in teaching him that spurring was to be expected, speed or no speed, and now he took the pain of it dully and stolidly, as an animal who finds that doing his best gains him no respite.

José was turned into a raving maniac. He bellowed and screamed, working his arms and his heels like one in a fit. He resembled a man on a sinking ship, who appeals to the ship. Richardson, too, cried madly to the black horse.

The spirit of the horse responded to these calls, and, quivering and breathing heavily, he made a great effort, a sort of final rush, not for himself apparently, but because he understood that his life's sacrifice, perhaps, had been invoked by these two men who cried to him in the universal tongue. Richardson had no sense of appreciation at this time—he was too frightened—but often now he remembers a certain black horse.

From the rear could be heard a yelling, and once a shot was fired—in the air, evidently. Richardson moaned as he looked back. He kept his hand on his revolver. He tried to imagine the brief tumult of his capture—the flurry of dust from the hoofs of horses pulled suddenly to their haunches, the shrill biting curses of the men, the ring of the shots, his own last contortion. He wondered, too, if he could not somehow manage to pelt that fat Mexican, just to cure his abominable egotism.

It was José, the terror-stricken, who at last discovered safety. Suddenly he gave a howl of delight, and astonished his horse into a new burst of speed. They were on a little ridge at the time, and the American at the top of it saw his servant gallop down the slope and into the arms, so to speak, of a small column of horsemen in grey and silver clothes. In the dim light of the early morning they were as vague as shadows, but Richardson knew them at once for a detachment of rurales, that crack cavalry corps of the Mexican army which polices the plain so zealously, being of themselves the law and the arm of it—a fierce and swift-moving body that knows little of prevention, but much of vengeance. They drew up suddenly, and the rows of great silver-trimmed sombreros bobbed in surprise.

Richardson saw José throw himself from his horse and begin to jabber at the leader of the party. When he arrived he found that his servant had already outlined the entire situation, and was then engaged in describing him, Richardson, as an American señor of vast wealth, who was the friend of almost every governmental potentate within two hundred miles. This seemed to profoundly impress the officer. He bowed gravely to Richardson and smiled significantly at his men, who unslung their carbines.

The little ridge hid the pursuers from view, but the rapid thud of their horses' feet could be heard. Occasionally they yelled and called to each other.

Then at last they swept over the brow of the hill, a wild mob of almost fifty drunken horsemen. When they discerned the pale-uniformed rurales they were sailing down the slope at top speed.

If toboggans half-way down a hill should suddenly make up their minds to turn around and go back, there would be an effect somewhat like that now produced by the drunken horsemen. Richardson saw the rurales serenely swing their carbines forward, and, peculiar-minded person that he was, felt his heart leap into his throat at the prospective volley. But the officer rode forward alone.

It appeared that the man who owned the best horse in this astonished company was the fat Mexican with the snaky moustache, and, in consequence, this gentleman was quite a distance in the van. He tried to pull up, wheel his horse, and scuttle back over the hill as some of his companions had done, but the officer called to him in a voice harsh with rage.

"——!" howled the officer. "This señor is my friend, the friend of my friends. Do you dare pursue him, ——? ——! ——! ——! ——!" These lines represent terrible names, all different, used by the officer.

The fat Mexican simply grovelled on his horse's neck. His face was green; it could be seen that he expected death.

The officer stormed with magnificent intensity: "——! ——! ——!"

Finally he sprang from his saddle and, running to the fat Mexican's side, yelled: "Go!" and kicked the horse in the belly with all his might. The animal gave a mighty leap into the air, and the fat Mexican, with one wretched glance at the contemplative rurales, aimed his steed for the top of the ridge. Richardson again gulped in expectation of a volley, for, it is said, this is one of the favourite methods of the rurales for disposing of objectionable people. The fat, green Mexican also evidently thought that he was to be killed while on the run, from the miserable look he cast at the troops. Nevertheless, he was allowed to vanish in a cloud of yellow dust at the ridge-top.

José was exultant, defiant, and oh! bristling with courage. The black horse was drooping sadly, his nose to the ground. Richardson's little animal, with his ears bent forward, was staring at the horses of the rurales as if in an intense study. Richardson longed for speech, but he could only bend forward and pat the shining, silken shoulders. The little horse turned his head and looked back gravely.

W. H. Hudson

STORY OF A PIEBALD HORSE

This is all about a piebald. People there are like birds that come down in flocks, hop about chattering, gobble up their seed, then fly away, forgetting what they have swallowed. I love not to scatter grain for such as these. With you, friend, it is different. Others may laugh if they like at the old man of many stories, who puts all things into his copper memory. I can laugh, too, knowing that all things are ordered by destiny; otherwise I might sit down and cry.

The things I have seen! There was the piebald that died long ago; I could take you to the very spot where his bones used to lie bleaching in the sun. There is a nettle growing on the spot. I saw it yesterday. What important things are these to remember and talk about! Bones of a dead horse and a nettle; a young bird that falls from its nest in the night and is found dead in the morning: puff-balls blown about by the wind: a little lamb left behind by the flock bleating at night amongst the thorns and thistles, where only the fox or wild dog can hear it! Small matters are these, and our lives, what are they? And the people we have known, the men and women who have spoken to us and touched us with warm hands—the bright eyes and red lips! Can we cast these things like dead leaves on the fire? Can we lie down full of heaviness because of them, and sleep and rise in the morning without them? Ah, friend!

Let us to the story of the piebald. There was a cattle-marking at neighbour Sotelo's estancia, and out of a herd of three thousand herd we had to part all the yearlings to be branded. After that, dinner and a dance. At sunrise we gathered, about thirty of us; all friends and neighbours, to do the work. Only with us came one person nobody knew. He joined us when we were on our way to the cattle; a young man, slender, well-formed, of pleasing countenance and dressed as few could dress in those days. His horse also shone with silver trappings. And what an animal! Many horses have I seen in this life, but never one with such a presence as this young stranger's piebald.

Arrived at the herd, we began to separate the young animals, the men riding in couples through the cattle, so that each calf when singled out could be driven by two horsemen, one on each side, to prevent it from doubling back. I happened to be mounted on a demon with a fiery mouth—there was no making him work, so I had to leave the parters and stand with little to do, watching the yearlings already parted, to keep them from returning to the herd.

Presently neighbour Chapaco rode up to me. He was a good-hearted man, well-spoken, half Indian and half Christian; but he also had another half, and that was devil.

"What! neighbour Lucero, are you riding on a donkey or a goat, that you remain here doing boy's work?"

I began telling him about my horse, but he did not listen; he was looking at the parters.

"Who is that young stranger?" he asked.

"I see him to-day," I replied, "and if I see him again to-morrow then I shall have seen him twice."

"And in what country of which I have never heard did he learn cattle-parting?" said he.

"He rides," I answered, "like one presuming on a good horse. But he is safe, his fellow-worker has all the danger."

"I believe you," said Chapaco. "He charges furiously and hurls the heifer before his comrade, who has all the work to keep it from doubling, and all the danger, for at any moment his horse may go over it and fall. This our young stranger does knowingly, thinking that no one here will resent it. No, Lucero, he is presuming more on his long knife than on his good horse."

Even while we spoke, the two we were watching rode up to us. Chapaco saluted the young man, taking off his hat, and said—"Will you take me for a partner, friend?"

"Yes; why not, friend?" returned the other; and together the two rode back to the herd.

Now I shall watch them, said I to myself, to see what this Indian devil intends doing. Soon they came out of the herd driving a very small animal. Then I knew what was coming. "May your guardian angel be with you to avert a calamity, young stranger!" I exclaimed. Whip and spur those two came towards me like men riding a race and not parting cattle. Chapaco kept close to the calf, so that he had the advantage, for his horse was well trained. At length he got a little ahead, then, quick as lightning, he forced the calf round square before the other. The piebald struck it full in the middle, and fell because it had to fall. But, Saints in Heaven! Why did not the rider save himself? Those who were watching saw him throw up his feet to tread his horse's neck and leap away; nevertheless man, horse, and calf came down together. They ploughed the ground for some distance, so great had been their speed, and the man was under. When we picked him up he was senseless, the blood flowing from his mouth. Next morning, when the sun rose and God's light fell on the earth, he expired.

Of course there was no dancing that night. Some of the people, after eating, went away; others remained sitting about all night, talking in low tones, waiting for the end. A few of us were at his bedside watching his white face and closed eyes. He breathed, and that was all. When the sunlight came over the world he opened his eyes, and Sotelo asked him how he did. He took no notice, but presently his lips began to move, though they seemed to utter no sound. Sotelo bent his ear down to listen. "Where does she live?" he asked. He could not answer—he was dead.

"He seemed to be saying many things," Sotelo told us, "but I understood only this—'Tell her to forgive me . . . I was wrong. She loved him from the first. . . . I was jealous and hated him . . . Tell Elaria not to grieve—Anacleto will be good to her.' Alas! my friends, where shall I find his relations to deliver this dying message to them?"

The Alcalde came that day and made a list of the dead man's possessions, and bade Sotelo take charge of them till the relations could be found. Then, calling all the people together, he bade each person cut on his whip-handle and on the sheath of his knife the mark branded on the flank of the piebald, which was in shape like a horse-shoe with a cross inside, so that it might be shown to all strangers, and made known through the country until the dead man's relations should hear of it.

When a year had gone by, the Alcalde told Sotelo that, all inquiries having failed, he could now take the piebald and the silver trappings for himself. Sotelo would not listen to this, for he was a devout man and coveted no person's property, dead or alive. The horse and things, however, still remained in his charge.

Three years later I was one afternoon sitting with Soleto, taking maté, when his herd of dun mares were driven up. They came galloping and neighing to the corral and ahead of them, looking like a wild horse, was the piebald, for no person ever mounted him.

"Never do I look on that horse," I remarked, "without remembering the fatal marking, when its master met his death."

"Now you speak of it," said he, "let me inform you that I am about to try a new plan. That noble piebald and all those silver trappings hanging in my room are always reproaching my conscience. Let us not forget the young stranger we put under ground. I have had many masses said for his soul's repose, but that does not quite satisfy me. Somewhere there is a place where he is not forgotten. Hands there are, perhaps, that gather wild flowers to place them with lighted candles before the image of the Blessed Virgin; eyes there are that weep and watch for his coming. You know how many travellers and cattle-drovers going to Buenos Ayres from the south call for refreshment at the *pulperia*. I intend taking the piebald and trying him every day at the gate there. No person calling will fail to notice the horse, and some day perhaps some traveller will recognise the brand on its flank and will be able to tell us what department and what estancia it comes from."

I did not believe anything would result from this, but said nothing, not wishing to discourage him.

Next morning the piebald was tied up at the gate of the *pulperia*, at the road side, only to be released again when night came, and this was repeated every day for a long time. So fine an animal did not fail to attract the attention of all strangers passing that way, still several weeks went by and nothing was discovered. At length, one evening, just when the sun was setting, there appeared a troop of cattle driven by eight men. It had come a great distance, for the troop was a large one—about nine hundred head—and they moved slowly, like cattle that had been many days on the road. Some of the men came in for refreshments; then the store-keeper noticed that one remained outside leaning on the gate.

"What is the capatas doing that he remains outside?" said one of the men.

"Evidently he has fallen in love with that piebald," said another, "for he cannot take his eyes off it."

At length the capatas, a young man of good presence, came in and sat down on a bench. The others were talking and laughing about the strange things they had all been doing the day before; for they had been many days and nights on the road, only nodding a little in their saddles, and at length becoming delirious from want of sleep, they had begun to act like men that are half-crazed.

"Enough of the delusions of yesterday," said the capatas, who had been silently listening to them, "but tell me, boys, am I in the same condition to-day?"

"Surely not!" they replied. 'Thanks to those horned devils being so tired and footsore, we all had some sleep last night."

"Very well then," said he, "now you have finished eating and drinking, go back to the troop, but before you leave look well at that piebald tied at the gate. He that is not a cattle-drover may ask, 'How can my eyes deceive me?' but I know that a crazy brain makes us see many strange things when the drowsy eyes can only be held open with the fingers."

The men did as they were told, and when they had looked well at the piebald, they all shouted out, "He has the brand of the estancia de Silva on his flank, and no counter-brand—claim the horse, capatas, for he is yours." And after that they rode away to the herd.

"My friend," said the capatas to the store-keeper, "will you explain how you came possessed of this piebald horse?"

Then the other told him everything, even the dying words of the young stranger, for he knew all.

The capatas bent down his head, and covering his face shed tears. Then he said, "And you died thus, Torcuato, amongst strangers! From my heart I have forgiven you the wrong you did me. Heaven rest your soul, Torcuato; I cannot forget that we were once brothers. I, friend, am that Anacleto of whom he spoke with his last breath."

Sotelo was then sent for, and when he arrived, and the *pulperia* was closed for the night, the capatas told his story, which I will give you in his own words, for I was also present to hear him. This is what he told us:—

I was born on the southern frontier. My parents died when I was very small, but Heaven had compassion on me and raised up one to shelter me in my orphanhood. Don Loreto Silva took me to his estancia on the Sarandi, a stream half a day's journey from Tandil, towards the setting sun. He treated me like one of his own children, and I took the name of Silva. He had two other children, Torcuato, who was about the same age as myself, and his daughter, Elaria, who was younger. He was a widower when he took charge of me, and died when I was still a youth. After his death we moved to Tandil, where we had a house close to the little town; for we were all minors, and the property had been left to be equally divided between us when we should be of age. For four years we lived happily together; then when we were of age we preferred to keep the property undivided. I proposed that we should go and live on the estancia, but Torcuato would not consent, liking the place where we were living best. Finally, not being able to persuade him, I resolved to go and attend to the estancia myself. He said that I could please myself and that he should stay where he was with Elaria. It was only when I told Elaria of these things that I knew how much I loved her. She wept and implored me not to leave her.

"Why do you shed tears, Elaria?" I said; "is it because you love me? Know, then, that I also love you with all my heart, and if you will be mine, nothing can ever make us unhappy. Do not think that my absence at the estancia will deprive me of this feeling which has ever been growing up in me."

"I do love you, Anacleto," she replied, "and I have also known of your love for a long time. But there is something in my heart which I cannot impart to you; only I ask you, for the love you bear me, do not leave me, and do not ask me why I say this to you."

After this appeal I could not leave her, nor did I ask her to tell me her secret. Torcuato and I were friendly, but not as we had been before this difference. I had no evil thoughts of him; I loved him and was with him continually; but from the moment I announced to him that I had changed my mind about going to the estancia, and was silent when he demanded the reason, there was a something in him which made it different between us. I could not open my heart to him about Elaria, and sometimes I thought that he also had a secret which he had no intention of sharing with me. This coldness did not, however, distress me very much, so great was the happiness I now experienced, knowing that I possessed Elaria's love. He was much away from the house, being fond of amusements, and he had also begun to gamble. About three months passed in this way, when one morning Torcuato, who was saddling his horse to go out, said, "Will you come with me, to-day, Anacleto?"

"I do not care to go," I answered.

"Look, Anacleto," said he; "once you were always ready to accompany me to a race or dance or cattle-marking. Why have you ceased to care for these things? Are you growing devout before your time, or does my company no longer please you?"

"It is best to tell him everything and have done with secrets," said I to myself, and so replied—

"Since you ask me, Torcuato, I will answer you frankly. It is true that I now take less pleasure than formerly in these pastimes; but you have not guessed the reason rightly."

"What then is this reason of which you speak?"

"Since you cannot guess it," I replied, "know that it is love."

"Love for whom?" he asked quickly, and turning very pale.

"Do you need ask? Elaria," I replied.

I had scarcely uttered the name before he turned on me full of rage.

"Elaria!" he exclaimed. "Do you dare tell me of love for Elaria! But you are only a blind fool, and do not know that I am going to marry her myself."

"Are you mad, Torcuato, to talk of marrying your sister?"

"She is no more my sister than you are my brother," he returned. "I" he continued, striking his breast passionately, "am the only child of my father, Loreto Silva. Elaria, whose mother died in giving her birth, was adopted by my parents. And because she is going to be my wife, I am willing that she should have a share of the property; but you, a miserable foundling, why were you lifted up so high? Was it not enough that you were clothed and fed till you came to man's estate? Not a hand's-breadth of the estancia land should be yours by right, and now you presume to speak of love for Elaria."

My blood was on fire with so many insults, but I remembered all the benefits I had received from his father, and did not raise my hand against him. Without more words he left me. I then hastened to Elaria and told her what had passed.

"This," I said, "is the secret you would not impart to me. Why, when you knew these things, was I kept in ignorance?"

"Have pity on me, Anacleto," she replied, crying. "Did I not see that you two were no longer friends and brothers, and this without knowing of each other's love? I dared not open my lips to you or to him. It is always a woman's part to suffer in silence. God intended us to be poor, Anacleto, for we were both born of poor parents, and had this property never come to us, how happy we might have been!"

"Why do you say such things, Elaria? Since we love each other, we cannot be unhappy, rich or poor."

"Is it a little matter," she replied, "that Torcuato must be our bitter enemy? But you do not know every thing. Before Torcuato's father died, he said he wished his son to marry me when we came of age. When he spoke about it we were sitting together by his bed."

"And what did you say, Elaria?" I asked, full of concern.

"Torcuato promised to marry me. I only covered my face, and was silent, for I loved you best even then, though I was almost a child, and my heart was filled with grief at his words. After we came here, Torcuato reminded me of his father's words. I answered that I did not wish to marry him, that he was only a brother to me. Then he said that we were young and he could wait until I was of another mind. This is all I have to say; but how shall we three live together any longer? I cannot bear to part from you, and every moment I tremble to think what may happen when you two are together."

"Fear nothing." I said. "To-morrow morning you can go to spend a week at some friend's house in the town; then I will speak to Torcuato, and tell him that since we cannot live in peace together we must separate. Even if he answers with insults I shall do nothing to grieve you, and if he refuses to listen to me, I shall send some person we both respect to arrange all things between us."

This satisfied her, but as evening approached she grew paler, and I knew she feared Torcuato's return. He did not, however, come back that night. Early the next morning she was ready to leave. It was an easy walk to town, but the dew was heavy on the grass, and I saddled a horse for her to ride. I had just lifted her to the saddle when Torcuato appeared. He came at great speed, and throwing himself off his horse, advanced to us. Elaria trembled and seemed ready to sink upon the earth to hide herself like a partridge that has seen the hawk. I prepared myself for insults and perhaps violence. He never looked at me; he only spoke to her.

"Elaria," he said, "something has happened—something that obliges me to leave this house and neighbourhood at once. Remember when I am away that my father, who cherished you and enriched you with his bounty, and who also cherished and enriched this ingrate, spoke to us from his dying bed and made me promise to marry you. Think what his love was; do not forget that his last wish is sacred, and that Anacleto has acted a base, treacherous part in trying to steal you from me. He was lifted out of the mire to be my brother and equal in everything except this. He has got a third part of my inheritance—let that satisfy him; your own heart, Elaria, will tell you that a marriage with him would be a crime before God and man. Look not for my return to-morrow nor for many days. But if you two begin to laugh at my father's dying wishes, look for me, for then I shall not delay to come back to you, Elaria, and to you, Anacleto. I have spoken."

He then mounted his horse and rode away. Very soon we learned the cause of his sudden departure. He had quarrelled over his cards and in a struggle that followed had stabbed his adversary to the heart. He had fled to escape the penalty. We did not believe that he would remain long absent; for Torcuato was very young, well off, and much liked, and this was, moreover, his first offence against the law. But time went on and he did not return, nor did any message from him reach us, and we at last concluded that he had left the country. Only now after four years have I accidentally discovered his fate through seeing his piebald horse.

After he had been absent over a year, I asked Elaria to become my wife. "We cannot marry till Torcuato returns," she said. "For if we take the property that ought to have been all his, and at the same time disobey his father's dying wish, we shall be doing an evil thing. Let us take care of the property till he returns to receive it all back from us; then, Anacleto, we shall be free to marry."

I consented, for she was more to me than lands and cattle. I put the estancia in order and leaving a trustworthy person in charge of everything I invested my money in fat bullocks to resell in Buenos Ayres, and in this business I have been employed ever since. From the estancia I have taken nothing, and now it must all come back to us—his inheritance and ours. This is a bitter thing and will give Elaria great grief.

Thus ended Anacleto's story, and when he had finished speaking and still seemed greatly troubled in his mind, Sotelo said to him, "Friend, let me advise you what to do. You will now shortly be married to the woman you love and probably some day a son will be born to you. Let him be named Torcuato, and let Torcuato's inheritance be kept for him. And if God gives you no son, remember what was done for you and for the girl you are going to marry, when you were orphans and friendless, and look out for some unhappy child in the same condition, to protect and enrich him as you were enriched."

"You have spoken well," said Anacleto. "I will report your words to Elaria, and whatever she wishes done that I will do."

So ends my story, friend. The cattle-drover left us that night and we saw no more of him. Only before going he gave the piebald and the silver trapping to Sotelo. Six months after his visit, Sotelo also received a letter from him to say that his marriage with Elaria had taken place; and the letter was accompanied with a present of seven cream-coloured horses with black manes and hoofs.

Bret Harte

CHU CHU

I DO not believe that the most en-
thusiastic lover of that "useful and noble animal," the horse, will claim
for him the charm of geniality, humor, or expansive confidence. Any
creature who will not look you squarely in the eye—whose only oblique
glances are inspired by fear, distrust, or a view to attack; who has no way
of returning caresses, and whose favorite expression is one of head-lifting
disdain, may be "noble" or useful," but can be hardly said to add to the
gayety of nations. Indeed it may be broadly stated that, with the single
exception of gold-fish, of all animals kept for the recreation of mankind
the horse is alone capable of exciting a passion that shall be absolutely
hopeless. I deem these general remarks necessary to prove that my un-

reciprocated affection for Chu Chu was not purely individual or singular. And I may add that to these general characteristics she brought the waywardness of her capricious sex.

She came to me out of the rolling dust of an emigrant wagon, behind whose tail-board she was gravely trotting. She was a half-broken filly—in which character she had at different times unseated everybody in the train—and, although covered with dust, she had a beautiful coat, and the most lambent gazelle-like eyes I had ever seen. I think she kept these latter organs purely for ornament—apparently looking at things with her nose, her sensitive ears, and, sometimes, even a slight lifting of her slim near foreleg. On our first interview I thought she favored me with a coy glance, but as it was accompanied by an irrelevant "Look out!" from her owner, the teamster, I was not certain. I only know that after some conversation, a good deal of mental reservation, and the disbursement of considerable coin, I found myself standing in the dust of the departing emigrant wagon with one end of a forty-foot riata in my hand, and Chu Chu at the other.

I pulled invitingly at my own end, and even advanced a step or two toward her. She then broke into a long disdainful pace, and began to circle round me at the extreme limit of her tether. I stood admiring her free action for some moments—not always turning with her, which was tiring—until I found that she was gradually winding herself up *on me*! Her frantic astonishment when she suddenly found herself thus brought up against me was one of the most remarkable things I ever saw, and nearly took me off my legs. Then, when she had pulled against the riata until her narrow head and prettily arched neck were on a perfectly straight line with it, she as suddenly slackened the tension and conde-scended to follow me, at an angle of her own choosing. Sometimes it was on one side of me, sometimes on the other. Even then the sense of my dreadful contiguity apparently would come upon her like a fresh discov-ery, and she would become hysterical. But I do not think that she really *saw* me. She looked at the riata and sniffed it disparagingly; she pawed some pebbles that were near me tentatively with her small hoof; she started back with a Robinson Crusoe-like horror of my footprints in the wet gully, but my actual personal presence she ignored. She would sometimes pause, with her head thoughtfully between her forelegs, and apparently say: "There is some extraordinary presence here: animal, vegetable, or mineral—I can't make out which—but it's not good to eat, and I loathe and detest it."

When I reached my house in the suburbs, before entering the "fifty vara" lot inclosure, I deemed it prudent to leave her outside while I informed the household of my purchase; and with this object I tethered her by the long riata to a solitary sycamore which stood in the centre of the road, the crossing of two frequented thoroughfares. It was not long, however, before I was interrupted by shouts and screams from that vicinity, and on returning thither I found that Chu Chu, with the assistance of her riata, had securely wound up two of my neighbors to the tree, where they presented the appearance of early Christian martyrs. When I released them it appeared that they had been attracted by Chu Chu's graces, and had offered her overtures of affection, to which she had characteristically rotated with this miserable result. I led her, with some difficulty, warily keeping clear of the riata, to the inclosure, from whose fence I had previously removed several bars. Although the space was wide enough to have admitted a troop of cavalry she affected not to notice it, and managed to kick away part of another section on entering. She resisted the stable for some time, but after carefully examining it with her hoofs, and an affectedly meek outstretching of her nose, she consented to recognize some oats in the feed-box—without looking at them—and was formally installed. All this while she had resolutely ignored my presence. As I stood watching her she suddenly stopped eating; the same reflective look came over her. "Surely I am not mistaken, but that same obnoxious creature is somewhere about here!" she seemed to say, and shivered at the possibility.

It was probably this which made me confide my unreciprocated affection to one of my neighbors—a man supposed to be an authority on horses, and particularly of that wild species to which Chu Chu belonged. It was he who, leaning over the edge of the stall where she was complacently and, as usual, obliviously munching, absolutely dared to toy with a pet lock of hair which she wore over the pretty star on her forehead.

"Ye see, captain," he said, with jaunty easiness, "hosses is like wimmen; ye don't want ter use any standoffishness or shyness with *them*; a stiddy but keerless sort o' familiarity, a kind o' free but firm handlin', jess like this, to let her see who's master"—

We never clearly knew *how* it happened; but when I picked up my neighbor from the doorway, amid the broken splinters of the stall rail, and a quantity of oats that mysteriously filled his hair and pockets, Chu Chu was found to have faced around the other way, and was contemplating her forelegs, with her hind ones in the other stall. My neighbor spoke of damages while he was in the stall, and of physical coercion when he was out of it again. But here Chu Chu, in some marvelous way, righted herself, and my neighbor departed hurriedly with a brimless hat and an unfinished sentence.

My next intermediary was Enriquez Saltello—a youth of my own age, and the brother of Consuelo Saltello, whom I adored. As a Spanish Californian he was presumed, on account of Chu Chu's half-Spanish origin, to have superior knowledge of her character, and I even vaguely believed that his language and accent would fall familiarly on her ear. There was the drawback, however, that he always preferred to talk in a marvelous English, combining Castilian precision with what he fondly believed to be Californian slang.

"To confer then as to thees horse, which is not—observe me—a Mexican plug! Ah, no! You can your boots bet on that. She is of Castilian stock—believe me and strike me dead! I will myself at different times overlook and affront her in the stable, examine her as to the assault, and why she should do thees thing. When she is of the exercise I will also accost and restrain her. Remain tranquil, my friend! When a few days shall pass much shall be changed, and she will be as another. Trust your oncle to do thees thing! Comprehend me? Everything shall be lovely, and the goose hang high!"

Conformably with this he "overlooked" her the next day, with a cigarette between his yellow-stained fingertips, which made her sneeze in a silent pantomimic way, and certain Spanish blandishments of speech which she received with more complacency. But I don't think she ever even looked at him. In vain he protested that she was the "dearest" and "littlest" of his "little loves"—in vain he asserted that she was his patron saint, and that it was his soul's delight to pray to her; she accepted the compliment with her eyes fixed upon the manger. When he had exhausted his whole stock of endearing diminutives, adding a few playful and more audacious sallies, she remained with her head down, as if inclined to meditate upon them. This he declared was at least an improvement on her former performances. It may have been my own jealousy, but I fancied she was only saying to herself, "Gracious! can there be *two* of them?"

"Courage and patience, my friend," he said, as we were slowly quitting the stable. "Thees horse is yonge, and has not yet the habitude of the person. To-morrow, at another season, I shall give to her a foundling" ("fondling," I have reason to believe, was the word intended by Enriquez)—"and we shall see. It shall be as easy as to fall away from a log. A leetle more of this chin music which your friend Enriquez possesses, and some tapping of the head and neck, and you are there. You are ever the right side up. Houp la! But let us not precipitate this thing. The more haste, we do not so much accelerate ourselves."

He appeared to be suiting the action to the word as he lingered in the doorway of the stable. "Come on," I said.

"Pardon," he returned, with a bow that was both elaborate and evasive, "but you shall yourself precede me—the stable is *yours*."

"Oh, come along!" I continued impatiently. To my surprise he seemed to dodge back into the stable again. After an instant he reappeared.

"Pardon! but I am re-strain! Of a truth, in this instant I am grasp by the mouth of thees horse in the coattail of my dress! She will that I should remain. It would seem"—he disappeared again—"that"—he was out once more—"the experiment is a sooccess! She reciprocate! She is, of a truth, gone on me. It is lofe!"—a stronger pull from Chu Chu here sent him in again—"but"—he was out now triumphantly with half his garment torn away—"I shall coquet."

Nothing daunted, however, the gallant fellow was back next day with a Mexican saddle, and attired in the complete outfit of a vaquero. Overcome though *he* was by heavy deerskin trousers, open at the side from the knees down, and fringed with bullion buttons, an enormous flat sombrero, and a stiff, short embroidered velvet jacket, I was more concerned at the ponderous saddle and equipments intended for the slim Chu Chu. That these would hide and conceal her beautiful curves and contour, as well as overweight her, seemed certain; that she would resist them all to the last seemed equally clear. Nevertheless, to my surprise, when she was led out, and the saddle thrown deftly across her back, she was passive. Was it possible that some drop of her old Spanish blood responded to its clinging embrace? She did not either look at it or smell it. But when Enriquez began to tighten the cinch or girth a more singular thing occurred. Chu Chu visibly distended her slender barrel to twice its dimensions; the more he pulled the more she swelled, until I was actually ashamed of her. Not so Enriquez. He smiled at us, and complacently stroked his thin mustache.

"Eet is ever so! She is the child of her grandmother! Even when you shall make saddle thees old Castilian stock, it will make large—it will become a balloon! Eet is a trick—eet is a leetle game—believe me. For why?"

I had not listened, as I was at that moment astonished to see the saddle slowly slide under Chu Chu's belly, and her figure resume, as if by magic, its former slim proportions. Enriquez followed my eyes, lifted his shoulders, shrugged them, and said smilingly, "Ah, you see!"

When the girths were drawn in again with an extra pull or two from the indefatigable Enriquez, I fancied that Chu Chu nevertheless secretly enjoyed it, as her sex is said to appreciate tight lacing. She drew a deep sigh, possibly of satisfaction, turned her neck, and apparently tried to glance at her own figure—Enriquez promptly withdrawing to enable her to do so easily. Then the dread moment arrived. Enriquez, with his hand on her mane, suddenly paused and, with exaggerated courtesy, lifted his hat and made an inviting gesture.

"You will honor me to precede."

I shook my head laughingly.

"I see," responded Enriquez gravely. "You have to attend the obsequies of your aunt who is dead, at two of the clock. You have to meet your broker who has bought you feefty share of the Comstock lode—at thees moment—or you are loss! You are excuse! Attend! Gentlemen, make your bets! The band has arrived to play! 'Ere we are!"

With a quick movement the alert young fellow had vaulted into the saddle. But, to the astonishment of both of us, the mare remained perfectly still. There was Enriquez bolt upright in the stirrups, completely overshadowing by his saddle-flaps, leggings, and gigantic spurs the fine proportions of Chu Chu, until she might have been a placid Rosinante, bestridden by some youthful Quixote. She closed her eyes, she was going to sleep! We were dreadfully disappointed. This clearly would not do. Enriquez lifted the reins cautiously! Chu Chu moved forward slowly— then stopped, apparently lost in reflection.

"Affront her on thees side."

I approached her gently. She shot suddenly into the air, coming down again on perfectly stiff legs with a springless jolt. This she instantly followed by a succession of other rocket-like propulsions, utterly unlike a leap, all over the inclosure. The movements of the unfortunate Enriquez were equally unlike any equitation I ever saw. He appeared occasionally over Chu Chu's head, astride of her neck and tail, or in the free air, but never *in* the saddle. His rigid legs, however, never lost the stirrups, but came down regularly, accentuating her springless hops. More than that, the disproportionate excess of rider, saddle, and accoutrements was so great that he had, at times, the appearance of lifting Chu Chu forcibly from the ground by superior strength, and of actually contributing to her exercise! As they came toward me, a wild tossing and flying mass of hoofs and spurs, it was not only difficult to distinguish them apart, but to ascertain how much of the jumping was done by Enriquez separately. At last Chu Chu brought matters to a close by making for the low-stretching branches of an oak-tree which stood at the corner of the lot. In a few moments she emerged from it—but without Enriquez

I found the gallant fellow disengaging himself from the fork of a branch in which he had been firmly wedged, but still smiling and confident, and his cigarette between his teeth. Then for the first time he removed it, and seating himself easily on the branch with his legs dangling down, he blandly waved aside my anxious queries with a gentle reassuring gesture.

"Remain tranquil, my friend. Thees does not count! I have conquer—you observe—for why? I have *never* for once *arrive at the ground*! Consequent she is disappoint! She will ever that I *should*! But I have got her when the hair is not long! Your oncle Henry"—with an angelic wink—"is fly! He is ever a bully boy, with the eye of glass! Believe me. Behold! I am here! Big Injun! Whoop!"

He leaped lightly to the ground. Chu Chu, standing watchfully at a little distance, was evidently astonished at his appearance. She threw out her hind hoofs violently, shot up into the air until the stirrups crossed each other high above the saddle, and made for the stable in a succession of rabbit-like bounds—taking the precaution to remove the saddle, on entering, by striking it against the lintel of the door.

"You observe," said Enriquez blandly, "she would make that thing of *me*. Not having the good occasion, she ees dissatisfied. Where are you now?"

Two or three days afterwards he rode her again with the same result—accepted by him with the same heroic complacency. As we did not, for certain reasons, care to use the open road for this exercise, and as it was impossible to remove the tree, we were obliged to submit to the inevitable. On the following day I mounted her—undergoing the same experience as Enriquez, with the individual sensation of falling from a third-story window on top of a countinghouse stool, and the variation of being projected over the fence. When I found that Chu Chu had not accompanied me, I saw Enriquez at my side.

"More than ever it is become necessary that we should do thees things again," he said gravely, as he assisted me to my feet. "Courage, my noble General! God and Liberty! Once more on to the breach! Charge, Chestare, charge! Come on, Don Stanley! 'Ere we are!"

He helped me none too quickly to catch my seat again, for it apparently had the effect of the turned peg on the enchanted horse in the Arabian Nights, and Chu Chu instantly rose into the air. But she came down this time before the open window of the kitchen, and I alighted easily on the dresser. The indefatigable Enriquez followed me.

"Won't this do?" I asked meekly.

"It ees *better*—for you arrive *not* on the ground," he said cheerfully; "but you should not once but a thousand times make trial! Ha! Go and win! Nevare die and say so! 'Eave ahead! 'Eave! There you are!"

Luckily, this time I managed to lock the rowels of my long spurs under her girth, and she could not unseat me. She seemed to recognize the fact after one or two plunges, when, to my great surprise, she suddenly sank to the ground and quietly rolled over me. The action disengaged my spurs, but, righting herself without getting up, she turned her beautiful head and absolutely *looked* at me!—still in the saddle. I felt myself blushing! But the voice of Enriquez was at my side.

"Errise, my friend; you have conquer! It is *she* who has arrive at the ground! *You* are all right. It is done; believe me, it is feenish! No more shall she make thees thing. From thees instant you shall ride her as the cow—as the rail of thees fence—and remain tranquil. For she is a-broke! Ta-ta! Regain your hats, gentlemen! Pass in your checks! It is ovar! How are you now?" He lit a fresh cigarette, put his hands in his pockets, and smiled at me blandly.

For all that, I ventured to point out that the habit of alighting in the fork of a tree, or the disengaging of one's self from the saddle on the ground, was attended with inconvenience, and even ostentatious display. But Enriquez swept the objections away with a single gesture. "It is the *preencipal*—the bottom fact—at which you arrive. The next come of himself! Many horse have achieve to mount the rider by the knees, and relinquish after thees same fashion. My grandfather had a barb of thees kind—but she has gone dead, and so have my grandfather. Which is sad and strange! Otherwise I shall make of them both an instant example!"

I ought to have said that although these performances were never actually witnessed by Enriquez's sister—for reasons which he and I thought sufficient—the dear girl displayed the greatest interest in them, and, perhaps aided by our mutually complimentary accounts of each other, looked upon us both as invincible heroes. It is possible also that she overestimated our success, for she suddenly demanded that I should *ride* Chu Chu to her house, that she might see her. It was not far; by going through a back lane I could avoid the trees which exercised such a fatal fascination for Chu Chu. There was a pleading, childlike entreaty in

Consuelo's voice that I could not resist, with a slight flash from her lustrous dark eyes that I did not care to encourage. So I resolved to try it at all hazards.

My equipment for the performance was modeled after Enriquez's previous costume, with the addition of a few fripperies of silver and stamped leather out of compliment to Consuelo, and even with a faint hope that it might appease Chu Chu. *She* certainly looked beautiful in her glittering accoutrements, set off by her jet-black shining coat. With an air of demure abstraction she permitted me to mount her, and even for a hundred yards or so indulged in a mincing maidenly amble that was not without a touch of coquetry. Encouraged by this, I addressed a few terms of endearment to her, and in the exuberance of my youthful enthusiasm I even confided to her my love for Consuelo, and begged her to be "good" and not disgrace herself and me before my Dulcinea. In my foolish trustfulness I was rash enough to add a caress, and to pat her soft neck. She stopped instantly with an hysteric shudder. I knew what was passing through her mind: she had suddenly become aware of my baleful existence.

The saddle and bridle Chu Chu was becoming accustomed to, but who was this living, breathing object that had actually touched her? Presently her oblique vision was attracted by the fluttering movement of a fallen oak-leaf in the road before her. She had probably seen many oak-leaves many times before; her ancestors had no doubt been familiar with them on the trackless hills and in field and paddock, but this did not alter her profound conviction that I and the leaf were identical, that our baleful touch was something indissolubly connected. She reared before that innocent leaf, she revolved round it, and then fled from it at the top of her speed.

The lane passed before the rear wall of Saltellos' garden. Unfortunately, at the angle of the fence stood a beautiful madroño-tree, brilliant with its scarlet berries, and endeared to me as Consuelo's favorite haunt, under whose protecting shade I had more than once avowed my youthful passion. By the irony of fate Chu Chu caught sight of it, and with a succession of spirited bounds instantly made for it. In another moment I was beneath it, and Chu Chu shot like a rocket into the air. I had barely time to withdraw my feet from the stirrups, to throw up one arm to protect my glazed sombrero and grasp an overhanging branch with the other, before Chu Chu darted off. But to my consternation, as I gained a secure perch on the tree, and looked about me, I saw her—instead of running away—quietly trot through the open gate into Saltellos' garden.

Need I say that it was to the beneficent Enriquez that I again owed my salvation? Scarcely a moment elapsed before his bland voice rose in a concentrated whisper from the corner of the garden below me. He had divined the dreadful truth!

"For the love of God, collect to yourself many kinds of thees berry! All you can! Your full arms round! Rest tranquil. Leave to your ole oncle to make for you a delicate exposure. At the instant!"

He was gone again. I gathered, wonderingly, a few of the larger clusters of parti-colored fruit, and patiently waited. Presently he reappeared, and with him the lovely Consuelo—her dear eyes filled with an adorable anxiety.

"Yes," continued Enriquez to his sister, with a confidential lowering of tone but great distinctness of utterance, "it is ever so with the American! He will ever make *first* the salutation of the flower or the fruit, picked to himself by his own hand, to the lady where he call. It is the custom of the American hidalgo! My God—what will you? *I* make it not—it is so! Without doubt he is in this instant doing thees thing. That is why he have let go his horse to precede him here; it is always the etiquette to offer these things on the feet. Ah! behold! it is he!—Don Francisco! Even now he will descend from thees tree! Ah! You make the blush, little sister (archly)! I will retire! I am discreet; two is not company for the one! I make tracks! I make tracks! I am gone!"

How far Consuelo entirely believed and trusted her ingenious brother I do not know, nor even then cared to inquire. For there was a pretty mantling of her olive cheek, as I came forward with my offering, and a certain significant shyness in her manner that were enough to throw me into a state of hopeless imbecility. And I was always miserably conscious that Consuelo possessed an exalted sentimentality, and a predilection for the highest mediæval romance, in which I knew I was lamentably deficient. Even in our most confidential moments I was always aware that

I weakly lagged behind this daughter of a gloomily distinguished ancestry, in her frequent incursions into a vague but poetic past. There was something of the dignity of the Spanish châtelaine in the sweetly grave little figure that advanced to accept my specious offering. I think I should have fallen on my knees to present it, but for the presence of the all-seeing Enriquez. But why did I even at that moment remember that he had early bestowed upon her the nickname of "Pomposa?" This, as Enriquez himself might have observed, was "sad and strange."

I managed to stammer out something about the madroño berries being at her "disposicion" (the tree was in her own garden!), and she took the branches in her little brown hand with a soft response to my unutterable glances.

But here Chu Chu, momentarily forgotten, executed a happy diversion. To our astonishment she gravely walked up to Consuelo and, stretching out her long slim neck, not only sniffed curiously at the berries, but even protruded a black under lip towards the young girl herself. In another instant Consuelo's dignity melted. Throwing her arms around Chu Chu's neck she embraced and kissed her. Young as I was, I understood the divine significance of a girl's vicarious effusiveness at such a moment, and felt delighted. But I was the more astonished that the usually sensitive horse not only submitted to these caresses, but actually responded to the extent of affecting to nip my mistress's little right ear.

This was enough for the impulsive Consuelo. She ran hastily into the house, and in a few moments reappeared in a bewitching riding-skirt gathered round her jimp waist. In vain Enriquez and myself joined in earnest entreaty: the horse was hardly broken for even a man's riding yet; the saints alone could tell what the nervous creature might do with a woman's skirt flapping at her side! We begged for delay, for reflection, for at least time to change the saddle—but with no avail! Consuelo was determined, indignant, distressingly reproachful! Ah, well! if Don Pancho (an ingenious diminutive of my Christian name) valued his horse so highly—if he were jealous of the evident devotion of the animal to herself, he would— But here I succumbed! And then I had the felicity of holding that little foot for one brief moment in the hollow of my hand, of readjusting the skirt as she threw her knee over the saddle-horn, of clasp-

ing her tightly—only half in fear—as I surrendered the reins to her grasp.
And to tell the truth, as Enriquez and I fell back, although I had insisted
upon still keeping hold of the end of the riata, it was a picture to admire.
The petite figure of the young girl, and the graceful folds of her skirt,
admirably harmonized with Chu Chu's lithe contour, and as the mare
arched her slim neck and raised her slender head under the pressure of the
reins, it was so like the lifted velvet-capped toreador crest of Consuelo
herself, that they seemed of one race.

"I would not that you should hold the riata," said Consuelo petu-
lantly.

I hesitated—Chu Chu looked certainly very amiable—I let go. She
began to amble towards the gate, not mincingly as before, but with a
freer and fuller stride. In spite of the incongruous saddle the young girl's
seat was admirable. As they neared the gate she cast a single mischievous
glance at me, jerked at the rein, and Chu Chu sprang into the road at a
rapid canter. I watched them fearfully and breathlessly, until at the end of
the lane I saw Consuelo rein in slightly, wheel easily, and come flying
back. There was no doubt about it; the horse was under perfect control.
Her second subjugation was complete and final!

Overjoyed and bewildered, I overwhelmed them with congratulations; Enriquez alone retaining the usual brotherly attitude of criticism,
and a superior toleration of a lover's enthusiasm. I ventured to hint to
Consuelo (in what I believed was a safe whisper) that Chu Chu only
showed my own feelings towards her.

"Without doubt," responded Enriquez gravely. "She have of herself
assist you to climb to the tree to pull to yourself the berry for my sister."

But I felt Consuelo's little hand return my pressure, and I forgave
and even pitied him.

From that day forward, Chu Chu and Consuelo were not only firm
friends but daily companions. In my devotion I would have presented the
horse to the young girl, but with flattering delicacy she preferred to call
it mine.

"I shall erride it for you, Pancho," she said. "I shall feel," she
continued, with exalted although somewhat vague poetry, "that it is of
you! You lofe the beast—it is therefore of a necessity *you*, my Pancho! It is

your soul I shall erride like the wings of the wind—your lofe in this beast shall be my only cavalier forever."

I would have preferred something whose vicarious qualities were less uncertain than I still felt Chu Chu's to be, but I kissed the girl's hand submissively. It was only when I attempted to accompany her in the flesh, on another horse, that I felt the full truth of my instinctive fears. Chu Chu would not permit any one to approach her mistress's side. My mounted presence revived in her all her old blind astonishment and disbelief in my existence; she would start suddenly, face about, and back away from me in utter amazement as if I had been only recently created, or with an affected modesty as if I had been just guilty of some grave indecorum towards her sex which she really could not stand. The frequency of these exhibitions in the public highway were not only distressing to me as a simple escort, but as it had the effect on the casual spectators of making Consuelo seem to participate in Chu Chu's objections, I felt that, as a lover, it could not be borne. Any attempt to coerce Chu Chu ended in her running away. And my frantic pursuit of her was open to equal misconstruction.

"Go it, miss, the little dude is gainin' on you!" shouted by a drunken teamster to the fightened Consuelo, once checked me in mid-career.

Even the dear girl herself saw the uselessness of my real presence, and after a while was content to ride with "my soul."

Notwithstanding this, I am not ashamed to say that it was my custom, whenever she rode out, to keep a slinking and distant surveillance of Chu Chu on another horse, until she had fairly settled down to her pace. A little nod of Consuelo's round black-and-red toreador hat, or a kiss tossed from her riding-whip, was reward enough!

I remember a pleasant afternoon when I was thus awaiting her in the outskirts of the village. The eternal smile of the Californian summer had begun to waver and grow less fixed; dust lay thick on leaf and blade; the dry hills were clothed in russet leather; the trade-winds were shifting to the south with an ominous warm humidity; a few days longer and the rains would be here. It so chanced that this afternoon my seclusion on the roadside was accidentally invaded by a village belle—a Western young lady somewhat older than myself, and of flirtatious reputation. As she persistently and—as I now have reason to believe—mischievously lingered, I had only a passing glimpse of Consuelo riding past at an unaccustomed speed which surprised me at the moment. But as I reasoned later that she was only trying to avoid a merely formal meeting, I thought no more about it. It was not until I called at the house to fetch Chu Chu at the usual hour, and found that Consuelo had not yet returned, that a recollection of Chu Chu's furious pace again troubled me. An hour passed—it was getting towards sunset, but there were no signs of Chu Chu or her mistress. I became seriously alarmed. I did not care to reveal my fears to the family, for I felt myself responsible for Chu Chu. At last I desperately saddled my horse, and galloped off in the direction she had taken. It was the road to Rosario and the hacienda of one of her relations, where she sometimes halted.

The road was a very unfrequented one, twisting like a mountain river; indeed, it was the bed of an old water-course, between brown hills of wild oats, and debouching at last into a broad blue lake-like expanse of alfalfa meadows. In vain I strained my eyes over the monotonous level; nothing appeared to rise above or move across it. In the faint hope that she might have lingered at the hacienda, I was spurring on again when I heard a slight splashing on my left. I looked around. A broad patch of fresher-colored herbage and a cluster of dwarfed alders indicated a hidden spring. I cautiously approached its quaggy edges, when I was shocked by what appeared to be a sudden vision! Mid-leg deep in the centre of a greenish pool stood Chu Chu! But without a strap or buckle of harness upon her—as naked as when she was foaled!

For a moment I could only stare at her in bewildered terror. Far from recognizing me, she seemed to be absorbed in a nymph-like contemplation of her own graces in the pool. Then I called, "Consuelo!" and galloped frantically around the spring. But there was no response, nor was there anything to be seen but the all-unconscious Chu Chu. The pool, thank Heaven! was not deep enough to have drowned any one; there were no signs of a struggle on its quaggy edges. The horse might have come from a distance! I galloped on, still calling. A few hundred yards further I detected the vivid glow of Chu Chu's scarlet saddle-blanket, in the brush near the trail. My heart leaped—I was on the track. I called again; this time a faint reply, in accents I knew too well, came from the field beside me!

Consuelo was there! reclining beside a manzanita bush which screened her from the road, in what struck me, even at that supreme moment, as a judicious and picturesquely selected couch of scented Indian grass and dry tussocks. The velvet hat with its balls of scarlet plush was laid carefully aside; her lovely blue-black hair retained its tight coils undisheveled, her eyes were luminous and tender. Shocked as I was at her apparent helplessness, I remember being impressed with the fact that it gave so little indication of violent usage or disaster.

I threw myself frantically on the ground beside her.

"You are hurt, Consita! For Heaven's sake, what has happened?"

She pushed my hat back with her little hand, and tumbled my hair gently.

"Nothing. *You* are here, Pancho—eet is enofe! What shall come after thees—when I am perhaps gone among the grave—make nothing! *You* are here—I am happy. For a little, perhaps—not mooch."

"But," I went on desperately, "was it an accident? Were you thrown? Was it Chu Chu?"—for somehow, in spite of her languid posture and voice, I could not, even in my fears, believe her seriously hurt.

"Beat not the poor beast, Pancho. It is not from *her* comes thees thing. She have make nothing—believe me! I have come upon your assignation with Miss Essmith! I make but to pass you—to fly—to never come back! I have say to Chu Chu, 'Fly!' We fly many miles. Sometimes together, sometimes not so mooch! Sometimes in the saddle, sometimes on the neck! Many things remain in the road; at the end, I myself remain! I have say, 'Courage, Pancho will come!' Then I say, 'No, he is talk with Miss Essmith!' I remember not more. I have creep here on the hands. Eet is feenish!"

I looked at her distractedly. She smiled tenderly, and slightly smoothed down and rearranged a fold of her dress to cover her delicate little boot.

"But," I protested, "you are not much hurt, dearest. You have broken no bones. Perhaps," I added, looking at the boot, "only a slight sprain. Let me carry you to my horse; I will walk beside you, home. Do, dearest Consita!"

She turned her lovely eyes towards me sadly.

"You comprehend not, my poor Pancho! It is not of the foot, the ankle, the arm, or the head that I can say, 'She is broke!' I would it were even so. But"—she lifted her sweet lashes slowly—"I have derrange my inside. It is an affair of my family. My grandfather have once toomble over the bull at a rodeo. He speak no more; he is dead. For why? He has derrange his inside. Believe me, it is of the family. You comprehend? The Saltellos are not as the other peoples for this. When I am gone, you will bring to me the berry to grow upon my tomb, Pancho; the berry you have picked for me. The little flower will come too, the little star will arrive, but Consuelo, who lofe you, she will come not more! When you are happy and talk in the road to the Essmith, you will not think of me. You will not see my eyes, Pancho; thees little grass"—she ran her plump little fingers through a tussock—"will hide them; and the small animals in the black coats that lif here will have sorrow—but you will not. It ees better so! My father will not that I, a Catholique, should marry into a camp-meeting, and lif in a tent, and make howl like the coyote." (It was one of Consuelo's bewildering beliefs that there was only one form of dissent,—Methodism!) "He will not that I should marry a man who possess not the many horses, ox, and cow, like him. But *I* care not. *You* are my only religion, Pancho! I have enofe of the horse, and ox, and cow when *you* are with me! Kiss me, Pancho. Perhaps it is for the last time— the feenish! Who knows?"

There were tears in her lovely eyes; I felt that my own were growing dim; the sun was sinking over the dreary plain to the slow rising of the wind; an infinite loneliness had fallen upon us, and yet I was miserably conscious of some dreadful unreality in it all. A desire to laugh, which I felt must be hysterical, was creeping over me; I dared not speak. But her dear head was on my shoulder, and the situation was not unpleasant.

Nevertheless, something must be done! This was the more difficult as it was by no means clear what had already been done. Even while I supported her drooping figure I was straining my eyes across her shoulder for succor of some kind. Suddenly the figure of a rapid rider appeared upon the road. It seemed familiar. I looked again—it was the blessed Enriquez! A sense of deep relief came over me. I loved Consuelo; but never before had lover ever hailed the irruption of one of his beloved's family with such complacency.

"You are safe, dearest; it is Enriquez!"

I thought she received the information coldly. Suddenly she turned upon me her eyes, now bright and glittering.

"Swear to me at the instant, Pancho, that you will not again look upon Miss Essmith, even for once."

I was simple and literal. Miss Smith was my nearest neighbor, and, unless I was stricken with blindness, compliance was impossible. I hesitated—but swore.

"Enofe—you have hesitate—I will no more."

She rose to her feet with grave deliberation. For an instant, with the recollection of the delicate internal organization of the Saltellos on my mind, I was in agony lest she should totter and fall, even then, yielding up her gentle spirit on the spot. But when I looked again she had a hairpin between her white teeth, and was carefully adjusting her toreador hat. And beside us was Enriquez—cheerful, alert, voluble, and undaunted.

"Eureka! I have found! We are all here! Eet is a leetle public—eh? a leetle to much of a front seat for a tête-à-tête, my yonge friends," he said, glancing at the remains of Consuelo's bower, "but for the accounting of taste there is none. What will you? The meat of the one man shall envenom the meat of the other. But" (in a whisper to me) "as to thees horse—thees Chu Chu, which I have just pass—why is she undress? Surely you would not make an exposition of her to the traveler to suspect! And if not, why so?"

I tried to explain, looking at Consuelo, that Chu Chu had run away, that Consuelo had met with a terrible accident, had been thrown, and I feared had suffered serious internal injury. But to my embarrassment Consuelo maintained a half-scornful silence, and an inconsistent freshness of healthful indifference, as Enriquez approached her with an engaging smile.

"Ah, yes, she have the headache, and the molligrubs. She will sit on the damp stone when the gentle dew is falling. I comprehend. Meet me in the lane when the clock strike nine! But," in a lower voice, "of thees undress horse I comprehend nothing! Look you—it is sad and strange."

He went off to fetch Chu Chu, leaving me and Consuelo alone. I do not think I ever felt so utterly abject and bewildered before in my life. Without knowing why, I was miserably conscious of having in some way offended the girl for whom I believed I would have given my life, and I had made her and myself ridiculous in the eyes of her brother. I had again failed in my slower Western nature to understand her high romantic Spanish soul! Meantime she was smoothing out her riding-habit, and looking as fresh and pretty as when she first left her house.

"Consita," I said hesitatingly, "you are not angry with me?"

"Angry?" she repeated haughtily, without looking at me. "Oh, no! Of a possibility eet is Mees Essmith who is angry that I have interroopt her tête-à-tête with you, and have send here my brother to make the same with me."

"But," I said eagerly, "Miss Smith does not even know Enriquez!"

Consuelo turned on me a glance of unutterable significance.

"Ah!" she said darkly, "you *tink*!"

Indeed I *knew*. But here I believed I understood Consuelo, and was relieved. I even ventured to say gently, "And you are better?"

She drew herself up to her full height, which was not much.

"Of my health, what is it? A nothing. Yes! Of my soul let us not speak."

Nevertheless, when Enriquez appeared with Chu Chu she ran towards her with outstretched arms. Chu Chu protruded about six inches of upper lip in response—apparently under the impression, which I could quite understand, that her mistress was edible. And, I may have been mistaken, but their beautiful eyes met in an absolute and distinct glance of intelligence!

During the home journey Consuelo recovered her spirits, and parted from me with a magnanimous and forgiving pressure of the hand. I do not know what explanation of Chu Chu's original escape was given to

Enriquez and the rest of the family; the inscrutable forgiveness extended to me by Consuelo precluded any further inquiry on my part. I was willing to leave it a secret between her and Chu Chu. But, strange to say, it seemed to complete our own understanding, and precipitated, not only our love-making, but the final catastrophe which culminated that romance. For we had resolved to elope. I do not know that this heroic remedy was absolutely necessary from the attitude of either Consuelo's family or my own; I am inclined to think we preferred it, because it involved no previous explanation or advice. Need I say that our confidant and firm ally was Consuelo's brother—the alert, the linguistic, the ever happy, ever ready Enriquez! It was understood that his presence would not only give a certain mature respectability to our performance—but I do not think we would have contemplated this step without it. During one of our riding excursions we were to secure the services of a Methodist minister in the adjoining county, and later, that of the mission padre—when the secret was out.

"I will gif her away," said Enriquez confidently; "it will on the instant propitiate the old shadbelly who shall perform the affair, and withhold his jaw. A little chin music from your uncle 'Arry shall finish it! Remain tranquil and forget not a ring! One does not always, in the agony and dissatisfaction of the moment, a ring remember. I shall bring two in the pocket of my dress."

If I did not entirely participate in this roseate view it may have been because Enriquez, although a few years my senior, was much younger-looking, and with his demure deviltry of eye, and his upper lip close shaven for this occasion, he suggested a depraved acolyte rather than a responsible member of a family. Consuelo had also confided to me that her father—possibly owing to some rumors of our previous escapade—had forbidden any further excursions with me alone. The innocent man did not know that Chu Chu had forbidden it also, and that even on this momentous occasion both Enriquez and myself were obliged to ride in opposite fields like out-flankers. But we nevertheless felt the full guilt of disobedience added to our desperate enterprise. Meanwhile, although pressed for time, and subject to discovery at any moment, I managed at certain points of the road to dismount and walk beside Chu Chu (who did not seem to recognize me on foot), holding Consuelo's hand in my own, with the discreet Enriquez leading my horse in the distant field. I retain a very vivid picture of that walk—the ascent of a gentle slope towards a prospect as yet unknown, but full of glorious possibilities; the tender dropping light of an autumn sky, slightly filmed with the promise of the future rains, like foreshadowed tears, and the half-frightened, half-serious talk into which Consuelo and I had insensibly fallen. And then, I don't know how it happened, but as we reached the summit Chu Chu suddenly reared, wheeled, and the next moment was flying back along the road we had just traveled, at the top of her speed! It might have been that, after her abstracted fashion, she only at that moment detected my presence; but so sudden and complete was her evolution that before I could regain my horse from the astonished Enriquez she was already a quarter of a mile on the homeward stretch, with the frantic Consuelo pulling hopelessly at the bridle. We started in pursuit. But a horrible despair seized us. To attempt to overtake her, to even follow at the same rate of speed, would only excite Chu Chu and endanger Consuelo's life. There was absolutely no help for it, nothing could be done; the mare had taken her determined long, continuous stride; the road was a straight, steady descent all the way back to the village; Chu Chu had the bit between her teeth, and there was no prospect of swerving her. We could only follow hopelessly, idiotically, furiously, until Chu Chu dashed triumphantly into the Saltellos' courtyard, carrying the half-fainting Consuelo back to the arms of her assembled and astonished family.

It was our last ride together. It was the last I ever saw of Consuelo before her transfer to the safe seclusion of a convent in Southern California. It was the last I ever saw of Chu Chu, who in the confusion of that rencontre was overlooked in her half-loosed harness, and allowed to escape through the back gate to the fields. Months afterwards it was said that she had been identified among a band of wild horses in the Coast Range, as a strange and beautiful creature who had escaped the brand of the rodeo and had become a myth. There was another legend that she had been seen, sleek, fat, and gorgeously caparisoned, issuing from the gateway of the Rosario patio, before a lumbering Spanish cabriolé in which a short, stout matron was seated—but I will have none of it. For there are days when she still lives, and I can see her plainly still climbing the gentle slope towards the summit, with Consuelo on her back, and myself at her side, pressing eagerly forward towards the illimitable prospect that opens in the distance.

Ambrose Bierce

RACE AT LEFT BOWER

"It's all very well fer you Britishers to go assin' about the country tryin' to strike the trail o' the mines you've salted down yer loose carpital in," said Colonel Jackhigh, setting his empty glass on the counter and wiping his lips with his coat sleeve; "but w'en it comes to hoss racin', w'y I've got a cayuse ken lay over all the thurrerbreds yer little mantel-ornyment of a island ever panned out—bet yer britches I have! Talk about yer Durby winners—w'y this pisen little beast o' mine'll take the bit in her teeth and show 'em the way to the horizon like she was takin' her mornin' stroll and they was tryin' to keep an eye on her to see she didn't do herself an injury—that's w'at she

375

would! And she haint never run a race with anything spryer'n an Injun in all her life; she's a green amatoor, *she* is!

"Oh, very well," said the Englishman with a quiet smile; "it is easy enough to settle the matter. My animal is in tolerably good condition, and if yours is in town we can have the race to-morrow for any stake you like, up to a hundred dollars."

"That's jest the figger," said the colonel; "dot it down, barkeep. But it's like slarterin' the innocents," he added, half-remorsefully, as he turned to leave; "it's bettin' on a dead sure thing—that's what it is! If my cayuse knew wa't I was about she'd go and break a laig to make the race a fair one."

So it was arranged that the race was to come off at three o'clock the next day, on the *mesa,* some distance from town. As soon as the news got abroad, the whole population of Left Bower and vicinity knocked off work and assembled in the various bars to discuss it. The Englishman and his horse were general favorites, and aside from the unpopularity of the colonel, nobody had ever seen his "cayuse." Still the element of patriotism came in, making the betting very nearly even.

A race-course was marked off on the *mesa* and at the appointed hour every one was there except the colonel. It was arranged that each man should ride his own horse, and the Englishman, who had acquired something of the free-and-easy bearing that distinguishes the "mining sharp," was already atop of his magnificent animal, with one leg thrown carelessly across the pommel of his Mexican saddle, as he puffed his cigar with calm confidence in the result of the race. He was conscious, too, that he possessed the secret sympathy of all, even of those who had felt it their duty to bet against him. The judge, watch in hand was growing impatient, when the colonel appeared about a half-mile away, and bore down upon the crowd. Everyone was eager to inspect his mount; and such a mount as it proved to be was never before seen, even in Left Bower!

You have seen "perfect skeletons" of horses often enough, no doubt, but this animal was not even a perfect skeleton; there were bones missing here and there which you would not have believed the beast could have spared. "Little" the colonel had called her! She was not an inch less than eighteen hands high, and long out of all reasonable proportion. She was so hollow in the back that she seemed to have been bent in a machine. She had neither tail nor mane, and her neck, as long as a man, stuck straight up into the air, supporting a head without ears. Her eyes had an expression in them of downright insanity, and the muscles of her face were afflicted with periodical convulsions that drew back the corners of the mouth and wrinkled the upper lip so as to produce a ghastly grin every two or three seconds. In color she was "claybank," with great blotches of white, as if she had been pelted with small bags of flour. The crookedness of her legs was beyond all comparison, and as to her gait it was that of a blind camel walking diagonally across innumerable deep ditches. Altogether she looked like the crude result of Nature's first experiment in equifaction.

As this libel on all horses shambled up to the starting post there was a general shout; the sympathies of the crowd changed in the twinkling of an eye! Everyone wanted to bet on her, and the Englishman himself was only restrained from doing so by a sense of honor. It was growing late, however, and the judge insisted on starting them. They got off very well together, and seeing the mare was unconscionably slow the Englishman soon pulled his animal in and permitted the ugly thing to pass him, so as to enjoy a back view of her. That sealed his fate. The course had been marked off in a circle of two miles in circumference and some twenty feet wide, the limits plainly defined by little furrows. Before the animals had gone a half mile both had been permitted to settle down into a comfortable walk, in which they continued three-fourths of the way round the ring. Then the Englishman thought it time to whip up and canter in.

But he didn't. As he came up alongside the "Lightning Express," as the crowd had begun to call her, that creature turned her head diagonally backward and let fall a smile. The encroaching beast stopped as if he had been shot! His rider plied whip, and forced him again forward upon the track of the equine hag, but with the same result.

The Englishman was now alarmed; he struggled manfully with rein and whip and shout, amidst the tremendous cheering and inextinguishable laughter of the crowd, to force his animal past, now on this side, now on that, but it would not do. Prompted by the fiend in the concavity of her back, the unthinkable quadruped dropped her grins right and left with such seasonable accuracy that again and again the competing beast was struck "all of a heap" just at the moment of seeming success. And, finally, when by a tremendous spurt his rider endeavored to thrust him by, within half a dozen lengths of the winning post, the incarnate nightmare turned squarely about and fixed upon him a portentous stare— delivering at the same time a grimace of such prodigious ghastliness that the poor thoroughbred, with an almost human scream of terror, wheeled about, and tore away to the rear with the speed of the wind, leaving the colonel an easy winner in twenty minutes and ten seconds.

Rudyard Kipling

THE DAY'S WORK

A Walking Delegate

According to the custom of Vermont, Sunday afternoon is salting-time on the farm, and, unless something very important happens, we attend to the salting ourselves. Dave and Pete, the red oxen, are treated first; they stay in the home meadow, ready for work on Monday. Then come the cows, with Pan, the calf, who should have been turned into veal long ago, but survived on account of his manners; and, lastly, the horses, scattered through the seventy acres of the Back Pasture.

You must go down by the brook that feeds the clicking, bubbling water-ram; up through the sugar-bush, where the young maple undergrowth closes round you like a shallow sea; next follow the faint line of an old country-road running past two green hollows fringed with wild rose that mark the cellars of two ruined houses; then by Lost Orchard, where nobody ever comes except in cider-time; then across another brook, and so into the Back Pasture. Half of it is pine and hemlock and spruce, with sumach and little juniper-bushes, and the other half is grey rock and boulder and moss, with green streaks of brake and swamp; but the horses like it well enough—our own, and the others that are turned down there to feed at fifty cents a week. Most people walk to the Back Pasture, and find it very rough work; but one can get there in a buggy, if the horse knows what is expected of him. The safest conveyance is our coupé. This began life as a buckboard, and we bought it for five dollars from a sorrowful man who had no other sort of possessions; and the seat came off one night when we were turning a corner in a hurry. After that alteration it made a beautiful salting-machine, if you held tight, because there was nothing to catch your feet when you fell out, and the slats rattled tunes.

One Sunday afternoon we went out with the salt as usual. It was a broiling hot day, and we could not find the horses anywhere till we let Tedda Babler, the bob-tailed mare who throws up the dirt with her big hoofs exactly as a tedder throws hay, have her head. Clever as she is, she tipped the coupé over in a hidden brook before she came out on a ledge of rock where all the horses had gathered and were switching flies. The Deacon was the first to call to her. He is a very dark iron-grey four-year-old, son of Grandee. He has been handled since he was two, was driven in a light cart before he was three, and now ranks as an absolutely steady lady's horse—proof against steam rollers, grade-crossings, and street processions.

'Salt!' said the Deacon, joyfully. 'You're dreffle late, Tedda.'

'Any—any place to cramp the coupé?' Tedda panted. 'It draws turr'ble this weather. I'd 'a' come sooner, but they didn't know what they wanted—ner haow. Fell out twice, both of them. I don't understand sech foolishness.'

'You look consider'ble het up. Guess you'd better cramp her under them pines, an' cool off a piece.'

Tedda scrambled on the ledge, and cramped the coupé in the shade of a tiny little wood of pines, while my companion and I lay down among the brown, silky needles, and gasped. All the home horses were gathered round us, enjoying their Sunday leisure.

There were Rod and Rick, the seniors on the farm. They were the regular road-pair, bay with black points, full brothers, aged, sons of a Hambletonian sire and a Morgan dam. There were Nip and Tuck, seal-browns, rising six, brother and sister, Black Hawks by birth, perfectly matched, just finishing their education, and as handsome a pair as man could wish to find in a forty-mile drive. There was Muldoon, our ex-car-horse, bought at a venture, and any colour you choose that is not white; and Tweezy, who comes from Kentucky, with an affliction of his left hip, which makes him a little uncertain how his hind legs are moving. He and Muldoon had been hauling gravel all the week for our new road. The Deacon you know already. Last of all, and eating something, was our faithful Marcus Aurelius Antoninus, the black buggy-horse, who had seen us through every state of weather and road, the horse who was always standing in harness before some door or other—a philosopher with the appetite of a shark and the manners of an archbishop. Tedda Gabler was a new 'trade', with a reputation for vice which was really the result of bad driving. She had one working gait, which she could hold till further notice; a Roman nose; a large, prominent eye; a shaving-brush of a tail; and an irritable temper. She took her salt through her bridle; but the others trotted up nuzzling and wickering for theirs, till we emptied it on the clean rocks. They were all standing at ease, on three legs for the most part, talking the ordinary gossip of the Back Pasture—about the scarcity of water, and gaps in the fence, and how the early windfalls tasted that season—when little Rick blew the last few grains of his allowance into a crevice, and said:

'Hurry, boys! Might ha' knowed that livery-plug would be around.'

We heard a clatter of hoofs, and there climbed up from the ravine below a fifty-center transient—a wall-eyed, yellow frame-house of a horse, sent up to board from a livery-stable in town, where they called him 'The Lamb', and never let him out except at night and to strangers.

My companion, who knew and had broken most of the horses, looked at the ragged hammerhead as it rose, and said quietly:

'Nice beast. Man-eater, if he gets the chance—see his eye. Kicker, too—see his hocks. Western horse.'

The animal lumbered up, snuffling and grunting. His feet showed that he had not worked for weeks and weeks, and our creatures drew together significantly.

'As usual,' he said, with an underhung sneer—'bowin' your heads before the Oppressor, that comes to spend his leisure gloatin' over you.'

'Mine's done,' said the Deacon; he licked up the remnant of his salt, dropped his nose in his master's hand, and sang a little grace all to himself. The Deacon has the most enchanting manners of any one I know.

'An' fawnin' on them for what is your inalienable right. It's humiliatin',' said the yellow horse, sniffing to see if he could find a few spare grains.

'Go daown hill, then, Boney,' the Deacon replied. 'Guess you'll find somefin' to eat still, if yer hain't hogged it all. You've ett more'n any three of us today—an' day 'fore that—an' the last two months—sence you've been here.'

'I am not addressin' myself to the young an' immature. I am speakin' to those whose opinion *an'* experience commands respect.'

I saw Rod raise his head as though he were about to make a remark; then he dropped it again, and stood three-cornered, like a plough-horse. Rod can cover his mile in a shade under three minutes on an ordinary road to an ordinary buggy. He is tremendously powerful behind, but, like most Hambletonians, he grows a trifle sullen as he gets older. No one can love Rod very much; but no one can help respecting him.

'I wish to wake *those*,' the yellow horse went on, 'to an abidin' sense o' their wrongs an' their injuries an' their outrages.'

'Haow's that?' said Marcus Aurelius Antoninus, dreamily. He thought Boney was talking of some kind of feed.

'An' when I say outrages and injuries'—Boney waved his tail furiously—'I mean 'em, too. Great Oats! That's just what I *do* mean, plain an' straight.'

'The gentleman talks quite earnest,' said Tuck, the mare, to Nip, her brother. 'There's no doubt thinkin' broadens the horizons o' the mind. His language is right lofty.'

'Hesh, sis,' Nip answered. 'He hain't widened nothin' 'cep' the circle he's ett in pasture. They feed words fer beddin' where he comes from.'

'It's elegant talkin', though,' Tuck returned, with an unconvinced toss of her pretty, lean, little head.

The yellow horse heard her, and struck an attitude which he meant to be extremely impressive. It made him look as though he had been badly stuffed.

'Now I ask you—I ask you without prejudice an' without favour— what has Man the Oppressor ever done for you? Are you not inalienably entitled to the free air o' heaven, blowin' acrost this boundless prairie?'

'Hev ye ever wintered here?' said the Deacon, merrily, while the others snickered. 'It's kinder cool.'

'Not yet,' said Boney. 'I come from the boundless confines o' Kansas, where the noblest of our kind have their abidin'-place among the sunflowers on the threshold o' the settin' sun in his glory.'

'An' they sent you ahead as a sample?' said Rick, with an amused quiver of his long, beautifully-groomed tail, as thick and as fine and as wavy as a quadroon's back hair.

'Kansas, sir, needs no adver*tise*ment. Her native sons rely on themselves an' their native sires. Yes, sir.'

Then Tweezy lifted up his wise and polite old face. His affliction makes him bashful as a rule, but he is ever the most courteous of horses.

'Excuse me, suh,' he said slowly, 'but, unless I have been mis-infohmed, most of your prominent siahs, suh, are impo'ted from Kentucky; an' *I'm* from Paduky.'

There was the least little touch of pride in the last words.

'Any horse dat knows beans,' said Muldoon, suddenly (he had been standing with his hairy chin on Tweezy's broad quarters), 'gets outer Kansas 'fore dey crip his shoes. I blew in dere frum Ioway in de days o' me youth an' innocence, and I wuz grateful when dey boxed me fer N'York. You can't tell *me* anything about Kansas I don't wanter fergit. De

Belt Line stables ain't no Hoffman House, but dey're Vanderbilt's 'longside o' Kansas.'

'What the horses o' Kansas think today, the horses of America will think tomorrow; an' I tell *you* that when the horses of America rise in their might, the day o' the Oppressor is ended.'

There was a pause, till Rick said, with a little grunt:

'Ef you put it that way, every one of us has riz in his might, 'cep' Marcus, mebbe. Marky, 'j ever rise in yer might?'

'Nope,' said Marcus Aurelius Antoninus, thoughtfully quidding over a mouthful of grass. 'I seen a heap o' fools try, though.'

'You admit that you riz?' said the Kansas horse, excitedly. 'Then why—why in Kansas did you ever go under again?'

'Horse can't walk on his hind legs *all* the time,' said the Deacon. 'Not when he's jerked over on his back 'fore he knows what fetched him. We've all done it, Boney,' said Rick. 'Nip an' Tuck, they tried it, spite o' what the Deacon told 'em; and the Deacon, he tried it, spite o' what me an' Rod told him; an' me an' Rod tried it, spite o' what Grandee told us; an' I guess Grandee he tried it, spite o' what his dam told him. It's the same old circus from generation to generation. Colt can't see why he's called on to back. Same old rearin' on end—straight up. Same old feelin' that you've bested 'em this time. Same old little yank at yer mouth when you're up good an' tall. Same old Pegasus-act, wonderin' where you'll 'light. Same old whop when you hit the dirt with your head where your tail should be, and your in'ards shook up like a bran-mash. Same old voice in your ear, 'Waal, ye little fool, an' what did you reckon to make by that?' We're through with risin' in our might on this farm. We go to pole er single, accordin' ez we're hitched.'

'An' Man the Oppressor sets an' gloats over you, same as he's settin' now. Hain't that been your experience, madam?'

This last remark was addressed to Tedda, and any one could see with half an eye that poor, old, anxious, fidgety Tedda, stamping at the flies, must have left a wild and tumultuous youth behind her.

"Pends on the man,' she answered, shifting from one foot to the other, and addressing herself to the home horses. 'They abused me dreffle when I was young. I guess I was sperrity an' nervous some, but they didn't allow for that. 'Twas in Monroe County, Noo York, an' sence then till I come here, I've run away with more men than 'ud fill a boardin'-house. Why, the man that sold me here he says to the boss, s' he: 'Mind, now, I've warned you. 'Twon't be none of my fault if she sheds you daown the road. Don't you drive her in a top-buggy, ner 'thout winkers,' s' he, 'ner 'thout this bit, ef you look to come home behind her.' 'N' the fust thing the boss did was to git the top-buggy.'

'Can't say as I like top-buggies,' said Rick; 'they don't balance good.'

"Suit me to a harr,' said Marcus Aurelius Antoninus. 'Top-buggy means the baby's in behind, an' I kin stop while she gathers the pretty flowers—yes, an' pick a maouthful, too. The women-folk all say I hev to be humoured, an'—I don't kerry things to the sweatin'-point.'

"Course I've no pre*ju*dice against a top-buggy s' long's I can see it,' Tedda went on quickly. 'It's ha'f-seein' the pesky thing bobbin' an balancin' behind the winkers gets on *my* nerves. Then the boss looked at the bit they'd sold with me, an' s' he: 'Jiminy Christmas! This 'ud make a clothes-horse stan' 'n end!' Then he gave me a plain bar bit, an' fitted it 's if there was some feelin' to my maouth.'

'Hain't ye got any, Miss Tedda?' said Tuck, who has a mouth like velvet, and knows it.

'Might 'a' had, Miss Tuck, but I've forgot. Then he give me an open bridle—my style's an open bridle—an'—I dunno as I ought to tell this by rights—he gave—me—a kiss.'

'My!' said Tuck, 'I can't tell fer the shoes o' me what makes some men so fresh.'

'Pshaw, sis,' said Nip, 'what's the sense in actin' so? *You* git a kiss reg'lar's hitchin'-up time.'

'Well, you needn't tell, smarty,' said Tuck, with a squeal and a kick.

'I'd heard o' kisses, o' course,' Tedda went on, 'but they hadn't come my way specially. I don't mind tellin' I was that took aback at that man's doin's he might ha' lit fire-crackers on my saddle. Then we went out jest's if a kiss was nothin', an' I wasn't three strides into my gait 'fore I felt the boss knoo his business, an' was trustin' me. So I studied to please him, an' he never took the whip from the dash—a whip drives me plumb distracted—an' the upshot was that—waal, I've come up the Back Pasture today, an' the coupé's tipped clear over twice, an' I've waited till 'twuz fixed each time. You kin judge for yourselves. I don't set up to be no better than my neighbours—specially with my tail snipped off the way 'tis—but I want you all to know Tedda's quit fightin' in harness or out of it, 'cep' when there's a born fool in the pasture, stuffin' his stummick with board that ain't rightly hisn, 'cause he hain't earned it.'

'Meanin' me, madam?' said the yellow horse.

'Ef the shoe fits, clinch it,' said Tedda, snorting. '*I* named no names, though, to be sure, some folks are mean enough an' greedy enough to do 'thout 'em.'

'There's a deal to be forgiven to ignorance,' said the yellow horse, with an ugly look in his blue eye.

'Seemin'ly, yes; or some folks 'ud ha' been kicked raound the pasture 'bout onct a minute sence they came—board er no board.'

'But what you do *not* understand, if you will excuse me, madam, is that the whole principle o' servitood, which includes keep an' feed, starts from a radically false basis; an' I am proud to say that me an' the majority o' the horses o' Kansas think the entire concern should be relegated to the limbo of exploded superstitions. I say we're too progressive for that. I say we're too enlightened for that. 'Twas good enough's long's we didn't think, but naow—but naow—a new loominary has arisen on the horizon!'

'Meanin' you?' said the Deacon.

'The horses o' Kansas are behind me with their multitoodinous thunderin' hoofs, an' we say, simply but grandly, that we take our stand with all four feet on the inalienable rights of the horse, pure and simple—the high-toned child o' nature, fed by the same wavin' grass, cooled by the same ripplin' brook—yes, an' warmed by the same gen'rous sun as falls impartially on the outside an' the *in*side of the pampered machine o' the trottin'-track, or the bloated coupé-horses o' these yere Eastern cities. Are we not the same flesh and blood?'

'Not by a bushel an' a half,' said the Deacon, under his breath. 'Grandee never was in Kansas.'

'My! Ain't that elegant, though, abaout the wavin' grass an' the ripplin' brooks?' Tuck whispered in Nip's ear. 'The gentleman's real convincin', *I* think.'

'I say we *are* the same flesh an' blood! Are we to be separated, horse from horse, by the artificial barriers of a trottin'-record, or are we to look down upon each other on the strength o' the gifts o' nature—an extry inch below the knee, or slightly more powerful quarters? What's the use o' them advantages to you? Man the Oppressor comes along, an' sees you're likely an' good-lookin', an' grinds you to the face o' the earth. What for? For his own pleasure: for his own convenience! Young an' old, black an' bay, white an' grey, there's no distinctions made between us. We're ground up together under the remorseless teeth o' the engines of oppression!'

'Guess his brichin' must ha' broke goin' daownhill,' said the Deacon. 'Slippery road, maybe, an' the buggy come onter him, an' he didn't know 'nough to hold back. That don't feel like teeth, though. Maybe he busted a shaft, an' it pricked him.'

'An' I come to you from Kansas, wavin' the tail o' friendship to all an' sundry, an' in the name of the uncounted millions o' pure-minded high-toned horses now strugglin' towards the light o' freedom, I say to you, rub noses with us in our sacred an' holy cause. The power is yourn. Without you, I say, Man the Oppressor cannot move himself from place to place. Without you he cannot reap, he cannot sow, he cannot plough.'

'Mighty odd place, Kansas!' said Marcus Aurelius Antoninus. 'Seemin'ly they reap in the spring an' plough in the fall. Guess it's right fer them, but 'twould make me kinder giddy.'

'The produc's of your untirin' industry would rot on the ground if you did not weakly consent to help them. *Let* 'em rot, I say! Let him call you to the stables in vain an' nevermore! Let him shake his ensnarin' oats under your nose in vain! Let the Brahmas roost in the buggy, an' the rats run riot round the reaper! Let him walk on his two hind feet till they blame well drop off! Win no more soul-destroyin' races for his pleasure! Then, an' not till then, will Man the Oppressor know where he's at. Quit workin', fellow-sufferers an' slaves! Kick! Rear! Plunge! Lie down on the shafts, an' woller! Smash an' destroy! The conflict will be but short, an' the victory is certain. After that we can press our inalienable rights to eight quarts o' oats a day, two good blankets, an' a fly-net an' the best o' stablin'.'

The yellow horse shut his yellow teeth with a triumphant snap; and Tuck said, with a sigh: 'Seems 's if somethin' ought to be done. Don't seem right, somehow—oppressin' us an' all—to my way o' thinkin'.'

Said Muldoon, in a far-away and sleepy voice: 'Who in Vermont's goin' to haul de inalienable oats? Dey weigh like Sam Hill, an' sixty bushel at dat allowance ain't goin' to last t'ree weeks here. An' dere's de winter hay for five mont's!'

'We can settle those minor details when the great cause is won,' said the yellow horse. 'Let us return simply but grandly to our inalienable rights—the right o' freedom on these yere verdant hills, an' no invijjus distinctions o' track an' pedigree.'

'What in stables 'jer call an invijjus distinction?' said the Deacon, stiffly.

'Fer one thing, bein' a bloated, pampered trotter jest because you happen to be raised that way, an' couldn't no more help trottin' than eatin'.'

'Do ye know anythin' about trotters?' said the Deacon.

'I've seen 'em trot. That was enough for me. *I* don't want to know any more. Trottin' 's immoral.'

'Waal, I'll tell you this much. They don't bloat, an' they don't pamp—much. I don't hold out to be no trotter myself, though I am free to say I had hopes that way—oncet. But I *do* say, fer I've seen 'em trained, that a trotter don't trot with his feet; he trots with his head; an' he does more work—ef you know what *that* is—in a week then you er your sire ever done in all your lives. He's everlastingly at it, a trotter is; an' when he isn't, he's studyin' haow. You seen 'em trot? Much you hev! You was hitched to a rail, back o' the stand, in a buckboard with a soap-box nailed on the slats, an' a frowsy buff'lo atop, while your man peddled rum for lemonade to little boys as thought they was actin' manly, till you was both run off the track and jailed—you intoed, shufflin', sway-backed, wind-suckin' skate, you!'

'Don't get het up, Deacon,' said Tweezy, quietly. 'Now, suh, would you consider a fox-trot, an' single-foot, an' rack, an' pace, *an'* amble, distinctions not worth distinguishin'? I assuah you, gentlemen, there was a time befo' I was afflicted in my hip, if you'll pardon me, Miss Tuck, when I was quite celebrated in Paduky for *all* those gaits; an' in my opinion the Deacon's co'rect when he says that a ho'se of any position in society gets his gaits by his haid, an' not by—his, ah, limbs, Miss Tuck. I reckon I'm very little good now, but I'm rememberin' the things I used to do befo' I took to transpo'tin' real estate with the help and assistance of this gentleman here.' He looked at Muldoon.

'Invijjus arterficial hind-legs!' said the ex-car-horse, with a grunt of contempt. 'On de Belt Line we don't reckon no horse wuth his keep 'less he kin switch de car off de track, run her round on de cobbles, an' dump her in ag'in ahead o' de truck what's blockin' him. Dere is a way o' swinging yer quarters when de drivers says, "Yank her out, boys!" dat takes a year to learn. Onct yer git onter it, youse kin yank a cable-car outer a manhole. I don't advertise myself fer no circus-horse, but I knew dat trick better than most, an' dey was good to me in de stables, fer I saved time on de Belt—an' time's what dey hunt in N' York.'

'But the simple child o' nature—' the yellow horse began.

'Oh, go an' unscrew yer splints! You're talkin' through yer bandages,' said Muldoon, with a horse-laugh. 'Dere ain't no loose-box for de simple child o' nature on de Belt Line, wid de *Paris* comin' in an' de *Teutonic* goin' out, an' de trucks an' de coupés sayin' things, an' de heavy freight movin' down fer de Boston boat 'bout t'ree o'clock of an August afternoon, in de middle of a hot wave when de fat Kanucks an' Western horses drops dead on de block. De simple child o' nature had better chase himself inter de water. Every man at de end of his lines is mad or loaded or silly, an' de cop's madder an' loadeder an' sillier dan de rest. Dey all take it outer de horses. Dere's no wavin' brooks ner ripplin' grass on de Belt Line. Run her out on de cobbles wid de sparks flyin', an' stop when de cop slugs you on de bone o' yer nose. Dat's N' York; see?'

'I was always told s'ciety in Noo York was dreffle refined an' high-toned,' said Tuck. 'We're lookin' to go there one o' these days, Nip an' me.'

'Oh, *you* won't see no Belt business where you'll go, miss. De man dat wants you'll want you bad, an' he'll summer you on Long Island er at Newport, wid a winky-pinky silver harness an' an English coachman. You'll make a star-hitch, you an' yer brother, miss. But I guess you won't have no nice smooth bar bit. Dey checks 'em, an' dey bangs deir tails, an' dey bits 'em, de city folk, an' dey says it's English, ye know, an dey darsen't cut a horse loose 'ca'se o' de cops. N' York's no place fer a horse, 'less he's on de Belt, an' can go round wid de boys. Wisht *I* was in de Fire Department!'

'But did you never stop to consider the degradin' servitood of it all?' said the yellow horse.

'You don't stop on de Belt, cully. You're stopped. An' we was all in de servitood business, man an' horse, an' Jimmy dat sold de papers. Guess de passengers weren't out to grass neither, by de way dey acted. I done my turn, an' I'm none o' Barnum's crowd; but any horse dat's worked on de Belt four years don't train wid no simple child o' nature—not by de whole length o' N' York.'

'But can it be possible that with your experience, and at your time of life, you do not believe that all horses are free and equal?' said the yellow horse.

'Not till dey're dead,' Muldoon answered quietly. 'An' den it depends on de gross total o' buttons an' mucilage dey gits outer youse at Barren Island.'

'They tell me you're a prominent philosopher.' The yellow horse turned to Marcus. 'Can *you* deny a basic and pivotal statement such as this?'

'I don't deny anythin',' said Marcus Aurelius Antoninus, cautiously; 'but ef you *ast* me, I should say 'twuz more different sorts o' clipped oats of a lie than anythin' I've had my teeth into since I wuz foaled.'

'Are you a horse?' said the yellow horse.

'Them that knows me best 'low I am.'

'Ain't *I* a horse?'

'Yep; one kind of.'

'Then ain't you an' me equal?'

'How fer kin you go in a day to a loaded buggy, drawin' five hundred pounds?' Marcus asked carelessly.

'That has nothing to do with the case,' the yellow horse answered excitedly.

'There's nothing I know hez more to do with the case,' Marcus replied.

'Kin ye yank a full car outer de tracks ten times in de mornin'?' said Muldoon.

'Kin ye go to Keene—forty-two mile in an afternoon—with a mate,' said Rick, 'an' turn out bright an' early next mornin'?'

'Was there evah any time in your careah, suh—I am not referrin' to the present circumstances, but our mutual glorious past—when you could carry a pretty girl to market hahnsome, an' let her knit all the way on account o' the smoothness o' the motion?' said Tweezy.

'Kin you keep your feet through the West River Bridge, with the narrer-gage comin' in on one side, an' the Montreal flyer the other, an' the old bridge teetrin' between?' said the Deacon. 'Kin you put your nose down on the cow-catcher of a locomotive when you're waitin' at the depot an' let 'em play 'Curfew shall not ring tonight' with the big brass bell?'

'Kin you hold back when the brichin' breaks? Kin you stop fer orders when your nigh hind leg's over your trace an' ye feel good of a frosty mornin'?' said Nip, who had only learned that trick last winter, and thought it was the crown of horsely knowledge.

'What's the use o' talkin'?' said Tedda Gabler, scornfully. 'What kin ye do?'

'I rely on my simple rights—the inalienable rights o' my unfettered horsehood. An' I am proud to say I have never, since my first shoes, lowered myself to obeyin' the will o' man.'

'Must ha' had a heap o' whips broke over yer yaller back,' said Tedda. 'Hev ye found it paid any?'

'Sorrer has been my portion since the day I was foaled. Blows an' boots an' whips an' insults—injury, outrage, an' oppression. I would not endoor the degradin' badges o' servitood that connect us with the buggy an' the farm-wagon.'

'It's amazin' difficult to draw a buggy 'thout traces er collar er breast-strap er somefin',' said Marcus. 'A Power-machine for sawin' wood is 'most the only thing there's no straps to. I've helped saw's much as three cord in an afternoon in a Power-machine. Slep', too, most o' the time, I did; but 'tain't half as inter*e*stin' ez goin' daown-taown in the Concord.'

'Concord don't hender *you* goin' to sleep any,' said Nip. 'My throat-lash! D' you remember when you lay down in the sharves last week, waitin' at the piazza?'

'Pshaw! That didn't hurt the sharves. They wuz good an' wide, an' I lay down keerful. The folks kep' me hitched up nigh an hour 'fore they started; an' larfed—why, they all but lay down themselves with larfin'. Say, Boney, if you've got to be hitched *to* anything that goes on wheels, you've got to be hitched *with* somefin'.'

'Go an' jine a circus,' said Muldoon, 'an' walk on your hind legs. All de horses dat knows too much to work [he pronounced it 'woik', New York fashion] jine de circus.'

'I am not sayin' anythin' again' work,' said the yellow horse; 'work is the finest thing in the world.'

'Seems too fine fer some of us,' Teddy snorted.

'I only ask that each horse should work for himself, an' enjoy the profit of his labours. Let him work intelligently, an' not as a machine.'

'There ain't no horse that works like a machine,' Marcus began.

'There's no way o' workin' that doesn't mean goin' to pole or sin-gle—they never put me in the Power-machine—er under saddle,' said Rick.

'Oh, shucks! We're talkin' same ez we graze,' said Nip, 'raound an' raound in circles. Rod, we hain't heard from you yet, an' you've more knowhow than any span here.'

Rod, the off-horse of the pair, had been standing with one hip lifted, like a tired cow; and you could only tell by the quick flutter of the haw across his eye, from time to time, that he was paying any attention to the argument. He thrust his jaw out sidewise, as his habit is when he pulls, and changed his leg. His voice was hard and heavy, and his ears were close to his big, plain Hambletonian head.

'How old are you?' he said to the yellow horse.

'Nigh thirteen, I guess.'

'Mean age; ugly age; I'm gettin' that way myself. How long hev ye been pawin' this fire-fanged stable litter?'

'If you mean my principles, I've held 'em sence I was three.'

'Mean age; ugly age; teeth give heaps o' trouble then. Set a colt to actin' crazy fer a while. *You*'ve kep' it up, seemin'ly. D'ye talk much to your neighbours fer a steady thing?'

'I uphold the principles o' the Cause wherever I am pastured.'

'Done a heap o' good, I guess?'

'I am proud to say I have taught a few of my companions the principles o' freedom an' liberty.'

'Meaning they ran away er kicked when they got the chanst?'

'I was talkin' in the abstac', an' not in the concrete. My teachin's educated them.'

'What a horse, specially a young horse, hears in the abstrac', he's liable to do in the Concord. You wuz handled late, I presoom.'

'Four, risin' five.'

'That's where the trouble began. Driv' by a woman, like ez not—eh?'

'Not fer long,' said the yellow horse, with a snap of his teeth.

'Spilled her?'

'I heerd she never drove again.'

'Any children?'

'Buckboards full of 'em.'

'Men too?'

'I have shed conside'ble men in my time.'

'By kickin'?'

'Any way that came along. Fallin' back over the dash is as handy as most.'

'They must be turr'ble afraid o' you daown-taown?'

'They've sent me here to get rid o' me. I guess they spend their time talkin' over my campaigns.'

'*I* wanter know!'

'Yes, *sir*. Now, all you gentlemen have asked me what I can do. I'll just show you. See them two fellers lyin' down by the buggy?'

'Yep; one of 'em owns me. T'other broke me,' said Rod.

'Get 'em out here in the open, an' I'll show you something. Lemme hide back o' you peoples, so's they won't see what I'm at.'

'Meanin' ter kill 'em?' Rod drawled. There was a shudder of horror through the others; but the yellow horse never noticed.

'I'll catch 'em by the back o' the neck, an pile-drive 'em a piece. They can suit 'emselves about livin' when I'm through with 'em.'

'Shouldn't wonder ef they did,' said Rod.

The yellow horse had hidden himself very cleverly behind the others as they stood in a group, and was swaying his head close to the ground with a curious scythe-like motion, looking sideways out of his wicked eyes. You can never mistake a maneater getting ready to knock a man down. We had had one to pasture the year before.

'See that?' said my companion, turning over on the pineneedles. 'Nice for a woman walking 'cross lots, wouldn't it be?'

'Bring 'em out!' said the yellow horse, hunching his sharp back. 'There's no chance among them tall trees. Bring out the—oh! Ouch!'

It was a right-and-left kick from Muldoon. I had no idea that the old car-horse could lift so quickly. Both blows caught the yellow horse full and fair in the ribs, and knocked the breath out of him.

'What's that for?' he said angrily, when he recovered himself; but I noticed he did not draw any nearer to Muldoon than was necessary.

Muldoon never answered, but discoursed to himself in the whining grunt that he uses when he is going down-hill in front of heavy load. We call it singing; but I think it's something much worse, really. The yellow horse blustered and squealed a little, and at last said that, if it was a horse-fly that had stung Muldoon, he would accept an apology.

'You'll get it,' said Muldoon, 'in de sweet by-and-by—all de apology you've any use for. Excuse me interruptin' you, Mr. Rod, but I'm like Tweezy—I've a Southern drawback in me hind legs.'

'Naow, I want you all here to take notice, and you'll learn something,' Rod went on. 'This yaller-backed skate comes to our pastur'—'

'Not havin' paid his board,' put in Tedda.

'Not havin' earned his board, an' talks smooth to us abaout ripplin' brooks an' wavin' grass, an' his high-toned, pure-souled horsehood, which don't hender him sheddin' women an' childern, an' fallin' over the dash onter men. You heard his talk, an' you thought it mighty fine, some o' you.'

Tuck looked guilty here, but she did not say anything.

'Bit by bit he goes on ez you have heard.'

'I was talkin' in the abstrac',' said the yellow horse, in an altered voice.

'Abstrac' be switchèd! Ez I've said, it's this yer blamed abstrac' business that makes the young uns cut up in the Concord; an' abstrac' or no abstrac', he crep' on an' on till he comes to killin' plain an' straight—killin' them as never done him no harm, jest beca'se they owned horses.'

'An' knowed how to manage 'em,' said Tedda. 'That makes it worse.'

'Waal, he didn't kill 'em, anyway,' said Marcus. 'He'd ha' been half killed ef he had tried.'

'Makes no differ,' Rod answered. 'He meant to; an' ef he hadn't—s'pose we want the Back Pasture turned into a biffin'-ground on our only day er rest? 'S'pose *we* want *our* men walkin' round with bits er lead pipe an' a twitch, an' their hands full o' stones to throw at us, same's if we wuz hogs er hooky keows? More'n that, leavin' out Tedda here—an' I guess it's more her maouth than her manners stands in her light—there ain't a horse on this farm that ain't a woman's horse, an' proud of it. An' this yer bog-spavined Kansas sunflower goes up an' daown the length o' the country, traded off and traded on, boastin' ez he's shed women—an' childern. I don't say ez a woman in a buggy ain't a fool. I don't say ez she ain't the lastin'est kind er fool, ner I don't say a child ain't worse—spattin' the lines an' standin' up an' hollerin'—but I *do* say, 'tain't none of our business to shed 'em daown the road.'

'We don't,' said the Deacon. 'The baby tried to git some o' my tail for a sooveneer last fall when I was up to the haouse, an' I didn't kick. Boney's talk ain't goin' to hurt us any. We ain't colts.'

'Thet's what you *think*. Bimeby you git into a tight corner, 'Lection day er Valley Fair, like's not, daown-taown, when you're all het an' lathery, an' pestered with flies, an' thirsty, an' sick o' bein' worked in an' aout 'tween buggies. *Then* somethin' whispers inside o' yer winkers, bringin' up all that talk abaout servitood an' inalienable truck an' sech like, an' jest then a Militia gun goes off, er your wheels hit, an'—waal, you're only another horse ez can't be trusted. I've been there time an' again. Boys— fer I've seen you all bought er broke—on my solemn repitation fer a three-minute clip, I ain't givin' you no bran-mash o' my own fixin'. I'm tellin' you my experiences, an' I've had ez heavy a load an' ez high a check's any horse here. I wuz born with a splint on my near fore ez big's a walnut, an' the cussed, three-cornered Hambletonian temper that sours up an' curdles daown ez you git older. I've favoured my splint; even little Rick he don't know what it's cost me to keep my end up sometimes; an' I've fit my temper in stall an' harness, hitched up an' at pasture, till the sweat trickled off my hoofs, an' they thought I wuz off condition, an' drenched me.'

'When my affliction came,' said Tweezy, gently, 'I was very near to losin' my manners. Allow me to extend to you my sympathy, suh.'

Rick said nothing, but he looked at Rod curiously. Rick is a sunny-tempered child who never bears malice, and I don't think he quite understood. He gets his temper from his mother, as a horse should.

'I've been there too, Rod,' said Tedda. 'Open confession's good for the soul, an' all Monroe County knows I've had my experiences.'

'But if you will excuse me, suh, that pusson'—Tweezy looked unspeakable things at the yellow horse—'that pusson who has insulted our intelligences comes from Kansas. An' what a ho'se of his position, an' Kansas at that, says cannot, by any stretch of the halter, concern gentlemen of *our* position. There's no shadow of equal'ty, suh, not even for one kick. He's beneath our contempt.'

'Let him talk,' said Marcus. 'It's always interestin' to know what another horse thinks. It don't tech us.'

'An' he talks so, too,' said Tuck. 'I've never heard anythin' so smart for a long time.'

Again Rod stuck out his jaws sidewise, and went on slowly, as though he were slugging on a plain bit at the end of a thirty-mile drive:

'I want all you here ter understand thet ther' ain't no Kansas, ner no Kentucky, ner yet no Vermont, in *our* business. There's jest two kind o' horse in the United States—them ez can an' will do their work after bein' properly broke an' handled, an' them ez won't. I'm sick an' tired o' this everlastin' tail-switchin' an' wickerin' abaout one State er another. A horse kin be proud o' his State, an' swap lies abaout it in stall or when he's hitched to a block, ef he keers to put in fly-time that way; but he hain't no right to let that pride o' hisn interfere with his work, ner to make it an excuse fer claimin' he's different. That's colt's talk, an' don't you fergit it, Tweezy. An', Marcus, you remember that bein' a philosopher, an' anxious to save trouble—fer you *are*—don't excuse you from jumpin' with all your feet on a slack-jawed, crazy clay-bank like Boney here. It's leavin' 'em alone that gives 'em their chance to ruin colts an' kill folks. An', Tuck, waal, you're a mare anyways—but when a horse comes along an' covers up all his talk o' killin' with ripplin' brooks, an' wavin' grass, an' eight quarts of oats a day free, *after* killin' his man, don't you be run away with by his yap. You're too young an' too nervous.'

'I'll—I'll have nervous prostration sure ef there's a fight here,' said Tuck, who saw what was in Rod's eye; 'I'm—I'm that sympathetic I'd run away clear to next caounty.'

'Yep; I know that kind o' sympathy. Jest lasts long enough to start a fuss, an' then lights aout to make new trouble. I hain't been ten years in harness fer nuthin'. Naow, we're goin' to keep school with Boney fer a spell.'

'Say, look a-here, you ain't goin' to hurt me, are you? Remember, I belong to a man in town,' cried the yellow horse, uneasily. Muldoon kept behind him so that he could not run away.

'I know it. There must be some pore delooded fool in this State hez a right to the loose end o' your hitchin'-strap. I'm blame sorry fer him, but he shall hev his rights when we're through with you,' said Rod.

'If it's all the same, gentlemen, I'd ruther change pasture. Guess I'll do it now.'

'Can't always have your 'druthers. Guess you won't,' said Rod.

'But look a-here. All of you ain't so blame unfriendly to a stranger. S'pose we count noses.'

'What in Vermont fer?' said Rod, putting up his eyebrows. The idea of settling a question by counting noses is the very last thing that ever enters the head of a well-broken horse.

'To see how many's on my side. Here's Miss Tuck, anyway, an' Colonel Tweezy yonder's neutral; an' Judge Marcus, an' I guess the Reverend [the yellow horse meant the Deacon] might see that I had my rights. He's the likeliest-lookin' trotter I've ever set eyes on. Pshaw, boys! You ain't goin' to pound *me,* be you? Why, we've gone round in pasture, all colts together, this month o' Sundays, hain't we, as friendly as could be. There ain't a horse alive—I don't care who he is—has a higher opinion o' you, Mr. Rod, than I have. Let's do it fair an' true an' above the exe. Let's count noses same's they do in Kansas.' Here he dropped his voice a little and turned to Marcus: 'Say, Judge, there's some green food I know, back o' the brook, no one hain't touched yet. After this little *fracas* is fixed up, you an' me'll make up a party an' 'tend to it.'

Marcus did not answer for a long time, then he said: 'There's a pup up to the haouse 'bout eight weeks old. He'll yap till he gits a lickin', an' when he sees it comin' he lies on his back an' yowls. But he don't go through no cir*kit*uous nose-counting first. I've seen a noo light sence Rod spoke. You'll better stand up to what's served. I'm goin' to philsophize all over your carcass.'

'*I*'m goin' to do yer up in brown paper,' said Muldoon. 'I can fit you on apologies.'

'Hold on. Ef we all biffed you now, these same men you've been so dead anxious to kill 'ud call us off. Guess we'll wait till they go back to the haouse, an' you'll have time to think cool an' quiet,' said Rod.

'Have you no respec' whatever fer the dignity o' our common horsehood?' the yellow horse squealed.

'Nary respec' onless the horse kin do something. America's paved with the kind er horse you are—jist plain yaller-dog horse—waitin' ter be whipped inter shape. We call 'em yearlings an' colts when they're young. When they're aged we pound 'em—in this pastur'. Horse, sonny, is what you start from. We know all about horse here, an' he ain't any high-toned, pure-souled child o' nature. Horse, plain horse, same ez you, is chock-full o' tricks, an' meannesses, an' cussednesses, an' shirkin's, an' monkey-shines, which he's took over from his sire an' his dam, an' thickened up with his own special fancy in the way o' goin' crooked. Thet's *horse,* an' thet's about his dignity an' the size of his soul 'fore he's been broke an' raw-hided a piece. Now we ain't goin' to give ornery unswitched *horse,* that hain't done nawthin' wuth a quart of oats sence he wuz foaled, pet names that would be good enough for Nancy Hanks, or Alix, or Directum, who *hev.* Don't you try to back off acrost them rocks. Wait where you are! Ef I let my Hambletonian temper git the better o' me I'd frazzle you out finer than rye-straw inside o' three minutes, you woman-scarin', kid-killin', dash-breakin', unbroke, unshod, ungaited, pastur'-hoggin', saw-backed, shark-mouthed, hair-trunk-thrown-in-intrade son of a bronco an' a sewin'-machine!'

'I think we'd better get home,' I said to my companion when Rod had finished; and we climbed into the coupé, Tedda whinnying, as we bumped over the ledges: 'Well, I'm dreffle sorry I can't stay fer the sociable; but I hope an' trust my friends 'll take a ticket for me.'

'Bet your natchul!' said Muldoon, cheerfully, and the horses scattered before us, trotting into the ravine.

Next morning we sent back to the livery-stable what was left of the yellow horse. It seemed tired, but anxious to go.

Washington Irving

GOVERNOR MANCO AND THE SOLDIER

While Govenor Manco, or "the one-armed," kept up a show of military state in the Alhambra, he became nettled at the reproaches continually cast upon his fortress, of being a nestling place of rogues and contrabandistas. On a sudden, the old potentate determined on reform and setting vigorously to work, ejected whole nests of vagabonds out of the fortress and the gipsy caves with which the surrounding hills are honeycombed. He sent out soldiers, also, to patrol the avenues and footpaths, with orders to take up all suspicious persons.

One bright summer morning, a patrol, consisting of the testy old corporal who had distinguished himself in the affair of the notary, a trumpeter and two privates, was seated under the garden wall of the

Generalife, beside the road which leads down from the mountain of the sun, when they heard the tramp of a horse, and a male voice singing in rough, though not unmusical tones, an old Castilian campaigning song.

Presently they beheld a sturdy, sunburnt fellow, clad in the ragged garb of a foot-soldier, leading a powerful Arabian horse, caparisoned in the ancient Moresco fashion.

Astonished at the sight of a strange soldier descending, steed in hand, from that solitary mountain, the corporal stepped forth and challenged him.

"Who goes there?"

"A friend."

"Who and what are you?"

"A poor soldier just from the wars, with a cracked crown and empty purse for a reward."

By this time they were enabled to view him more narrowly. He had a black patch across his forehead, which, with a grizzled beard, added to a certain dare-devil cast of countenance, while a slight squint threw into the whole an occasional gleam of roguish good humor.

Having answered the questions of the patrol, the soldier seemed to consider himself entitled to make others in return. "May I ask," said he, "what city is that which I see at the foot of the hill?"

"What city!" cried the trumpeter; "come, that's too bad. Here's a fellow lurking about the mountain of the sun, and demands the name of the great city of Granada!"

"Granada! Madre di Dios! can it be possible?"

"Perhaps not!" rejoined the trumpeter; "and perhaps you have no idea that yonder are the towers of the Alhambra."

"Son of the trumpet," replied the stranger, "do not trifle with me; if this be indeed the Alhambra, I have some strange matters to reveal to the governor."

"You will have an opportunity," said the corporal, "for we mean to take you before him." By the time the trumpeter had seized the bridle of the steed, the two privates had each secured an arm of the soldier, the corporal put himself in front, gave the word, "Forward—march!" and away they marched for the Alhambra.

The sight of a ragged foot-soldier and a fine Arabian horse, brought in captive by the patrol, attracted the attention of all the idlers of the fortress, and of those gossip groups that generally assemble about wells and fountains at early dawn. The wheel of the cistern paused in its rotations, and the slipshod servant-maid stood gaping, with pitcher in hand, as the corporal passed by with his prize. A motley train gradually gathered in the rear of the escort.

Knowing nods and winks and conjectures passed from one to another. "It is a deserter," said one; "A contrabandista," said another; "A bandalero," said a third;—until it was affirmed that a captain of a desperate band of robbers had been captured by the prowess of the corporal and his patrol. "Well, well," said the old crones, one to another, "captain or not, let him get out of the grasp of old Governor Manco if he can, though he is but one-handed."

Governor Manco was seated in one of the inner halls of the Alhambra, taking his morning's cup of chocolate in company with his confessor, a fat Franciscan friar, from the neighboring convent. A demure, dark-eyed damsel of Malaga, the daughter of his housekeeper, was attending upon him. The world hinted that the damsel, who, with all her demureness, was a sly buxom baggage, had found out a soft spot in the iron heart of the old governor, and held complete control over him. But let that pass— the domestic affairs of these mighty potentates of the earth should not be too narrowly scrutinized.

When word was brought that a suspicious stranger had been taken lurking about the fortress, and was actually in the outer court, in durance of the corporal, waiting the pleasure of his excellency, the pride and stateliness of office swelled the bosom of the governor. Giving back his chocolate cup into the hands of the demure damsel, he called for his basket-hilted sword, girded it to his side, twirled up his mustaches, took his seat in a large high-backed chair, assumed a bitter and forbidding aspect, and ordered the prisoner into his presence. The soldier was brought in, still closely pinioned by his captors, and guarded by the corporal. He maintained, however, a resolute self confident air, and returned the sharp, scrutinizing look of the governor with an easy squint, which by no means pleased the punctilious old potentate.

"Well, culprit," said the governor, after he had regarded him for a moment in silence, "what have you to say for yourself—who are you?"

"A soldier, just from the wars, who has brought away nothing but scars and bruises."

"A soldier—humph—a foot-soldier by your garb. I understand you have a fine Arabian horse. I presume you brought him too from the wars, besides your scars and bruises."

"May it please your excellency, I have something strange to tell about that horse. Indeed I have one of the most wonderful things to relate. Something too that concerns the security of this fortress, indeed of all Granada. But it is a matter to be imparted only to your private ear, or in presence of such only as are in your confidence."

The governor considered for a moment, and then directed the corporal and his men to withdraw, but to post themselves outside of the door, and be ready at a call. "This holy friar," said he, "is my confessor, you may say any thing in his presence—and this damsel," nodding towards the handmaid, who had loitered with an air of great curiosity, "this damsel is of great secrecy and discretion, and to be trusted with any thing."

The soldier gave a glance between a squint and a leer at the demure handmaid. "I am perfectly willing," said he, "that the damsel should remain."

When all the rest had withdrawn, the soldier commenced his story. He was a fluent, smooth-tongued varlet, and had a command of language above his apparent rank.

"May it please your excellency," said he, "I am, as I before observed, a soldier, and have seen some hard service, but my term of enlistment being expired, I was discharged, not long since, from the army at Valladolid, and set out on foot for my native village in Andalusia. Yesterday evening the sun went down as I was traversing a great dry plain of Old Castile."

"Hold," cried the governor, "what is this you say? Old Castile is some two or three hundred miles from this."

"Even so," replied the soldier, coolly; "I told your excellency I had strange things to relate; but not more strange than true; as your excellency will find, if you will deign me a patient hearing."

"Proceed, culprit," said the governor, twirling up his mustaches.

"As the sun went down," continued the soldier, "I cast my eyes about in search of quarters for the night, but as far as my sight could reach, there were no signs of habitation. I saw that I should have to make my bed on the naked plain, with my knapsack for a pillow; but your excellency is an old soldier, and knows that to one who has been in the wars, such a night's lodging is no great hardship."

The governor nodded assent, as he drew his pocket handkerchief out of the basket-hilt, to drive away a fly that buzzed about his nose.

"Well, to make a long story short," continued the soldier, "I trudged forward for several miles until I came to a bridge over a deep ravine, through which ran a little thread of water, almost dried up by the summer heat. At one end of the bridge was a Moorish tower, the upper end all in ruins, but a vault in the foundation quite entire. Here, thinks I, is a good place to make a halt; so I went down to the stream, took a hearty drink, for the water was pure and sweet, and I was parched with thirst; then, opening my wallet, I took out an onion and a few crusts, which were all my provisions, and seating myself on a stone on the margin of the stream, began to make my supper; intending afterwards to quarter myself for the night in the vault of the tower; and capital quarters they would have been for a campaigner just from the wars, as your excellency, who is an old soldier, may suppose."

"I have put up gladly with worse in my time," said the governor, returning his pocket-handkerchief into the hilt of his sword.

"While I was quietly crunching my crust," pursued the soldier, "I heard something stir within the vault; I listened—it was the tramp of a horse. By and by a man came forth from a door in the foundation of the tower, close by the water's edge, leading a powerful horse by the bridle. I could not well make out what he was by the starlight. It had a suspicious look to be lurking among the ruins of a tower, in that wild solitary place. He might be a mere wayfarer, like myself; he might be a contrabandista;

he might be a bandalero! what of that? thank heaven and my poverty, I had nothing to lose; so I sat still and crunched my crusts.

"He led his horse to the water, close by where I was sitting, so that I had a fair opportunity of reconnoitering him. To my surprise he was dressed in a Moorish garb, with a cuirass of steel, and a polished skull-cap that I distinguished by the reflection of the stars upon it. His horse, too, was harnessed in the Moresco fashion, with great shovel stirrups. He led him, as I said, to the side of the stream, into which the animal plunged his head almost to the eyes, and drank until I thought he would have burst.

" 'Comrade,' said I, 'your steed drinks well; it's a good sign when a horse plunges his muzzle bravely into the water.'

" 'He may well drink,' said the stranger, speaking with a Moorish accent; 'it is a good year since he had his last draught.'

" 'By Santiago,' said I, 'that beats even the camels I have seen in Africa. But come, you seem to be something of a soldier, will you sit down and take part of a soldier's fare?' In fact, I felt the want of a companion in this lonely place, and was willing to put up with an infidel. Besides, as your excellency well knows, a soldier is never very particular about the faith of his company, and soldiers of all countries are comrades on peaceable ground."

The governor again nodded assent.

"Well, as I was saying, I invited him to share my supper, such as it was, for I could not do less in common hospitality. 'I have no time to pause for meat or drink,' said he, 'I have a long journey to make before morning.'

" 'In which direction?' said I.

" 'Andalusia,' said he.

" 'Exactly my route,' said I, 'so, as you won't stop and eat with me, perhaps you will let me mount and ride with you. I see your horse is of a powerful frame, I'll warrant he'll carry double.'

" 'Agreed,' said the trooper; and it would not have been civil and soldierlike to refuse, especially as I had offered to share my supper with him. So up he mounted, and up I mounted behind him.

" 'Hold fast,' said he, 'my steed goes like the wind.'

" 'Never fear me,' said I, and so off we set.

"From a walk the horse soon passed to a trot, from a trot to a gallop, and from a gallop to a harum-scarum scamper. It seemed as if rocks, trees, houses, every thing, flew hurry-scurry behind us.

" 'What town is this?' said I.

" 'Segovia,' said he; and before the word was out of his mouth, the towers of Segovia were out of sight. We swept up the Guadarama mountains, and down by the Escurial; and we skirted the walls of Madrid, and we scoured away across the plains of La Mancha. In this way we went up hill and down dale, by towers and cities, all buried in deep sleep, and across mountains, and plains, and rivers, just glimmering in the starlight.

"To make a long story short, and not to fatigue your excellency, the trooper suddenly pulled up on the side of a mountain. 'Here we are,' said he, 'at the end of our journey.' I looked about, but could see no signs of habitation; nothing but the mouth of a cavern. While I looked I saw multitudes of people in Moorish dresses, some on horseback, some on foot, arriving as if borne by the wind from all points of the compass, and hurrying into the mouth of the cavern like bees into a hive. Before I could ask a question the trooper struck his long Moorish spurs into the horse's flanks, and dashed in with the throng. We passed along a steep winding way, that descended into the very bowels of the mountain. As we pushed on, a light began to glimmer up, by little and little, like the first glimmerings of day, but what caused it I could not discern. It grew stronger and stronger, and enabled me to see every thing around. I now noticed, as we passed along, great caverns, opening to the right and left, like halls in an arsenal. In some there were shields, and helmets, and cuirasses, and lances, and cimeters, hanging against the walls; in others there were great heaps of warlike munitions, and camp equipage lying upon the ground.

"It would have done your excellency's heart good, being an old soldier, to have seen such grand provision for war. Then, in other caverns, there were long rows of horsemen armed to the teeth, with lances raised and banners unfurled, all ready for the field; but they all sat motionless in their saddles like so many statues. In other halls were warriors sleeping on the ground beside their horses, and foot-soldiers in groups ready to fall into the ranks. All were in old-fashioned Moorish dresses and armor.

"Well, your excellency, to cut a long story short, we at length entered an immense cavern, or I may say palace, of grotto work, the walls of which seemed to be veined with gold and silver, and to sparkle with diamonds and sapphires and all kinds of precious stones. At the upper end sat a Moorish king on a golden throne, with his nobles on each side, and a guard of African blacks with drawn cimeters. All the crowd that continued to flock in, and amounted to thousands and thousands, passed one by one before his throne, each paying homage as he passed. Some of the multitude were dressed in magnificent robes, without stain or blemish and sparkling with jewels; others in burnished and enamelled armor; while others were in mouldered and mildewed garments, and in armor all battered and dented and covered with rust.

"I had hitherto held my tongue, for your excellency well knows it is not for a soldier to ask many questions when on duty, but I could keep silent no longer.

" 'Prithee, comrade,' said I, 'what is the meaning of all this?'

" 'This,' said the trooper, 'is a great and fearful mystery. Know, O Christian, that you see before you the court and army of Boabdil the last king of Granada.'

" 'What is this you tell me?' cried I. 'Boabdil and his court were exiled from the land hundreds of years agone, and all died in Africa.'

" 'So it is recorded in your lying chronicles,' replied the Moor, 'but know that Boabdil and the warriors who made the last struggle for Granada were all shut up in the mountain by powerful enchantment. As for the king and army that marched forth from Granada at the time of the surrender, they were a mere phantom train, or spirits and demons permitted to assume those shapes to deceive the Christian sovereigns. And furthermore let me tell you, friend, that all Spain is a country under the power of enchantment. There is not a mountain cave, not a lonely watchtower in the plains, nor ruined castle on the hills, but has some spellbound warriors sleeping from age to age within its vaults, until the sins are expiated for which Allah permitted the dominion to pass for a time out of the hands of the faithful. Once every year, on the eve of St. John, they are released from enchantment, from sunset to sunrise, and permitted to repair here to pay homage to their sovereign; and the crowds which you beheld swarming into the cavern are Moslem warriors from their haunts in all parts of Spain. For my own part, you saw the ruined tower of the bridge in Old Castile, where I have now wintered and summered for many hundred years, and where I must be back again by daybreak. As to the battalions of horse and foot which you beheld drawn up in array in the neighboring caverns, they are the spell-bound warriors of Granada. It is written in the book of fate, that when the enchantment is broken, Boabdil will descend from the mountain at the head of this army, resume his throne in the Alhambra and his sway of Granada, and gathering together the enchanted warriors, from all parts of Spain, will reconquer the Peninsula and restore it to Moslem rule.'

" 'And when shall this happen?' said I.

" 'Allah alone knows: we had hoped the day of deliverance was at hand; but there reigns at present a vigilant governor in the Alhambra, a staunch old soldier, well known as Governor Manco. While such a warrior holds command of the very outpost, and stands ready to check the first irruption from the mountain, I fear Boabdil and his soldiery must be content to rest upon their arms.' "

Here the governor raised himself somewhat perpendicularly, adjusted his sword, and twirled up his mustaches.

"To make a long story short, and not to fatigue your excellency, the trooper, having given me this account, dismounted from his steed.

" 'Tarry here,' said he, 'and guard my steed while I go and bow the knee to Boabdil.' So saying, he strode away among the throng that pressed forward to the throne.

" 'What's to be done?' thought I, when thus left to myself, 'shall I wait here until this infidel returns to whisk me off on his goblin steed, the Lord knows where; or shall I make the most of my time and beat a retreat from this hobgoblin community?' A soldier's mind is soon made up, as your excellency well knows. As to the horse, he belonged to an avowed enemy of faith and the realm, and was a fair prize according to the rules of war. So hoisting myself up from the crupper into the saddle, I turned the reins, struck the Moorish stirrups into the sides of the steed, and put him to make the best of his way out of the passage by which he had entered. As we scoured by the halls where the Moslem horsemen sat in motionless battalions, I thought I heard the clang of armor and a hollow murmur of voices. I gave the steed another taste of the stirrups and doubled my speed. There was now a sound behind me like a rushing blast; I heard the clatter of a thousand hoofs; a countless throng overtook me. I was borne along in the press, and hurled forth from the mouth of the cavern, while thousands of shadowy forms were swept off in every direction by the four winds of heaven.

"In the whirl and confusion of the scene I was thrown senseless to the earth. When I came to myself I was lying on the brow of a hill, with the Arabian steed standing beside me; for in falling, my arm had slipped within the bridle, which, I presume, prevented his whisking off to Old Castile.

"Your excellency may easily judge of my surprise, on looking round, to behold hedges of aloes, and Indian figs and other proofs of a southern climate, and to see a great city below me, with towers, and palaces, and a grand cathedral.

"I descended the hill cautiously, leading my steed, for I was afraid to mount him again, lest he should play me some slippery trick. As I descended I met with your patrol, who let me into the secret that it was Granada that lay before me; and that I was actually under the walls of the Alhambra, the fortress of the redoubted Governor Manco, the terror of all enchanted Moslems. When I heard this, I determined at once to seek your excellency, to inform you of all that I had seen, and to warn you of the perils that surround and undermine you, that you may take measures in time to guard your fortress, and the kingdom itself, from this intestine army that lurks in the very bowels of the land."

"And prithee, friend, you who are a veteran campaigner, and have seen so much service," said the governor, "how would you advise me to proceed, in order to prevent this evil?"

"It is not for a humble private of the ranks," said the soldier, modestly, "to pretend to instruct a commander of your excellency's sagacity, but it appears to me that your excellency might cause all the caves and entrances into the mountain to be walled up with solid mason work, so that Boabdil and his army might be completely corked up in their subterranean habitation. If the good father, too," added the soldier, reverently bowing to the friar, and devoutly crossing himself, "would consecrate the barricadoes with his blessing, and put up a few crosses and relics and images of saints, I think they might withstand all the power of infidel enchantments."

"They doubtless would be of great avail," said the friar.

The governor now placed his arm a-kimbo, with his hand resting on the hilt of his Toledo, fixed his eye upon the soldier, and gently wagging his head from one side to the other.

"So, friend," said he, "then you really suppose I am to be gulled with this cock-and-bull story about enchanted mountains and enchanted Moors? Hark, ye, culprit!—not another word. An old soldier you may be, but you'll find you have an older soldier to deal with, and one not easily outgeneralled. Ho! guards there! put this fellow in irons."

The demure handmaid would have put in a word in favor of the prisoner, but the governor silenced her with a look.

As they were pinioning the soldier, one of the guards felt something of bulk in his pocket, and drawing it forth, found a long leathern purse that appeared to be well filled. Holding it by one corner, he turned out the contents upon the table before the governor, and never did freebooter's bag make more gorgeous delivery. Out tumbled rings, and jewels, and rosaries of pearls, and sparkling diamond crosses, and a profusion of ancient golden coin, some of which fell jingling to the floor, and rolled away to the uttermost parts of the chamber.

For a time the functions of justice were suspended; there was a universal scramble after the glittering fugitives. The governor alone, who was imbued with true Spanish pride, maintained his stately decorum, though his eye betrayed a little anxiety until the last coin and jewel was restored to the sack.

The friar was not so calm; his whole face glowed like a furnace, and his eyes twinkled and flashed at sight of the rosaries and crosses.

"Sacrilegious wretch that thou art!" exclaimed he; "what church or sanctuary hast thou been plundering of these sacred relics?"

"Neither one nor the other, holy father. If they be sacrilegious spoils, they must have been taken, in times long past, by the infidel trooper I have mentioned. I was just going to tell his excellency when he interrupted me, that on taking possession of the trooper's horse, I unhooked a leathern sack which hung at the saddle-bow, and which I presume contained the plunder of his campaigning in days of old, when the Moors overran the country."

"Mighty well; at present you will make up your mind to take up your quarters in a chamber of the vermilion tower, which, though not under a magic spell, will hold you as safe as any cave of your enchanted Moors."

"Your excellency will do as you think proper," said the prisoner, coolly. "I shall be thankful to your excellency for any accommodation in the fortress. A soldier who has been in the wars, as your excellency well knows, is not particular about his lodgings: provided I have a snug dungeon and regular rations, I shall manage to make myself comfortable. I would only entreat that while your excellency is so careful about me, you would have an eye to your fortress, and think on the hint I dropped about stopping up the entrances to the mountain."

Here ended the scene. The prisoner was conducted to a strong dungeon in the vermilion tower, the Arabian steed was led to his excellency's stable, and the trooper's sack was deposited in his excellency's strong box. To the latter, it is true, the friar made some demur, questioning whether the sacred relics, which were evidently sacrilegious spoils, should not be placed in custody of the church; but as the governor was peremptory on the subject, and was absolute lord in the Alhambra, the friar discreetly dropped the discussion, but determined to convey intelligence of the fact to the church dignitaries in Granada.

To explain these prompt and rigid measures on the part of old Governor Manco, it is proper to observe, that about this time the Alpuxarra mountains in the neighborhood of Granada were terribly infested by a gang of robbers, under the command of a daring chief named Manuel Borasco, who were accustomed to prowl about the country, and even to enter the city in various disguises, to gain intelligence of the departure of convoys of merchandise, or travellers with well-lined purses, whom they took care to waylay in distant and solitary passes of the road. These repeated and daring outrages had awakened the attention of government, and the commanders of the various posts had received instructions to be on the alert, and to take up all suspicious stragglers. Governor Manco was particularly zealous in consequence of the various stigmas that had been cast upon his fortress, and he now doubted not he had entrapped some formidable desperado of this gang.

In the mean time the story took wind, and became the talk, not merely of the fortress, but of the whole city of Granada. It was said that the noted robber Manuel Borasco, the terror of the Alpuxarras, had fallen into the clutches of old Governor Manco, and been cooped up by him in a dungeon of the vermilion towers; and every one who had been robbed by him flocked to recognize the marauder. The vermilion towers, as is well known, stand apart from the Alhambra on a sister hill, separated from the main fortress by the ravine down which passes the main avenue. There were no outer walls, but a sentinel patrolled before the tower. The window of the chamber in which the soldier was confined was strongly grated, and looked upon a small esplanade. Here the good folks of Granada repaired to gaze at him, as they would at a laughing hyena, grinning through the cage of a menagerie. Nobody, however, recognized him for Manuel Borasco, for that terrible robber was noted for a ferocious physiognomy, and had no means the good-humored squint of the prisoner. Visitors came not merely from the city, but from all parts of the country; but nobody knew him, and there began to be doubts in the minds of the common people whether there might not be some truth in his story. That Boabdil and his army were shut up in the mountain, was an old tradition which many of the ancient inhabitants had heard from their fathers. Numbers went up to the mountain of the sun, or rather of St. Elena, in search of the cave mentioned by the soldier; and saw and peeped into the deep dark pit, descending, no one knows how far, into the mountain, and which remains there to this day—the fabled entrance to the subterranean abode of Boabdil.

By degrees the soldier became popular with the common people. A freebooter of the mountains is by no means the opprobrious character in

Spain that a robber is in any other country: on the contrary, he is a kind of chivalrous personage in the eyes of the lower classes. There is always a disposition, also, to cavil at the conduct of those in command, and many began to murmur at the high-handed measures of old Governor Manco, and to look upon the prisoner in the light of a martyr.

The soldier, moreover, was a merry, waggish fellow, that had a joke for every one who came near his window, and a soft speech for every female. He had procured an old guitar also, and would sit by his window and sing ballads and love-ditties to the delight of the women of the neighborhood, who would assemble on the esplanade in the evenings and dance boleros to his music. Having trimmed off his rough beard, his sunburnt face found favor in the eyes of the fair, and the demure handmaid of the governor declared that his squint was perfectly irresistible. This kind-hearted damsel had from the first evinced a deep sympathy in his fortunes, and having in vain tried to mollify the governor, had set to work privately to mitigate the rigor of his dispensations. Every day she brought the prisoner some crumbs of comfort which had fallen from the governor's table, or been abstracted from his larder, together with, now and then, a consoling bottle of choice Val de Peñas, of rich Malaga.

While this petty treason was going on, in the very centre of the old governor's citadel, a storm of open war was brewing up among his external foes. The circumstance of a bag of gold and jewels having been found upon the person of the supposed robber, had been reported, with many exaggerations, in Granada. A question of territorial jurisdiction was immediately started by the governor's inveterate rival, the captain-general. He insisted that the prisoner had been captured without the precincts of the Alhambra, and within the rules of his authority. He demanded his body therefore, and the *spolia opima* taken with him. Due information having been carried likewise by the friar to the grand inquisitor of the crosses, and rosaries, and other relics contained in the bag, he claimed the culprit as having been guilty of sacrilege, and insisted that his plunder was due to the church, and his body to the next auto da fe. The feuds ran high; the governor was furious, and swore, rather than surrender his captive, he would hang him up within the Alhambra, as a spy caught within the purlieus of the fortress.

The captain-general threatened to send a body of soldiers to transfer the prisoner from the vermilion tower to the city. The grand inquisitor was equally bent upon dispatching a number of the familiars of the Holy Office. Word was brought late at night to the governor of these machinations. "Let them come," said he, "they'll find me beforehand with them; he must rise bright and early who would take in an old soldier." He accordingly issued orders to have the prisoner removed, at daybreak, to the donjon keep within the walls of the Alhambra. "And d'ye hear, child," said he to his demure handmaid, "tap at my door, and wake me before cock-crowing, that I may see to the matter myself."

The day dawned, the cock crowed, but nobody tapped at the door of the governor. The sun rose high above the mountain-tops, and glittered in at his casement, ere the governor was awakened from his morning dreams by his veteran corporal, who stood before him with terror stamped upon his iron visage.

"He's off! he's gone!" cried the corporal, grasping for breath.

"Who's off—who's gone?"

"The soldier—the robber—the devil, for aught I know; his dungeon is empty, but the door locked: no one knows how he has escaped out of it."

"Who saw him last?"

"Your handmaid, she brought him his supper."

"Let her be called instantly."

Here was new matter of confusion. The chamber of the demure damsel was likewise empty, her bed had not been slept in: she had doubtless gone off with the culprit, as she had appeared, for some days past, to have frequent conversations with him.

This was wounding the old governor in a tender part, but he had scarce time to wince at it, when new misfortunes broke upon his view. On going into his cabinet he found his strong box open, the leather purse of the trooper abstracted, and with it, a couple of corpulent bags of doubloons.

But how, and which way had the fugitives escaped? An old peasant who lived in a cottage by the road-side, leading up into the Sierra, declared that he had heard a tramp of a powerful steed just before daybreak, passing up into the mountains. He had looked out at his casement, and could just distinguish a horseman, with a female seated before him.

"Search the stables!" cried Governor Manco. The stables were searched; all the horses were in their stalls, excepting the Arabian steed. In his place was a stout cudgel tied to the manger, and on it a label bearing these words, "A gift to Governor Manco, from an Old Soldier."

Booth Tarkington

WHITEY

Penrod and Sam made a gloomy discovery one morning in mid-October. All the week had seen amiable breezes and fair skies until Saturday, when, about breakfast-time, the dome of heaven filled solidly with gray vapour and began to drip. The boys' discovery was that there is no justice about the weather.

They sat in the carriage-house of the Schofields' empty stable; the doors upon the alley were open, and Sam and Penrod stared torpidly at the thin but implacable drizzle which was the more irritating because there was barely enough of it to interfere with a number of things they had planned to do.

"Yes; this is *nice!*" Sam said, in a tone of plaintive sarcasm. "This is a *perty* way to do!" (He was alluding to the personal spitefulness of the elements.) "I'd like to know what's the sense of it—ole sun pourin' down every day in the week when nobody needs it, then cloud up and rain all Saturday! My father said it's goin' to be a three days' rain."

"Well, nobody with any sense cares if it rains Sunday and Monday," said Penrod. "I wouldn't care if it rained every Sunday as long as I lived; but I just like to know what's the reason it had to go and rain to-day. Got all the days o' the week to choose from and goes and picks on Saturday. That's a fine biz'nuss!"

"Well, in vacation—" Sam began, but at a sound from a source invisible to him he paused. "What's that?" he said, somewhat startled.

It was a curious sound, loud and hollow and unhuman, yet it seemed to be a cough. Both boys rose, and Penrod asked uneasily:

"Where'd that noise come from?"

"It's in the alley," said Sam.

Perhaps if the day had been bright, both of them would have stepped immediately to the alley doors to investigate; but their actual procedure was to move a little distance in the opposite direction. The strange cough sounded again.

"*Say!*" Penrod quavered. "What *is* that?"

Then both boys uttered smothered exclamations and jumped, for the long, gaunt head which appeared in the doorway was entirely unexpected. It was the cavernous and melancholy head of an incredibly thin, old, whitish horse. This head waggled slowly from side to side; the nostrils vibrated; the mouth opened, and the hollow cough sounded again.

Recovering themselves, Penrod and Sam underwent the customary human reaction from alarm to indignation.

"What you want, you ole horse, you?" Penrod shouted. "Don't you come coughin' around *me!*"

And Sam, seizing a stick, hurled it at the intruder.

"Get out o' here!" he roared.

The aged horse nervously withdrew his head, turned tail, and made a rickety flight up the alley, while Sam and Penrod, perfectly obedient to inherited impulse, ran out into the drizzle and uproariously pursued.

They were but automatons of instinct, meaning no evil. Certainly they did not know the singular and pathetic history of the old horse who had wandered into the alley and ventured to look through the open door.

This horse, about twice the age of either Penrod or Sam, had lived to find himself in a unique position. He was nude, possessing neither harness nor halter; all he had was a name, Whitey, and he would have answered to it by a slight change of expression if any one had thus properly addressed him. So forlorn was Whitey's case, he was actually an independent horse; he had not even an owner. For two days and a half he had been his own master.

Previous to that period he had been the property of one Abalene Morris, a person of colour, who would have explained himself as engaged in the hauling business. On the contrary, the hauling business was an insignificant side line with Mr. Morris, for he had long ago given himself, as utterly as fortune permitted, to that talent which, early in youth, he had recognized as the greatest of all those surging in his bosom. In his waking thoughts and in his dreams, in health and in sickness, Abalene Morris was the dashing and emotional practitioner of an art probably more than Roman in antiquity. Abalene was a crap-shooter. The hauling business was a disguise.

A concentration of events had brought it about that, at one and the same time, Abalene, after a dazzling run of the dice, found the hauling business an actual danger to the preservation of his liberty. He won seventeen dollars and sixty cents, and within the hour found himself in trouble with an officer of the Humane Society on account of an altercation with Whitey. Abalene had been offered four dollars for Whitey some ten days earlier; wherefore he at once drove to the shop of the junk-dealer who had made the offer and announced his acquiescence in the sacrifice.

"*No,* suh!" said the junk-dealer, with emphasis. "I aweady done got me a good mule fer my deliv'ry hoss, 'n'at ole Whitey hoss ain' wuff no fo' dollah nohow! I 'uz a fool when I talk 'bout th'owin' money roun' that a-way. *I* know what *you* up to, Abalene. Man come by here li'l bit ago tole me all 'bout white man try to 'rest you, ovah on the avvynoo. Yessuh; he say white man goin' to git you yit an' th'ow you in jail 'count o' Whitey. White man tryin' to fine out who you *is.* He say, nemmine, he'll know Whitey ag'in, even if he don' know you! He say he ketch you by the hoss; so you come roun' tryin' fix me up with Whitey so white man grab me, th'ow *me* in 'at jail. G'on 'way f'um hyuh, you Abalene! You cain' sell an' you cain' give Whitey to no cullud man 'n 'is town. You go an' drowned 'at ole hoss, 'cause you sutny goin' to jail if you git ketched drivin' him."

The substance of this advice seemed good to Abalene, especially as the seventeen dollars and sixty cents in his pocket lent sweet colours to life out of jail at this time. At dusk he led Whitey to a broad common at the edge of town, and spoke to him finally.

"G'on, 'bout you biz'nis," said Abalene; "you ain' *my* hoss. Don' look roun' at me, 'cause *I* ain' got no 'quaintance wif you. I'm a man o' money, an' I got my own frien's; I'm a-lookin' fer bigger cities, hoss. You got you biz'nis an' I got mine. Mista' Hoss, good-night!"

Whitey found a little frosted grass upon the common and remained there all night. In the morning he sought the shed where Abalene had kept him, but that was across the large and busy town, and Whitey was hopelessly lost. He had but one eye, a feeble one, and his legs were not to be depended upon; but he managed to cover a great deal of ground, to have many painful little adventures, and to get monstrously hungry and thirsty before he happened to look in upon Penrod and Sam.

When the two boys chased him up the alley they had no intention to cause pain; they had no intention at all. They were no more cruel than Duke, Penrod's little old dog, who followed his own instincts, and making his appearance hastily through a hole in the back fence, joined the pursuit with sound and fury. A boy will nearly always run after anything that is running, and his first impulse is to throw a stone at it. This is a survival of primeval man, who must take every chance to get his dinner. So, when Penrod and Sam drove the hapless Whitey up the alley, they were really responding to an impulse thousands and thousands of years old—an impulse founded upon the primordial observation that whatever runs is likely to prove edible. Penrod and Sam were not "bad"; they were never that. They were something which was not their fault; they were historic.

At the next corner Whitey turned to the right into the cross-street; thence, turning to the right again and still warmly pursued, he zig-zagged down a main thoroughfare until he reached another cross-street, which ran alongside the Schofield's yard and brought him to the foot of the alley he had left behind in his flight. He entered the alley, and there his dim eye fell upon the open door he had previously investigated. No memory of it remained, but the place had a look associated in his mind with hay, and as Sam and Penrod turned the corner of the alley in panting yet still vociferous pursuit, Whitey stumbled up the inclined platform before the open doors, staggered thunderously across the carriage-house and through another open door into a stall, an apartment vacant since the occupancy of Mr. Schofield's last horse, now several years deceased.

The two boys shrieked with excitement as they beheld the coinci-dence of this strange return. They burst into the stable, making almost as much noise as Duke, who had become frantic at the invasion. Sam laid hands upon a rake.

"You get out o' there, you ole horse, you!" he bellowed. "I ain't afraid to drive him out. I——"

"*Wait* a minute!" shouted Penrod. "Wait till I——"

Sam was manfully preparing to enter the stall.

"You hold the doors open," he commanded, "so's they won't blow shut and keep him in here. I'm goin' to hit him with——"

"Quee-*yut!*" Penrod shouted, grasping the handle of the rake so that Sam could not use it. "Wait a *minute,* can't you." He turned with ferocious voice and gestures upon Duke. *"Duke!"* And Duke, in spite of his excitement, was so impressed that he prostrated himself in silence, and then unobtrusively withdrew from the stable. Penrod ran to the alley doors and closed them.

"My gracious!" Sam protested. "What you goin' to do?"

"I'm goin' to keep this horse," said Penrod, whose face showed the strain of a great idea.

"What *for?*"

"For the reward," said Penrod simply.

Sam sat down in the wheelbarrow and stared at his friend almost with awe.

"My gracious," he said, "I never thought o' that. How—how much do you think we'll get, Penrod?"

Sam's thus admitting himself to a full partnership in the enterprise met no objection from Penrod, who was absorbed in the contemplation of Whitey.

"Well," he said judicially, "we might get more and we might get less."

Sam rose and joined his friend in the doorway opening upon the two stalls. Whitey had preëmpted the nearer, and was hungrily nuzzling the old frayed hollows in the manger.

"Maybe a hundred dollars—or sumpthing?" Sam asked in a low voice.

Penrod maintained his composure and repeated the new-found expression which had sounded well to him a moment before. He recognized it as a symbol of the non-committal attitude that makes people looked up to. "Well"—he made it slow, and frowned—"we might get more and we might get less."

"More'n a hundred *dollars?*" Sam gasped.

"Well," said Penrod, "we might get more and we might get less." This time, however, he felt the need of adding something. He put a question in an indulgent tone, as though he were inquiring, not to add to his own information but to discover the extent of Sam's. "How much do you think horses are worth, anyway?"

"I don't know," said Sam frankly, and unconsciously, he added, "They might be more and they might be less."

"Well, when our ole horse died," said Penrod, "papa said he wouldn't take five hundred dollars for him. That's how much *horses* are worth!"

"My gracious!" Sam exclaimed. Then he had a practical afterthought. "But maybe he was a better horse than this'n. What colour was he?"

"He was bay. Looky here, Sam"—and now Penrod's manner changed from the superior to the eager—"you look what kind of horses they have in the circus, and you bet a circus has the *best* horses, don't it? Well, what kind of horses do they have in a circus? They have some black and white ones, but the best they have are white all over. Well, what kind of a horse is this we got here? He's perty near white right now, and I bet if we washed him off and got him fixed up nice he *would* be white. Well, a bay horse is worth five hundred dollars, because that's what papa said, and this horse————"

Sam interrupted rather timidly.

"He—he's awful bony, Penrod. You don't guess that'd make any—"

Penrod laughed contemptuously.

"Bony! All he needs is a little food and he'll fill right up and look good as ever. You don't know much about horses, Sam, I expect. Why, *our* ole horse—"

"Do you expect he's hungry now?" asked Sam, staring at Whitey.

"Let's try him," said Penrod. "Horses like hay and oats the best, but they'll eat most anything."

"I guess they will. He's trying to eat that manger up right now, and I bet it ain't good for him."

"Come on," said Penrod, closing the door that gave entrance to the stalls. "We got to get this horse some drinkin'-water and some good food."

They tried Whitey's appetite first with an autumnal branch which they wrenched from a hardy maple in the yard. They had seen horses nibble leaves, and they expected Whitey to nibble the leaves of this branch, but his ravenous condition did not allow him time for cool discriminations. Sam poked the branch at him from the passageway, and Whitey, after one backward movement of alarm, seized it venomously.

"Here! You stop that!" Sam shouted. "You stop that, you ole horse, you!"

"What's the matter?" called Penrod from the hydrant, where he was filling a bucket. "What's he doin' now?"

"Doin! He's eatin' the wood part, too! He's chewin' up sticks as big as baseball bats! He's crazy!"

Penrod rushed to see this sight, and stood aghast.

"Take it away from him, Sam!" he commanded sharply.

"Go on, take it away from him yourself!" was the prompt retort of his comrade.

"You had no biz'nuss to give it to him," said Penrod. "Anybody with any sense ought to know it'd make him sick. What'd you want to go and give it to him for?"

"Well, you didn't say not to."

"Well, what if I didn't? I never said I did, did I? You go on in that stall and take it away from him."

"*Yes*, I will!" Sam returned bitterly. Then, as Whitey had dragged the remains of the branch from the manger to the floor of the stall, Sam scrambled to the top of the manger and looked over. "There ain't much left to *take* away! He's swallered it all except some splinters. Better give him the water to try and wash it down with." And, as Penrod complied, "My gracious, look at that horse *drink!*"

They gave Whitey four buckets of water, and then debated the question of nourishment. Obviously, this horse could not be trusted with branches, and, after getting their knees black and their backs sodden, they gave up trying to pull enough grass to sustain him. Then Penrod remembered that horses like apples, both "cooking-apples" and "eating-apples," and Sam mentioned the fact that every autumn his father received a barrel of "cooking-apples" from a cousin who owned a farm. That barrel was in the Williams' cellar now, and the cellar was providentially supplied with "outside doors," so that it could be visited without going through the house. Sam and Penrod set forth for the cellar.

They returned to the stable bulging, and, after a discussion of Whitey's digestion (Sam claiming that eating the core and seeds, as Whitey did, would grow trees in his inside), they went back to the cellar for supplies again—and again. They made six trips, carrying each time a capacity cargo of apples, and still Whitey ate in a famished manner. They were afraid to take more apples from the barrel, which began to show conspicuously the result of their raids, wherefore Penrod made an unostentatious visit to the cellar of his own house. From the inside he opened a window and passed vegetables out to Sam, who placed them in a bucket and carried them hurriedly to the stable, while Penrod returned in a casual manner through the house. Of his *sang-froid* under a great strain it is sufficient to relate that, in the kitchen, he said suddenly to Della, the cook, "Oh, look behind you!" and by the time Della discovered that there was nothing unusual behind her, Penrod was gone, and a loaf of bread from the kitchen table was gone with him.

Whitey now ate nine turnips, two heads of lettuce, one cabbage, eleven raw potatoes, and the loaf of bread. He ate the loaf of bread last and he was a long time about it; so the boys came to a not unreasonable conclusion.

"Well, sir, I guess we got him filled up at last!" said Penrod. "I bet he wouldn't eat a saucer of ice-cream now, if we'd give it to him!"

"He looks better to me," said Sam, staring critically at Whitey. "I think he's kind of begun to fill out some. I expect he must like us, Penrod; we been doin' a good deal for this horse."

"Well, we got to keep it up," Penrod insisted rather pompously. "Long as *I* got charge o' this horse, he's goin' to get good treatment."

"What we better do now, Penrod?"

Penrod took on the outward signs of deep thought.

"Well, there's plenty to *do,* all right. I got to think."

Sam made several suggestions, which Penrod—maintaining his air of preoccupation—dismissed with mere gestures.

"Oh, *I* know!" Sam cried finally. "We ought to wash him so's he'll look whiter'n what he does now. We can turn the hose on him acrost the manger."

"No; not yet," said Penrod. "It's too soon after his meal. You ought to know that yourself. What we got to do is to make up a bed for him—if he wants to lay down or anything."

"Make up a what for him?" Sam echoed, dumfounded. "What you talkin' about? How can—"

"Sawdust," said Penrod. "That's the way the horse we used to have used to have it. We'll make this horse's bed in the other stall, and then he can go in there and lay down whenever he wants to."

"How we goin' to do it?"

"Look, Sam; there's the hole into the sawdust-box! All you got to do is walk in there with the shovel, stick the shovel in the hole till it gets full of sawdust, and then sprinkle it around on the empty stall."

"All *I* got to do!" Sam cried. "What are you goin' to do?"

"I'm goin' to be right here," Penrod answered reassuringly. "He won't kick or anything, and it isn't goin' to take you half a second to slip around behind him to the other stall."

"What makes you think he won't kick?"

"Well, I *know* he won't, and besides, you could hit him with the shovel if he tried to. Anyhow, I'll be right here, won't I?"

"I don't care where you are," Sam said earnestly. "What difference would that make if he ki—"

"Why, you were goin' right in the stall," Penrod reminded him. "When he first came in, you were goin' to take the rake and—"

"I don't care if I was," Sam declared. "I was excited then."

"Well, you can get excited now, can't you?" his friend urged. "You can just as easy get—"

He was interrupted by a shout from Sam, who was keeping his eye upon Whitey throughout the discussion.

"Look! Looky there!" And undoubtedly renewing his excitement, Sam pointed at the long, gaunt head beyond the manger. It was disappearing from view. "Look!" Sam shouted. "He's layin' down!"

"Well, then," said Penrod, "I guess he's goin' to take a nap. If he wants to lay down without waitin' for us to get the sawdust fixed for him, that's his lookout, not ours."

On the contrary, Sam perceived a favourable opportunity for action.

"I just as soon go and make his bed up while he's layin' down," he volunteered. "You climb up on the manger and watch him, Penrod, and I'll sneak in the other stall and fix it all up nice for him, so's he can go in there any time when he wakes up, and lay down again, or anything; and if he starts to get up, you holler and I'll jump out over the other manger."

Accordingly, Penrod established himself in a position to observe the recumbent figure. Whitey's breathing was rather laboured but regular, and, as Sam remarked, he looked "better," even in his slumber. It is not to be doubted that, although Whitey was suffering from a light attack of colic, his feelings were in the main those of contentment. After trouble, he was solaced; after exposure, he was sheltered; after hunger and thirst, he was fed and watered. He slept.

The noon whistles blew before Sam's task was finished, but by the time he departed for lunch there was made a bed of such quality that Whitey must needs have been a born faultfinder if he complained of it. The friends parted, each urging the other to be prompt in returning, but Penrod got into threatening difficulties as soon as he entered the house.

"Penrod," said his mother, "what did you do with that loaf of bread Della says you took from the table?"

"Ma'am? *What* loaf o' bread?"

"I believe I can't let you go outdoors this afternoon," Mrs. Schofield said severely. "If you were hungry, you know perfectly well all you had to do was to—"

"But I wasn't hungry; I—"

"You can explain later," said Mrs. Schofield. "You'll have all afternoon."

Penrod's heart grew cold.

"I *can't* stay in," he protested. "I've asked Sam Williams to come over."

"I'll telephone Mrs. Williams."

"Mamma!" Penrod's voice became agonized. "I *had* to give that bread to a—to a poor ole man. He was starving and so were his children and his wife. They were all just *starving*—and they couldn't wait while I took time to come and ask you, mamma. I *got* to go outdoors this afternoon. I *got* to! Sam's—"

She relented.

In the carriage-house, half an hour later, Penrod gave an account of the episode.

"Where'd we been, I'd just like to know," he concluded, "if I hadn't got out here this afternoon?"

"Well, I guess I could managed him all right," said Sam. "I was in the passageway, a minute ago, takin' a look at him. He's standin' up again. I expect he wants more to eat."

"Well, we got to fix about that," said Penrod. "But what I mean— if I'd had to stay in the house, where would we been about the most important thing in the whole biz'nuss?"

"What you talkin' about?"

'Well, why can't you wait till I tell you?" Penrod's tone had become peevish. For that matter, so had Sam's; they were developing one of the little differences, or quarrels, that composed the very texture of their friendship.

"Well, why don't you tell me, then?"

"Well, how can I?" Penrod demanded. "You keep talkin' every minute."

"I'm not talkin' *now*, am I?" Sam protested. "You can tell me *now*, can't you? I'm not talk—"

"You are too!" shouted Penrod. "You talk all the time! You—"

He was interrupted by Whitey's peculiar cough. Both boys jumped and forgot their argument.

"He means he wants some more to eat, I bet," said Sam.

"Well, if he does, he's got to wait," Penrod declared. "We got to get the most important thing of all fixed up first."

"What's that, Penrod?"

"The reward," said Penrod mildly. "That's what I was tryin' to tell you about, Sam, if you'd ever give me half a chance."

"Well, I *did* give you a chance. I kept *tellin'* you to tell me, but—"

"You never! You kept sayin'—"

They renewed this discussion, protracting it indefinitely; but as each persisted in clinging to his own interpretation of the facts, the question still remained unsettled. It was abandoned, or rather, it merged into another during the later stages of the debate, this other being concerned with which of the debaters had the least "sense." Each made the plain statement that if he were more deficient than his opponent in that regard, self-destruction would be his only refuge. Each declared that he would "rather die than be talked to death"; and then, as the two approached a point bluntly recriminative, Whitey coughed again, whereupon they were miraculously silent, and went into the passageway in a perfectly amiable manner.

"I got to have a good look at him, for once," said Penrod, as he stared frowningly at Whitey. "We got to fix up about that reward."

"I want to take a good ole look at him myself," said Sam.

After supplying Whitey with another bucket of water, they returned to the carriage-house and seated themselves thoughtfully. In truth, they were something a shade more than thoughtful; the adventure to which they had committed themselves was beginning to be a little overpowering. If Whitey had been a dog, a goat, a fowl, or even a stray calf, they would have felt equal to him; but now that the earlier glow of their wild daring had disappeared, vague apprehensions stirred. Their "good look" at Whitey had not reassured them—he seemed large, Gothic, and unusual.

Whisperings within them began to urge that for boys to undertake an enterprise connected with so huge an animal as an actual horse was perilous. Beneath the surface of their musings, dim but ominous prophecies moved; both boys began to have the feeling that, somehow, this affair was going to get beyond them and that they would be in heavy trouble before it was over—they knew not why. They knew why no more than they knew why they felt it imperative to keep the fact of Whitey's presence in the stable a secret from their respective families, but they did begin to realize that keeping a secret of that size was going to be attended with some difficulty. In brief, their sensations were becoming comparable to those of the man who stole a house.

Nevertheless, after a short period given to unspoken misgivings, they returned to the subject of the reward. The money-value of bay horses, as compared to white, was again discussed, and each announced his certainty that nothing less than " a good ole hunderd dollars" would be offered for the return of Whitey.

But immediately after so speaking they fell into another silence, due to sinking feelings. They had spoken loudly and confidently, and yet they knew, somehow, that such things were not to be. According to their knowledge, it was perfectly reasonable to suppose that they would receive this fortune, but they frightened themselves in speaking of it; they knew that they *could* not have a hundred dollars for their own. An oppression, as from something awful and criminal, descended upon them at intervals.

Presently, however, they were warmed to a little cheerfulness again by Penrod's suggestion that they should put a notice in the paper. Neither of them had the slightest idea how to get it there, but such details as that were beyond the horizon; they occupied themselves with the question of what their advertisement ought to "say." Finding that they differed irreconcilably, Penrod went to a cache of his in the sawdust-box and brought two pencils and a supply of paper. He gave one of the pencils and several sheets to Sam; then both boys bent themselves in silence to the labour of practical composition. Penrod produced the briefer paragraph. (See Fig. I.) Sam's was more ample. (See Fig. II.)

Neither Sam nor Penrod showed any interest in what the other had written, but both felt that something praiseworthy had been accomplished. Penrod exhaled a sigh, as of relief, and, in a manner he had observed his father use sometimes, he said:

FOND FIG II

Horse on Saturday morning anwer can get him by applyng at. stable bhind Mr Schofield. You will have to proov he is your horse he is whit with kind of brown speked speks. and worout tail. Tail he is geting good care and food reward $10. $20. sevnty five cents Eache one or we will keep him long enuf.

?

"Thank goodness, *that's* off my mind, anyway!"

"What we goin' do next, Penrod?" Sam asked deferentially, the borrowed manner having some effect upon him.

"I don't know what *you're* goin' to do," Penrod returned, picking up the old cigarbox which had contained the paper and pencils. "*I'm* goin' to put mine in here, so's it'll come in handy when I haf to get at it."

"Well, I guess I'll keep mine there, too," said Sam. Thereupon he deposited his scribbled slip beside Penrod's in the cigarbox, and the box was solemnly returned to the secret place whence it had been taken.

"There, *that's* 'tended to!" said Sam, and, unconsciously imitating his friend's imitation, he gave forth audibly a breath of satisfaction and relief. Both boys felt that the financial side of their great affair had been conscientiously looked to, that the question of the reward was settled, and that everything was proceeding in a businesslike manner. Therefore, they were able to turn their attention to another matter.

This was the question of Whitey's next meal. After their exploits of the morning, and the consequent imperilment of Penrod, they decided that nothing more was to be done in apples, vegetables, or bread; it was evident that Whitey must be fed from the bosom of nature.

"We couldn't pull enough o' that frostbit ole grass in the yard to feed him," Penrod said gloomily. "We could work a week and not get enough to make him swaller more'n about twice. All we got this morning, he blew most of it away. He'd try to scoop it in toward his teeth with his lip, and then he'd haf to kind of blow out his breath, and after that all the grass that'd be left was just some wet pieces stickin' to the outsides of his face. Well, and you know how he acted about that maple branch. We can't trust him with branches."

Sam jumped up.

"'*I* know!" he cried. "There's lots of leaves left on the branches. We can give them to him."

"I just said—"

"I don't mean the branches," Sam explained. "We'll leave the branches on the trees, but just pull the leaves off the branches and put 'em in the bucket and feed 'em to him out of the bucket."

Penrod thought this plan worth trying, and for three-quarters of an hour the two boys were busy with the lower branches of various trees in the yard. Thus they managed to supply Whitey with a fair quantity of wet leaves, which he ate in a perfunctory way, displaying little of his earlier enthusiasm. And the work of his purveyors might have been more tedious if it had been less damp, for a boy is seldom bored by anything that involves his staying-out in the rain without protection. The drizzle had thickened; the leaves were heavy with water, and at every jerk the branches sent fat drops over the two collectors. They attained a noteworthy state of sogginess.

Finally, they were brought to the attention of the authorities indoors, and Della appeared upon the back porch.

"Musther Penrod," she called, "y'r mamma says ye'll c'm in the house this minute an' change y'r shoes an' stockin's an' everythun' else ye got on! D'ye hear me?"

Penrod, taken by surprise and unpleasantly alarmed, darted away from the tree he was depleting and ran for the stable.

"You tell her I'm dry as toast!" he shouted over his shoulder.

Della withdrew, wearing the air of a person gratuitously insulted; and a moment later she issued from the kitchen, carrying an umbrella. She opened it and walked resolutely to the stable.

"She says I'm to bring ye in the house," said Della, "an' I'm goin' to bring ye!"

Sam had joined Penrod in the carriage-house, and, with the beginnings of an unnamed terror, the two beheld this grim advance. But they did not stay for its culmination. Without a word to each other they hurriedly tiptoed up the stairs to the gloomy loft, and there they paused, listening.

They heard Della's steps upon the carriage-house floor.

"Ah, there's plenty places t'hide in," they heard her say; "but I'll show ye! She tole me to bring ye, and I'm—"

She was interrupted by a peculiar sound—loud, chilling, dismal, and unmistakably not of human origin. The boys knew it for Whitey's cough, but Della had not their experience. A smothered shriek reached their ears; there was a scurrying noise, and then, with horror, they heard Della's footsteps in the passageway that ran by Whitey's manger. Immediately there came a louder shriek, and even in the anguish of knowing their secret discovered, they were shocked to hear distinctly the words, "O Lard in hivvin!" in the well-known voice of Della. She shrieked again, and they heard the rush of her footfalls across the carriage-house floor. Wild words came from the outer air, and the kitchen door slammed violently. It was all over. She had gone to "tell."

Penrod and Sam plunged down the stairs and out of the stable. They climbed the back fence and fled up the alley. They turned into Sam's yard, and, without consultation, headed for the cellar doors, nor paused till they found themselves in the farthest, darkest, and gloomiest recess of the cellar. There, perspiring, stricken with fear, they sank down upon the earthen floor, with their moist backs against the stone wall.

Thus with boys. The vague apprehensions that had been creeping upon Penrod and Sam all afternoon had become monstrous; the unknown was before them. How great their crime would turn out to be (now that it was in the hands of grown people), they did not know, but, since it concerned a horse, it would undoubtedly be considered of terrible dimensions.

Their plans for a reward, and all the things that had seemed both innocent and practical in the morning, now staggered their minds as manifestations of criminal folly. A new and terrible light seemed to play upon the day's exploits; they had chased a horse belonging to strangers, and it would be said that they deliberately drove him into the stable and there concealed him. They had, in truth, virtually stolen him, and they had stolen food for him. The waning light through the small window above them warned Penrod that his inroads upon the vegetables in his own cellar must soon be discovered. Della, that Nemesis, would seek them in order to prepare them for dinner, and she would find them not. But she would recall his excursion to the cellar, for she had seen him when he came up; and also the truth would be known concerning the loaf of bread. Altogether, Penrod felt that his case was worse than Sam's—until Sam offered a suggestion which roused such horrible possibilities concerning the principal item of their offense that all thought of the smaller indictments disappeared.

"Listen, Penrod," Sam quavered: "What—what if that—what if that ole horse maybe b'longed to a—policeman!" Sam's imagination was not of the comforting kind. "What'd they—do to us, Penrod, if it turned out he was some policeman's horse?"

Penrod was able only to shake his head. He did not reply in words, but both boys thenceforth considered it almost inevitable that Whitey *had* belonged to a policeman, and in their sense of so ultimate a disaster, they ceased for a time to brood upon what their parents would probably do to them. The penalty for stealing a policeman's horse would be only a step short of capital, they were sure. They would not be hanged; but vague, looming sketches of something called the penitentiary began to flicker before them.

It grew darker in the cellar, so that finally they could not see each other.

"I guess they're huntin' for us by now," Sam said huskily. "I don't—I don't like it much down here, Penrod."

Penrod's hoarse whisper came from the profound gloom:

"Well, who ever said you did?"

"Well—" Sam paused; then he said plaintively, "I wish we'd never *seen* that dern ole horse."

"It was every bit his fault," said Penrod. "*We* didn't do anything. If he hadn't come stickin' his ole head in our stable, it'd never happened at all. Ole fool!" He rose. "I'm goin', to get out of here; I guess I've stood about enough for one day."

"Where—where you goin', Penrod? You aren't goin' *home*, are you?"

"No; I'm not! What you take me for? You think I'm crazy?"

"Well, where *can* we go?"

How far Penrod's desperation actually would have led him is doubtful, but he made this statement:

"I don't know where *you're* goin' but *I'm* goin' to walk straight out in the country till I come to a farmhouse and say my name's George and live there!"

"I'll do it too," Sam whispered eagerly. "I'll say my name's Henry."

"Well, we better get started," said the executive Penrod. "We got to get away from here, anyway."

But when they came to ascend the steps leading to the "outside doors," they found that those doors had been closed and locked for the night.

"It's no use," Sam lamented, "and we can't bust 'em, 'cause I tried to, once before. Fanny always locks 'em about five o'clock—I forgot. We got to go up the stairway and try to sneak out through the house."

They tiptoed back, and up the inner stairs. They paused at the top, then breathlessly stepped out into a hall which was entirely dark. Sam touched Penrod's sleeve in warning, and bent to listen at a door.

Immediately that door opened, revealing the bright library, where sat Penrod's mother and Sam's father.

It was Sam's mother who had opened the door.

"Come into the library, boys," she said. "Mrs. Schofield is just telling us about it."

And as the two comrades moved dumbly into the lighted room, Penrod's mother rose, and, taking him by the shoulder, urged him close to the fire.

"You stand there and try to dry off a little, while I finish telling Mr. and Mrs. Williams about you and Sam," she said. "You'd better make Sam keep near the fire, too, Mrs. Williams, because they both got wringing wet. Think of their running off just when most people would have wanted to stay! Well, I'll go on with the story, then. Della told me all about it, and what the cook next door said *she'd* seen, how they'd been trying to pull grass and leaves for the poor old thing all day—and all about the apples they carried from *your* cellar, and getting wet and working in the rain as hard as they could—and they'd given him a loaf of bread! Shame on you, Penrod!" She paused to laugh, but there was a little moisture round her eyes, even before she laughed. "And they'd fed him on potatoes and lettuce and cabbage and turnips out of *our* cellar! And I wish you'd see the sawdust bed they made for him! Well, when I'd telephoned, and the Humane Society man got there, he said it was the most touching thing he ever knew. It seems he *knew* this horse, and had been looking for him. He said ninety-nine boys out of a hundred would have chased the poor old thing away, and he was going to see to it that this case didn't go unnoticed, because the local branch of the society gives little silver medals for special acts like this. And the last thing he said before he led the poor old horse away was that he was sure Penrod and Sam would each be awarded one at the meeting of the society next Thursday night."

. . . On the following Saturday morning a yodel sounded from the sunny sidewalk in front of the Schofields' house, and Penrod, issuing forth, beheld the familiar figure of Samuel Williams in waiting.

Upon Sam's breast there glittered a round bit of silver suspended by a white ribbon from a bar of the same metal. Upon the breast of Penrod was a decoration precisely similar.

" 'Lo, Penrod," said Sam. "What you goin' to do?"

"Nothin'."

"I got mine on," said Sam.

"I have, too," said Penrod. "I wouldn't take a hundred dollars for mine."

"I wouldn't take two hundred for mine," said Sam.

Each glanced pleasantly at the other's medal. They faced each other without shame. Neither had the slightest sense of hypocrisy either in himself or in his comrade. On the contrary!

Penrod's eyes went from Sam's medal back to his own; thence they wandered, with perhaps a little disappointment, to the lifeless street and to the empty yards and spectatorless windows of the neighbourhood. Then he looked southward toward the busy heart of the town, where the multitudes were.

"Let's go down and see what time it is by the court-house clock," said Penrod.

Alfred Ollivant

THE BROWN MARE

I

He used to bring her home when he came on his winter's leave in the years before the War, to hunt with the South Down: for she was an unusually fine performer across country. And it was there I met her.

A tall upstanding creature, sixteen hands and over, very high at the withers, not quite clean-bred and yet showing breeding in every line. She did not really carry bone enough for the heavy Wealden clay, in which your horse sinks up to his hocks at every stride; but the Major was clearly always pleased when the big iron-gray Granite had strained a sinew and he could fall back on the mare for an extra day. And little sturdy Humbleton, the very British groom, with the blue eyes, the chestnut hair, and stolid way, was just the same. When exercising, he always rode the mare for preference and led the gray. She was honest and she was kind, with the heart of a woman and the manners of a lady. Yet except for a general air of breeding I do not think you would have singled her out in a crowd.

Kitty came first into the Major's stable when after a long spell at the War Office he went back to regimental work and took over the command of a Field Battery. I think he picked her out of the ranks: maybe the trumpeter had been riding her.

In that stable other horses came and went. The mare stayed; and her reputation grew.

At the big Aldershot meeting the Major entered her for the Artillery Point-to-point. He was never hard on his horses, and didn't ride her out. She was not placed. Afterwards he heard the whole Brigade had been backing her.

When the Major got his Jacket and took command of the Black Horse Battery at the Wood, Humbleton and the mare went with him. She was not black: she was brown. Therefore he could not ride her on ceremonial parades as his first charger. So he bought a sporting little black horse with a short back, Dandy by name, on which he rode with nodding plume at the head of his Troop down Park Lane, across Piccadilly and the Mall, to fire salutes on Horse Guards Parade.

But if she was no longer his first charger she was still first in his heart; and for long days on Salisbury Plain during autumn manoeuvers she had not her equal.

There followed three quiet years of preparation, the Black Horse Battery doing the Musical Drive at Olympia, swirling at the gallop in rhythmic figures interlaced about the famous bronze Gundamuck gun which the Troop had lost when covering the retreat from Cabul in the first Afghan War and recovered forty years later in the second. The Battery drove to the admiration of connoisseurs, artists, and the London crowd; and then would march down to Salisbury Plain to break records there in the mimic business of war.

Then came the reality; and the Major had to make the sacrifice of his life, and break up in a moment the fighting unit which through three laborious years he had trained to the point of perfection. Immediately on mobilization he was called upon to send all his horses, all his men and half his officers to complete the strength of a first-for-service Battery at Alder-shot. He stood with folded arms on the barrack-square and watched his famous black teams, shining in the sun, and beloved of Londoners, file out of the gate. The subalterns said they thought the Major's heart would break. It was perhaps a little comfort to him that when horses and men arrived at Aldershot the Major of the first-for-service Battery there asked his own gun-team drivers to give place to the newcomers.

"These are the drivers of the Black Horse Troop," he said.

The only men left the Major were Humbleton and his batman; the only horses Dandy and the mare. For the rest he had his guns; his non-commissioned officers; a couple of subalterns, reservists, and the pick of all the horses that were streaming into London with which to build up a new Battery.

II

He had two months in which to do it; and he did it.

In those days there was no tarrying. The Germans were knocking at the Gates of Calais.

At the beginning of October the Black Horse Battery, its horses no longer black, many-coloured, many-cornered, but a hard and handy crowd, disembarked at Zeebrugge with the Seventh Division in the romantic and desperate endeavour to relieve Antwerp; and the officers of the Guards Brigade to which the Battery was attached muttered among themselves that if it was no longer the Battery of Olympia days it was still the best Horse Battery in England.

Antwerp fell the day they landed. The Immortal Division, 20,000 strong, marched out to meet the enemy much as David went to meet Goliath. In a perilously thin-drawn-out line it flung itself across the path of the German herds driving bull-headed, hundred thousands of them, for the sea and the island that lay across the Channel.

General French sent word to the valiant Division that he would reinforce them in five hours. Those reinforcements took five days to come. But the Division held; though at the end of the stress it had but forty officers left out of the four hundred who had disembarked at Zeebrugge six weeks before.

In those tremendous days the Black Horse Battery played its fiery part in support of the First Battalion of the Grenadier Guards. Tried in that white-hot furnace, Guardsmen and Gunners proved worthy of each other and of the traditions of their great regiments. There was no rest by night or day for officers, men, or horses.

Kitty, the mare, took it all very calmly. Back with the limbers, on the sheltered side of the ridge on which the guns were barking, she stretched her long neck, bowed a knee, and grazed the Flemish turf at ease much as on Salisbury Plain. The hubbub across the ridge, her master's fierce peremptory voice, the occasional burst of shrapnel near by, disturbed her little.

Now and then the trumpeter, handing over the mare and his own horse to the care of Humbleton, would crawl to the top of the ridge and watch the Battery in action beyond, pounding away at the grey-coats struggling in the valley. He didn't see much: for the guns were roughly dug in. But once he saw a farmhouse which the Major was using for observation post crash down in headlong ruin.

"Gosh!" muttered the trumpeter. "Spotted 'im. He's done."

Then the long, lean Major came running out of the dust and débris.

The trumpeter returned at the trot to his horses.

"Old man ain't 'alf nippy," he reported to Humbleton.

"He ain't so old neether, then," answered Humbleton, who took no liberties with his master himself, and allowed none.

"Ain't he, then?" retorted the trumpeter who must have the last word even in the mouth of Hell. "I'll lay he's older than he were twenty year ago, then."

Once on that last desperate day, when the one skeleton Cavalry Brigade held in reserve was dashing here and there to make good as best it might gaps in the broken line, the Major got his guns up under a wall to cover the Guards' counter-attack launched as a forlorn hope. The Germans saw him and swept the wall away with a tidal wave of fire.

It was *Rear limber up!* and the gun-teams came up at the gallop.

In the hubbub and tumult of shells, shouts, of gunners furiously handling gun-wheels, of drivers with outstretched whip-hands quieting their teams, of bloody men disengaging bloody and floundering horses, Kitty, the mare, was steady as a rock.

"Got her, sir?" gasped the trumpeter, as he toppled off his own horse.

"Right," said the Major, toe in his stirrup, and swung into his saddle. *"Battle column, gallop!"*

And somehow or other the Battery swung clear.

Those were astounding days. For three weeks the officers and men of that Battery never had their clothes off, and for days together the horses were never unharnessed. But whoever else went short Kitty, the mare, never suffered. Humbleton saw to that, and to be just the mare saw to herself in her large and sensible way, grazing when opportunity offered, and snatching *bonne bouches* from ruined haystacks.

After the first terrible six weeks the Armies settled down to trench warfare. It was not the game for Horse Artillery; but the Black Horse Battery played it with zest all through that first winter.

The horses stood out in the open and thrived. Kitty grew a coat like a bear's; and the saddle sank into her back as into a drift of brown snow. But campaigning suited her as it did her black companion Dandy.

Then came promotion.

The Major, now a Brevet-Lieutenant-Colonel, took command of a Field Artillery Brigade. That did not last for long. Within a few weeks he and Humbleton and the two horses were back with the Horse Artillery, the Colonel now commanding a Brigade.

III

The Headquarters of the Brigade was in a château some thirty miles behind the firing line.

When the turn of the Cavalry Division, to which the Brigade was attached, came for a spell in the trenches, horses and guns made a long forced march by night and took up their positions early in December of the second winter of the War.

They had three months in the trenches—months of sleet and rain, of dogged endurance, infinitely dull, varied by lurid nightmare interludes.

When towards the end of February they were relieved nobody in the Division regretted it.

That was the time of the heavy snows; and all reliefs were made of necessity at night.

The Horse Artillery started for the thirty-mile trek home at midnight, the long thin line of guns, their wheels thick with snow, trailing worm-like through the white dimness that muffled the noise of their going and made the procession strangely ghost-like.

Wagons and kits were to follow later.

The Colonel gave his Brigade an hour's start.

It was just one when his batman came to the door of his much-shelled lodging and announced that Humbleton and the horses were outside.

The Colonel, busy destroying papers, went to the door, accompanied by his terrier Bruiser. The little groom, in his goat-skin coat, stood outside in the snow, the horses in hand. Dandy stretched a neck to greet his little friend, the terrier, standing three-legged, and shivering in the snow, while the mare nibbled tentatively at a pile of wood close by.

"Don't let her eat that!" ordered the Colonel ferociously.

He always spoke to his servants as if they were his mortal enemies and he wished them to know he knew it. And they took more from him than they would have done from many a man with a smoother tongue and a smaller heart. It was just the old man's way, they said among themselves. And he had the qualities which ensured respect if they did not win love. He was just, consistent, and in the heart of him considerate. So, to the surprise of many, they always stuck to him.

The Colonel went back to his room with Bruiser, and piled on layer upon layer of clothes: sweaters, hunting-waistcoats, Norfolk jackets, towards the top a suit of oilskins, and over all a Burberry.

In multitudinous pockets he stuffed an electric torch, a flask, a thermos, a map, a ball of string, an extra pair of gloves, a muffler, and other odds and ends. The lean Colonel, now a very portly man, gave certain curt instructions to his batman, tied Bruiser, who was to follow with the kits, to the leg of the table, and mounted Dandy: for he knew of old that the mare was not clever in the snow.

Then he set off into the night, Humbleton and the mare following in his wake.

Once clear of the village the Colonel looked around. In that little distance he had already gained greatly on the other pair.

He waved for the groom to come up alongside.

"Leg her up!" he ordered gruffly. "Keep her alongside me."

Side by side master and man rode along through the night, the snow coating them heavily.

"She's walking abominably," said the Colonel.

"Yes, sir," answered Humbleton, who never wasted words, least of all on his master.

Laboriously the Colonel disengaged his electric torch and flashed it on the mare.

What he saw he didn't like.

The snow was heavy on her shoulders, thick in her ears, plastering her heavy coat; and she was slouching along disconsolately, her head down, as though smelling out a track.

It's that wood's poisoned her, thought the Colonel; but he didn't say anything.

"Does she feel all right?" he asked.

"Yes, sir," answered Humbleton.

Twelve miles out they stopped at a little *estaminet* for a water and feed.

Dandy tucked into his nose-bag greedily. The mare would not look at hers.

"Come on, missus," said Humbleton.

He warmed some water, making a weak gruel, sprinkled bran on the top, and held the bucket to her nostrils temptingly.

She breathed on it, her breath mingling with the steam, but would not touch it.

The Colonel walked round her with anxious eyes, pulled her ears, hand-rubbed her cold pasterns.

It's that wood, he thought.

Then he rummaged in his multitudinous pockets. After long search he produced a thermometer and took her temperature.

It was 103; and there was still a twenty-mile march before them.

He got her a ball and gave it her.

There was no stabling at the *estaminet;* and nothing for it therefore but to go on.

He swung into his saddle again.

The track lay before them invisible save for the half-obliterated furroughs left by the gun-wheels. The snow came waving across them in white curtains that almost seemed to lighten the darkness. The moustaches of both men froze and were thatched with snow. The two white-cloaked figures laboured along side by side like two phantom horsemen with feet of lead.

The mare seemed to come on a little better.

Every now and then the Colonel said—

"How's she feel now?"

And Humbleton answered—

"Very queer, sir."

At length they came to the foot of a long bare ridge, stretching interminably before them, smooth and bleak and white as a shroud, great curtains of snow flapping dismally across its desolate face.

The mare stopped.

Both men dismounted. The Colonel with a hoof-picker, disengaged with difficulty from a remote interior pocket, emptied her hoofs of the balling snow.

He thought she was going to lie down; and once she lay down on that slope he knew he would never get her up again.

He and Humbleton, crouching in the snow, hand-rubbed her legs and flanks. Then they started leading her up the slope.

The two men were wonderfully kind and patient with the suffering creature; far more kind and patient with her than with each other.

The forlorn little group toiled desolately up the slope, now engulfed in a billow of waving white, now emerging into blotted dimness, the wind rollicking away with terrible laughter in the valley below. The horses, with windy tails tucked-in and strewn about their flanks, plodded on with downward heads, shaking the snow from their ears like big dogs with a rattle of accoutrements that sounded weirdly in the night.

Honest and kind as always, the mare was doing her dumb best; and both men knew it. One on either side, they shouldered her up the slope, easing her, halting her, talking to her, coaxing her on a step at a time, as a nurse teaching a child to walk. And every now and then she rubbed her snowy head against one man or the other, as though recognizing their love, and wishing to tell them about it.

Somehow or other they bolstered her up to the top of that Ridge of Windy Death.

Down in the valley, on the other side, the Colonel hoped he might find a Cavalry Division and some shelter for the mare.

He was right.

As they descended the slope, the mare walking more easily, they found themselves among friends.

The Gunners were in possession of the valley.

Officers and men with lanterns came to the rescue. Most of them knew the Colonel; many of them the mare. A veterinary surgeon was found and pulled out of his bed. The mare was given a roomy box in a farm. She revived somewhat. Willing hands bedded her down in bracken. Humbleton set to work to warm and dry her. The Colonel took her temperature and found it less.

The light was just stealing over the white-bosomed hills and snow-thatched roofs when he swung into the saddle to ride the last long stage to his Headquarters alone.

The mare was playing with some hay, and Humbleton was rugging her up, as he left her.

IV

All that day he was busy, and no news came through; but a horse of his Orderly Officer died partly from exposure and partly from eating wood, the vet. said.

Next morning early the Colonel rode off to the valley where the mare was to see how things were going.

As he rode up to the yard of the farm, Humbleton, looking in his goat-skin like a little clean-shaven Robinson Crusoe, came ploughing through the snow to meet him.

He looked very dogged and did not catch the Colonel's eye.

"Well?" said the Colonel.

"Mare's dead, sir," answered the little man.

"Indeed!" said the Colonel rudely. "What time?"

"Two o'clock this morning."

The Colonel said nothing and dismounted.

Heavily he walked through the slush of the farmyard towards the loose-box and entered.

Honest and kind in death as in life, the brown mare lay on her side, rough of coat, her long flat neck stretched out, her long thin legs slightly crooked, her shoes upturned and shining, looking strangely pathetic.

Over her head Humbleton had scrawled in chalk upon a beam:

KITTY:
Died for her country,
1 March, 1916.

The Colonel stood above her.

He was glad she had such a thick bed of bracken to rest upon.

Then he bent and felt her heart.

One of those strange and overwhelming waves of emotion, of which we cannot trace the origin, came surging up out of the inland ocean of his being and choked him.

He kicked the bracken about with his feet, and blew his nose.

Then he said—

"We shall miss her, Humbleton."

The little groom, standing in his goat-skin jacket in the door, his back towards his master, looked out over the snow and answered nothing.

William Dean Howells

BUYING A HORSE

If one has money enough, there seems no reason why one should not go and buy such a horse as he wants. This is the commonly accepted theory, on which the whole commerce in horses is founded, and on which my friend proceeded.

He was about removing from Charlesbridge, where he had lived many happy years without a horse, farther into the country, where there were charming drives and inconvenient distances, and where a horse would be very desirable, if not quite necessary. But as a horse seemed at first an extravagant if not sinful desire, he began by talking vaguely round, and rather hinting than declaring that he thought somewhat of buying. The professor to whom he first intimated his purpose flung himself from his horse's back to the grassy border of the sidewalk where my friend stood, and said he would give him a few points. "In the first place don't buy a horse that shows much daylight under him, unless you buy a horse-doctor *with* him; get a short-legged horse; and he ought to be short and thick in the barrel,"—or words to that effect. "Don't get a horse with a narrow forehead: there are horsefools as well as the other kind, and you want a horse with room for brains. And look out that he's *all right forward.*"

"What's that?" asked my friend, hearing this phrase for the first time.

"That he isn't tender in his fore-feet,—that the hoof isn't contracted," said the professor, pointing out the well-planted foot of his own animal.

"What ought I to pay for a horse?" pursued my friend, struggling to fix the points given by the professor in a mind hitherto unused to points of the kind.

"Well, horses are cheap, now; and you ought to get a fair family horse— You want a family horse?"

"Yes."

"Something you can ride and drive both? Something your children can drive?"

"Yes, yes."

"Well, you ought to get such a horse as that for a hundred and twenty-five dollars."

This was the figure my friend had thought of; he drew a breath of relief. "Where did you buy your horse?"

"Oh, I always get my horses"—the plural abashed my friend—"at the Chevaliers'. If you throw yourself on their mercy, they'll treat you well. I'll send you a note to them."

"Do!" cried my friend, as the professor sprang upon his horse, and galloped away.

My friend walked home encouraged; his purpose of buying a horse had not seemed so monstrous, at least to this hardened offender. He now began to announce it more boldly; he said right and left that he wished to buy a horse, but that he would not go above a hundred. This was not true, but he wished to act prudently, and to pay a hundred and twenty-five only in extremity. He carried the professor's note to the Chevaliers', who duly honored it, understood at once what my friend wanted, and said they would look out for him. They were sorry he had not happened in a little sooner,—they had just sold the very horse he wanted. I may as well say here that they were not able to find him a horse, but that they used him with the strictest honor, and that short of supplying his want they were perfect.

In the mean time the irregular dealers began to descend upon him, as well as amateurs to whom he had mentioned his wish for a horse, and his premises at certain hours of the morning presented the effect of a horse-fair, or say rather a museum of equine bricabrac. At first he blushed at the spectacle, but he soon became hardened to it, and liked the excitement of driving one horse after another round the block, and deciding upon him. To a horse, they had none of the qualities commended by the professor, but they had many others which the dealers praised. These persons were not discouraged when he refused to buy, but cheerfully returned the next day with others differently ruinous. They were men of a spirit more obliging than my friend has found in other walks. One of them, who paid him a prefatory visit in his library, in five minutes augmented from six to seven hundred and fifty pounds the weight of a pony-horse, which he wished to sell. ("What you want," said the Chevaliers, "is a pony-horse," and my friend, gratefully catching at the phrase, had gone about saying he wanted a pony-horse. After that, hulking brutes of from eleven to thirteen hundred pounds were every day brought to him as pony-horses.) The same dealer came another day with a mustang, in whom was no fault, and who had every appearance of speed, but who was only marking time as it is called in military drill, I believe, when he seemed to be getting swiftly over the ground; he showed a sociable preference for the curbstone in turning corners, and was condemned, to be replaced the next evening by a pony-horse that a child might ride or drive, and that especially would not shy. Upon experiment, he shied half across the road, and the fact was reported to the dealer. He smiled compassionately. "What did he shy *at?*"

"A wheelbarrow."

"Well! I never see the hoss *yet* that *wouldn't* shy at a wheelbarrow."

My friend owned that a wheelbarrow was of an alarming presence, but he had his reserves respecting the self-control and intelligence of this pony-horse. The dealer amiably withdrew him, and said that he would bring next day a horse—if he could get the owner to part with a family pet—that *would* suit; but upon investigation it appeared that this treasure was what is called a calico-horse, and my friend, who was without the ambition to figure in the popular eye as a stray circus-rider, declined to see him.

These adventurous spirits were not squeamish. They thrust their hands into the lathery mouths of their brutes to show the state of their teeth, and wiped their fingers on their trousers or grass afterwards, without a tremor, though my friend could never forbear a shudder at the sight. If sometimes they came with a desirable animal, the price was far beyond his modest figure; but generally they seemed to think that he did not want a desirable animal. In most cases, the pony-horse pronounced sentence upon himself by some gross and ridiculous blemish; but sometimes my friend failed to hit upon any tenable excuse for refusing him. In such an event, he would say, with an air of easy and candid comradery, "Well, now, what's the matter with him?" And then the dealer, passing his hand down one of the pony-horse's fore-legs, would respond, with an upward glance of searching inquiry at my friend, "Well, he's a leetle mite tender for'a'd."

I am afraid my friend grew to have a cruel pleasure in forcing them to this exposure of the truth; but he excused himself upon the ground that they never expected him to be alarmed at this tenderness forward, and that their truth was not a tribute to virtue, but was contempt of his ignorance. Nevertheless, it was truth; and he felt that it must be his part thereafter to confute the common belief that there is no truth in horse-trades.

These people were not usually the owners of the horses they brought, but the emissaries or agents of the owners. Often they came merely to show a horse, and were not at all sure that his owner would part with him on any terms, as he was a favorite with the ladies of the family. An impenetrable mystery hung about the owner, through which he sometimes dimly loomed as a gentleman in failing health, who had to give up his daily drives, and had no use for the horse. There were cases in which the dealer came secretly, from pure zeal, to show a horse whose owner supposed him still in the stable, and who must be taken back before his absence was noticed. If my friend insisted upon knowing the owner and conferring with him, in any of these instances, it was darkly admitted that he was a gentleman in the livery business over in Somerville or down in the Lower Port. Truth, it seemed, might be absent or present in a horse-trade, but mystery was essential.

The dealers had a jargon of their own, in which my friend became an expert. They did not say that a horse weighed a thousand pounds, but ten hundred; he was not worth a hundred and twenty-five dollars, but one and a quarter; he was not going on seven years old, but was coming seven. There are curious facts, by the way, in regard to the age of horses which are not generally known. A horse is never of an even age: that is, he is not six, or eight, or ten, but five, or seven, or nine years old; he is sometimes, but not often, eleven; he is *never* thirteen; his favorite time of life is seven, and he rarely gets beyond it, if on sale. My friend found the number of horses brought into the world in 1871 quite beyond computation. He also found that most hard-working horses were sick or ailing, as most hard-working men and women are; that perfectly sound horses are as rare as perfectly sound human beings, and are apt, like the latter, to be vicious.

He began to have a quick eye for the characteristics of horses, and could walk round a proffered animal and scan his points with the best. "What," he would ask, of a given beast, "makes him let his lower lip hang down in that imbecile manner?"

"Oh, he's got a parrot-mouth. Some folks like 'em." Here the dealer would pull open the creature's flabby lips, and discover a beak like that of a polyp; and the cleansing process on the grass or trousers would take place.

Of another. "What makes him trot in that spread-out, squatty way, behind?" he demanded, after the usual tour of the block.

"He travels wide. Horse men prefer that."

They preferred any ugliness or awkwardness in a horse to the opposite grace or charm, and all that my friend could urge, in meek withdrawal from negotiation, was that he was not of an educated taste. In the course of long talks, which frequently took the form of warnings, he became wise in the tricks practiced by all dealers except his interlocutor. One of these, a device for restoring youth to an animal nearing the dangerous limit of eleven, struck him as peculiarly ingenious. You pierce the forehead, and blow into it with a quill; this gives an agreeable fullness, and erects the drooping ears in a spirited and mettlesome manner, so that a horse coming eleven will look for a time as if he were coming five.

After a thorough course of the volunteer dealers, and after haunting the Chevaliers' stables for several weeks, my friend found that not money alone was needed to buy a horse. The affair began to wear a sinister aspect. He had an uneasy fear that in several cases he had refused the very horse he wanted with the *aplomb* he had acquired in dismissing undesirable beasts. The fact was he knew less about horses than when he began to buy, while he had indefinitely enlarged his idle knowledge of men, of their fatuity and hollowness. He learned that men whom he had always envied their brilliant omniscience in regard to horses, as they drove him out behind their dashing trotters, were quite ignorant and helpless in the art of buying; they always got somebody else to buy their horses for them. "Find a man you can trust," they said, "and then put yourself in his hands. And *never* trust anybody about the health of a horse. Take him to a veterinary surgeon, and have him go all over him."

My friend grew sardonic; then he grew melancholy and haggard. There was something very strange in the fact that a person unattainted of crime, and not morally disabled in any known way, could not take his money and buy such a horse as he wanted with it. His acquaintance began to recommend men to him. "If you want a horse, Captain Jenks is your man." "Why don't you go to Major Snaffle? He'd take pleasure in it." But my friend, naturally reluctant to trouble others, and sickened by long failure, as well as maddened by the absurdity that if you wanted a horse you must first get a man, neglected this really good advice. He lost his interest in the business, and dismissed with lack-lustre indifference the horses which continued to be brought to his gate. He felt that his position before the community was becoming notorious and ridiculous. He slept badly; his long endeavor for a horse ended in nightmares.

One day he said to a gentleman whose turn-out he had long admired, "I wonder if you couldn't find me a horse!"

"Want a horse?"

"Want a horse! I thought my need was known beyond the sun. I thought my want of a horse was branded on my forehead."

This gentleman laughed, and then he said, "I've just seen a mare that would suit you. I thought of buying her, but I want a match, and this mare is too small. She'll be round here in fifteen minutes, and I'll take you out with her. Can you wait?"

"Wait!" My friend laughed in his turn.

The mare dashed up before the fifteen minutes had passed. She was beautiful, black as a coal; and kind as a kitten, said her driver. My friend thought her head was rather big. "Why, yes, she's a *pony*-horse; that's what I like about her."

She trotted off wonderfully, and my friend felt that the thing was now done.

The gentleman, who was driving, laid his head on one side, and listened. "Clicks, don't she?"

"She *does* click," said my friend obligingly.

"Hear it?" asked the gentleman.

"I *don't* hear it. What *is* clicking?"

"Oh, striking the heel of her fore-foot with the toe of her hind-foot. Sometimes it comes from bad shoeing. Some people like it. I don't myself." After a while he added, "If you can get this mare for a hundred and twenty-five, you'd better buy her."

"Well, I will," said my friend. He would have bought her, in fact, if she had clicked like a noiseless sewing-machine. But the owner, remote as Medford, and invisibly dealing, as usual, through a third person, would not sell her for one and a quarter; he wanted one and a half. Besides, another Party was trying to get her; and now ensued a negotiation which for intricacy and mystery surpassed all the others. It was conducted in my friend's interest by one who had the difficult task of keeping the owner's imagination in check and his demands within bounds, for it soon appeared that he wanted even more than one and a half for her. Unseen and inaccessible, he grew every day more unmanageable. He entered into relations with the other Party, and it all ended in his sending her out one day after my friend had gone into the country, and requiring him to say at once that he would give one and a half. He was not at home, and he never saw the little mare again. This confirmed him in the belief that she was the very horse he ought to have had.

People had now begun to say to him, "Why don't you advertise? Advertise for a gentleman's pony-horse and phaeton and harness complete. You'll have a perfect procession of them before night." This proved true. His advertisement, mystically worded after the fashion of those things, found abundant response. But the establishments which he would have taken he could not get at the figure he had set, and those which his money would buy he would not have. They came at all hours of the day; and he never returned home after an absence without meeting the reproach that *now* the very horse he wanted had just been driven away, and would not be brought back, as his owner lived in Billerica, and only happened to be down. A few equipages really appeared desirable, but in regard to these his jaded faculties refused to work: he could decide nothing; his volition was extinct; he let them come and go.

It was at this period that people who had at first been surprised that he wished to buy a horse came to believe that he had bought one, and were astonished to learn that he had not. He felt the pressure of public opinion.

He began to haunt the different sale-stables in town, and to look at horses with a view to buying at private sale. Every facility for testing them was offered him, but he could not make up his mind. In feeble wantonness he gave appointments which he knew he should not keep, and, passing his days in an agony of multitudinous indecision, he added to the lies in the world the hideous sum of his broken engagements. From time to time he forlornly appeared at the Chevaliers', and refreshed his corrupted nature by contact with their sterling integrity. Once he ventured into their establishment just before an auction began, and remained dazzled by the splendor of a spectacle which I fancy can be paralleled only by some dream of a mediaeval tournament. The horses, brilliantly harnessed, accurately shod, and standing tall on burnished hooves', their necks curved by the check rein and their black and blonde manes flowing over the proud arch, lustrous and wrinkled like satin, were ranged in a glittering hemicycle. They affected my friend like the youth and beauty of his earliest evening parties; he experienced a sense of bashfulness, of sickening personal demerit. He could not have had the audacity to bid on one of those superb creatures, if all the Chevaliers together had whispered him that here at last was the very horse.

I pass over an unprofitable interval in which he abandoned himself to despair, and really gave up the hope of being able ever to buy a horse. During this interval he removed from Charlesbridge to the country, and found himself, to his self-scorn and self-pity, actually reduced to hiring a livery horse by the day. But relief was at hand. The carpenter who had remained to finish up the new house after my friend had gone into it bethought himself of a firm in his place who brought on horses from the West, and had the practice of selling a horse on trial, and constantly replacing it with other horses till the purchaser was suited. This seemed an ideal arrangement, and the carpenter said that he *thought* they had the very horse my friend wanted.

The next day he drove him up, and the upon the plan of successive exchanges till the perfect horse was reached, my friend bought him for one and a quarter, the figure which he had kept in mind from the first. He bought a phaeton and harness from the same people, and when the whole equipage stood at his door, he felt the long-delayed thrill of pride and satisfaction. The horse was of the Morgan breed, a bright bay, small and round and neat, with a little head tossed high, and a gentle yet alert movement. He was in the prime of youth, of the age of which every horse desires to be, and was just coming seven. My friend had already taken him to a horse-doctor, who for one dollar had gone all over him, and pronounced him sound as a fish, and complimented his new owner upon his acquisition. It all seemed too good to be true. As Billy turned his soft eye on the admiring family group, and suffered one of the children to smooth his nose while another held a lump of sugar to his dainty lips, his amiable behavior restored my friend to his peace of mind and his long-lost faith in a world of reason.

The ridiculous planet, wavering bat-like through space, on which it had been impossible for an innocent man to buy a suitable horse was a dream of the past, and he had the solid, sensible old earth under his feet once more. He mounted into the phaeton and drove off with his wife; he returned and gave each of the children a drive in succession. He told them that any of them could drive Billy as much as they liked, and he quieted a clamor for exclusive ownership on the part of each by declaring that Billy belonged to the whole family. To this day he cannot look back to those moments without tenderness. If Billy had any apparent fault, it was an amiable indolence. But this made him all the safer for the children, and it did not really amount to laziness. While on sale he had been driven in a provision cart, and had therefore the habit of standing un-hitched. One had merely to fling the reins into the bottom of the phaeton and leave Billy to his own custody. His other habit of drawing up at kitchen gates was not confirmed, and the fact that he stumbled on his way to the doctor who pronounced him blameless was reasonably attrib-uted to a loose stone at the foot of the hill; the misstep resulted in a barked shin, but a little wheel-grease, in a horse of Billy's complexion, easily removed the evidence of this.

It was natural that after Billy was bought and paid for, several extremely desirable horses should be offered to my friend by their owners, who came in person, stripped of all the adventitious mystery of agents and middle-men. They were gentlemen, and they spoke the English ha-bitual with persons not corrupted by horses. My friend saw them come and go with grief; for he did not like to be shaken in his belief that Billy was the only horse in the world for him, and he would have liked to purchase their animals, if only to show his appreciation of honor and frankness and sane language. Yet he was consoled by the possession of Billy, whom he found increasingly excellent and trustworthy. Any of the family drove him about; he stood unhitched; he was not afraid of cars; he was as kind as a kitten; he had not, as the neighboring coachman said, a voice, though he seemed a little loively in coming out of the stable sometimes. He went well under the saddle; he was a beauty, and if he had a voice, it was too great satisfaction in his personal appearance.

One evening after tea, the young gentleman, who was about to drive Billy out, stung by the reflection that he had not taken blackberries and cream twice, ran into the house to repair the omission, and left Billy, as usual unhitched at the door. During his absence, Billy caught sight of his stable, and involuntarily moved towards it. Finding himself unchecked, he gently increased his pace; and when my friend, looking up from the melon-patch which he was admiring, called out, "Ho, Billy! Whoa, Billy!" and headed him off from the gap, Billy profited by the circumstance to turn into the pear orchard. The elastic turf under his unguided hoof seemed to exhilarate him; his pace became a trot, a canter, a gallop, a tornado; the reins fluttered like ribbons in the air; the phaeton flew ruining after. In a terrible cyclone the equipage swept round the neighbor's house, vanished, reappeared, swooped down his lawn, and vanished again. It was incredible.

My friend stood transfixed among his melons. He knew that his neighbor's children played under the porte-cochère on the other side of the house which Billy had just surrounded in his flight, and probably. . . . My friend's first impulse was not to go and see, but to walk into his own house, and ignore the whole affair. But you cannot really ignore an affair of that kind. You must face it, and commonly it stares you out of countenance. Commonly, too, it knows how to choose its time so as to disgrace as well as crush its victim. His neighbor had people to tea, and long before my friend reached the house the host and his guests were all out on the lawn, having taken the precaution to bring their napkins with them.

"The children!" gasped my friend.

"Oh, they were all in bed," said the neighbor, and he began to laugh. That was right; my friend would have mocked at the calamity if it had been his neighbor's. "Let us go and look up your phaeton." He put his hand on the naked flank of a fine young elm, from which the bark had just been stripped. "Billy seems to have passed this way."

At the foot of a stone-wall four feet high lay the phaeton, with three wheels in the air, and the fourth crushed flat against the axle; the willow back was broken, the shafts were pulled out, and Billy was gone.

"Good thing there was nobody in it," said the neighbor.

"Good thing it didn't run down some Irish family, and get you in for damages," said a guest.

It appeared, then, that there were two good things about this disaster. My friend had not thought there were so many, but while he rejoiced in this fact, he rebelled at the notion that a sorrow like that rendered the sufferer in any event liable for damages, and he resolved that he never would have paid them. But probably he would.

Some half-grown boys got the phaeton right-side up, and restored its shafts and cushions, and it limped away with them towards the carriage-house. Presently another half-grown boy came riding Billy up the hill. Billy showed an inflated nostril and an excited eye, but physically he was unharmed, save for a slight scratch on what was described as the off hind-leg; the reader may choose which leg this was.

"The worst of it is," said the guest, "that you never can trust 'em after they've run off once."

"Have some tea?" said the host to my friend.

"No, thank you," said my friend, in whose heart the worst of it rankled; and he walked home embittered by his guilty consciousness that Billy ought never to have been left untied. But it was not this self-reproach; it was not the mutilated phaeton; it was not the loss of Billy, who must now be sold; it was the wreck of settled hopes, the renewed suspense of faith, the repetition of the tragical farce of buying another horse, that most grieved my friend.

Billy's former owners made a feint of supplying other horses in his place, but the only horse supplied was an aged veteran with the scratches, who must have come seven early in our era, and who, from his habit of getting about on tip-toe, must have been tender for'a'd beyond anything of my friend's previous experience. Probably if he could have waited they might have replaced Billy in time, but their next installment from the West produced nothing suited to his wants but a horse with the presence and carriage of a pig, and he preferred to let them sell Billy for what he would bring, and to trust his fate elsewhere. Billy had fallen nearly one half in value, and he brought very little—to his owner; though the new purchaser was afterwards reported to value him at much more than what my friend had paid for him. These things are really mysteries; you cannot fathom them; it is idle to try. My friend remained grieving over his own folly and carelessness, with a fond hankering for the poor little horse he had lost, and the belief that he should never find such another. Yet he was not without a philanthropist's consolation. He had added to the stock of harmless pleasures in a degree of which he could not have dreamed. All of his acquaintance knew that he had bought a horse, and they all seemed now to conspire in asking him how he got on with it. He was forced to confess the truth. On hearing it, his friends burst into shouts of laughter, and smote their persons, and stayed themselves against lamp-posts and house-walls. They begged his pardon, and then they began again, and shouted and roared anew. Since the gale which blew down the poet——'s chimneys and put him to the expense of rebuilding them, no joke so generally satisfactory had been offered to the community. My friend had, in his time, achieved the reputation of a wit by going about and saying, "Did you know——'s chimneys had blown down?" and he had now himself the pleasure of causing the like quality of wit in others.

Having abandoned the hope of getting anything out of the people who had sold him Billy, he was for a time, the prey of an inert despair, in which he had not even spirit to repine at the disorder of a universe in which he could not find a horse. No horses were now offered to him, for it had become known throughout the trade that he had bought a horse. He had therefore to set about counteracting this impression with what feeble powers were left him. Of the facts of that period he remembers with confusion and remorse the trouble to which he put the owner of the pony-horse, Pansy, whom he visited repeatedly in a neighboring town at a loss of time and money to himself, and with no result but to embarrass Pansy's owner in his relations with people who had hired him and did not wish him sold. Something of the old baffling mystery hung over Pansy's whereabouts; he was with difficulty produced and when *en evidence* he was not the Pansy my friend had expected. He paltered with his regrets; he covered his disappointment with what pretenses he could; and he waited till he could telegraph back his adverse decision. His conclusion was that, next to proposing marriage, there was no transaction of life that involved so many delicate and complex relations as buying a horse and that the rupture of a horse-trade was little less embarrassing and distressing to all concerned than a broken engagement. There was a terrible intimacy in the affair; it was alarmingly personal. He went about sorrowing for the pain and disappointment he had inflicted on many amiable people of all degrees who had tried to supply him with a horse.

"Look here," said his neighbor, finding him in this low state, "why don't you get a horse of the gentleman who furnishes mine?" This had been suggested before, and my friend explained that he had disliked to make trouble. His scruples were lightly set aside, and he suffered himself to be entreated. The fact was he was so discouraged with his attempt to buy a horse that if any one had now given him such a horse as he wanted he would have taken it.

One sunny, breezy morning his neighbor drove my friend over to the beautiful farm of the good genius on whose kindly offices he had now fixed his languid hopes. I need not say what the landscape was in mid-August, or how, as they drew near the farm, the air was enriched with the breath of vast orchards of early apples,—apples that no forced fingers rude shatter from their stems, but that ripen and mellow untouched, till they drop into the straw with which the orchard aisles are bedded; it is the poetry of horticulture; it is Art practicing the wise and gracious patience of Nature, and offering to the Market a Summer Sweeting of the Hesperides.

The possessor of this luscious realm at once took my friend's case into consideration; he listened, the owner of a hundred horses, with gentle indulgence to the shapeless desires of a man whose wildest dream was *one* horse. At the end he said, "I see you want a horse that can take care of himself."

"No," replied my friend, with the inspiration of despair. "I want a horse that can take care of me."

The good genius laughed, and turned the conversation. Neither he nor my friend's neighbor was a man of many words, and like taciturn people they talked in low tones. The three moved about the room and looked at the Hispano-Roman pictures; they had a glass of sherry; from time to time something was casually murmured about Frank. My friend felt that he was in good hands, and left the affair to them. It ended in a visit to the stable, where it appeared that this gentleman had no horse to sell among his hundred which exactly met my friend's want, but that he proposed to lend him Frank while a certain other animal was put in training for the difficult office he required of a horse. One of the men was sent for Frank, and in the mean time my friend was shown some gaunt and graceful thoroughbreds, and taught to see the difference between them and the plebeian horse. But Frank, though no thoroughbred, eclipsed these patricians when he came. He had a little head, and a neck gallantly arched; he was black and plump and smooth; and though he carried himself with a petted air, and was a dandy to the tips of his hooves, his knowing eye was kindly. He turned it upon my friend with the effect of understanding *his* case at a glance.

It was in this way that for the rest of the long, lovely summer peace was reestablished in his heart. There was no question of buying or selling Frank; there were associations that endeared him beyond money to his owner; but my friend could take him without price. The situation had its humiliation for a man who had been arrogantly trying to buy a horse, but he submitted with grateful meekness, and with what grace Heaven granted him; and Frank gayly entered upon the peculiar duties of his position. His first duty was to upset all preconceived notions of the advantage of youth in a horse. Frank was not merely not coming seven or nine, but his age was an even number,—he was sixteen; and it was his owner's theory, which Frank supported, that if a horse was well used he was a good horse till twenty-five.

The truth is that Frank looked like a young horse; he was a dandy without any of the ghastliness which attends the preservation of youth in old beaux of another species. When my friend drove him in the rehabilitated phaeton he felt that the turn-out was stylish, and he learned to consult certain eccentricities of Frank's in the satisfaction of his pride. One of these was a high reluctance to be passed on the road. Frank was as lazy as a horse—but lazy in a self-respectful, aesthetic way—as ever was; yet if he heard a vehicle at no matter how great distance behind him (and he always heard it before his driver), he brightened with resolution and defiance, and struck out with speed that made competition difficult. If my friend found that the horse behind was likely to pass Frank, he made a merit of holding him in. If they met a team, he lay back in his phaeton, and affected not to care to be going faster than a walk, any way.

One of the things for which he chiefly prized Frank was his skill in backing and turning. He is one of those men who become greatly perturbed when required to back and turn a vehicle; he cannot tell (till too late) whether he ought to pull the right rein in order to back to the left, or *vice versa;* he knows, indeed, the principle, but he becomes paralyzed in its application. Frank never was embarrassed, never confused. My friend had but to say, "Back, Frank!" and Frank knew from the nature of the ground how far to back and which way to turn. He has thus extricated my friend from positions in which it appeared to him that no earthly power could relieve him.

In going up hill Frank knew just when to give himself a rest, and at what moment to join the party in looking about and enjoying the prospect. He was also an adept in scratching off flies, and had a precision in reaching an insect anywhere in his van with one of his rear hooves which few of us attain in slapping mosquitoes. This action sometimes disquieted persons in the phaeton, but Frank knew perfectly well what he was about, and if harm had happened to the people under his charge my friend was sure that Frank could have done anything short of applying arnica and telegraphing to their friends. His varied knowledge of life and his long experience had satisfied him that there were very few things to be afraid of in this world. Such womanish weaknesses as shying and starting were far from him, and he regarded the boisterous behavior of locomotives with indifference. He had not, indeed, the virtue of one horse offered to my friend's purchase, of standing unmoved, with his nose against a passing express train; but he was certainly not afraid of the cars.

Frank was by no means what Mr. Emerson calls a mush of concession; he was not merely amiable; he had his moments of self-assertion, his touches of asperity. It was not safe to pat his nose, like the erring Billy's; he was apt to bring his handsome teeth together in proximity to the caressing hand with a sharp click and a sarcastic grin. Not that he ever did, or ever would really bite. So, too, when left to stand long under fly-haunted cover, he would start off afterwards with alarming vehemence; and he objected to the saddle. On the only occasion when any of my friend's family mounted him, he trotted gayly over the grass towards the house, with the young gentleman on his back; then, without warning, he stopped short, a slight tremor appeared to pass over him, and his rider continued the excursion some ten feet farther, alighting lump-wise on a bunch of soft turf which Frank had selected for his reception.

The summer passed, and in the comfort of Frank's possession my friend had almost abandoned the idea of ever returning him to his owner. He had thoughts of making the loan permanent, as something on the whole preferable to a purchase. The drives continued quite into December, over roads as smooth and hard as any in June, and the air was delicious. The first snow brought the suggestion of sleighing; but that cold weather about Christmas dispersed these gay thoughts, and restored my friend to virtue. Word came from the stable that Frank's legs were swelling from standing so long without going out, and my friend resolved to part with an animal for which he had no use. I do not praise him for this; it was no more than his duty; but I record his action in order to account for the fact that he is again without a horse, and now, with the opening of the fine weather, is beginning once more to think of buying one.

But he is in no mood of arrogant confidence. He has satisfied himself that neither love nor money is alone adequate to the acquisition: the fates also must favor it. The horse which Frank's owner has had in training may or may not be just the horse he wants. He does not know; he humbly waits; and he trembles at the alternative of horses, mystically summoned from space, and multitudinously advancing upon him, parrot-mouthed, pony-gaited, tender for'a'd, and traveling wide behind.